MW00812983

Clinical
Behavior
Analysis

Dedication

To Megan and Tim

Clinical Behavior Analysis

Editor:
Michael J. Dougher

Context Press
Reno, Nevada

Clinical Behavior Analysis / edited by Michael J. Dougher
   p. 306 cm.
   Includes bibliographical references
   ISBN 1-878978-38-1

   1. Behavioral assessment. 2. Behavior therapy. 3. Cognitive therapy.

   I. Dougher, Michael J. 1950-

   RC473.B43C58   1999
   616.89--dc21   99-43532   CIP

© 2000 CONTEXT PRESS
933 Gear Street, Reno, NV 89503-2729

All rights reserved.

No part of this book may be reproduced, stored in a retrieval system, or transmitted in
any form or by any means, electronic, mechanical, photocopying, microfilming,
recording, or otherwise, without written permission from the publisher.

Printed in the United States of America

Forward

Clinical behavior analysis is a relatively recent and rapidly growing branch of applied behavior analysis. Although they share many of the same philosophical assumptions, the two fields differ in terms of the types of interventions, clinical disorders, and treatment settings that characterize them. Applied behavior analysis focuses on the use of contingency management procedures to treat severely impaired populations such as autistic, brain injured, and developmentally delayed children and adults in residential treatment settings, special schools and hospitals. Clinical behavior analysis focuses on the use of verbally based interventions to treat verbally competent clients who seek outpatient treatment. The types of disorders treated by clinical behavior analysts include anxiety, depression, personality disorders, substance abuse, stress disorders, and relationship difficulties. While applied behavior analysis has flourished since its beginning in the early 1960s, it is only recently that behavior analysts have more fully addressed the issues faced by verbally competent clients seeking therapeutic assistance.

Because of the substantive differences between the two fields, the applied behavior analysis literature has been of only limited use to those working in the emerging field of clinical behavior analysis. Although the mainstream clinical literature, is concerned with the same substantive issues, the philosophical assumptions, theories, underlying principles, objectives, and methods of clinical behavior analysis are so fundamentally different from those of other clinical approaches, including behavior therapy, that these literatures have also been of limited use to clinical behavior analysts. In the end, clinical behavior analysts have had to develop their own literature.

The seeds of clinical behavior analysis were planted years ago in the writings of Skinner (1953; 1957; 1974), Ferster (1972a; 1972b; 1973;), Goldiamond (1974), and Hawkins (1986). Since then, an increasing number of behavior analysts have turned their attention to clinically relevant behavioral phenomena. Two sets of events have been particularly important to the development of the field. First is the relatively recent and rapid increase in basic research on verbal behavior. The research on rule-governance, stimulus equivalence, derived stimulus relations and the transformation of stimulus functions has been particularly relevant. This work, much of which has been conducted by clinical behavior analysts themselves, has led to an enhanced understanding of complex human behavior and provided the empirical foundation upon which the unique contributions made by behavior analysts to clinical contexts are based.

The second set of events that significantly affected the growth and direction of clinical behavior analysis was the development of Kohlenberg and Tsai's Functional Analytic Psychotherapy (FAP, 1994) and Hayes' Acceptance and Commitment Therapy (ACT, Hayes & Wilson, 1994; Hayes, Stosahl, & Wilson, 1999). To a large extent, FAP relies on direct contingency shaping of clinically relevant behaviors. However, it incorporates a basic premise of psychodynamic therapies that the best place to observe and modify these behaviors is within the therapeutic session. Moreover, FAP actively seeks to establish intense, curative, emotional reactions within the therapeutic relationship. ACT, on the other hand, stems directly from a radical behavioral perspective on private experience and recent research on derived stimulus relations. Its aim is to help clients openly experience both private and public events as they are and without distortion. Perhaps surprisingly, its objectives and some of its techniques are similar to those advocated by Buddhism, Gestalt therapies and existential therapies.

Although they differ in their objectives and in the types and focus of the interventions they employ, FAP and ACT represent the first fully articulated, verbally based, comprehensive, outpatient oriented treatment approaches based upon behavior analytic principles. By demonstrating the unique contributions that behavior analysis can make to the clinical context, these two therapies have provided tremendous impetus to the development of the field. Acceptance based procedures, in particular, have recently proliferated and have been applied to the treatment of a wide-variety of disorders (see Hayes, Jacobson, Follette, & Dougher, 1994).

In the past decade, an increasing number of scholar/practitioners have contributed to the developing field of clinical behavior analysis. These writers have drawn upon long-standing behavior analytic principles and recent advances in verbal behavior research to explain the development of a variety of clinical disorders, advocate alternative approaches to clinical assessment and classification, develop new therapeutic interventions, and suggest new treatment goals. The field has grown enormously and it is fair to say at this point that clinical behavior analysis has made some unique contributions to the fields of psychopathology, clinical assessment and psychotherapy. The purpose of this book is to bring together in a single place a sampling of the work that constitutes the growing field of clinical behavior analysis.

The first four chapters of the book focus on the distinguishing characteristics of behavior analysis and the recent research on language and verbal behavior upon which much of the field is based. In Chapter 1, Michael Dougher and Steven Hayes provide an historical perspective on the development of clinical behavior analysis and lay out the underlying philosophical and theoretical assumptions that distinguish it from other clinical approaches, including behavior therapy and cognitive behavior therapy. In Chapter 2, Kelly Wilson and John Blackledge discuss the clinical relevance of recent behavior analytic research on language and verbal behavior. These authors make the argument that recent data draw into question Skinner's definition of verbal behavior, and they offer an alternative definition, which they suggest provides a better framework for understanding important clinical phenomena. In the next chapter, Dermot Barnes, Ian Stewart, Simon Dymond, and Bryan Roche attempt to bring some clarity to the term "self," one of the most frequently used but poorly understood terms in psychology. These authors rely on recent developments in Relational Frame Theory to provide an account of the development of the concept of self and related clinical disorders. In

Chapter 4, Jacqueline Pistorello, Victoria Follette, and Steven Hayes describe the long-term effects of childhood sexual abuse and attempt to explain these effects by appeal to the concept of derived stimulus relations

The next five chapters focus more directly on the assessment and treatment of specific disorders. In Chapter 5, William Follette, Amy Naugle and Peter Linnerooth distinguish between functional (behavioral) and more traditional approaches to clinical assessment and diagnosis. They go on to describe the basic assumptions, principles, processes, and objectives of functional assessment, and suggest how this approach can enhance treatment utility and bring some clarity to the difficult issue of psychological health. In Chapter 6, Madelon Bolling, Robert Kohlenberg, and Chauncey Parker provide a behavior analytic account of some basic cognitive therapy terms and then describe how FAP can enhance cognitive therapies for depression. In the next chapter, John Forsyth relies on recent developments in verbal research to elucidate the core processes and functional similarities among the various anxiety disorders and to suggest different methods for assessing, classifying and treating these disorders. In Chapter 8, Sara Berns, the late Neil Jacobson, and Andrew Christensen describe their attempts to improve upon the success rates of traditional behavioral couple therapy by incorporating acceptance-based procedures. These authors describe various strategies for promoting acceptance in couple therapy and present some outcome data that support the advantages of their integrated treatment approach. In Chapter 9, Jane Smith and Robert Meyers describe the Community Reinforcement Approach to treating alcohol problems. Unlike some of the other treatment procedures described in this book, the Community Reinforcement Approach relies less on verbally based interventions and more on utilizing a broad spectrum of reinforcement contingencies in clients' existing social environments to affect behavior change. Particularly impressive are the effects of these procedures with homeless alcoholics.

The next two chapters demonstrate the extension of clinical behavior analysis beyond the typical clinical context. In Chapter 10, Laura Little and Tracy Simpson report the effects of applying acceptance based interventions with college athletes. They challenge the conventional wisdom that enhanced athletic performance results from feelings of confidence and positive thoughts and show that the performance of intercollegiate softball players can be enhanced by changing the context of their self-talk. In Chapter 11, Barbara Kistenmacher and Anthony Biglan advocate expanding the clinical research paradigm by adopting a public health perspective. The authors argue that behavior analysis is well suited to assist a public policy approach to clinical disorders, and they describe how this approach can be used to decrease the prevalence of marital conflict.

The last two chapters concern the relevance to clinical behavior analysis of two fundamental issues in the psychotherapy literature: the therapeutic relationship and clinical interpretation. In Chapter 12, Barbara Kohlenberg discusses the role of the therapeutic relationship in clinical behavior analysis and offers an explanation for the common finding that much of the improvement in therapy stems directly from the nature of the relationship between the therapist and client. She also addresses the thorny issue of emotions in the therapy context. In Chapter 13, David Perkins, Lucianne Hackbert, and Michael Dougher discuss the role of interpretation in clinical behavior analysis. In that regard, they describe different types of clinical interpretations and the processes by which they may contribute to therapeutic change.

References

Ferster, C. B. (1972a). An experimental analysis of clinical phenomena. *The Psychological Record, 22,* 1-16.

Ferster, C. B. (1972b). Psychotherapy from the standpoint of a behaviorist. In J. D. Keehn (Ed.), *Psychopathology in animals: Research and clinical implications* (pp. 279-304). New York: Academic Press.

Ferster, C. B. (1973). A functional analysis of depression. *American Psychologist, 28,* 857-870.

Goldiamond, I. (1974). Toward a constructional approach to social problems: Ethical and constitutional issues raised by applied behavior analysis. *Behaviorism, 2,* 1-85.

Hawkins, R. P. (1986). Selection of target behaviors. In R. O. Nelson & S. C. Hayes (Eds.), *Conceptual foundations of behavioral assessment* (pp. 331-385). New York: Guilford.

Hayes, S. C., Jacobson, N. S., Follette, V. M., & Dougher, M. J. (1994). *Acceptance and change: Current content and context in psychotherapy.* Reno, NV: Context Press.

Hayes, S. C., Stosahl, K. D., & Wilson, K. G. (1999). *Acceptance and Commitment Therapy: An experiential approach to behavior change.* New York: Guilford Press.

Hayes, S. C., & Wilson, K. G. (1994). Acceptance and Commitment Therapy: Altering the verbal support for experiential avoidance. *The Behavior Analyst, 17,* 289-303.

Kohlenberg, R. J., & Tsai, M. (1991). *Functional Analytic Psychotherapy: Creating intense and curative therapeutic relationships.* New York: Plenum.

Skinner, B. F. (1953). *Science and human behavior.* New York: The Free Press/ Macmillan.

Skinner, B. F. (1957). *Verbal behavior.* New York: Appleton-Century-Crofts.

Skinner, B. F. (1974). *About behaviorism.* New York: Alfred A. Knopf.

Table of Contents

Chapter 1

Clinical Behavior Analysis

Michael J. Dougher
University of New Mexico
Steven C. Hayes
University of Nevada

Clinical behavior analysis is a relatively new field. Although Skinner (1953; 1957) and Ferster (1973) laid the conceptual foundations of a behavior-analytic approach to traditional clinical problems decades ago, it is only recently that behavior analysts have more fully addressed the issues faced by verbally-competent clients seeking therapeutic assistance. Now that has changed and the last decade has witnessed an enormous expansion of the field. Clinical behavior analysis is now in a position to offer unique and important conceptual and methodological contributions to the broadly defined field of psychotherapy.

It may be useful at this point to define clinical behavior analysis and to describe some of its distinguishing characteristics. Clinical behavior analysis can generally be defined as the application of the assumptions, principles and methods of modern functional contextual behavior analysis to "traditional clinical issues." By traditional clinical issues we mean the range of problems, settings, and issues typically confronted by clinical psychologists working in outpatient settings. They include the identification of the variables and processes that play a role in the development, maintenance, and treatment of clinical disorders. To a degree clinical behavior analysis is redundant with applied behavior analysis, but historical factors require a distinction between the two fields based both on populations and on philosophical and theoretical development.

Applied behavior analysis emerged in the 1960's, at a time when direct contingency principles defined basic behavior analysis. Applied behavior analysis focused on severely impaired populations such as autistic, brain injured, and developmentally delayed children and adults. Often these clinical populations were treated in residential treatment settings, special schools and hospitals where there is a good deal of direct control over the contingencies of reinforcement affecting clients' behavior. Direct contingency management procedures comprise the bulk of the clinical interventions reported in the applied behavior analysis literature.

Conversely, clinical behavior analysis arose in the 1990's, at a time when derived stimulus relations, rule-governance, and other issues involving language and cognition were emerging as key topics in basic behavior analysis. While not abandoning direct contingencies, these findings and principles lent themselves to applications focused on the clinical problems presented by verbally capable clients who see a therapist in a typical outpatient setting once or twice a week to receive "psychotherapy" or "counseling" for their depression, anxiety, substance abuse, or interpersonal distress. Therapists working with these clients have relatively little direct control over the contingencies of reinforcement affecting clients' behavior outside the clinical context, and typically rely on verbally based interventions to affect therapeutic change (see Kohlenberg, Tsai, and Dougher, 1993).

In the long run the two literatures may recombine, because there are no necessary philosophical differences between them, but the targets, technologies and specific principles are different enough that they may remain distinct merely for reasons of convenience. Issues of psychological acceptance, meaning, commitment, relationships, and so on are just not applicable to persons with little or no verbal abilities. The issues involved in reducing, say, the self-injurious behavior of an autistic child have little to do with the issues involved in reducing, say, the panic attacks suffered by an agoraphobic. There is an intense need for a rigorous literature in behavior analysis that is directly applicable to traditional clinical problems.

Because the existing applied behavior analysis literature has had relatively little to say to clinicians working with verbally competent clients in outpatient settings, clinical behavior analysts have historically turned to the behavior therapy or cognitive-behavior therapy literatures as their primary source of information. However, for many reasons, these literatures are often unsatisfying. As traditionally defined cognitive-behavior therapy is concerned with many of the relevant substantive issues, but it can be philosophically, conceptually and methodologically alien to behavior analysis. Where behavior analysis is contextualistic, functionalistic, monistic, non-mentalistic, non-reductive, and idiographic, cognitive-behavior therapy is often mechanistic, structuralistic, dualistic, mentalistic, reductive and nomothetic.

These differences are not between "good" assumptions versus "bad" assumptions. By definition, assumptions are pre-analytic—they permit analysis, but they cannot themselves be fully justified by that same analysis. Nevertheless, it does no good to pretend that basic differences are not present, and thus there is no reason to think that behavior analytically oriented clinicians will be satisfied with the cognitive behavioral literature as a basis for their work. The traditional behavior therapy literature is sometimes closer, but even here the philosophical and conceptual differences can be profound, particularly when procedures and analyses are based on warmed-over SR principles and assumptions. Indeed, clinical behavior analysts are sometimes more comfortable with traditions outside of the behavioral and cognitive behavioral camps (e.g., Gestalt therapy), precisely because there is a greater degree of overlap in philosophical assumptions. Because philosophical assumptions are so critical to an understanding of the nature of clinical behavior analysis, they will be discussed separately below. Before that, however, it would be useful at this point to discus the history of the behavior therapy movement to put the emerging field of clinical behavior analysis in some historical context.

History of the Behavior Therapy Movement

Because some of the contemporary issues in the behavior therapy movement have their roots in positions taken by John B. Watson, the father of behavioral psychology, we will begin there. Watson presented a unique mix of views drawn from American pragmatism, evolutionary biology, functionalism, and reflexology. His most important contribution was a shift in the focus of psychology from the mind and its components as studied through introspection, to the study of overt behavior and its context (Watson, 1913; 1924). He made two core arguments for this shift. First, he claimed that mind did not exist, and, therefore, all that psychologists can study is overt behavior. Second, he argued that psychology as a science could not study mind, even if mind existed, because there would never be a scientifically acceptable method to do so. The first position is usually called Watsonian metaphysical behaviorism, while the latter is termed methodological behaviorism.

Few psychologists ever embraced Watsonian metaphysical behaviorism. Contrary to popular view, Watson himself embraced the study of thinking, emotion, and the like (e.g., Watson, 1920), but he could hold to his metaphysical claim because he a) defined "behavior" as muscle movements and glandular secretions (Watson, 1924, e.g., p. 14), and b) believed that seemingly private events were actually behavior so defined (e.g., he believed that thinking was sub-vocal speech). Conversely, methodological behaviorism became the dominant approach in American psychology. Oddly, however, it provided a philosophical foundation for the later emergence of more sophisticated forms of mentalism, since the claim was merely that mental events could not be directly studied scientifically. Eventually, researchers realized that this left the door open as to whether mental events could be studied indirectly, and ingenious methods were devised seemingly to do so.

Watson was not a therapist, but he conducted a few studies demonstrating the applicability of behavioral principles to clinical issues (e.g., Watson & Rayner's, 1920, famous case of "Little Albert"), before his affair and 1920 marriage to his graduate student Rosalie Rayner forced him prematurely and permanently out of academic life. Watson's applied work is of importance in the current context because it showed the natural alliance within the behavioral movement between basic theory and applied research. This was usual for theoretical approaches of the time. Indeed, one of the common criticisms of Watson's original behavior manifesto (Watson, 1913) was that his view was that of an applied technologist, not a real scientist.

From Watson's time to the 1950's a large number of behavioral principles were identified in the laboratories of psychologists studying learning, including all of the principles of operant and classical conditioning, and the associationistic principles of the SR learning theorists. When applied behavioral work burst on the scene in the late 1950's and early 1960's, there was a huge backlog of basic knowledge ready to be explored for its applied implications. Behavior therapy quickly emerged, in two distinct varieties. Applied behavior analysis began in the United States and was closely related to the operant psychology of B. F. Skinner. It included early leaders such as Donald Baer, Todd Risley, Teodoro Ayllon, and Nathan Azrin. The first applied behavior analysis journal, the *Journal of Applied Behavior Analysis*, was founded in 1968.

A second wing emerged in Britain and South Africa, and was associated with the methodological behaviorism of the S-R learning theorists. It included such people as Joseph Wolpe, Arnold Lazarus, Stanley Rachman, Hans Eysenck, M. B. Shapiro, and others. At one time both wings sometimes called themselves "behavior modifiers" but this second wing quickly settled on the term "behavior therapy" (even though this term was apparently coined by Ogden Lindsley, a student of B. F. Skinner's). The first behavior therapy journal, *Behaviour Research and Therapy*, was founded in England in 1963. The first US-based behavior therapy journal, *Behavior Therapy*, was founded in 1970 by the Association for the Advancement of Behavior Therapy.

Of the two wings, applied behavior analysis had far fewer adherents. As Mahoney, Kazdin, & Lesswing (1974, p. 15) put it, "Methodological behaviorism is much more characteristic of contemporary behavior modifiers than is radical behaviorism." Both wings were strongly empirically oriented, however. Franks and Wilson (1974) argued that the common element in behavior therapies was an adherence to "operationally defined learning theory and conformity to well established experimental paradigms" (p. 7).

Although both were empirically oriented, the two wings were quite different in their focus and background. Originally, behavior analysts tended to be experimental or developmental psychologists. They worked in applied areas, but not in areas commonly associated with clinical psychology. Behavior therapists were usually clinical psychologists and worked in outpatient settings. Behavior analysts focused on work with children (often in schools, group homes, or other non-traditional settings) and institutionalized clients. Behavior therapists tended to work with adults in outpatient settings. Behavior analytic techniques relied on staff, teachers, parents, or others to deliver direct contingencies (e.g., token economies; time out) while behavior therapy focused on how therapists could replace old associations with new ones (e.g., through systematic desensitization). Over time, applied behavior analysis focused more on severe problems in less verbal populations, while behavior therapy focused on the use of psychotherapy to alleviate anxiety, depression, and problems of that kind.

Philosophically, applied behavior analysis was and is dominantly contextualistic and developmental. Actions of organisms are situated, both historically and by the current context - they evolve over time and emerge in certain specific circumstances. The position is epigenetic: the relevant context for behavior includes the structure of the organism itself, but no one part of the situational features of an interaction eliminate the importance of other features. In the early days the behavior therapy wing tended to be neo-behavioristic, and associationistic. Philosophically, the approach was and is mechanistic: systems are analyzed in terms of discrete parts, relations, and forces that are presumed to pre-exist as part of a grand mechanical system. Applied behavior analysis has stayed remarkably consistent over the years, although with perhaps more and more emphasis on developmental disabilities, in part because of the large number of behavior analysts employed in such settings. The biggest change is the quite recent one represented by the present volume: the rise of clinical behavior analysis.

Behavior therapy went through a major change in the mid and late 1970's. SR psychology had by then collapsed into basic cognitive psychology. The change was not one of philosophy, both were fairly mechanistic, but of the liberalization of theory and the adoption of a new mechanical metaphor, the computer, to guide theory and research. Early cognitive mediational accounts of behavior change began to emerge (e.g., Bandura, 1969) and then fairly quickly blossomed into the cognitive therapy movement (e.g., Mahoney, 1974; Meichenbaum, 1977). The theorizing became more mediational and the techniques more oriented toward detection and alteration of thoughts. In the modern era, behavior therapy, cognitive behavior therapy, cognitive therapy, applied behavior analysis, and now clinical behavior analysis all coexist within behavioral psychology as distinct but overlapping traditions. Of these, clinical behavior analysis is clearly the new kid on the block.

Characteristics of Behavior Analysis

There are several characteristics that distinguish behavior analysis from more mainstream approaches to psychology, including behavior therapy and cognitive behavior therapy. These characteristics are partly philosophical in nature, involving metaphysical, epistemological, and ontological assumptions, but they also involve certain empirical principles and methodological preferences. In an effort to elucidate these characteristics, they will be contrasted with the corresponding characteristics that we believe define mainstream psychology.

Contextualism vs. Mechanism

Contextualism and mechanism are two of four primary coherent world hypotheses or world-views described in 1942 by the philosopher Stephen C. Pepper. We focus on these two world-views because it is our contention that they represent the philosophical core of behavior analysis and much of mainstream psychology, respectively. Contextualism as the philosophical core of behavior analysis has been discussed extensively in previous writings by Hayes and others (e.g., Hayes, Hayes, & Reese, 1988; Morris, 1988), and these sources should be consulted for more in-depth treatments of the topic. A convenient way of contrasting the two perspectives is to compare their respective root metaphors and truth criteria. The root metaphor of mechanism is, appropriately enough, the machine. Mechanists see the universe and the events within it as machine-like, a collection of independent parts that operate together. Newton's metaphor of the universe as a clock illustrates this perspective. Understanding the machine requires an analysis of its basic parts and the principles by which they operate. From this perspective, one can be said to know how a car works when one has identified the important parts and how they operate together to make the car work. An important aspect of this perspective is that the parts of the machine can be understood independently of each other. That is, there is no interdependence among the parts of the machine. Carburetors do what carburetors do regardless of what distributors or alternators do.

The truth criterion of mechanism is correspondence or the extent to which what we observe about the world matches or corresponds with our mechanical model of it. A rigorous type of correspondence, and one that is regularly employed in science, is prediction. To the extent that an analysis of an event allows for the prediction of that event, the analysis is true or correct. For example, the theory that matter is comprised of atoms is true to the extent it allows for better predictions than competing theories of matter.

As is the case with most sciences, mainstream psychology is and has been mechanistic. Nowhere is this more evident than in cognitive psychology, where behavior is explained by postulating cognitive entities or mechanisms that are said to cause behavior. Contemporary models of the mind are based on computers. The information-processing model of memory, which divides memory into three types of memory stores (sensory, short-term, and long-term) and postulates various processes (e.g., attention, rehearsal, encoding) by which information is transferred from one memory store to another is a case in point. The truth of this model is the extent to which it allows for the prediction of behavior, for example, in memory experiments. Another example, perhaps with more clinical relevance, is Bandura's (e.g., 1977) construct of self-efficacy. Self-efficacy is a cognitive entity (a belief) or process, which is said to partially explain individual differences in behavior. Relying on this construct, social-cognitive psychologists might appeal to differences in self-efficacy to explain why one student studies diligently and achieves a good grade in a course and another student does not. From a mechanistic perspective, the extent to which differences in self-efficacy beliefs can predict differences in the grades obtained by students in the course, self-efficacy theory is true.

The root metaphor of contextualism is the ongoing act in context. The emphasis here is not on the act alone, but an act in and with its context or setting. Events or acts are interdependent with their contexts, and neither can be understood alone. They reciprocally define each other. An event makes sense only in terms of its situation. Contextualists would argue that even such basic physical entities as velocity and space can be known or understood only from a situated perspective. As it pertains to behavior, the contextualist position is that it is most meaningfully understood only with respect to its context. In turn, behavioral contexts are best understood in relation to their effects on behavior. Behavior analysis' contextualism is exemplified by its adoption of the two-term contingency as the basic unit of analysis. The two terms in the contingency, behavior and consequences, are interdependently defined. Behavior is defined in terms of the consequences it produces, and consequences are defined in terms of their effects on behavior. The same topographical response, e.g., driving a car, can be defined quite differently depending upon the consequences controlling the driving. Thus, going to the store, testing out a new set of spark plugs, and rushing to the emergency room are all quite different behaviors, despite the fact that each involves the topographically defined act of driving a car. A behavioral consequence is defined as a reinforcer only if it increases the frequency of the behaviors that produces it. It is this interdependence of the two terms in a contingency that render it a basic unit.

The truth criterion of contextualism is successful working or effective action. Statements about the world are true to the extent that they allow for more effective action than other statements. This criterion is similar to that adopted by William James (1907) and other pragmatic philosophers (e.g., Peirce, 1940) and, for this reason, contextualism is very closely aligned with philosophical pragmatism. This truth criterion is also similar to Skinner's (1957) position that the goals of science are prediction and control. Control and effective action are virtually synonymous, and while other schools in psychology have adopted prediction as a goal, only behavior analysis had adopted both prediction and control. At least with regard to human behavior, the term control has some fairly negative connotations, and is probably technically inaccurate (see Hayes, 1993). For these reasons, the term influence seems preferable to control.

It is critical to an understanding of behavior analysis to see that the adoption of effective action, or prediction and influence as a truth criterion necessarily limits the kind of explanations that are considered legitimate. For example, although measurements of self-efficacy may very well allow for the prediction of behavior, they do not necessarily allow for its influence. In order to influence behavior, one must know and have access to the determinants of self-efficacy beliefs. Unless these are specified, self-efficacy cannot be considered an adequate explanation of behavior. Thus, the behavior analyst's objection to self-efficacy theory is not that it is not useful or does not allow for prediction, it is that it does not allow for effective action with respect to the behavior in question (see Biglan, 1987; Dougher, 1995, Hawkins, 1995; and Lee, 1995, for further discussion of the behavior analytic objections to self-efficacy theory, and Bandura, 1996, for a reply). As will be made clear below, the adoption of effective action as a truth criterion is also at the heart of behavior analysis' objection to structuralism, dualism, mentalism, and reductionism.

Structuralism vs. Functionalism

Structuralism is related to mechanism and refers to approaches in psychology that seek to identify and understand the basic structure or nature of the underlying entities that are said to cause behavior. Since Wundt established the first psychology laboratory in the late 1800's, mainstream psychology has been primarily structuralistic in its approach to studying behavior. Although the introspective methods of the early structuralists have been abandoned, modern cognitive psychology is still concerned with identifying the essential structures of the mind. Moreover, one of the "hottest" areas in contemporary psychology is cognitive neuroscience, which attempts to explain behavior and cognition by identifying relevant underlying brain structures. The structuralism of cognitive-behavior therapy is revealed by its attempts to explain behavior by appeal to such cognitive structures as beliefs, expectancies, and schema.

Functionalism, on the other hand, is related to contextualism, and attempts to explain behavior by appeal to its function or purpose. It is worthwhile pointing out here that functionalism does not necessarily follow from contextualism. Indeed, Hayes (1993) has identified two types of contextualism: descriptive contextualism and functional contextualism, and the distinctions between them are important for an understanding of the relation between contextualism and functionalism. One critical distinction is that descriptive contextualists tend to adopt more personal, abstract goals for their analyses. They tend to be philosophers rather than psychologists, and they generally seek a personal sense of coherence or understanding that comes from an appreciation of the interdependent participation of parts or aspects in the whole event. Functional contextualists tend to adopt more directly practical goals and often are interested in developing solutions to specified problems. Functionalism suits the purposes of functional contextualists because the emphasis on the functions of events frequently points to their controlling variables.

Skinner's (1957) approach to the study of verbal behavior exemplified the underlying functionalism of behavior analysis. Where mainstream psychology identifies verbal behavior by its form or structure (vocal), Skinner defined verbal behavior in terms of its function. Rather than behavior that emanates from the vocal chords, Skinner defined verbal behavior as any behavior, vocal or otherwise, that is maintained by its effects on an audience. Structuralistic and functionalistic approaches are concerned with primarily different aspects of verbal behavior. Where linguists and cognitive psychologists are interested in the grammatical and syntactical structure of language, behavior analysts are interested in the current and historical stimulus conditions that evoke and maintain verbal behavior. The distinction between structuralistic and functionalistic approaches to the study of language is reflected even in the basic units of analysis adopted by the two approaches. The basic unit of analysis in linguistics and cognitive approaches to language, the morpheme, is structurally defined, while the basic units in behavioral analyses of verbal behavior, e.g., mands, tact, and autoclitics, are functionally defined, (see Skinner, 1957, for an extended discussion of these issues). Parenthetically, keeping these distinctions in mind might have led to a more reasonable and productive exchange between cognitivists and behavior analysts on the issue of how language is acquired (see Chomsky's 1959 critique of Skinner's book, *Verbal Behavior* and MacCorquodale's 1970 reply).

Because a functional approach to the study of behavior focuses on the determinants and effects of behavior, it facilitates the objectives of prediction and influence. Identifying the determinants of behavior often allows for effective action with respect to that behavior. In addition, when behavior is defined in terms of its functions, then the covariation of functionally similar but topographically different behaviors begins to make sense. This has important clinical implications. For example, faced with situations that produce strong emotional reactions, individuals may respond in a number of topographically different ways. They may drink or use drugs, throw themselves into their work, become socially isolated, solicit comfort from family and friends, become housebound, or engage in ritualistic or compulsive behaviors. On the basis of their appearance or form, these behaviors are very different. Functionally, however, they are quite similar. From a clinical perspective, it may be more useful to classify behaviors in terms of their function rather than their form, and to aim treatment interventions at the functional causes of disorders. In this situation, interventions aimed at the emotional avoidance underlying the various behaviors may be most effective.

Monism vs. Dualism

Although monism and dualism are classical ontological positions about the nature of reality, the discussion here is not so lofty. It is concerned with the nature and scientific legitimacy of private events. By private events, we are referring to the collection of experiences, responses and acts that are observable only to the individual who "has" them. These are more commonly referred to as feelings, emotions, thoughts, images, self-talk, beliefs, expectancies, memories, attributions, etc. One of the most persistent misunderstandings of behavior analysis is that it wants to restrict psychology to the study of publicly observable behavior and relegate private events beyond the scope of scientific analysis (Dougher, 1993; Hayes & Brownstein, 1986; Moore, 1980). Quite to the contrary, behavior analysis explicitly includes private events as legitimate subjects of scientific inquiry (Skinner, 1974). It is able to do so because private events are seen as instances of behavior. For behavior analysts, behavior is anything and everything an integrated organism does that can be orderly related to its environment, and private events certainly fall within that definition. Private events are accorded no special status because they occur within the skin and are not publicly observable. Their ontological status is the same as publicly observable behavior. That is, they are real, physical reactions to real, physical events. In that sense, behavior analysts are monistic with respect to their treatment of private events.

Although very few mainstream psychologists would adopt a position of literal dualism, they do tend to talk about private events in ways that suggests a metatheoretical dualism (see Hayes & Brownstein, 1986). For example, private events are often referred to as mental or cognitive events, structures or processes. The exact meanings of the terms mental and cognitive are not typically specified, but something other than physical is often implied. Moreover, there is a clear bifurcation in the ways private and public behaviors are treated scientifically that suggests a scientific and even an epistemological dualism. In the traditions of positivism, operationism, and methodological behaviorism (Day, 1969; Moore, 1980; Skinner, 1945) mainstream psychology has tended to divide psychological phenomenon into the private and public, and, in an attempt to maintain scientific status, it has confined itself to the latter. Private events are not studied directly, but instead are categorized as hypothetical constructs and operationally defined. Thus, anxiety and depression are defined in terms of scores on tests that purportedly measure them. Likewise, self-efficacy beliefs are not considered to be real entities. Rather, they are hypothetical constructs that are defined in terms of the methods or operations used to measure them.

One problem that arises from this dualistic view of private events is that it is difficult to stipulate how these events actually influence other behavior, both private and public. How, for example, do schema influence people to act in particular ways? Conversely, if we assume that depression results from faulty beliefs or schema, then we are faced with the question of how drugs, which are physical stimuli, alter beliefs or schema, which are mental or cognitive in nature. If we take a monistic view of private events and see them as instances of behavior, then this problem becomes one of specifying behavior-behavior relationships (Hayes & Brownstein, 1986). While this can be technically challenging, it is, at least, not philosophically questionable.

Mentalism vs. Non-mentalism

From a behavior analytic view, the most serious problem arising from a dualistic position on private events occurs when these events are given causal status. The attempt to explain behavior by appeal to inner states, processes, or constructs is called mentalism. It is difficult to find a term that is the opposite of mentalism, so we will simply use the term non-mentalism. Behavior analysis is non-mentalistic in its insistence that causal explanations of behavior should be restricted to external and, preferably, accessible events. It is important to note that this does not restrict scientific study to external or publicly observable behaviors, nor does it deny that internal or private events have any influence on behavior. Rather, it is the position that explanations of behavior are most useful when they stipulate the external, observable, and, accessible or manipulable determinants of behavior. Again, this position directly stems from the behavior analytic goals of prediction and influence.

Explanations of behavior that are based on inner states or structures such as anxiety, depression, beliefs, expectancies or schema can, in fact, allow for prediction. If we know that an individual is anxious or lacking in self-efficacy, it increases our ability to predict her behavior in certain situations. On the other hand, if the goal is to influence behavior, then it is critical to know the external, accessible determinants of that behavior, because behavior can be influenced only by manipulating its determinants (see Hayes & Brownstein, 1986 for a detailed development of this point). At best, mentalistic explanations point to correlated internal events, but they do not specify the external determinants of behavior. The behavior-analytic objection to mentalism, then, is not that it invokes private events, but that it does not facilitate and may even interfere with the goals of prediction and influence.

Reductionism vs. Non-reductionism

Reductionism generally refers to attempts to explain events by appeal to a lower level of analysis. In psychology, the prototypic example of reductionism is the attempt to explain behavior by appeal to physiological processes. One problem with reductionism, of course, is that it is easy to continue moving to lower levels of analyses ad infinitum. Just as there are underlying physiological processes associated with any behavior, there are underlying biochemical processes associated with all physiological processes, and underlying physical processes associated with all chemical processes. In the end, the phenomenon of interest and the level of analysis that defines psychology disappear.

Recently, there has been an increase in attempts to explain behavior by appeal to biological processes. Genetic explanations are increasingly offered for behavior, and behavioral and cognitive neuroscience may be the most rapidly growing fields in psychology. There is no doubt that advances in behavior genetics, behavioral neuroscience and physiological psychology have been and will continue to be very useful to behavior analysts. After all, behavior is biological. But even if we knew in detail the biological processes involved in every behavior, it still would be critical to know the conditions that cause these processes to occur if we want to be able to influence behavior. For this reason, behavior analysis has rejected reductionism, preferring instead to keep scientific analysis at the level of environment-behavior relations.

Nomothetic vs. Idiographic Methods

As is clear from even a cursory review of almost any psychology journal and by the almost universal requirement that psychology graduate students pass courses in inferential statistics, mainstream psychology relies on nomothetic methods. Despite calls for the increased use of single-subject designs in clinical research (Barlow, Hayes, & Nelson, 1984)) the vast majority of studies reported in clinical journals, including behaviorally oriented clinical journals, use between-group designs and inferential statistics. On the other hand, behavior analytic studies typically, but not always, use idiographic or single-subject methods. The reason, again, stems from its goals of prediction and influence. The intent of most behavior analytic studies is to demonstrate the precise experimental control over the behavior of individual subjects. Nomothetic methods, on the other hand, seek to determine whether measured relationships among variables are statistically significant. This determination is generally made on the basis of averaged group data, and the behavior of individual subjects is typically ignored. Nomothetic methods are simply ill suited to the objectives of most behavior analytic research.

An issue that frequently arises in this regard concerns the generalizeability of the results of single-subject studies. How can one know whether the effects obtained for one or a few subjects will generalize to others? The issue of generalizeability in idiographic approaches is addressed through experimental replication. To the extent that research findings can be replicated across subjects, the findings are generalizeable and, therefore, can be said to have scope as well as precision. However, what is replicated across studies is not the effect of a topographically or formally defined intervention, but the effect of a functionally defined intervention. For example, reinforcement has been shown repeatedly to be an effective method of changing behavior. But the specific stimuli that function as reinforcers change from individual to individual and over time for the same individual. For this reason, applied researcher often use different stimuli as reinforcers across time, subjects and responses. Obviously, then, what generalize across reinforcement studies are not the specific stimuli that function as reinforcers. What generalizes is the principle of reinforcement.

Because idiographic replication studies focus on functionally defined interventions, researchers are faced with the task of tailoring their interventions to individual subjects. For example, applied researchers using reinforcement procedures must find stimuli that function effectively as reinforcers for each of the participants in their studies. This process can be quite useful to the extent that it forces clinical researchers to grapple with and perhaps identify the principles and variables that determine the generalizeability of their interventions. This process also makes idiographic methods especially well suited to clinical research. Clinical work, after all, is typically done with individual clients, and working clinicians are generally less interested in knowing the statistical significance of a clinical intervention than they are in knowing how to maximize the effectiveness of an intervention for a particular client. When clinical researchers are forced to address these issues, it helps working clinicians with the task of tailoring interventions to the needs and circumstances of their individual clients.

Clinical Behavior Analysis and the Principles of Behavior Analysis

We mentioned earlier that clinical behavior analysis applies the principles of the experimental analysis of behavior to clinical contexts. Although the principles of reinforcement, punishment, schedule effects, and stimulus control are certainly applicable to clinical contexts (e.g., Kohlenberg & Tsai, 1991), of particular relevance to clinical behavior analysis is the recent research in the area of verbal behavior. Clients and therapist interact verbally. Clients report their histories, describe their problems, articulate their private experiences, express their hypotheses about the causes of their issues, and declare their expectations and goals for therapy. Therapists listen, interpret, explore, question, clarify, explain, educate, offer alternative formulations, provide metaphors, encourage, challenge, comfort, reinforce, and schedule future appointments. All of this is verbal.

It could be argued that the defining characteristic of being human is our capacity to interact verbally. Despite fascinating reports of primate symbol use, no species comes even close to humans in their verbal facility, complexity, and capacity. Obviously, this verbal ability confers great evolutionary advantage to our species. On the down side, however, it may very well be responsible for a number of clinical disorders.

At a deep level, clinical behavior analysis is the name not just for a new set of techniques, or a new population and problem focus for behavior analysis. It is the name for a new substantive concern. Exactly what divides institutionalized populations and the developmentally disabled from outpatient clinical populations is the expanded relevance of verbal behavior both in the development of problems and in their remediation. "Psychotherapy" is dominantly verbal therapy and the "mind" is a name for a collection of verbal processes. In that sense, "psychopathology" is dominantly verbal pathology and "mental" illness is verbal illness. Thus, clinical behavior analysis is a field that studies modern behavior analytic approaches to verbal events and develops the applied implications of these approaches in the areas of psychopathology and its remediation.

It is not by accident that many of the most vigorous labs in clinical behavior analysis also produce and consume contemporary research on verbal behavior, derived stimulus relations, rule-governance, and the like. Clinical behavior analysts cannot look to the theories of cognitive psychologists and therapists for guidance, even though clinical behavior analysts are intensely interested in language and cognition as behaviorally defined. There is a huge difference between cognitive psychology and a behaviorally sensible psychology of cognition. From the point of view of behavior analysis, an adequate analysis of language and cognition requires that we approach this area as a behavioral phenomenon; that we view it as a kind of interaction between whole organisms (not brains) and the historical and current situational environment, and that we measure our understanding of it by the degree to which we can predict and influence such interactions with precision, scope, and depth.

Behavior analysis is one of the few fields in psychology that maintain a broad and effective alliance between basic and applied wings. Clinical behavior analysts feel quite comfortable moving some of their effort toward generating the basic knowledge about verbal processes that is needed for their clinical work. A good example is the transformation of stimulus functions through equivalence classes and other derived relations. A large proportion of the research in this area has come from the laboratories of clinical behavior analysts. The transformation of stimulus functions through derived stimulus relations is one of the most obviously applicable areas of basic behavior analytic research into language processes-so when basic behavior analysts were not moving rapidly enough in this area, the clinical behavior analysts simply stepped in. It is a very positive thing that clinical behavior analysts have been willing to do basic behavior analysis when basic knowledge has been lacking. The fact that they have confirms the view that clinical behavior analysis is a field substantively oriented toward the development of modern behavior analytic approaches to verbal events. As such, clinical behavior analysis spans the range of areas within behavior analysis: basic, applied, theoretical, and philosophical.

References

Bandura, A. (1969). *Principles of behavior modification.* New York: Holt, Rinehart and Winston.

Bandura, A. (1977). Self efficacy: Toward a unifying theory of behavior change. *Psychological Review, 84,* 191-215.

Bandura, A. (1996). Comments on the crusade against the causal efficacy of human thought. *Journal of Behavior Therapy and Experimental Psychiatry, 28,* 1-15.

Barlow, D. H., Hayes, S. C., & Nelson, R. O. (1984). *The scientist practitioner: Research and accountability in clinical and educational settings.* New York: Pergamon.

Biglan, A. (1987). A behavior analytic critique of Bandura's self-efficacy theory. *The Behavior Analyst, 10,* 1-6.

Chomsky, N. (1959). A review of *Verbal Behavior* by B. F. Skinner. *Language, 35,* 26-58.

Day, W. F. (1969). On the difference between radical and methodological behaviorism. *Behaviorism, 11,* 89-102.

Dougher, M. J. (1993). On the advantages and implications of a radical behavioral perspective on private events. *The Behavior Therapist,* 204-206.

Dougher, M. J. (1995). A bigger picture: Cause and cognition in relation to differing scientific frameworks. *Journal of Behavior Therapy and Experimental Psychiatry, 26,* 215-219.

Ferster, C. B. (1973). A functional analysis of depression. *American Psychologist, 28,* 857-870.

Franks, C. M. & Wilson, G. T. (1974). *Annual review of behavior therapy: Theory and practice.* New York: Brunner/Mazel.

Hawkins, R. M. F. (1992). Self Efficacy: A predictor but not a cause of behavior. *Journal of Behavior Therapy and experimental Psychiatry, 23,* 251-256.

Lee, C. (1992). On cognitive theories and causation in human behavior. *Journal of Behavior Therapy and Experimental Psychiatry, 23,* 257-268.

Hayes, S. C. (1993). Analytic goals and the varieties of scientific contextualism. In S. C. Hayes, L. J. Hayes, H. W. Reese, and T. R. Sarbin (Eds.), *Varieties of Scientific Contextualism* (pp. 11-27). Reno, NV: Context Press.

Hayes, S. C., & Brownstein, A. J. (1986). Mentalism, behavior-behavior relations, and a behavior analytic view of the purpose of science. *The Behavior Analyst, 9,* 175-190.

Hayes, S. C., Hayes, L. J., & Reese, H. W. (1988). Finding the philosophical core: A review of Stephen C. Pepper's *World Hypotheses. Journal of the Experimental Analysis of Behavior, 50,* 97-111.

James, W. (1907; reprinted in 1981). *Pragmatism.* Indianapolis, IN: Hackett.

Kohlenberg, R. J., & Tsai, M. (1991). *Functional Analytic Psychotherapy: Creating intense and curative therapeutic relationships.* New York: Plenum.

Kohlenberg, R. J., Tsai, M. & Dougher, M. J. (1993). The dimensions of clinical behavior analysis. *The Behavior Analyst,* 271-282.

MacCorquodale, K. (1970). On Chomsky's review of Skinner's *Verbal Behavior. Journal of the Experimental Analysis of Behavior, 13,* 83-100.

Mahoney, M. J. (1974). *Cognition and behavior modification.* Cambridge, MA: Ballinger.

Mahoney, M. J., Kazdin, A. E. & Lesswing, N. J. (1974). Behavior modification: Delusion or deliverance? In C. M. Franks & G. T. Wilson (Eds.), Annual Review of Behavior Therapy: Theory and Practice (pp. 11-40). New York: Brunner/Mazel.

Meichenbaum. D. H. (1977). *Cognitive-behavior modification: An integrative approach.* New York: Plenum.

Moore, J. (1980). On behaviorism and private events. *The Psychological Record*, 30, 459-475

Morris, E. K. (1988). Contextualism: The world view of behavior analysis. *Journal of Experimental Child Psychology*, 46, 289-323.

Pepper, S. C. (1942). *World hypotheses*. Berkeley: University of California Press.

Peirce, C. S. (1940). *Philosophical writings of Peirce*. (J. Buchler, Ed) New York: Dover.

Skinner, B. F. (1945). The operational analysis of psychological terms. *Psychological Review*, 52, 270-277, 291-294.

Skinner, B. F. (1953). *Science and human behavior*. New York: The Free Press/ Macmillan.

Skinner, B. F. (1957). *Verbal behavior*. New York: Appleton-Century-Crofts.

Skinner, B. F. (1974). *About behaviorism*. New York: Alfred A. Knopf, Inc

Watson, J. B. (1913). Psychology as a behaviorist views it. *Psychological Review, 20*, 158-177.

Watson, J. B. (1920). Is thinking merely the action of language mechanisms? *British Journal of Psychology, 11*, 87-104.

Watson, J. B. (1924). *Behaviorism*. New York: Norton.

Watson, J. B., & Raynor, R. (1920). Conditioned emotional reactions. *Journal of Experimental Psychology, 3*, 1-14.

Chapter 2

Recent Developments in the Behavioral Analysis of Language: Making Sense of Clinical Phenomena

Kelly G. Wilson
John T. Blackledge
University of Nevada

Verbal behavior and related topics, such as the treatment of the problem of private events, have been persistently interesting topics for behavior analysts since Skinner's earliest work (e.g., Day, 1969; Moore, 1975; Skinner, 1945, 1953, 1957). However, all this talk about talk has born little fruit in the domain of applied problems. In part this is the result of Skinner's eloquent, but we think premature analysis of verbal behavior and the implications of that analysis for understanding the impact of private events (Friman, Hayes, & Wilson, 1998; Hayes & Hayes, 1992; Hayes & Wilson, 1993; Wilson & Hayes, in press). A strategy was adopted early on in behavior analysis where behavior among infrahumans was studied and it was assumed that these principles would apply to humans in a straightforward manner. This "continuity strategy" (Hayes & Hayes, 1992) has produced potent behavior change strategies in some applied areas, such as developmental disabilities. However, it has left other areas virtually untouched. The realm of adult outpatient psychotherapy is one such area.

In 1938, Skinner speculated that the principles derived from work with laboratory animals would be adequate to the task of analyzing all behavior, with the possible exception of verbal behavior. By 1957, when Skinner published *Verbal Behavior*, he had become convinced that even verbal behavior could be analyzed using principles of operant and respondent conditioning. However, whereas Skinner's original analyses in *Behavior of Organisms* (1938), and subsequent analyses of schedules of reinforcement (Ferster & Skinner, 1957), were based upon extensive empirical findings, his analyses of verbal behavior (Skinner, 1957) and topics such as scientific behavior, problem solving, government, psychotherapy, and economics (e.g., Skinner, 1953, 1989) were entirely interpretive efforts, and benefited little from *direct* empirical analyses.

Skinner was sensitive to the problems of premature theory building and cautioned against it (1972/1950). Absent relevant data, a powerful, parsimonious, and general theory of behavior, such as Skinner's, can be extended to almost any area of human functioning and produce reasonably coherent, plausible explanations of behavior. Actual data, though, are notoriously less cooperative than a good theory. Data generation can exert a selective effect upon theorizing. Data that persistently fail to fit theory, in the best cases, cause the theorist to alter their theorizing. Ironically, Skinner's own analyses of verbal behavior and other complex human functioning may provide a case study in the hazards of engaging in extrapolation of principles to domains without experimental work that supports and shapes the analyses.

Skinner on Verbal Behavior and the Social/Verbal Community

In the most general sense, we are fully in agreement with Skinner's views on verbal behavior. He saw verbal behavior as operant behavior that is shaped and supported by a social context. For a clinical psychologist interested in a pragmatic science of behavior, contextual approaches to understanding behavior are preferable to analyses that locate the causes of behavior in some mental netherworld that is susceptible neither to direct observation, nor to direct manipulation.

The particulars of Skinner's analysis, however, are problematic. Consider, for example, Skinner's claim that the self-awareness, generated by the verbal community, has adaptive advantage. According to Skinner:

> Self-knowledge is of social origin. It is only when a person's private world becomes important to others that it is made important to him. It then enters into the control of the behavior called knowing....self-knowledge has a special value to the individual himself. A person who has been 'made aware of himself' is in a better position to predict and control his own behavior. (1974, p. 31)

According to Skinner's analysis, the verbal community shapes up a discriminative repertoire with respect to one's own public and private responses (1945). Skinner's claim that this repertoire enhances self-control ought to be particularly interesting to clinicians. We work long and hard to help our clients get control of their lives. Skinner seems to be saying that if an individual becomes aware of the contingencies controlling their behavior, they may be more effective in controlling their lives. Sometimes we describe contingencies that are affecting the client and give advice on behaviors that could generate more positive outcomes. Skinner rightly points out though that direct advice has limits in the clinic:

> Not every problem can be solved by applying a rule, however, and therapists need to take a further step and teach their clients how to construct their own rules. That means teaching them something about the analysis of behavior. (Skinner, 1989, p.81)

Behavior analysts have sometimes attempted to teach clients to do functional analyses of their own circumstances, and to then organize contingencies that would support desired behavior. On the face of it, it seems obvious that knowledge about the contingencies controlling one's own behavior would be useful. Obviousness, though, is not the same as a behavioral analysis. Therefore, we turn our attention to the last sentence in the Skinner quotation regarding self-knowledge, and ask: Why would self-knowledge put an individual in a better position to predict and control his or her own behavior? Asked in a more technical way, why would discriminations regarding one's own responding (either public or private) have behavior regulatory functions over subsequent responding?

Perplexing Clinical Questions

In the following section, we will examine several clinical questions that illustrate the problem with Skinner's direct contingency analysis of the aspect of verbal behavior called self-knowledge. What are the expected and actual outcomes of becoming self-aware? We will contrast clinical examples with several experimental analogues to demonstrate what we think is a critical omission in Skinner's account of verbal behavior. Finally, we will discuss some of the clinical implications of emerging analyses.

Consider the following two scenarios. First, a survivor of childhood sexual abuse, upon disclosing the abuse, reports reexperiencing aspects of the abuse. Over the course of treatment, she describes various aspects of her abuse history with her therapist. Her functioning in a variety of areas gradually improves. Second, a man who has been inconsistent in his contact with his daughter finds it difficult to discuss his relationship with his daughter in therapy? As he describes his relationship with his daughter, he sees that his avoidance of contact alleviates pain over the short term, but increases pain over the long term. Having recognized this, he makes a plan to establish regular contact, follows it, and recaptures that relationship. Several clinical questions emerge as we attempt a behavioral analysis of these scenarios:

- Why would it be aversive for the sexual abuse survivor to talk about her history of abuse?
- Why would it make a difference for her to talk about her history?
- In the second scenario, why would it be painful for the avoidant father to talk about his avoidance?
- Why would descriptions of short and long term contingencies affecting the avoidant father's behavior alter the relative effectiveness of those contingencies?

Why is it Painful for the Abuse Survivor to Talk about a Painful History?

Anyone who has treated survivors of childhood sexual abuse has observed how difficult it often is to talk about their abuse history. Why would this be so? At first blush, it seems obvious that when the individual talks about the abuse, some of the psychological functions of the abuse are psychologically present in the telling. Reporting seems to subject the client to a sort of reliving of the abuse. But why, in *technical behavioral terms* might this be so? To illustrate the problem, consider a couple of experimental preparations.

Transfer of Function: An Experimental Analogue

Imagine a choice preparation in which a pigeon is placed in an operant chamber containing two keys – one red and one green. A tone is sounded, and on half of the trials, the tone is followed by a shock. The two keys are then illuminated. The pigeon is reinforced for pecking the red key if it was just shocked, and the green key if it was not. This is a straightforward discrimination task in which the pigeon is asked to "self-report" whether it was just shocked or not. Would it be any more difficult to train the pigeon to report that it had just been shocked as opposed to not having been shocked? No. The shock may have been aversive, but the report should not be.

In a standard classical conditioning paradigm involving a tone followed by a shock, the stimulus functions of the shock inhere in the tone, but not visa versa. We know this because if we reverse the order–shock to tone – we do not get elicitation upon presentation of the tone. Backward conditioning, even in the limited conditions in which it appears to occur, is weak and transitory (Hall, 1984; Mackintosh, 1974). In the preparation described, the tone, which precedes the shock might come to have some of the stimulus functions of the shock, since the shock is correlated .50 with the tone and .00 with the absence of the tone. However,

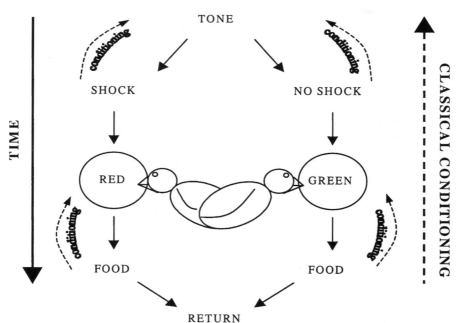

Figure 1. The direction of conditioning leads to the tone acquiring some of the stimulus functions of the shock. **Both** the red and green keys should acquire some of the stimulus functions of the food, but **neither** should acquire the stimulus functions of the shock.

if the red key were to acquire any stimulus functions in this preparation it would acquire the stimulus functions of the food, which reliably follows red-key-pecking-after-shock. Whereas we would expect the tone to take on conditioned aversive functions, we would expect the red key (and the green key) to take on conditioned reinforcing functions (see Figure 1 for a detailed diagram showing the direction of conditioning and transfer of function).

Subtle Differences in Transfer of Function: A Second Analogue

Consider a second experimental preparation that would show more precisely the transfer of stimulus function from the reinforcer to the operant chamber's keys

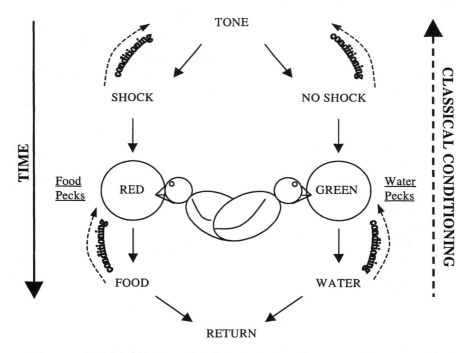

Figure 2. Again, the direction of conditioning leads to the tone acquiring some of the stimulus functions of the shock, but here the red key acquires some of the stimulus functions of the food while the green key acquires some of the stimulus functions of the water. This preparation would be expected to lead to two different pecking topographies as result of the interaction of operant and respondent conditioning processes.

(see Figure 2). Imagine in this instance that the pigeon was both food *and* water deprived. Imagine further that pecks on the red key were reinforced with food and pecks on the green key were reinforced with water. Jenkins and Moore (1973) demonstrated that the topography of pigeon's key pecks differed subtly depending on the type of consequence delivered. Thus, in this example, we would expect that the psychological functions acquired by the keys would be different. Again though, neither would be expected to acquire conditioned aversive functions. Instead we would expect the pigeon to deliver "eating" pecks when reporting shock on the red key and "drinking" pecks when reporting the absence of shock on the green key (see Jenkins & Moore, 1973). The two reports would be different, but the difference would not be that shock reports would be aversive and no-shock reports would be nonaversive. The difference in the key pecks would be as a result of what *followed* the peck, not as a result of what preceded them.

The Aversiveness of Reporting Aversives Revisited

Now, reconsider the first clinical question posed: Why is it painful to report a painful history? The report necessarily follows the sexual abuse, so the report would not be expected to take on the functions of the abuse through classical conditioning. If anything, it should take on the socially reinforcing functions of the therapist delivering reassurance and comfort upon hearing the report. One might explain the aversive properties of the report by appealing to a history in which reporting, or even mentioning the abuse, was severely punished. This could indeed make reporting aversive; however, what would be psychologically present in the reporting would not be the sexual abuse that preceded the report, but instead, the punishment that had followed the report. One might also speculate that that the report would be aversive because the culture so disapproves of incest they may punish the victims of such crimes for talking about them. Here again though, the report ought to take on the psychological functions of the punishment that followed the report, not the event reported.

This is not what is seen clinically though. Clients often report reexperiencing aspects of the abuse when they begin talking about it. Indeed, reexperiencing is one of the hallmark symptoms of post-traumatic stress disorder – a not uncommon diagnosis among survivors. This is not to downplay the role of direct classical and operant conditioning effects. Events that preceded the abuse incidents might well become classically conditioned to the abuse. So, for example, individuals that look like the abuser, or wear the same cologne, might make psychologically present some aspects of the abuse (Figure 3, and see Wilson, Follette, Hayes, & Batten, 1996).

The Absent Father: Why is it Painful to Talk about Avoidance?

The same perplexity holds for the absent father. Say the father realized that avoiding his daughter allows him, over the short term, to avoid thinking about a failed marriage and a messy divorce. He might also realize that, over the long term, his relationship with his daughter is growing more and more distant. One could construe a missed visit to his daughter as a missed opportunity for reinforcement, but why would recounting a missed reinforcer be aversive? In order to illustrate the problem, consider yet another experimental analogue.

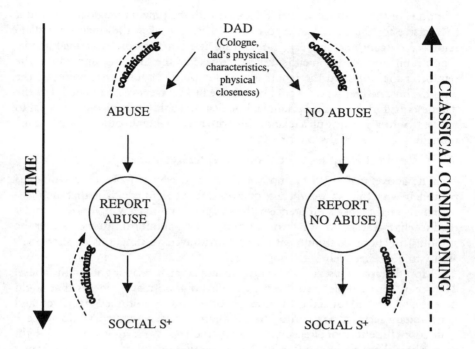

*Figure 3. In this example, given **only** respondent and operant conditioning effects, the direction of conditioning should lead to Dad acquiring some of the stimulus functions of the abuse, but the yes and no reports of abuse should **both** acquire some of the stimulus functions of the social reinforcement provided by the therapist. The reports ought to acquire appetitive, not aversive functions.*

The Pain of Reporting Impulsivity: Immediate and Delayed Reinforcement

Imagine a choice preparation in which a pigeon can obtain either a small immediate reinforcer or a large delayed reinforcer. The experimental literature suggests that immediacy of reinforcement is a potent variable in operant conditioning, and that we should expect the animal to select the small but immediate reinforcer (Rachlin & Green, 1972). Now suppose we alternately gave the pigeon access to the small and then large reinforcer then lit a red and a green key, alternately forcing the pigeon down the two links of the choice preparation. We could reinforce the pigeon for pecking the red key if it had just received the immediate small reinforcer and the green key if it had just received the delayed large reinforcer. This is a discrimination task similar to the one described in the first analogue. Now, if the pigeon is released into the operant chamber with both links of the choice available, we can "ask" it after the choice whether it had chosen the immediate small reinforcer or the delayed large reinforcer. As with the previous analogue, would it be aversive for the pigeon to report that it had just taken the small immediate reinforcer? Again, the answer is no, and for the same reasons described above. Opportunities to report on either key would take on the stimulus functions of the reinforcer that followed the report, not the impulsive choice that preceded the report. Thus, neither report would be expected to be aversive or avoided. For the dad described in the clinical example, however, it would likely be quite painful to realize that he was giving up a relationship with his daughter in order to avoid some immediate emotional discomfort.

Why Would it Help to Talk about an Aversive History?

The above analysis brings up questions as to why self-awareness would be painful. In what follows, we will raise questions about Skinner's claim that such self-awareness might make a difference within a direct contingency analysis. Consider the first clinical scenario. Why would simply talking about painful events alter the stimulus functions of stimuli with conditioned aversive functions or alter one's ability to deal effectively with those stimuli?

Most therapies for sexual abuse involve more than just talking about the abuse. They may, for example, also involve various homework assignments that could potentially lead to direct extinction processes on conditioned aversives and concomitant access to new reinforcers. However, as we have argued, we do not seek to discount the effects of direct conditioning processes. We simply seek to highlight areas where those analyses fall short. This is another one of those areas. Therapies for abuse tend to be multimodal and complex, but there are also experimental data that are supportive of our contention that *simply* talking may have an impact.

Consider, for example, the several dozen studies reviewed by Pennebaker (1997). The reviewed studies all involve assessing the effects of subjects' disclosures of disturbing and in some instances traumatic events. Among the studies, positive outcomes have been found in a remarkably diverse array of outcome measures, including reductions in physician visits, increased immune function, improved grade point average, more rapid re-employment following job loss, self-reported reductions in physical symptoms and psychological distress (see Pennebaker, 1997, for review, and also Wegner & Pennebaker, 1993, Pennebaker, et al., 1990), Pennebaker, 1995). It might be argued that social feedback and support received during disclosures could account for improvements; however, the studies reviewed by Pennebaker (1997) involve no feedback. Ironically, spending more time talking about a painful event may actually predict less time thinking about it. In a study by Pennebaker (1997) of widowed spouses, spending more time talking about the death of the spouse predicted both less illness and less rumination. These studies provide provocative evidence that simply talking about trauma can produce important positive improvements.

Would we expect such outcomes from the self-reports of nonhuman organisms? Consider the pigeon example described in Figure 1. Would we expect that any amount of "reporting" shock on the red key would alter the conditioned aversive functions of the tone? Or, would increasing the reinforcers available for reporting be expected to lessen the aversive properties of the tone? We think not. Increasing reinforcers might increase the strength of the reporting response, but would leave the stimulus functions of the tone intact. The only way we could alter the stimulus functions of the tone would be to alter the contingency that exists between the tone and what follows it. So, for example, we could sound the tone without delivering the shock until the conditioned aversive functions were extinguished, or better yet, we could stop the shock and schedule appetitive stimuli to follow the tone. This would lead not only to extinction of conditioned aversive functions, but also to the acquisition of conditioned appetitive functions. What, then, distinguishes the report of the pigeon from the report of the verbally competent human? We believe that the answer lies in the very definition of verbal behavior.

Verbal Behavior Defined?

For Skinner (1957), a behavior is considered verbal if its reinforcement is mediated by a listener conditioned precisely by a social community for this task, and non-verbal if otherwise reinforced. For example, the behavior of a rat trained by an experimenter to press a bar to receive food pellets would be explicitly verbal. According to Skinner, the experimental animal and the experimenter form a "small but genuine verbal community" (1957, p. 108), since reinforcement is mediated by the behavior of a 'listener' (the experimenter) and trained precisely by a social community (other researchers) to mediate such reinforcement. It is somewhat ironic, that because Skinner did not think that the behavior of the listener was verbal in any important sense (1957, p. 2), presumably only the rat, but not the experimenter in the above example, would be engaged in verbal behavior.

According to Skinner:

The basic processes and relations which give verbal behavior its special characteristics are now fairly well understood. Much of the experimental work responsible for this advance has been carried out on other species, but the results have proved to be surprisingly free of species restrictions. (1957, p. 3)

However, if this were so, why would we see the peculiar effects described in the clinical examples above? Where are the fruits of the application of these basic principles to the realm of verbal behavior? Forty plus years after the publication of *Verbal Behavior* we see little to help us in the clinic, at least in the realm of adult outpatient treatment. This stands in stark contrast to the dramatic development of applications in areas where verbal behavior is less central (e.g., developmental disabilities, infant feeding disorders, self-injurious behavior).

Recent Human Operant Data and the Tenability of Skinner's Analysis of Verbal Behavior

Skinner's analysis of verbal behavior, although a valiant effort given the available data, runs into difficulties when one considers some recent human operant data. After examining problems with Skinner's analysis of verbal behavior, we will see how these data may shed light on the perplexing clinical outcomes described above.

Skinner's Analysis of Verbal Behavior: The Example of the Tact

A close examination of the tact serves to illustrate difficulties with Skinner's analysis. Suppose a child says the word "water." In order to understand why, we must analyze the contingencies that have generated that bit of behavior. If the child says "water" in the presence of actual water, but not in its absence, and that utterance was shaped up by a history of generalized reinforcement for doing so, then it is a tact. To say that an utterance is a tact then is to say several things. Tacting is not simply another name for naming. Skinner invented new terms precisely to shed the excess baggage of lay terminology. The label tact is a technical term, and like other behavioral technical terms, it tells us something of the current environment (water is present) and also something of the child's history (reinforcement of the response in the presence of water and extinction in its absence).

The concept of the tact seems reasonable, and we can readily find examples in which children have been trained in much this way. In this account, the object (water) is the discriminative stimulus, the saying the word "water" is the response, and the reinforcing consequence is generally some form of praise or attention (e.g., "Good! That's right!"). Children do learn to name many things in this way, but is this *necessarily* the way they learn to do so?

Suppose we train the following: given the written word W-A-T-E-R, say "water," not "hat," and point to water, not hats. With these two trained relations (written word - oral name, written word - class of objects), four additional relations will likely emerge: being able to select the written word given either the oral name or the object, finding the object given the oral name, and saying the oral name given the object. Given this history, if the child now says "water" given actual water, is this a tact? We would say no. A tact is a technical term. Saying "water" in the presence of water in this case (assuming no other experience with these names, words, or objects) may be formally similar to a tact which involved direct discrimination training in the presence and absence of water; however, behavioral terms are defined functionally, not formally.

In this example, two relations among events were directly trained: saying "water" in the presence of the written word W-A-T-E-R and pointing to water in the presence of the written word W-A-T-E-R. The four additional relations that emerge (including saying "water" in the presence of actual water) are derived, rather than directly trained. The emergence of this pattern of derived relations is called an equivalence relation, and the written word W-A-T-E-R, the spoken word "water", and actual water are said to form an equivalence class (Sidman, 1971).

Skinner recognized the existence of these more indirect means of acquiring tacts. He suggests for example that a listener who hears that an amphora is a Greek vase with two handles might:

(1) say amphora when asked What is a Greek vase with two handles called?,

(2) say A Greek vase having two handles when asked What is an amphora?,

and (3) may point appropriately when asked Which of these is an amphora? (Skinner, 1957, p. 360)

Skinner suggests that this occurs as result of "a long history of verbal conditioning" (1957, p. 360), but does not offer a precise technical description of what this history might entail. We and some colleagues (Barnes, 1994; Friman, Hayes, & Wilson, 1998; Hayes & Hayes, 1992; Hayes & Wilson, 1993) have suggested that a history of reinforcement for deriving and combining stimulus relations and the contextually controlled transformation of stimulus functions among relatae is the defining property of this "long history," though some evidence suggests that it is not necessarily so long as was imagined by Skinner (e.g., Lipkens & Hayes, 1993).

It is not surprising that Skinner did not see the relevance of stimulus equivalence to his analysis of verbal behavior, since most of the empirical work on equivalence did not even begin until nearly 15 years after the publication of *Verbal Behavior* (1957) and nearly twenty years after his interpretive efforts in *Science and Human Behavior* (1953). Examination of the importance of stimulus equivalence in understanding psychological difficulties is even more recent (DeGrandpre & Bickel, 1993; Degrandpre, Bickel, & Higgins, 1992; Hayes & Hayes, 1992; Hayes & Wilson, 1993, 1995; Leslie, et al., 1993; Plaud, 1995; Roche & Barnes, 1997; Wilson & Hayes, in press).

What are Relational Stimulus Functions?

We have suggested that deriving and combining stimulus relations and contextually controlled transformation of stimulus functions among relatae provide insight into indirect acquisition of stimulus function. The particulars of this phenomenon are worth unpacking. We will begin with a simple stimulus equivalence example. Conditional discriminations can be trained in what is commonly known as a matching-to-sample paradigm. In a visual example of such a paradigm, an unfamiliar stimulus is presented. In addition, a set of perhaps 3 comparison stimuli are provided. The organism being trained is then reinforced for selecting the "correct" comparison stimulus. Comparison stimuli are arbitrarily assigned as either correct or incorrect by the experimenter. No formal property of the stimuli provides a basis for correctness (i.e., none of the stimuli are formally similar). In this way, the organism is taught that given stimulus A1, and comparisons B1, B2, and B3, pick B1, not B2 or B3. (See figure 4 for a visual example of the described preparation.) In further training, the organism might be taught that given the stimulus A1 and another set of comparisons, C1, C2, and C3, pick C1. Conditional discriminations can be easily trained in rats, dolphins and monkeys, as well as a variety of other nonhuman organisms (e.g., Herman & Thompson, 1982; Lashley, 1938; Nissen, 1951). This parallels language training in the normal environment, since there is no formal property that would connect, for example, actual water with either the written or spoken word water.

If a verbally-competent human is then exposed to a trial where B1 is presented as the sample stimulus, with A1 (which it has seen in previous training), A2, and A3

Figure 4. Example of matching-to-sample trial.

(with which the subject has no history of exposure) presented as comparisons, they will readily select A1. Similarly, if presented with a trial wherein C1 was presented as the sample, with B1, B2, and B3 as the comparisons, humans will readily select B1. This occurs in spite of the fact that the person has had no explicit training to make these selections. Note that in the C-B trial, the organism has never even seen the B and C stimuli at the same time. Although there is some controversy on this point, there has never been an unequivocal demonstration of this pattern of derived responding on the part of nonhumans (e.g., D'Amato, Salmon, Loukas, & Tomie, 1985; Lipkens, Kop, Matthijs, 1988; see also Hayes, 1989 and Saunders, 1989), or among non-language-competent individuals with developmental disabilities (Devany, Hayes, & Nelson, 1986).

The single possible exception is the unreplicated demonstration of equivalence in a single California sea lion (Schusterman & Kastak, 1993). If this were replicated, it could potentially lead to some interesting research into the requisite history necessary to generate equivalence and other derived stimulus relations. It would also lay to rest the conjecture by some theorists that equivalence is mediated by language.

In terms of economy, derived acquisition of stimulus function is a highly efficient learning process. Training two relations to a nonhuman generates two potential relational responses; whereas, training two relations to a human generates six. For the nonhuman, two unidirectional relations exist among three stimuli; for the human, a so-called "equivalence class" exists in which all members of the class are related to all other members, and that relationship is bidirectional.

In addition, for humans, if one member of the class is given some function all other members of that class may also acquire that stimulus function. So, if stimulus B1, in the equivalence class described above, were given a punishing function by pairing it with some existing punisher, stimulus C1 could be used in an operant task to punish responses the experimenter wishes to reduce (for a study involving transfer of consequential functions see Hayes, Kohlenberg, & Hayes, 1991).

A final feature of this relational responding which is relevant to its application to an analysis of language and other complex human behavior is that it is contextually controlled. Several studies (Bush, Sidman, & Derose, 1989; Gatch & Osborne, 1989; Wulfert & Hayes, 1988) have demonstrated that class membership of stimuli can be manipulated by contextual cues, such that a given stimulus is related to one set of stimuli in one condition and another given a change in context. The word "bat" occasions quite different responses when spoken in a cave as compared to a baseball diamond. Even the quality and intensity of the transfer of psychological function may differ according to context. For example, the spoken word "car" would be likely to engender decidedly different sets of responses if it were heard spoken in a conversational tone while looking out a window as opposed to being spoken loudly while standing in an intersection. Although we have spoken of relational responding thus far in terms of equivalence and non-equivalence, it has also been demonstrated to be the case with relations other than equivalence, such as oppositeness, difference, greater than/less than and sequencing relations (e.g., Dymond & Barnes, 1995; Roche & Barnes, 1997; Steele & Hayes, 1991; Wulfert & Hayes, 1988).

Consider, for example, Roche and Barnes (1997) recent demonstration of the transformation of sexual function among members of a relational network. In their study, relations of oppositeness and sameness were established among a group of five stimuli. When a pretrained contextual cue for sameness was present, and the A1 stimulus was the sample, the selection of the B1 and the C1 stimuli were reinforced. When a pretrained contextual cue for oppositeness was present, selection of the B2 and C2 stimuli was reinforced. Roche and Barnes found that when the B1 and B2 stimuli were then used in a respondent conditioning preparation with a nature and a sexually explicit film clip respectively, transformation of function occurred that was consistent with the trained and derived relations. That is, the C2 stimulus came to have conditioned sexual functions as assessed by changes in electrodermal activity.

We have spoken of members of a relational network as related. In fact, it would be more correct to say that the organism relates them, or responds relationally to them. There is considerable controversy on this topic (Horne & Lowe, 1996; Hayes & Wilson, 1996; Sidman, 1994). We and some colleagues have suggested that this relational responding is a form of operant behavior that is shaped quite early in human development (Barnes, 1996; Lipkens & Hayes, 1993; Hayes, et al., 1996). Relational Frame Theory is a contextual behavior theory. Therefore, the ultimate cause of this relational responding is not to be found in the organism. It is found in the organization of contingencies in the organism's history and current environment (see Hayes & Hayes, 1992; Hayes, Gifford, & Wilson, 1996; Hayes & Wilson, 1996, for a detailed account). Whether such an oranization of contingencies can be effective in generating this behavior in nonhumans is somewhat controvercial. However, it does appear to be difficult, if not impossible (i.e., Hayes, 1989, but see also comments above on Schusterman & Kastak, 1993).

Derived stimulus relations lead to behavioral functions that are extremely indirect. The psychological functions of an event in a relational network alter, under some contextual conditions, the functions of other events in such a network. Such transformations of stimulus functions have been shown in many studies (e.g., Dougher et al., 1994; Dymond & Barnes, 1995; Hayes, Kohlenberg, & Hayes, 1991). Thus, the functions of a given event are determined not just by the direct history an individual has with that event, but also by how it participates in derived relations with other events. Taken together, these empirical findings suggest that animal models of stimulus control are likely to be inadequate for the purpose of making sense of the complex, indirectly acquired, contextually controlled acquisition of stimulus function possible among verbally competent humans.

An Alternate Definition of Verbal Behavior

These seemingly unique features of relational responding suggest an alternative definition of verbal behavior that we believe does a better job of highlighting what is unique about this form of behavior. Relational stimulus functions are those functions that a stimulus has, not as result of direct training, but rather as result of participation in some relational response. From this perspective, relational stimulus functions are central to understanding complex human behavior and are the defining feature of verbal behavior. *A stimulus is a verbal stimulus if it has some of its stimulus functions as a result of its participation in a relational frame – that is, if some of its stimulus functions are derived. Thus, a behavior is defined as verbal if the stimulus functions controlling it are derived.*

Returning to Skinner's example, the behavior of the rat is nonverbal, since it's bar pressing response is controlled quite directly by a history of reinforcement for doing so. The experimenter, by contrast, is almost certainly engaging in verbal behavior. Although such laboratory work may have been directly reinforced by various instructors, providing reinforcement for the rat – listening to the rat as it were – is also likely to be under the control of some reinforcers that have never been contacted directly, such as finishing a Ph.D. or getting a publication.

Revisiting Clinical Questions

Having discussed verbal behavior and the relation between verbal behavior and relationally acquired stimulus function, we can return to our clinical questions and see how this analysis bears upon the perplexity seen in clinical cases.

Why is it aversive to talk about an aversive history?

From a Relational Frame perspective, this outcome ought not be the least surprising. At the simplest level, words used to report a trauma participate in equivalence relations with actual traumatic events. For members of the English speaking verbal community, the spoken or written word "rape" participates in an equivalence relation with actual occasions of forced sexual intercourse. Without any direct experience with actual rape, any of us could easily identify a case of rape were we to witness it. Even for those fortunate enough not to have been touched personally by such an event, the stimulus functions inherent in the word are probably aversive. Rape participates in a variety of frames through which it is related indirectly to other words such as "repellent," "immoral," and the like. The word may elicit some physical symptoms such as nausea or emotional functions we might identify as anger or pity – particularly if the word is set in the context of a graphic description of a rape.

For the survivor, who has *actual* contact with a rape, the word may have profoundly aversive qualities. As described above, stimulus functions transfer among members of an equivalence class. For the survivor, the psychological functions are potent, and those that transfer to other members of the class (such as the word rape or certainly dramatic portrayals of rape) will also be quite potent. Reporting the sexual abuse will likely produce many of the stimulus functions inherent in the abuse itself. The rat's report of the shock is not in an equivalence relation with the shock, and since it follows the shock it will acquire none of the aversive psychological functions of the shock. For the rat, the report is not verbal. The report for the survivor is verbal and the fact that it is verbal makes all the difference.

Why would it help to talk about an aversive history?

Here again, a Relational Frame account sheds some light on the positive therapeutic effects of interventions involving talk about an aversive history. Studies such as Dougher et al. (1994) are especially informative. In the Dougher et al. study, equivalence classes were trained in which one member of the class was used in a classical conditioning preparation with a mild electric shock. As would be expected, not only did that particular member of the equivalence class come to have eliciting functions, but other members of that class came to have these functions as well. In addition, when one member of the class was presented in extinction, other members of the class failed to provoke elicited skin conductance.

In the instance of a history of sexual or other trauma, open, unpunished discussion by the victim of the trauma might well be expected to lead to extinction of some eliciting functions of the words. If this were to happen, other conditioned elicitors in a class with those words should also undergo extinction. Thus, over time, aversive, relationally conditioned elicitors should undergo extinction and ultimately produce less elicitation and less avoidance.

Why would it be painful for the avoidant father to talk about his avoidance?

It is worthwhile beginning the discussion of avoidance with the initial causes of the avoidance. The client's daughter is likely to participate in a rich set of relational responses having to do with marriage, family, and ultimately separation, divorce, and failure. Because of the bidirectional transformation of stimulus functions among related events, the daughter will almost certainly possess a mix of pleasant and unpleasant psychological functions. The daughter may have some painful functions as a result of direct training, but for a verbally competent human, she will have a far richer set of functions than would be seen in a nonhuman.

The father in the clinical example begins to recognize that his short-term relief from emotional pain is gained at the cost of his child's long-term loss of a father and his own long-term loss of that relationship. This situation is something like the short-term versus long-term contingency in the pigeon choice preparation. In some respects it is a particularly insidious set of contingencies, since the long-term negative consequence is not only likely to be delayed, it is likely to be incrementally incurred. If the father avoids on one occasion, no long-term loss of the relationship is likely. However, many instances of avoidance will likely accrue and eventually lead to a poor relationship. These are precisely the sort of "defective contingencies" which *can* come to be effective that caused Skinner to invoke the concept of rule-governed behavior in the first place.

The father's self-report of responding to the small short-term gain is function-ally different than the pigeon's report, and for the same reason as described in the sexual abuse example. Having verbally described the contingency – "accessing the short-term reinforcer (immediate relief) is equivalent to discarding the long-term reinforcer (a rich parent-child relationship)" – the reinforcing functions of imme-diate relief are transformed. Talking about an instance of avoiding will likely be aversive, because the words describing the avoidance are in an equivalence relation with the actual avoidance, and loss of the relationship is in an equivalence relation with the actual loss. When avoidance is verbally related as being in opposition with having a strong relationship, then the aversive properties of the actual loss should inhere in descriptions of behavior that cause the loss.

Why would articulating the alternative reinforcers alter the father's responding?

In the pigeon analogue of the immediate-small-reinforcer versus delayed-large-reinforcer, we would not expect self-reports to be aversive, and we would also not expect them to alter future choices. For the verbally competent human though, as a result of bidirectional transformation of function, the psychological functions of avoiding may be altered. Engaging in behavior that has previously produced short-term emotional relief may actually become aversive, since doing so is in a relation of opposition with having a strong relationship with his child. Skinner called rules contingency-specifying stimuli. What was not known at that time was the means by which verbal behavior could make defective contingencies effective. From a relational frame theory perspective, stimuli contained in a verbal formulation acquire the stimulus functions of the events to which they refer through the transformation of stimulus functions through relational networks such as those we have described.

Thus, if the father generates the rule "If I avoid seeing my daughter I will lose our close relationship," the stimulus functions of the actual loss are psychologically present in the rule, even though the actual loss may occur only incrementally and over a long period of time. As in the sexual abuse example, self-knowledge can be both painful and valuable. As Skinner suggested, self-knowledge may put a person in a better position to act effectively. Intuitively, it was clear that this was so. Recent analyses of complex human behavior provide the beginnings of a technical account of why this is so.

Conclusion

We have described some recent empirical and theoretical developments in the analysis of verbal behavior, and the ways these developments may inform our understanding of complex clinical problems. This work is in its infancy. Although stimulus equivalence research has been going on for over 25 years, its clinical implications have only recently begun to be examined. Most studies of derived relational responding have involved arbitrarily-configured visual stimuli or non-sense syllables. Although some have seen the potential implications, actual data with functionally potent stimuli are few. We know little about the flexibility and stability or contextual control over transformation of stimulus function for emotionally impactful stimuli such as those described in the clinical examples we have used. Behavior analysis is uniquely notable for clinical advances based upon behavioral principles developed under well-controlled laboratory conditions. The behavioral principles developed during the first half of this century have paid generous dividends. Recent developments we have described can provide a basis for continuation of this tradition. There is much work to be done in the laboratory, the clinic, and in illuminating the connection between findings in both these arenas.

References

Barnes, D. (1996). Naming as a technical term: Sacrificing behavior analysis at the altar of popularity? *Journal of the Experimental Analysis of Behavior, 65(1)*, 264-267, 341-353.

Bush, K. M., Sidman, M., & de-Rose, T. (1989). Contextual control of emergent equivalence relations. *Journal of the Experimental Analysis of Behavior, 51(1)*, 29-45.

D'Amato, M. R., Salmon, D. P., Loukas, E., & Tomie, A. (1985). Symmetry and transitivity of conditional relations in monkeys (Cebus apella) and pigeons (Columba livia). *Journal of the Experimental Analysis of Behavior, 44*, 35-47.

Day,W. F. (1969). Radical behaviorism in reconciliation with phenomenology. *Journal of the Experimental Analysis of Behavior, 12(2)*, 315-328.

Degrandpre, R. J. & Bickel, W. K. (1993). Stimulus control and drug dependence. *Psychological Record, 43*, 651-666.

Degrandpre, R. J., Bickel, W. K., & Higgins, S. T. (1992). Emergent equivalence relations between interoceptive (drug) and exteroceptive (visual) stimuli. *Journal of the Experimental Analysis of Behavior, 58(1)*, 9-18.

Devaney, J. M., Hayes, S. C., & Nelson, R. O. (1986). Equivalence class formation in language-able and language-disabled children. *Journal of the Experimental Analysis of Behavior, 46*, 243-257.

Dougher, M. J., Augustson, E., Markham, M. R., Greenway, D. E., & Wulfert, E. (1994). The transfer of respondent eliciting and extinction functions through stimulus equivalence classes. *Journal of the Experimental Analysis of Behavior, 62*, 331-351.

Dymond, S. & Barnes, D. (1995). A transformation of self-discrimination response functions in accordance with the arbitrarily applicable relations of sameness, more than, and less than. *Journal of the Experimental Analysis of Behavior, 64*, 163-184.

Ferster, C. B. & Skinner, B. F. (1957). *Schedules of Reinforcement.* New York: Appleton-Century-Crofts.

Friman, P. C., Hayes, S. C., & Wilson, K. G. (1998). Why behavior analysts should study emotion: The example of anxiety. *Journal of Applied Behavior Analysis, 31(1)*, 137-156.

Gatch, M. B. & Osborne, J. G. (1989). Transfer of contextual stimulus function via equivalence class development. *Journal of the Experimental Analysis of Behavior, 51*, 369-378.

Hall, J.F. (1984). Backward conditioning in Pavlovian type studies: Reevaluation and present status. *Pavlovian Journal of Biological Sciences, 19*, 163-168.

Hayes, S. C. (1989). Nonhumans have not yet shown stimulus equivalence. *Journal of the Experimental Analysis of Behavior, 51*, 385-392.

Hayes, S. C. & Hayes, L. J. (1992). Verbal relations and the evolution of behavior analysis. *American Psychologist, 47*, 1383-1395.

Hayes, S. C. & Wilson, K. G. (1993). Some applied implications of a contemporary behavior analytic account of verbal behavior. *The Behavior Analyst, 16*, 283-301.

Hayes, S. C. & Wilson, K. G. (1995). The role of cognition in complex human behavior: A contextualistic perspective. *Journal of Behavior Therapy and Experimental Psychiatry, 26*, 241-248.

Hayes, S. C. & Wilson, K. G. (1996). Criticisms of relational frame theory: Implications for a behavior analytic account of derived stimulus relations. *Psychological Record 46*, 221-236.

Hayes, S. C., Gifford, E. V., & Wilson, K. G. (1996). Stimulus Classes and Stimulus Relations: Arbitrarily Applicable Relational Responding as an Operant. To appear in T. Zental & P. Smeets (Eds.), *Stimulus class formation.* Oxford: Elsevier.

Hayes, S. C., Kohlenberg, B. K., & Hayes, L. J. (1991). The transfer of specific and general consequential functions through simple and conditional equivalence classes. *Journal of the Experimental Analysis of Behavior, 56,* 119-137.

Herman, L. M. & Thompson, R. K. (1982). Symbolic, identity and probe-delayed matching of sounds in the bottle-nosed dolphin. *Animal Learning and Behavior, 10,* 22-34.

Horne, P. J., & Lowe, C. F. (1996). On the origins of naming and other symbolic behavior. *Journal of the Experimental Analysis of Behavior, 65,* 185-241.

Jenkins, H. M., & Moore B. R. (1973). The form of the auto-shaped response with food or water reinforcers. *Journal of the Experimental Analysis of Behavior, 20 (2),* 163-181.

Lashley, K.S. (1938). Conditional reactions in the rat. *Journal of Psychology, 6,* 311-324.

Leslie, J. C., Tierney, K. J., Robinson, C. P., Keenan, M., Watt, A., & Barnes, D. (1993). Differences between clinically anxious and non-anxious subjects in a stimulus equivalence training task involving threat words. *Psychological Record, 43,* 153-161.

Lipkens, R., Hayes, S. C., & Hayes, L. J. (1993). Longitudinal study of derived stimulus relations in an infant. *Journal of Experimental Child Psychology, 56,* 201-239.

Lipkens, R., Kop, P. F. M., & Matthijs, W. (1988). A test of symmetry and transitivity in the conditional discrimination performances of pigeons. *Journal of the Experimental Analysis of Behavior, 49,* 395-409.

Mackintosh, N.J. (1974). *The psychology of animal learning.* New York: Academic Press.

Moore, J. (1975). On the principle of operationism in a science of behavior. *Behaviorism, 3(2),* 120-138.

Nissen, H. (1951). Analysis of complex conditional reaction in the chimpanzee. *Journal of Comparative and Physiological Psychology, 7,* 449-516.

Pennebaker, J. (1997). Writing about emotional experiences as a therapeutic process. *Psychological Science, 8(3),* 162-166.

Pennebaker, J. (1995). *Emotion, disclosure, and health.* Washington D.C.: American Psychological Association.

Pennebaker, J. W., Colder, M., & Sharp, L. K. (1990). Accelerating the coping process. *Journal of Personality and Social Psychology, 58(3),* 528-537.

Plaud, J. J. (1995). The formation of stimulus equivalences: fear-relevant versus fear-irrelevant stimulus classes. *Psychological Record, 45,* 207-222.

Rachlin, H., & Green, L. (1972). Commitment, choice, & self-control. *Journal of the Experimental Analysis of Behavior, 17,* 15-22.

Roche, B. & Barnes, D. (1997). A transformation of respondently conditioned stimulus function in accordance with arbitrarily applicable relations. *Journal of the Experimental Analysis of Behavior, 67(3)*, 275-301.

Saunders, K. J. (1989). Naming in conditional discrimination and stimulus equivalence. *Journal of the Experimental Analysis of Behavior, 51*, 379-384.

Schusterman, R. J. & Kastak, D. (1993). A California sea lion (Zalophus californianus) is capable of forming equivalence relations. *Psychological-Record, 43(4)*, 823-839.

Sidman, M. (1971). Reading and auditory-visual equivalences. *Journal of Speech and Hearing Research, 14*, 5-13.

Sidman, M. (1994). *Equivalence relations and behavior: A research story*. Boston: Authors Cooperative.

Skinner, B. F. (1938). *Behavior of organisms*. New York: Appleton-Century-Crofts.

Skinner, B. F. (1945). The operational analysis of psychological terms. *Psychological Review, 52*, 270-277.

Skinner, B. F. (1953). *Science and human behavior*. New York: MacMillan.

Skinner, B. F. (1957). *Verbal behavior*. N.Y.: Appleton-Century-Crofts.

Skinner, B. F. (1972). Are theories of learning necessary? As reprinted in *Cumulative record: A selection of papers*, 3rd edition. New York: Appleton-Century-Crofts. (Original work published 1950).

Skinner, B. F. (1974). *About behaviorism*. New York: Vintage Books.

Skinner, B. F. (1989). Teaching machines. *Science, Mar, 243(4898)*, 1535.

Steele, D. L. & Hayes, S. C. (1991). Stimulus equivalence and arbitrarily applicable relational responding. *Journal of the Experimental Analysis of Behavior, 56*, 519-555.

Wegner, D. M. & Pennebaker, J. W. (1993). Changing our minds: An introduction to mental control. In Wegner, D. M. & Pennebaker, J. W. (Eds.), *Handbook of mental control*. Englewood Cliffs, NJ: Prentice-Hall.

Wilson, K. G., Follette, V. M., Hayes, S. C., & Batten, S. V. (1996). Acceptance theory and the treatment of survivors of childhood sexual abuse. *National Center for PTSD Clinical Quarterly, 6(2)*, 34-37.

Wilson, K. G. & Hayes, S. C. (In press). Why it is crucial to understand thinking and feeling: An analysis and application to drug abuse. *The Behavior Analyst*.

Wulfert, E. & Hayes, S. C. (1988). The transfer of conditional sequencing through conditional equivalence classes. *Journal of the Experimental Analysis of Behavior, 50*, 125-144.

Chapter 3

A Behavior-Analytic Approach to Some of the Problems of Self: A Relational Frame Analysis

Dermot Barnes-Holmes
Ian Stewart
National University of Ireland, Maynooth
Simon Dymond
Anglia University Polytechnic
Bryan Roche
National University of Ireland, Maynooth

The term "self" seems to be one of the most frequently used in psychology. In the field of clinical psychology, for example, terms such as *self*-esteem, and *self*-image are of central theoretical importance. The behavior-analytic literature also employs terms such as "*self*-control," "*self*-monitoring" "*self*-reinforcement," and "*self*-discrimination." Despite the apparent ubiquity of the term "self," the exact nature of the behavior to which it refers often remains unclear. Given this lack of clarity, it would seem incumbent upon the behavioral research community to develop a precise, functional-analytic language for discussing "self," and related terms, upon which a conceptually coherent program of behavior-analytic research may be built. The purpose of this chapter is to outline the beginnings of a functional-analytic definition of "self," based on some relatively recent conceptual and empirical research conducted under the rubric of Relational Frame Theory (RFT) (e.g., Hayes, 1991, 1994; Hayes & Barnes, 1997). We will then illustrate the relevance of this research to an understanding of the concept of "self", as used in clinical behavior therapy, with a specific focus on three clinical phenomena; namely, negative self-concept, identity crisis, and self-acceptance. We will begin our behavioral approach to the understanding of self with the seminal work of B. F. Skinner.

The Traditional Behavioral Interpretation of Self

According to Skinner (1974):

> There is a difference between behaving and reporting that one is behaving or reporting the causes of one's behavior. In arranging conditions under which a person describes the public or private world in which he lives, a community generate that very special form of behavior called knowing (pp. 34-35).

In this way, "self-knowledge is of social origin," because "It is only when a person's private world becomes important to others that it becomes important to him." (Skinner, 1974, p. 35). By asking questions such as "How are you feeling?" and "What did you just do?" for example, other members of the verbal community shape an individual's ability to respond discriminatively towards his or her own behavior. From Skinner's perspective, therefore, a sense of self, or self-awareness, emerges when a person learns via verbal interactions to discriminate their own responding.

In order to examine this approach to self-awareness many researchers have investigated the way in which nonhuman subjects can show responding that is under the control of their own previous behavior. Many studies have, for example, looked at the way in which a nonhuman subject can discriminate their own behavior on a reinforcement schedule. In one such study, Lattal (1975) trained pigeons to peck either red or green, in a conditional discrimination task, depending upon whether they had earlier pecked for reinforcement on a differential-reinforcement-of-low-rate (DRL) schedule or had pecked for reinforcement on a differential-reinforcement-of-high-rate (DRO) schedule. In effect, these pigeons learned to report on their own behavior on the previous schedule task. Other studies have seen pigeons discriminate their own behavior with respect to interresponse times (Reynolds, 1966), temporal intervals (Reynolds & Catania, 1962), different fixed ratio values (Pliskoff & Goldiamond, 1966), and run-lengths (Shimp, 1982). These studies can be seen as nonhuman analogs of Skinner's definition of self-awareness, in that the experimental contingencies, in each case, successfully established an organism's discrimination of its own behavior.

The aforementioned studies show how a particular history of behavioral interactions may train a nonhuman subject to respond discriminatively to its own behavior, thus demonstrating "Skinnerian self-awareness." We, and other relational frame theorists would argue, however, that the biological and social evolution of human language transforms the highly limited form of self-awareness observed with nonhumans into an extremely complex form of behavior that requires a separate and very special treatment in its own right. In short, from the RFT perspective, human self-discrimination often involves arbitrarily applicable relational responding, and thus self-discrimination becomes very different from that described by Skinner. To appreciate this perspective on self-awareness, we must first consider the burgeoning research area of derived stimulus relations, and then consider the RFT approach to this type of research (e.g., Barnes, 1994; Barnes & Roche, 1996; Hayes, 1991; 1994; Hayes & Barnes, 1997).

Derived Relational Responding

Over the last twenty seven years behavioral researchers have been developing experimental procedures that generate untrained or derived behavior under laboratory conditions. This derived behavior is normally studied using a "matching-to-sample" format to train conditional discriminations among stimuli. In one preparation, for instance, one of three "sample" stimuli is presented to a subject along with each of three "comparison" stimuli. The samples and comparisons may take the form of nonsense syllables, geometrical shapes, or any stimulus event, with the sole restriction that samples and comparisons do not bear any consistent relationship to each other along a physical dimension (e.g., size or color). As is normal in the discussion of derived relational responding, we will designate the samples and comparisons using alphanumerics. A standard equivalence training procedure might involve reinforcing choosing comparisons B1, B2, and B3 in the presence of samples A1, A2, and A3, respectively, and reinforcing choosing C1, C2, and C3 in the presence B1, B2, and B3, respectively. What is important about this preparation is that given the foregoing training, humans with even relatively basic language skills (e.g., expressive naming) often spontaneously reverse the trained relations (i.e., they match A1, A2, and A3 to B1, B2, and B3, respectively, and match B1, B2, and B3 to C1, C2, and C3, respectively). When this reversal occurs, it is assumed that derived symmetrical stimulus relations have been demonstrated. Furthermore, subjects often also respond in accordance with derived transitive stimulus relations, without any further training (i.e., they will match C1, C2, and C3 to A1, A2, and A3, respectively). When both symmetry and transitivity emerge for a set of stimuli, it is assumed that the stimuli participate in an equivalence relation (Sidman, 1990, pp. 100-102; Sidman, 1992, pp. 18-19; see also Barnes, 1994). As an aside, there are many variations on the training and testing design described above. For instance, rather than training A-B and B-C relations, some experiments have involved training B-A and C-A, and then testing for B-C and C-B equivalence relations (these relations are described as equivalence because they combine both symmetry and transitivity).

Other derived or untrained behaviors have also been produced using stimulus equivalence procedures. For instance, when a simple discriminative function is trained to one stimulus in an equivalence class, that function will often transfer to other stimuli in the class, without explicit reinforcement. This derived transfer of function effect via equivalence relations has been shown with discriminative (Barnes & Keenan, 1993; Barnes, Browne, Smeets, & Roche, 1995; deRose, McIlvane, Dube, Galpin, & Stoddard, 1988; Gatch & Osborne, 1989; Kohlenberg, Hayes, & Hayes, 1991; Wulfert & Hayes, 1988), consequential (Hayes, Devany, Kohlenberg, Brownstein, & Shelby, 1987; Hayes, Kohlenberg, & Hayes, 1991), and respondent stimulus functions (Dougher, Auguston, Markham, Greenway, & Wulfert, 1994; Roche & Barnes, 1997). In Experiment 1 of Roche and Barnes (1997), for instance, a stimulus, C1, was paired with sexually explicit video material, and thus acquired sexual arousal functions (measured using electrodermal responses). Subjects were then trained in the following four stimulus relations: A1-B1, A2-B2, B1-C1, B2-C2. This was followed by equivalence testing (e.g., C1-A1 and C2-A2), and then by testing for the derived transfer of sexual arousal functions. The majority of subjects showed that the sexual arousal functions acquired by C1, also emerged for A1 in the absence of explicit pairing with sexual material.

Stimulus equivalence and derived transfer effects are not readily predicted using traditional behavioral concepts. For instance, in Pavolian or respondent conditioning preparations a conditioned stimulus (CS) predicts the onset of an unconditioned stimulus (UCS) and thus acquires some of its functions, but the UCS does not readily acquire the functions of the CS through backward conditioning (i.e., in respondent conditioning the CS-UCS relation is *unidirectional* (see Hall, 1996). In contrast, the relations between samples and comparisons in the equivalence procedure become *bi-directional* after training in one direction only (i.e., see sample -> pick comparison generates see comparison -> pick sample).

Equivalence and derived transfer are interesting, in large part, because they appear to parallel many natural language phenomena, including, for instance, naming behaviors. In the words of Hayes, Gifford, and Ruckstuhl (1996),

> If a child of sufficient verbal abilities is taught to point to a particular object given a particular written word, the child may point to the word given the object without specific training to do so. In an equivalence-type example, given training in the spoken word "candy" and actual candy, and between the written word CANDY and the spoken word "candy," a child will identify the written word CANDY as in an equivalence class with "candy," even though this performance has never actually been trained. In naming tasks, symmetry and transitivity between written words, spoken words, pictures, and objects are commonplace . . . (p. 285).

Moreover, research indicates that the derivation of stimulus relations, such as equivalence, is related to verbal ability (Barnes, McCullagh, & Keenan, 1990; Devany, Hayes, & Nelson, 1986), and that equivalence procedures can be utilized to teach reading skills (de Rose, de Souza, Rossito, & de Rose, 1992). To many behavior analysts, therefore, equivalence responding constitutes an empirical analog of the symbolic nature of natural language (e.g., Barnes, 1994, 1996; Barnes, Browne, Smeets, & Roche, 1995; Barnes & Holmes, 1991; Barnes & Hampson, 1993a, 1993b, 1997; Barnes, Hegarty, & Smeets, 1997; Barnes et al., 1990; Barnes, Lawlor, Smeets, & Roche, 1996; Barnes & Roche, 1996; Barnes, Smeets, & Leader, 1996; Biglan, 1995; Chase & Danforth, 1991; Dymond & Barnes, 1994, 1995, 1996; Hayes, 1991; Hayes, et al., 1996; Hayes & Hayes, 1989, 1992; Lipkens, 1992; Lipkens, Hayes, & Hayes, 1993; Steele & Hayes, 1991; Watt, Keenan, Barnes, & Cairns, 1991).

In spite of the fact that the study of stimulus equivalence has generated much excitement within the behavioral community, it must be recognized that equivalence is nothing more than a description of a set of procedures and a particular behavioral outcome; it does not constitute an explanation for the effect to which it refers. In our research program, therefore, we have adopted the concepts and some of the procedures of RFT. As described subsequently, this theory aims to explain equivalence, and derived relational responding more generally, and also hopes to provide a behavior-analytic approach to the study of human language (Barnes, 1994; Barnes & Holmes, 1991; Barnes & Roche, 1996; Hayes, 1991, Hayes & Barnes, 1997; Hayes & Hayes, 1989, 1992).

Relational Frame Theory

Relational frame theory explains equivalence, and other examples of derived relational responding, by drawing upon two familiar ideas in behavior analysis. The first of these is that a functional behavioral class is not defined in terms of a particular response topography. For instance, a cat may press a lever with its front paw, back paw, nose, tail, or even by sneezing on it if the lever is sensitive enough. Each of these response forms may thus become members of the same functional class. For the behavior analyst, therefore, class membership is defined by the functional relations established between responding and its antecedents and consequences, and thus responses in any given class may take on an infinite variety of forms.

The concept of a response class with an infinite variety of forms is a defining feature of operant behavior. It is also the case, however, that topographical and functional classes of behavior-environment interactions often overlap, and thus the two may sometimes be confused. Lever pressing, for instance, may be defined by the effect of activity upon the lever, but in actuality the vast majority of lever presses involve "pressing-type" movements. A lever-press might be registered by sneezing, but for all practical purposes these can be ignored. In some circumstances, however, the independence between topographical and functional classes becomes clearly apparent. The concept of generalized imitation (Baer, Peterson, & Sherman, 1967; Gewirtz & Stengle, 1968) provides one good example. If a young child is taught a generalized imitative repertoire, an almost infinite number of response topographies can be substituted for the topographies used in the earlier training. The behavior of imitating is thus generalized, in the sense that it is not limited to any particular response topography. Along similar lines, behavioral researchers have also suggested that it is possible to reinforce "generalized attending" (McIlvane, Dube, Kledaras, Iennaco, & Stoddard, 1990; McIlvane, Dube, & Callahan, 1995), despite that fact that *what* is being attended to will vary.

These and other examples (see Neuringer, 1986; Pryor, Haag, & O'Reilly, 1969) represent a simple extension of the three-term contingency (stimulus-response-consequence) as an analytic unit, but specific qualifiers are often inserted when classes are not easily defined topographically. That is, the class is described as "generalized," "higher order," or "overarching." These qualifiers are not intended to be technical terms, in that no additional mediational process leads to the formation of operants of this type. Instead, these qualifiers emphasize that a particular functional class cannot be defined by its response forms, a fact that is true in principle of functional classes more generally. As we shall see, RFT relies heavily on this concept of a functionally defined, generalized operant class.

The second feature of RFT is a simple extension of the fact that organisms can respond to relations among events. The study of such responding has a long history in behavioral psychology, but most of the research has focused on responding that is based upon the formal or structural properties of the related events. For example, mammals, birds, and even insects can be trained to choose a stimulus as the dimmest of several options (see Reese, 1968, for a relevant review). In effect, the behavior of complex organisms may be brought under the stimulus control of a particular property of a stimulus relationship along a formal stimulus dimension. Relational frame theory argues that this concept of relational responding may be extended to situations in which responding is brought under the contextual control of features of the situation besides the formal properties of the related events. Imagine, for example, a young child who is taught to respond to questions such as "Which cookie has more chocolate?" or "Which glass has more juice?" If a relational response can be brought under the control of environmental features besides the actual relative quantities, it could then be *arbitrarily applied* to other events when the formal properties of the related events do not occasion the relational response – for example, "p is more than q." In this case, the relational response may be controlled by contextual cues, such as the words "more than," rather than by the relative physical sizes of the letters. At this point, the key question for RFT is how does a relational response come to be arbitrarily applied?

According to the theory, arbitrarily applicable relational responding, such as equivalence, is produced, in part, by an appropriate history of multiple exemplar training (see Barnes & Holmes, 1991; Barnes, 1994, 1996; Barnes & Roche, 1996; Hayes, 1991, 1994; Hayes & Hayes, 1989, 1992). Learning to name objects and events in the environment constitutes one of the foundational and earliest developing types of arbitrarily applicable relational responding. Parents often utter the name of an object in the presence of their young child and then reinforce any orienting response that occurs towards the named object. This interaction may be described as, hear name A -> look at object B. Parents also often present an object to their young child and then model and reinforce an appropriate "tact" (Skinner, 1957). This interaction may be described as see object B -> hear and say name A (see Barnes, 1994, for a detailed discussion). During the early stages of such language learning, each interaction may require explicit reinforcement for it to become fully established in the behavioral repertoire of the child, but after a number of name-object and object-name exemplars have been reinforced, the generalized, operant response class of derived "naming" will be created. That is, the multiple-exemplar training establishes particular contextual cues as discriminative for the derived naming response. Suppose, for instance, a child with this multiple exemplar naming history is told "This is your pencil". Contextual cues, such as the word "is" and other features of the naming context, will now be discriminative for symmetrical responding between the name and the object. In the absence of further training, for example, the child will now point to the pencil when asked "Where is your pencil?" (name A -> object B) and will utter "pencil" when presented with the pencil and asked "What is this?" (object B -> name A).

Arbitrarily applicable relational responding may be brought to bear on any events, given appropriate contextual cues. From the RFT perspective, therefore, when the generalized operant of derived naming is established in the behavioral repertoire of a young child, and he or she is then exposed to a matching-to-sample preparation, contextual cues provided by this may be discriminative for equivalence responding. In fact, the matching-to-sample procedure itself may be a particularly potent contextual cue for equivalence responding because it is often used in preschool education exercises to teach word-to-picture equivalence's (see Barnes, 1994, and Barnes & Roche, 1996, for detailed discussions). Relational frame theory therefore defines equivalence as a generalized or higher-order operant response class, insofar as it emerges from a history of reinforcement across multiple exemplars, and once established any stimulus events, irrespective of form, may participate in an equivalence relation.

As indicated previously, RFT views stimulus equivalence and derived transfer as important for the behavior analysis of human language. To illustrate this view consider the following example. Suppose that a young boy on hearing that he is going on a "Ship" (Stimulus A), subsequently experiences an extreme bout of sea sickness. The boy may then learn at school that an "Ocean Liner" (Stimulus B) is a type of ship. Later, on hearing that he is going on an ocean liner, he may show signs of anxiety, and even sickness, despite having had no direct experience with ocean liners. This transfer of function effect is based on the explicit psychological function of A (the word "ship" was paired directly with the experience of sea sickness) and the derived relation between A and B. In effect, the child does not need to experience the possibly aversive consequences of traveling on an ocean liner in rough seas, in order to show signs of anxiety.

This nautical example illustrates one of the pivotal and most important assumptions of the relational frame account of verbal events – *a stimulus is rendered verbal by its participation in one or more derived stimulus relations, such as an equivalence class* (relations other than equivalence are outlined subsequently) (see Hayes & Hayes, 1989, 1992; Hayes & Wilson, 1993, pp. 286-289). In effect, relational frame theorists define a behavioral event as verbal when it involves, at least to some extent, a transfer of functions in accordance with arbitrarily applicable relations. As will be made clear in the current chapter, this functional definition of verbal events provides an important foundation for the experimental and conceptual analysis of human self-awareness.

Relational frame theory also argues that if equivalence can be approached as a type of generalized operant behavior, then so too should other relational activities, such as responding in accordance with the arbitrarily applicable relations of before and after, opposite, different, and so on. In fact, a number of studies have provided empirical support for this position, thereby radically increasing the number of behavioral phenomena that can emerge from trained relational responding (e.g., Barnes & Hampson, 1993a, 1993b, 1997; Barnes & Keenan, 1993; Dymond & Barnes, 1994; Roche & Barnes, 1996; Steele & Hayes, 1991). Before we consider the first of these studies, however, we will briefly describe the three defining features of arbitrarily applicable relational responding. This needs to be done because this type of relational responding involves behavioral patterns that are not easily captured by the language of equivalence alone (see Barnes & Roche, 1996; Hayes & Barnes, 1997). The concept of symmetry, for example, readily captures the bidirectional nature of relations involving equivalent stimuli (e.g., if A is the same as B then B is the same as A). But if A and B are related via a frame of comparison such that A is *less than* B, it does not follow that B is less than A, as required by "strict" symmetry (i.e., B is more than A). Insofar as the concept of symmetry does not easily capture such effects, a more generic nomenclature than that provided by equivalence research is needed to describe the many relations that may be derived between related stimuli. Arbitrarily applicable relational responding is therefore said to involve the following properties.

1. *Mutual entailment*: If a stimulus A is related to another stimulus B, in a particular context, then a relation between B and A is entailed in that context. If the relation is one of equivalence (e.g., A is the same as B), then so too is the entailed relation (e.g., B is the same as A). However, trained and entailed relations may be dissimilar. For instance, if A comes *before* B, then an *after* relation is entailed between B and A.

2. *Combinatorial entailment*: If a stimulus A bears some relation to B, and B bears a relation to another stimulus C, then a relation is entailed between A and C and another between C and A. For example, if A is *bigger than* B, and B is *bigger* than C, then a *bigger than* relation is entailed between A and C, and a *smaller than* relation is entailed between C and A. Mutually entailed relations may differ in their specificity. For example, if A is *taller than* B and A is *taller than* C, then the entailed relations between B and C and between C and B remain unspecified (i.e., B and C may be the same height, or one may be taller than the other).

3. *Transformation of stimulus functions*: If stimuli A and B are in a relation, and stimulus A has acquired some behavioral function, then in a context that selects specific stimulus functions of A as behaviorally relevant, the stimulus functions of B will be transformed in accordance with that relation. For instance, if a subject is taught that stimulus A is *more than* stimulus B, which elicits anxiety, then one would expect that in some contexts stimulus A will elicit more anxiety than B. That is, the different functions of A and B are determined by the nature of the relation that obtains between them.

To avoid possible confusion we should clarify our use of the terms transfer and transformation. When functions transform in accordance with equivalence relations, the term *transfer* is often used, rather than transformation (e.g., Barnes & Keenan, 1993). If stimuli A and B participate in an equivalence relation and an anxiety provoking function is established in B, the previously neutral function of A may be transformed in accordance with this relation, such that A also acquires an anxiety arousing function. In this case, however, it would also be acceptable to say that the anxiety function of B *transfers* to A (see Dymond & Barnes, 1995, 1996). Although the term *transfer* is appropriate here, the term transformation is generic to RFT because functions do not transfer in accordance with non-equivalence relations. If, for example, A is opposite to B, we would not expect an anxiety function in B to transfer to A. Instead, the function of A would be transformed in accordance with the opposite relation, such that it may actually *reduce* anxiety. For this reason, relational frame theorists generally use the term transformation.

In summary, arbitrarily applicable relational responding is characterized by patterns of responding involving mutual entailment, combinatorial entailment, and the transformation of stimulus functions.

The first relational frame study was reported in the early 1990's (Steele and Hayes, 1991). This study demonstrated that human teenage subjects could be trained and tested for responding in accordance with the three arbitrarily applicable relations of coordination (i.e., equivalence), opposition, and difference. Subjects were first trained to relate same stimuli (e.g., a large line with a large line) in the presence of one contextual cue, opposite stimuli (e.g., a large line with a small line) in the presence of a second contextual cue, and different stimuli (e.g., a small line with an oval) in the presence of a third contextual cue. The contextual control functions of SAME, OPPOSITE, and DIFFERENT were thus established for each of three abstract stimuli.

Subjects were then trained and tested in a number of related conditional discriminations, with each discrimination occurring in the presence of one of the three contextual cues (this part of the experiment was quite complex, and so a schematic representation of the trained and tested relations is presented in Figure 1). There were six trained relations, and these were as follows; [S] A1/*B1*-B2-B3, [S] A1/*C1*-C2-C3, [O] A1/B1-B2-*B3*, [O] A1/C1-C2-*C3*, [D] A1/B1-*B2*, [D] A1/C1-*C2*. The letters S, O, and D represent the visual forms that had been established as SAME, OPPOSITE, and DIFFERENT contextual cues, respectively, during pretraining. The stimulus A1 was the sample, and the B and C stimuli were the comparisons. Selecting B1 and C1 was reinforced in the presence of the SAME stimulus, selecting B3 and C3 was reinforced in the presence of the OPPOSITE stimulus, and selecting B2 and C2 was reinforced in the presence of the DIFFER-ENT stimulus (reinforced comparisons are underlined). To get a flavor of the test performances that emerged, consider three of the 15 tasks that were used to test for derived responding; [S] B1/C1-C2-C3, [S] B3/C1-C2-C3, [D] C1/B1-B2-N3 (N3 was a novel stimulus that had not been used during the training). Subjects selected C1, C3, and B2, respectively on these tasks, indicating response patterns in accordance with the frames of coordination, opposition, and distinction (i.e., if B1 and C1 are the same as A1, then B1 and C1 are the same; if B3 and C3 are opposite to A1 then B3 and C3 are the same; if B2 is different from A1, and C1 is the same as A1, then B2 is also different from C1). More recent research has replicated and considerably extended this initial study (e.g., Roche & Barnes, 1996; Dymond & Barnes, 1995, 1996).

Trained Relations

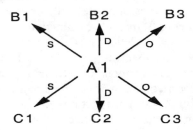

Tested Derived

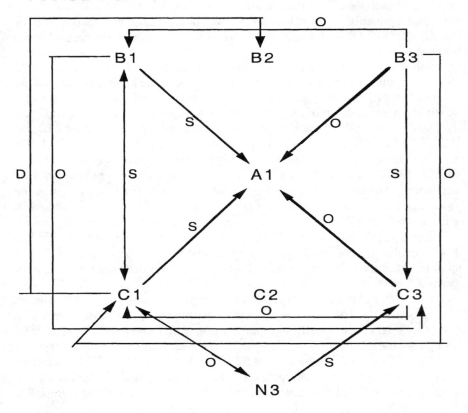

Figure 1. Schematic representation of the trained and tested relations from Steele and Hayes (1991). Letters S, O, and D indicate the arbitrarily applicable relations of sameness, opposition, and difference.

A Relational Frame Approach to Self: Verbal Self-Discrimination

Having described the main concepts, and some of the procedures of RFT, and having considered the earliest study to show responding in accordance with a variety of derived stimulus relations, we may now examine the utility of RFT in the analysis of self. In fact, a number of relatively recent studies by relational frame theorists approached the study of self-awareness by examining the transformation of self-discrimination response functions in accordance with equivalence and other derived relations (e.g., Dymond & Barnes 1994, 1995, 1996). In effect, this research combined the procedures used in earlier nonhuman studies (e.g. Lattal, 1975) with a number of methods used in the study of derived stimulus relations. In the first of these studies (Dymond & Barnes, 1994), subjects were first trained and tested for the formation of 3, 3-member equivalence classes (i.e. A1-B1-C1, A2-B2-C2, A3-B3-C3). Following the demonstration of equivalence responding, subjects were trained to emit two self-discrimination responses on two time-based schedules of reinforcement; if subjects did not emit an operant response then the choice of stimulus B1 was reinforced, but if they did emit one or more responses then reinforcement was contingent on choosing stimulus B2. Subjects were then tested for the transfer of these self-discrimination response functions via equivalence relations (i.e., no response -> choose C1; one or more responses -> choose C2). As predicted by RFT, all four subjects showed the formation of three equivalence relations and then the transfer of self-discrimination response functions via two of these relations. This was the first empirical demonstration of the derived transfer effect with self-discrimination response functions.

As previously stated, in order for a behavioral event to be defined as verbal by RFT it must involve, at least to some extent, a transfer (or transformation) of functions via arbitrarily applicable relations. It follows, then, that a transfer of self-discrimination response functions in accordance with such relations is defined by RFT as an example of *verbally* discriminating oneself. Thus, according to the RFT account of human self-awareness, a language-able human is not simply behaving with regard to his or her behavior, but is also behaving *verbally* with regard to his or her behavior (Hayes & Wilson, 1993). The crucial difference between humans and nonhumans, then, is a functional one. Although a nonhuman may learn to respond to its own behavior, it is simply performing a discrimination in which the original response (e.g., pecking according to a DRL or DRO schedule) becomes discriminative for the second (e.g., choosing either red or green keys; see Hineline & Wanchisen, 1989, p. 234). The responding of a verbally-able human, however, is often controlled by the participation of verbal events in derived stimulus relations and the various functions (e.g. "good" or "bad") that may transform in accordance with those relations. We believe that making a clear functional distinction, based on RFT, between verbal and non-verbal self-discrimination will provide an important foundation for developing a behavior-analytic understanding of human self-awareness. More importantly in the current context, however, is that this RFT, functional distinction may also provide key insights into the origins of a number of psychological problems that clients often present in therapy. For illustrative purposes we will present RFT interpretations of negative self-concept, identity crisis, and self-acceptance.

Negative Self-Concept

Imagine a young girl who is constantly criticized by her parents and told, for example, that she is "bad," "stupid," and "nothing but trouble." As this child comes into contact with the verbal community these negative descriptions of her may come to participate in equivalence relations, and other more general negative self-discriminations will be derived. For instance, the girl may respond to "bad" as "I am a worthless person," to "stupid" as "everyone laughs at me," and to "nothing but trouble" as "No one wants or loves me." Thus, as a young adult she may come to discriminate herself verbally (i.e., via derived relations) as unworthy of the affection and trust of others, and based on this "verbal construction" of self-worth she might avoid emotional intimacy because "no one could possibly want someone like me." In so doing, of course, her verbally constructed negative self-concept will gain support – in avoiding intimate relationships, the resultant loneliness provides the "proof" she needs to bolster her self-discrimination as not worthy of "real love." In summary, the RFT perspective sees psychological problems, such as this, as being the product of a history of behavioral interactions that give rise to networks of derived stimulus relations that allow the behavioral functions associated with negative descriptions of self to transfer and transform in accordance with those networks.

The foregoing interpretation suggests that the RFT approach can shed some light on the verbal nature of negative self-concept. Although the interpretation is clearly speculative at this point, the results of a recent study suggest that this approach to negative self-concept may well be useful. Using a stimulus-equivalence procedure, Barnes, et al. (1996) examined the effects of negative self-discriminations by mentally-retarded children with respect to non-retarded children (i.e., school mates). The retarded and nonretarded children were exposed to a "loaded" equivalence procedure, involving words germane to academic self-concept ('Slow' and 'Able') as B stimuli, and personal names (subjects own name and a fictional name) as C stimuli. Experimentally induced equivalence relations were intended to link each subject's own name to the word 'Able'. The study sought to determine whether or not the handicapped children would relate their own name to the word 'Slow' despite conditional discrimination training designed to produce an alternative derived performance (the assumption being that the retarded children would have previously learned, through interactions with the verbal community, to discriminate themselves as Slow). No significant differences between mildly mentally retarded and nonretarded subjects was found on neutral equivalence test performances (i.e., tests using abstract shapes). However, mildly mentally retarded subjects produced significantly lower levels of equivalence responding on the 'loaded' equivalence test by failing to match their own name to the word 'Able'. The results therefore supported the idea that preexperimentally established relations between the retarded subjects' own names and the descriptive term 'Slow' may have disrupted the formation of experimentally induced equivalence relations for some of the retarded subjects. Of course, a great deal more empirical work is needed in this area, but these preliminary data do appear promising.

Multiple relational frames. Up to this point we have looked only at equivalence relations. As explained previously, however, according to RFT equivalence responding is only one subcategory of derived stimulus relations. For RFT, then, a wide range of derived stimulus relations are involved in self-discrimination behaviors, and are thus relevant to an understanding of negative self-concept. One of the studies conducted by Dymond and Barnes (1995) is particularly pertinent in this regard. Four experimental subjects were pretrained in accordance with sameness, more-than and less-than relations (more-than and less-than relations being subcategories of the relational frame of comparison). The sameness pretraining employed procedures similar to those used by Steele and Hayes (1991) (i.e., reinforcement was provided for matching a short-line comparison to a short-line comparison in the presence of the SAME contextual cue). For the more-than and less-than relational pretraining, reinforcement was given for picking a comparison that was either more-than or less-than the sample along some physical dimension. As one example, choosing a 5-X comparison in the presence of a 10-X sample was reinforced given the LESS-THAN cue, whereas choosing a 20-X comparison in the presence of a 10-X sample was reinforced given the MORE-THAN cue. After successful pretraining, the subjects received training in six arbitrary relations, the following four relations being the most critical: SAME/A1-B1, SAME/A1-C1, LESS-THAN/A1-B2, MORE-THAN/A1-C2. Subjects were subsequently tested for seven derived relations, the following three relations being the most important: SAME/B1-C1, MORE-THAN/B1-C2, LESS-THAN/B1-B2 (see Figure 2).

The establishment of derived self-discrimination response functions in accordance with the relations of sameness, more-than, and less-than required that subjects acquire three response functions. They were thus provided, via three complex reinforcement schedules, with the behavioral repertoire necessary to show three performances: (i) No response, (ii) Just one response, and (iii) Just two responses. They were subsequently trained to pick the B1 stimulus after making a single response only. According to RFT, given the prior establishment of derived sameness, more-than, and less-than relations, a subject should go on to choose the following: (i) C1 after one response (because there is a transfer of functions via sameness from C1 to B1), (ii) B2 after no response (because B2 acquires a response function that is less than that of B1), and (iii) C2 after two responses (i.e. because C2 acquires a response function that is more than that of B1) (see Figure 2). In fact, the results showed that all four experimental subjects did indeed demonstrate the predicted transformation of self-discrimination response functions (see also Dymond & Barnes, 1996; Roche & Barnes, 1997).

We believe that the transformation of self-discrimination response functions in accordance with more-than and less-than relations, as just described, constitutes

Schematic Representation of Trained & Tested Relations (Dymond & Barnes, 1995)

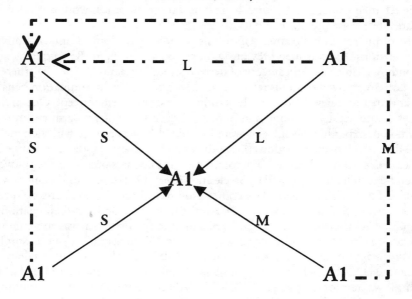

Figure 2. Schematic representation of the most crucial trained (solid lines) and tested (dashed lines) relations. Letters S, M, and L indicate the arbitrarily applicable relations of sameness, more-than, and less-than. The diagram also shows that a one-response function was trained using the B1 stimulus, and tests examined the transformation of the trained self-discrimination response function in accordance with the relations of sameness (C1, one response), more-than (C2, two responses), and less-than (B2, no response) (adapted from Dymond & Barnes, 1995; copyright 1995 by the Society for the Experimental Analysis of Behavior, Inc.).

a key behavioral process involved in the creation of negative self-concept via social comparison. Self-discriminations including "I'm worse than him", "She's much better than me", or "I'll never be as good as he is" may often develop via their participation in a number of different relational networks established and maintained by the language community. Imagine, for instance, a young boy who is repeatedly exposed to parental comments that compare him negatively to a sibling. For example, "You'll never measure up to your brother"; "Your reports are so bad in comparison with those of your brother"; or "Why can't you be more like brother — he's so good?" Such verbal comparisons may in later life contribute to the formation of more general self-criticisms in which the young man perceives himself as always *under* performing or doing *less* well than others. He might then find himself dropping out of college, quitting one job after another, and avoiding long-term emotional commitments because he has "verbally constructed" a future (i.e., derived a relational network) in which he underperforms in all of these areas (e.g., "What's the point in working hard, someone better will always be promoted over me."). Once again, the RFT perspective views the emergence of what is called negative self-concept as a relational activity that is produced in part through verbal interactions with significant others, such as parents.

Through such interactions, relational frames of comparison are established that lead an individual to discriminate him or herself as less worthy along a number of psychological dimensions (e.g., less intelligent, less hard working, less deserving of love, etc.). Negative self-concept, from the RFT perspective therefore, is essentially a relational or verbal process. The same approach also may be taken to a range of other psychological problems.

Identity Crisis

Why breaking up is hard to do. The RFT approach to self-discrimination also provides a unique interpretation of what it means to have an identity crisis. For illustrative purposes, we will consider an identity crisis for a man that may follow after a breakdown in his marriage. From the RFT perspective, the end of marriage requires that the man reframe himself as a single person. This transformation in his self-descriptive, verbal network will impact upon far reaching aspects of his so called self-identity. Perhaps he will begin to behave like a single person for a while, doing the things he used to do before he was married. Such changes in the way he thinks of himself and his lifestyle may also impact on the types of individuals to whom he is attracted (i.e., if he has become different following the break-up then those to whom he is similar and dissimilar will also change). For instance, he may be attracted to different types of people because they are *opposite to* his ex-partner on some dimension. Alternatively, if his self-description has not changed very much (i.e., in ordinary terms, he is in denial) perhaps he will look for his "old" partner in every woman he meets and continue to be attracted to women who are the *same as* her on some dimensions. Figure 3 outlines one hypothetical relational network that could support this type of "emotional stagnation" after a relationship has ended.

Figure 3 represents a hypothetical verbal network that characterizes a large part of the self-concept of a "family man" whose life is literally "built around" his partner and children. In this Figure the term "family man" is a verbal function. All of the other equivalent terms (e.g., children, hopeless romantic, married) are content of the category "family man" and so cannot exist without it. If, however, this man's wife deserts him then many of these relations are in jeopardy. Not only does her leaving make it impossible for this man to be a family man, but all of the equivalent terms at once also fail to apply (e.g., married, hopeless romantic). In addition, this man has not engaged in extra-familial activity and would appear to have no interests outside the home. Thus, with his wife's departure this man's family identity is lost and so too is a plethora of other terms in relation to which he defines himself. In effect, the functions of other nodes in this relational network are also transformed by her leaving.

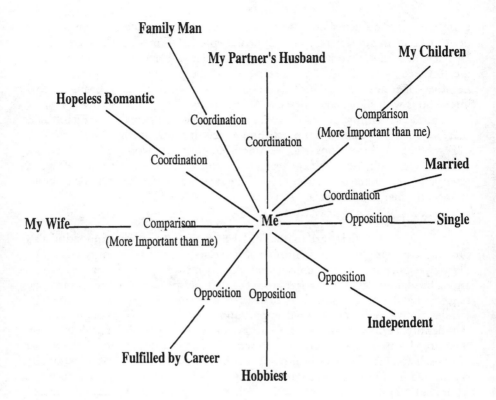

Figure 3. Some dimensions of a hypothetical relational network pertaining to the self-identity of a "family man."

When a network such as this is ripped apart by the departure of a loved one what is left is a psychological void. This "family man" is now a man in name only – the functions of his identity have literally fallen away. When relationship breakdown is viewed in this way, therefore, it is not difficult to see why such a man may contemplate suicide. After all, he has already been murdered psychologically. For RFT, therefore, the psychological turmoil created by an identity crisis is seen to be a largely verbal or relational process. In the current example, most of the relational/verbal responses made by the "family man" in his day-to-day life were destroyed when the central node (his wife) was removed from the network. The crisis, so to speak, is a crisis for the integrity of the relational network.

Self-Acceptance

The relational frames of Here and There and Now and Then: Extending the analysis to self-acceptance. Thus far, we have seen how Skinner's behavior-analytic interpretation of self-discrimination has been extended by incorporating the transformation of self-discrimination functions in accordance with arbitrarily applicable relations. Using this modern approach, it was then possible to offer some brief functional-analytic interpretations of human emotional problems that are normally bound up with what have been called "negative self-concept" and "identity crisis." Another important aspect of self that may yield to a relational frame interpretation is that of self-acceptance. According to RFT, the relational frames of "Here and There" and "Now and Then" are most relevant for such an interpretation (see Barnes & Roche, 1997a; Dymond & Barnes, 1997). Allow us to explain.

According to RFT, a young child will learn a variety of relational operants through his or her interactions with other language users (see Barnes, 1994; Dymond and Barnes, 1995; Hayes, 1991; Steele & Hayes, 1991). Relational frame theory considers the relational frames of "Here and There", and "Now and Then" as pivotal in developing a functional analysis of what it means to self-accept (see Barnes & Roche, 1997a). These two relational operants are established when a young girl, for example, is trained by other language users to discriminate her own perspective as unique. In effect, the young girl learns not just to discriminate her own behavior (i.e., to see that she sees) but also to discriminate that her own discriminating is *always* occurring from the same locus or perspective (i.e., she sees that her seeing is always from *her own perspective*). In the words of Hayes (1984):

> First, words such as "here" and "there" are acquired which do not refer to a specific thing but to a relation to the child's point of view. For example, "there" is always anywhere else but "here" and "here" is always "from this locus or point of view." Second, children are taught to distinguish their perspective from that of others. Young children have a hard time with the issue of perspective. For example, young children seated across from a doll will, when asked, report that the doll sees what they are seeing. Gradually, however, a sense of perspective emerges. A child learns what he or she sees is seen from a perspective. Similarly, a young child, asked what she had for breakfast, may respond with what her brother actually ate, but an older child will not make such a mistake. Through correction, ("No, that is what your brother ate. What did *you* eat?") a child must learn to see seeing from a consistent locus. . . Suppose a child can give correct answers to the question "what did you *x*?' where "*x*" is a wide variety of events such as eat, feel, watch, and so on. The events constantly change. In our terms, the seeing and the seeing seeing change. Only the locus does not. Thus, one consistency between the word "you" in such questions and behavior is not seeing or seeing seeing but the behavior of seeing that you see from a particular locus or perspective. Thus, in some real sense, "you" *are* the perspective (pp. 102-103; emphasis in original).

In brief, the girl's interaction with the verbal community establishes derived responding in accordance with the relational frames of "Here and There", and "Now and Then", and in so doing the girl learns to discriminate her own discriminating as being invariably located in the same positions in these relational frames (i.e., her discriminating acquires the relational functions of "Here" and "Now" rather than "There" and "Then"). This relational framing activity provides a constant perspective on the world, and it is this activity which gives rise to a sense of self.

Once established in the young girl's behavioral repertoire, the relational frames of "Here and There" and "Now and Then" will become an inherent aspect of almost all verbal events for her. She will always talk to another person from the perspective of Here and Now about events which occurred There and Then. Asking "How goes it?", for instance, locates the girl Here and Now and the listener There and Then, because she is asking Here and Now for a response from the listener that will occur There (wherever the listener is) and Then (whenever the listener replies). Even when the girl talks to herself she will likely respond in accordance with these relational frames. Suppose, for instance, that she solves a complex problem faster than anyone else in her class, and then exclaims to herself "I was really fast". In this example, the statement places the girl's current discrimination Here and Now (having solved the problem) talking about previous behavior, There and Then (actually solving the problem). To sum up, the relational frames of "Here and There" and "Now and Then" establish an ever-present division between the speaker (always Here and Now) and the spoken about (always There and Then).

The frames of "Here and There" and "Now and Then" play a very important role in our human ability to evaluate, judge, compare, contrast, etc. different events from a constant perspective. In the West, in particular, responding Here and Now to events There and Then as good, bad, better, worse, easy, difficult, and so on, is ongoing and ubiquitous. In fact, because evaluating is so pervasive we normally fail to discriminate our evaluating as evaluating. Instead, we usually discriminate our evaluations as reflecting the real or inherent properties of the events that we evaluate. In the language of RFT, the relational functions of Here and Now that become attached to our evaluations are rarely replaced by the relational functions of There and Then. For example, it is extremely rare that a person will evaluate (Here and Now) someone else as "devious," and then immediately discriminate that evaluation as being only an evaluation (located There and Then). In most circumstances, when a person is discriminated (Here and Now) as devious, this behavioral event is not then followed by the discrimination (Here and Now) that the previous evaluation (of deviousness) (now located There and Then) was simply an evaluation based on a personal history of likes and dislikes (e.g., someone else might discriminate the person as a great strategist, rather than devious). The fact that most of us do not usually discriminate our evaluations (occuring Here and Now) as evaluations (when they shift to There and Then) is an important factor in creating a barrier to self-acceptance.

In Acceptance and Commitment Therapy (ACT), a relatively recent RFT-based therapy, for instance, clients are encouraged to discriminate between experiential context (Here and Now) and experiential content (There and Then) (see Hayes, Strosahl, & Wilson, 1999; Hayes & Wilson, 1994; for a description of ACT). Experiential context refers to the fact that it is always *you* who is doing the discriminating (located Here and Now), and experiential content refers to the actual things and events that *you* discriminate or evaluate (located There and Then). As suggested above, most of us normally fail to recognize that our evaluations are evaluations (experiential content located There and Then) and thus are separate from our constant sense of perspective (experiential context located Here and Now). At one time, for example, we may evaluate someone as nice, but at a later time we may see them as bad (experiential content) – but it is the *same* you (experiential context) doing the evaluating. In an effort to establish a sense of separateness between experiential content and context, and thus facilitate self-acceptance, ACT clients are encouraged to adopt a verbal style in which evaluations of self are named, rather than simply stating the evaluation (see Hayes & Wilson, 1994). Using this new verbal style a client might say, for example, "*I'm having the evaluation that* I'm unlovable" as opposed to "I'm unlovable," or *I'm having the evaluation that* I'm a really bad person," rather than "I'm a really bad person." In getting a client to adopt this verbal style, negative evaluations of self are responded to as There and Then, rather than as Here and Now, because each self-evaluation is discriminated as an evaluation that will come and go, rather than as a "true" reflection of self. In this way, a sense of psychological distance is created between a client's negative evaluations of self (content located There and Then) and the client's sense of self (context located Here and Now). As a result, the client may experience a greater sense of self-acceptance, because when "bad stuff" shows up it is readily discriminated as ephemeral content (There and Then), rather than as constant and immutable context (Here and Now). For example, it is easier to accept the unpleasant thought, "I'm useless," if it is discriminated as a temporary evaluation, rather than as a true reflection of oneself.

There is as yet no basic empirical research to support the foregoing relational frame interpretation of self-acceptance. Nevertheless, we have used a teaching exercise that was developed to aid students in their understanding of the RFT interpretation of self-acceptance. This exercise will be presented here with a view to clarifying this interpretation. With this aim in mind, the reader is encouraged to attempt this exercise, either alone or, if possible, in a classroom setting (another version of this exercise, for teaching about the RFT interpretation of the "mystical experience," was presented by Barnes and Roche, 1997a).

A Teaching Exercise to Illustrate the RFT
Interpretation of Self-Acceptance

Participants in the following exercise would usually be students on a "Behavior Therapy" course for Psychiatric Nurses who have studied the basics of RFT. Such students would normally receive a simplified version of what has been covered thus far in this chapter and would then be encouraged to engage in an "RFT-based" exercise. They would be informed that the purpose of the exercise is to enable them to explore the difficulties inherent in transferring thoughts, feelings, and evaluations from Here and Now to There and Then in their relational framing activity, and that through contacting these difficulties at first hand they should gain a better appreciation of the RFT interpretation of self-acceptance. Before the start of the exercise, the participants would be reminded that responding to evaluations, and the like, as context (Here and Now) rather than as content (There and Then) is a relational operant that receives constant reinforcement from the earliest age, and as such is particularly difficult to extinguish.

The Exercise: Learning to Respond to Thoughts, Feelings, and Evaluations as Located There and Then rather than Here and Now

Teacher: OK, we're going to try an exercise based on RFT, to show how difficult it is to continually transfer thoughts, feelings, and evaluations from Here and Now to There and Then, in our relational framing activity. It seems simple enough; all you have to do is to let your thoughts, feelings, and evaluations appear and then flow past, without dwelling on them. The point of the exercise is to notice when your thoughts switch from There and Then back to Here and Now. When your thoughts are responded to as There and Then you are looking at them and taking note of them as mere unimportant thoughts, but when your thoughts are Here and Now you are caught up in them and as such you lose yourself in them. These descriptions may sound a bit strange, but by doing the exercise I think you will see what I mean. OK, I'm going to ask you to see yourself sitting by the side of a stream on a warm, sunny day. You see leaves float by on the surface of the water, and what I want you to do is to put each thought, feeling, or evaluation you have into a sentence which will be written on a leaf. If you prefer, you can put images rather than sentences on the leaves, because I know that some people find it easier to put thoughts into pictures rather than into words. OK, is everyone with me so far?

Students: General agreement [If anyone would prefer not to join in they may be allowed to leave].

Teacher: All right, in another minute or so we're going to do some pre-exercise relaxation, and then I'd like you to start putting your thoughts on the floating leaves. This isn't as easy as it might seem. You must try to watch the leaves float by carrying one thought after another without interrupting the process. But that's the tricky piece – you'll find it very difficult at first to do this without interruption, and it is this very point in the exercise that is the key. When you realize, as you eventually will at some stage, that the stream has disappeared and that you seem to be lost in your thoughts, I would like you to "back up" a few seconds and try to make contact again with what you were doing at the moment the stream disappeared. Then you should simply restart the process of putting your thoughts on leaves again until the next time that you get lost, and so on, and so on. The most important thing, though, is that you notice when the stream has disappeared, and then try to catch what was happening right before you got "lost." All right?

Students: General agreement [Again, if anyone would prefer not to join in, they may be allowed to leave].

Teacher: Just one further thing. If at some stage you start thinking "I'm not doing this right – I'm not getting the hang of it" then you should try putting *that* thought on a leaf and sending it floating down the stream. OK, then, first of all we're going to relax. Just close your eyes, feel yourself sitting comfortably in your chair, and listen to my voice. If your thoughts start "wandering" just return to the sound of my voice. All right, first turn your attention to yourself as you sit in this room. Imagine the room and yourself sitting in it exactly as you are doing. Now get inside your own skin – get in touch with your body. Notice the way it feels to sit in the chair – the shape that your body is making and the places where it makes contact with the chair. Notice any bodily sensations you may have. As you notice each one, just acknowledge it and then move on – don't dwell on the sensations, just move on [Pause]. OK, now imagine yourself sitting by the side of the stream. You are sitting comfortably up on the bank, watching the leaves float by. If the stream disappears or you find yourself on a leaf, or in the stream, or losing contact with this scene completely, then notice that and try to catch what you were doing at the moment you got lost. Then get back up on the bank again and put your thoughts on the floating leaves. (The group should be left to work on the exercise for about three to five minutes. They should be given enough time with as little interruption as possible. The teacher should try to get a feel for where the group are and then add appropriate comments as needed [e.g., "Just let the leaves continue to float along . . . and notice when this has stopped."]. Conversation with students should be avoided. Students who open their eyes should be told, calmly, to shut them again and to resume the exercise. If a student begins to talk then he/she should be told calmly that all comments should be left until after the exercise has finished, and that for the present time he/she should put what he/she wants to say on a leaf and let it float on down the stream.) OK, the last of the leaves is floating by now . . . we are beginning to come back to the room [Pause]. Imagine yourself sitting in the room and now imagine the room (the room should be described). When you are ready to come back into the room, then open your eyes. Right, welcome back.

Teacher: OK, how did that go? Has anyone got any comments to make?

Student 1: It was fairly tough to keep going without losing it. I'd be fine for a short time, and then I'd suddenly realize it was gone.

Teacher: So you lost the stream altogether.

Student 1: That's it – the exercise was left behind completely.

Teacher: Were you able to catch what you had been doing right before you lost track?

Student 1: Well yes, sort of. I was thinking that the exercise seemed very like a type of meditation and that this was a big change from the rest of the course, so far. Then I started to think about a meditation night class that I took years ago, and some of the people that I met on it. Then, suddenly, I remembered what I was supposed to be doing and that I hadn't put any of my recent thoughts on a leaf. Teacher: All right, that's great. So when the first thought turned up, the one about meditation and the course, was that on a leaf?

Student 1: Probably not.

Teacher: So where was it instead?

Student 1: Nowhere, really – I suppose that I got lost in it.

Teacher: Exactly! So in other words, your thought, located Here and Now, was about meditation, located There and Then. That's one way of putting it. Alternatively, we might say that you engaged in a piece of private verbal behavior, Here and Now, and then failed to discriminate it as behavior, There and Then. Instead, the thought remained Here and Now, and so you were caught up in it and were unaware of its existence as simply a thought. The stream and leaves were gone, and you were encompassed by the thought of meditation and the course. This thought was right Here and Now, instead of being away from you, There and Then.

Student 1: I can see what you're saying, it does make sense.

Teacher: Did you put the thought about your night classes in meditation on a leaf?

Student 1: As soon as I noticed that I'd "lost" the exercise, I imagined myself back beside the stream, and put the thought about "getting lost" on a leaf.

Teacher: How did you manage after that?

Student 1: Well, not too badly, I suppose. Every time I'd notice my thoughts wandering, I'd try to return to the stream and pick up where I'd left off.

Teacher: So, in other words you were switching all the time from responding to your thoughts as simply content, "There and Then," and then responding to them as context in the "Here and Now," and thus getting wrapped up in them.

Student 1 : Yes, that's what seemed to be happening.

Teacher: Great. Thanks for that. Your experience is a good example of how difficult it can be to maintain responding to our thoughts as mere content. Somebody else?

Student 2: I was doing fine until I started to think about going on holiday in two weeks time.

Teacher: Did you respond to that thought as content (There and Then) by putting it on a leaf, or did you respond to the thought as context (Here and Now) and get carried away by it?

Student 2: I got carried away.

Teacher: And so what happened to the stream you imagined?

Student 2: I just forgot it completely.

Teacher: Exactly. So it seems then, that when you responded to your thoughts as Here and Now (context) rather than as There and Then (content) you forgot about the stream. In other words, as soon as you stopped discriminating your thoughts as mere content they became all-encompassing context in which you became totally engrossed.

Student 2: Yeah, I see it – that's what was happening.

(Some of the remaining students' comments would be elicited and dealt with in much the same fashion, and then there would be a brief summing up as follows).

Teacher: Right, that's great. So at this stage, then, perhaps you've got a flavor of the kind of difficulties that are involved in responding to your thoughts, feelings, and evaluations as located There and Then (when you "distance" yourself from your thoughts) as opposed to Here and Now (when you become "wrapped up" in them).

The floating leaf exercise can be a very effective way of facilitating what we might call "self-acceptance." A common problem related to lack of self-acceptance is feeling bad about feeling bad. Some clients, for example, will start out by feeling anxious about a job interview or a date, or feeling down about a family quarrel, etc., but then very quickly they start to feel bad about having these negative emotions in the first place. Such clients often cycle into severe bouts of depression because they think that they are somehow abnormal in feeling so bad about what they perceive to be everyday normal things (the assumption being that "happy" people do not have these negative emotions). In effect, clients like this find it difficult to *accept* that sometimes they will feel bad. By getting such clients to practice the floating-leaf exercise, in the context of other therapeutic interventions, they often report finding it easier to catch themselves cycling into feeling bad about feeling bad. As a result, they find they can more readily accept the negative thoughts and emotions that show up during the course of day-to-day life without all of the self-recrimination that would normally follow. In short, they learn to accept the "bad" self (as content) by discriminating it as There and Then, rather than Here and Now. After the exercise, students are referred to Hayes and Wilson, (1993, 1994) for detailed coverage of the relationship between RFT and ACT.

Summary and Conclusion

We will conclude by reviewing very briefly the RFT approach to some of the problems of self. Self-awareness in humans is different from that seen in non-humans because although the latter may well demonstrate discrimination of their own behavior, only verbally-able humans can show a transformation of self-discrimination response functions in accordance with arbitrarily applicable relations that allows for novel or emergent self-discriminations. Such derived relations may contribute to negative psychological outcomes for the person involved, including what have been called "negative self-concept" and "identity crisis." With respect to self-acceptance, two important relational frames are Here and There, and Now and Then. Most Western speakers usually respond to their evaluations of the world as located Here and Now, a behavior pattern that, according to the RFT-based therapy ACT, often leads to unhappiness or even serious emotional problems. One important objective of ACT therapy then, is to encourage clients to respond repeatedly to their thoughts and feelings as located There and Then rather than Here and Now – a practice that may generate what is normally called greater *self-acceptance*.

Although the purely functional-analytic, relational frame approach to problems of self provides considerable scope for further empirical and conceptual
analyses, relatively little basic research has as yet been conducted to support the RFT
approach. Of primary importance in the generation of such research will be the
development of empirical procedures for the analysis of relational framing in
accordance with Here and There, and Now and Then. Some relevant work has
already been conducted by developmental researchers in the area of "perspective-
taking" (Vygotsky, 1978; Piaget, 1954; Rogoff, 1988), but as regards the RFT analysis
of self-acceptance much more will undoubtedly be needed. Nevertheless, in
focusing the empirical microscope on this issue we will be making serious inroads
into an area that has received scant attention from any empirically-based psychology. Success here would constitute a real coup for behavior analysis. We firmly
believe that we should not miss this golden opportunity.

References

Baer, D. M., Peterson, R. F., & Sherman, J. A. (1967). The development of imitation
by reinforcing behavioral similarity to a model. *Journal of the Experimental
Analysis of Behavior, 10,* 405-416.

Barnes, D. (1994). Stimulus equivalence and relational frame theory. *The Psychological Record, 44,* 91-124.

Barnes, D. (1996). Naming as a technical term: Sacrificing behavior analysis at the
altar of popularity. *Journal of the Experimental Analysis of Behavior, 65,* 264-267

Barnes, D., Browne, M., Smeets, P., & Roche, B. (1995). A transfer of functions and
a conditional transfer of functions through equivalence relations in three- to
six-year old children. *The Psychological Record, 45,* 405-430.

Barnes, D., & Holmes, Y. (1991). Radical behaviorism, stimulus equivalence, and
human cognition. *The Psychological Record, 41,* 19-31.

Barnes, D., & Hampson, P.J. (1993a). Stimulus equivalence and connectionism:
Implications for behavior analysis and cognitive science. *The Psychological
Record, 43,* 617-638.

Barnes, D., & Hampson, P.J. (1993b). Learning to learn: The contribution of
behavior analysis to connectionist models of inferential skill in humans. In G.
Orchard (Ed.), *Neural computing research and applications I* (pp. 129-138).
London, England, IOP.

Barnes, D., & Hampson, P.J. (1997). Connectionist models of arbitrarily applicable
relational responding: A possible role for the hippocampal system. In J. W.
Donohoe & V. P. Dorsel (Eds.), *Neural network models of cognition: Biobehavioral
foundations* (pp. 496-521). Netherlands: Elsevier.

Barnes, D., Hegarty, N., & Smeets, P. M. (1997). Relating equivalence relations to
equivalence relations: A relational framing model of complex human functioning. *The Analysis of Verbal Behavior, 14,* 57-83.

Barnes, D., & Keenan, M. (1993). A transfer of functions through derived arbitrary and non-arbitrary stimulus relations. *Journal of the Experimental Analysis of Behavior, 59*, 61-81.

Barnes, D., Lawlor, H., Smeets, & Roche, B. (1996). Stimulus equivalence and academic self-concept among mildly mentally handicapped and nonhandicapped children. *The Psychological Record, 46*, 87-107.

Barnes, D., McCullagh, P. D., & Keenan, M. (1990). Equivalence class formation in non-hearing impaired children and hearing impaired children. *The Analysis of Verbal Behavior, 8*, 19-30.

Barnes, D., & Roche, B. (1996). Relational frame theory and stimulus equivalence are fundamentally different: A reply to Saunders. *The Psychological Record, 46*, 489-508.

Barnes, D., & Roche, B. (1997a). A behavior-analytic approach to behavioral reflexivity. *The Psychological Record, 47*, 543-572.

Barnes, D., & Roche, B. (1997b). Relational frame theory and the experimental analysis of human sexuality. *Applied and Preventive Psychology, 6*, 117-135.

Barnes, D., Smeets, P.M., & Leader, G. (1996). New procedures for generating emergent matching performances in children and adults: Implications for stimulus equivalence. In T.R. Zentall & P.M. Smeets (Eds.), *Stimulus class formation in humans and animals* (pp. 153-171). Elsevier, Netherlands.

Biglan, A. (1995). *Changing cultural practices: A contextualist framework for intervention research*. Reno, NV.: Context Press.

Chase, P. N., & Danforth, J. S. (1991). The role of rules in concept learning. In L. J. Hayes & P. N. Chase (Eds.), *Dialogues on verbal behavior* (pp. 205-225). Reno, NV: Context Press.

Dougher, M. J., Auguston, E., Markham, M. R., Greenway, D. E., & Wulfert, E. (1994). The transfer of respondent eliciting and extinction functions through stimulus equivalence classes. *Journal of the Experimental Analysis of Behavior, 62*, 331-352.

de Rose, J. T., de Souza, D. G., Rossito, A. L., & de Rose, T. M. S. (1992). Stimulus equivalence and generalization in reading after matching-to-sample by exclusion. In S. C. Hayes & L. J. Hayes (Eds.), *Understanding verbal relations (pp. 69-82)*. Reno, NV: Context Press.

de Rose, J. C., McIlvane, W. J., Dube, W.V., Galpin, V. C., & Stoddard, L. T. (1988). Emergent simple discrimination established by indirect relation to differential consequences. *Journal of the Experimental Analysis of Behavior, 50*, 1-20.

Devany, J. M., Hayes, S. C., & Nelson, R. O. (1986). Equivalence class formation in language-able and language-disabled children. *Journal of the Experimental Analysis of Behavior, 46*, 243-257.

Dymond, S., & Barnes, D. (1994). A transfer of self-discrimination response functions through equivalence relations. *Journal of the Experimental Analysis of Behavior, 62*, 251-267.

Dymond, S., & Barnes, D. (1995). A transformation of self-discrimination response functions in accordance with the arbitrarily applicable relations of sameness, more-than, and less-than. *Journal of the Experimental Analysis of Behavior, 64,* 163-184.

Dymond, S., & Barnes, D. (1996). A transformation of self-discrimination response functions in accordance with the arbitrarily applicable relations of sameness and opposition. *The Psychological Record, 46,* 271-300.

Dymond, S., & Barnes, D. (1997). Behavior-analytic approaches to self-awareness. *The Psychological record, 47,* 181-201.

Gatch, M. B., & Osborne, J. G. (1989). Transfer of contextual stimulus function via equivalence class development. *Journal of the Experimental Analysis of Behavior, 51,* 369-378.

Gewirtz, J. L. & Stengle, K. G. (1968). Learning of generalized imitation as the basis for identification. *Psychological Review, 5,* 374-397.

Hayes, S. C. (1984). Making sense of spirituality. *Behaviorism, 12,* 99-110.

Hayes, S. C. (1991). A relational control theory of stimulus equivalence. In L. J. Hayes & P. N. Chase (Eds.), *Dialogues on verbal behavior: The first international institute on verbal relations,* (pp. 19-40). Reno, NV: Context Press.

Hayes, S. C. (1994). Relational frame theory: A functional approach to verbal events. In S. C. Hayes, L. J. Hayes, M. Sato, & K. Ono (Eds.), *Behavior analysis of language and cognition* (pp. 9-30). Reno, NV: Context Press.

Hayes, S. C., & Barnes, D. (1997). Analyzing derived stimulus relations requires more than the concept of stimulus class. *Journal of the Experimental Analysis of Behavior, 68,* 235-244.

Hayes, S. C., Devany, J. M., Kohlenberg, B. S., Brownstein, A. J., & Shelby, J. (1987). Stimulus equivalence and the symbolic control of behavior. *Revista Mexicana de Analisis de la Conducta, 13,* 361-374.

Hayes, S.C., Gifford, E.V., & Ruckstuhl, L.E. (1996). Relational frame theory and executive function: A behavioral approach. In G.R. Lyon & N.A. Krasnegor (Eds.), *Attention, memory, and executive function* (pp. 279-306). Baltimore, MD: Paul Brooks.

Hayes, S. C. & Hayes, L. J. (1989). The verbal action of the listener as a basis for rule-governance. In S. C. Hayes (Ed.), *Rule-governed behavior: Cognition, contingencies, and instructional control* (pp. 153-190). New York: Plenum.

Hayes, S. C. & Hayes, L. J. (1992). Verbal relations and the evolution of behavior analysis. *American Psychologist, 47,* 1383-1395.

Hayes, S. C., Kohlenberg, B. S., & Hayes, L. J. (1991). The transfer of specific and general consequential functions through simple and conditional equivalence relations. *Journal of the Experimental Analysis of Behavior, 56,* 119-137.

Hayes, S. C., Strosahl, K. D., & Wilson, K. G. (1999). *Acceptance and commitment therapy: An experiential approach to behavior change.* New York: Guilford.

Hayes, S. C. & Wilson, K. G. (1993). Some applied implications of a contemporary behavior-analytic view of verbal events. *The Behavior Analyst, 16,* 283-301.

Hayes, S. C. & Wilson, K. G. (1994). Acceptance and commitment therapy: Altering the verbal support for experiential avoidance. *The Behavior Analyst, 17,* 289-303.

Hall, G. (1996). Learning about associatively activated stimulus representations: Implications for acquired equivalence and perceptual learning. *Animal Learning and Behavior, 24,* 233-255.

Hineline, P. N., & Wanchisen, B. A. (1989). Correlated hypothesizing and the distinction between contingency-shaped and rule-governed behavior. In S.C. Hayes (Ed.), *Rule governed behavior: Cognition, contingencies, and instructional control,* (pp. 221-268). New York: Plenum.

Kohlenberg, B. S., Hayes, S. C., & Hayes, L. J. (1991). The transfer of contextual control over equivalence classes through equivalence classes: A possible model of social stereotyping. *Journal of the Experimental Analysis of Behavior, 56,* 505-518.

Lattal, K. A. (1975). Reinforcement contingencies as discriminative stimuli. *Journal of the Experimental Analysis of Behavior, 23,* 241-246.

Lipkens, R. (1992). *A behavior analysis of complex human functioning: Analogical reasoning.* Unpublished doctoral dissertation, University of Nevada, Reno.

Lipkens, R., Hayes, S. C., & Hayes, L. J. (1993). Longitudinal study of derived stimulus relations in an infant. *Journal of Experimental Child Psychology, 56,* 201-239.

McIlvane, W. J., Dube, W. V., Kledaras, J. B., Iennaco, F. M., & Stoddard, L. T. (1990). Teaching relational discrimination to individuals with mental retardation: Some problems and possible solutions. *American Journal on Mental Retardation, 95,* 283-296.

McIlvane, W. J., Dube, W. V., & Callahan, T .D. (1995). Attention: A behavior analytic perspective. In G.R. Lyon, & N.A. Krasnegor (Eds.), *Attention, memory, and executive function* (pp. 97-117). Paul H. Brookes: Baltimore, MA.

Neuringer, A. (1986). Can people behave randomly?: The role of feedback. *Journal of Experimental Psychology: General, 115,* 62-75.

Piaget, F. (1954). *The construction of reality in the child.* NY: Basic Books.

Pliskoff, S. S., & Goldiamond, I. (1966). Some discriminative properties of fixed ratio performance in the pigeon. *Journal of the Experimental Analysis of Behavior, 9,* 1-9.

Pryor, K. W., Haag, R., & O'Reilly, J. (1969). The creative porpoise: Training for novel behavior. *Journal of the Experimental Analysis of Behavior, 12,* 653-661.

Reese, H. W. (1968). *The perception of stimulus relations: Discrimination learning and transposition.* New York: Academic Press.

Reynolds, G. S. (1966). Discrimination and emission of temporal intervals by pigeons. *Journal of the Experimental Analysis of Behavior, 9,* 65-68.

Reynolds, G. S., & Catania, A. C. (1962). Temporal discrimination in pigeons. *Science, 135,* 314-315.

Roche, B. & Barnes, D. (1996). Arbitrarily applicable relational responding and sexual categorization: A critical test of the derived difference relation. *The Psychological Record, 46,* 451-475.

Roche, B. & Barnes, D. (1997). A transformation of respondently conditioned stimulus function in accordance with arbitrarily applicable relations. *Journal of the Experimental Analysis of Behavior, 67,* 275-301.

Rogoff, B., & Lave, F. (1988). *Everyday cognition: It's development in social context.* Cambridge MA: Harvard University Press.

Shimp, C. P. (1982). On metaknowledge in the pigeon: An organisms knowledge about it's own behavior. *Animal Learning and Behavior, 10,* 358-364.

Sidman, M. (1990). Equivalence relations: Where do they come from? In D. E. Blackman & H. Lejune (Eds.), *Behaviour analysis in theory and in practice: Contributions and controversies* (pp. 93-114). Hove, England: Erlbaum.

Sidman M. (1992). Equivalence relations: Some basic considerations. In S. C. Hayes and L. J. Hayes (Eds.), *Understanding verbal relations* (pp. 15-27). Reno, Nevada: Context Press.

Skinner, B. F. (1957). *Verbal behavior.* New York: Appleton-Century-Crofts.

Skinner, B. F. (1974, reprinted 1993). *About behaviorism.* London: Penguin.

Steele, D., & Hayes, S. C. (1991). Stimulus equivalence and arbitrarily applicable relational responding. *Journal of the Experimental Analysis of Behavior, 56,* 519-555.

Vygotsky, L.S. (1978). *Mind in society: The development of higher psychological processes.* Cambridge, MA: Harvard University Press.

Watt, A., Keenan, M., Barnes, D., & Cairns, E. (1991). Social categorization and stimulus equivalence. *The Psychological Record, 41,* 33-50.

Wulfert, E., & Hayes, S. C. (1988). Transfer of a conditional ordering response through conditional equivalence classes. *Journal of the Experimental Analysis of Behavior, 50,* 125-144.

Footnotes

Some of the material presented in this chapter is based on previously published work (Barnes & Roche, 1997a, 1997b; Dymond & Barnes, 1997).

The first author dedicates the current chapter to the memory of Pagan, best friend and companion – I will miss you old friend.

Chapter 4

Long-Term Correlates of Childhood Sexual Abuse: A Behavior Analytic Perspective

Jacqueline Pistorello
Victoria M. Follette
Steven C. Hayes
University of Nevada

Childhood sexual abuse (CSA) has received increased attention from clinicians and scientists alike within the last decade. This attention can easily be attributed to the significant number of individuals estimated to experience sexual abuse as children and to the documentation that CSA is a major risk factor for the development of many negative outcomes for both children and adults (Beitchman, Zucker, Hood, DaCosta, Akman, & Cassavia, 1992; Briere, 1988; Browne & Finkelhor, 1986; Polusny & Follette, 1995). Prevalence studies suggest that in the general population between 16% and 33% of women and 13% to 16% of men have experienced sexual abuse in childhood (cf. Polusny & Follette, 1995). Among clinical populations, between 35% and 75% of female and between 13% and 23% of male clients report a history of CSA (Briere & Runtz, 1991). Differences in prevalence rates across studies have been attributed to differences in sample composition and definitions of CSA (Browne & Finkelhor, 1986). For this chapter, the definition of sexual abuse will follow that utilized in two comprehensive reviews of correlates of CSA (Browne & Finkelhor, 1986; Polusny & Follette, 1995): "forced or coerced sexual behavior imposed on a child, and sexual activity between a child and a much older person, whether or not obvious coercion is involved."

Although not all adult survivors of sexual abuse present with the same mental health profile, the literature suggests that both men and women who were sexually abused as children are more likely than non-abused adults to report a broad range of maladaptive symptoms (e.g., Briere, 1988; 1992, Briere & Runtz, 1991, Briere & Zaidi, 1989; Cole & Putnam, 1992; Courtois, 1979; Harter, Alexander, & Neimeyer, 1988; Hunter, 1991; Meiselman, 1978; Rodriguez, Ryan, Kemp, & Foy, 1997, van der Kolk, Perry, & Herman, 1991; Wind & Silvern, 1992; Wyatt, Newcomb, & Rierderle, 1993). However, it is also important to note that a number of other distal variables, such as family environment and social support, may be associated with adult symptoms. Additionally, it is essential that clinicians and researchers not fail to consider the contribution of more proximal factors that could be associated with current distress.

The term "long-term correlates" refers to the symptoms observable in adults who experienced the sexual trauma as children. Although a wide range of immediate effects of CSA (better labeled as "initial effects" instead of "short-term effects," as these correlates are likely to persist beyond the first two years) have been reported in the literature (Browne & Finkelhor, 1986), those initial effects seen in children will not be discussed in this chapter. The focus of this chapter on adult survivors of child sexual abuse reflects the area of expertise of the authors. However, much of the concepts presented here are relevant to other forms of childhood trauma, such as child physical abuse and neglect and parental alcoholism. Additionally, the importance of contextual variables cannot be underestimated and is a growing area of research. Finally, empirical findings and theoretical developments from the fields of PTSD and adult sexual trauma will be incorporated, in view of the relevance of these findings to a conceptualization of CSA correlates.

Researchers have attempted to conceptualize the impact of CSA from a number of theoretical perspectives. These accounts have sometimes identified factors associated with the topography of the abuse, such as the onset and duration of the abuse, but these factors have not proved to be of substantial importance in understanding adult outcomes. Non-cognitive-behavioral accounts of the long-term correlates of CSA have emphasized developmental and attachment difficulties due to premature sexual experiences often perpetrated by family members, distortion of superego and development of attachments to sadistic love objects, particularly in parent-child incest, characteristics of family and society as dysfunctional systems, and the overwhelming sense of loss experienced by survivors (cf. Alexander, 1992; Cole & Putnam, 1992; Courtois, 1989; Vander-Mey, 1992), among others.

Cognitive accounts have focused on mediational effects of irrational cognitions (Frank, Anderson, Stewart, Dancu, Hughes, & West, 1988) and shattered core schemas (i.e., assumptions about oneself or the world) due to experience of the trauma (Resick & Schnicke, 1992). Finally, behavioral conceptualizations of correlates of CSA have primarily relied on both classical and operant conditioning (cf. Hoier et al., 1992).

Although these two conditioning principles provide a parsimonious way of understanding a wide range of long-term correlates of CSA, behaviorists have found them insufficient in accounting for the pervasiveness and diversity of long-term impacts of CSA, and have tended to incorporate cognitive models in their conceptualizations of these effects (e.g., Foa, Steketee, & Rothbaum, 1989; Hoier et al., 1992; Resick & Schnicke, 1992). Foa et al. (1989) has elaborated on a behavioral explanation of PTSD by incorporating information processing theory as a means of accounting for the pervasiveness of trauma effects. Another conceptualization of CSA effects "takes into account cognitive mediation processes related to outcomes of stress and trauma for victims, a theoretical position that is not typical of a radical behaviorist perspective" (Hoier et al., 1992, p. 101).

It is not surprising that behaviorists have turned to cognitive-behavioral models to explain more complex clinical phenomena, such as long-term correlates of CSA.

This appeal to other paradigms may have arisen out of perceived necessity, in attempting to ensure completeness of the analyses. Perhaps this recourse can be traced back to related criticisms that have plagued the behavior analysis field: that the rich workings of mental life might not be compatible with a science of human behavior solely based on physical law, and that paradigms based on animal behavior analysis fail to elucidate the role of the all important human cognitions (Vaugham, 1989).

There are at least two factors contributing to this turn to cognitive accounts. First, the role of private events in behavior analytic accounts of clinical phenomena remains a highly debated subject (see Dougher, 1993; Follette, 1993; Hayes, 1995), and many theorists have continued to argue that radical behaviorists downplay the importance of private events (Alford, Richards, & Hanych, 1995). Moreover, individuals presenting to treatment often report that aversive private events are associated with the onset and maintenance of various difficulties (e.g., Cummings, Gordon, & Marlatt, 1980). This was a body of evidence that clinical behaviorists could no longer ignore. The somewhat unclear position of behavior analysts regarding private events has been identified as an obstacle to accounting for complex phenomena, such as the impacts of CSA. While objecting to the non-causal position adopted by behavior analysts on private events, a critic noted: "what about clinical cases where the external cause is temporally distal, such as in adult clinical disorders related to childhood trauma?" (Alford et al., 1995, p. 58).

Second, and relatedly, the more well-established behavioral paradigms, such as classical and operant conditioning, have been insufficient to account for complex psychological phenomena involving verbal behavior (cf. Hayes & Wilson, 1993). Some have argued that as groundbreaking as Skinner's discussion on verbal behavior was, it was not *the* behavior-analytic account of verbal behavior, but rather *a* behavior-analytic account, and that recent empirical and theoretical developments from derived relational responding provide a useful alternative behavior-analytic account of verbal behavior (Hayes, 1994; Hayes & Wilson, 1993). While there is intuitive appeal for mentalistic structures, this must be measured against the cost in theoretical consistency, as some of these conceptualizations may be antithetical to the tenets and goals of behavior analysis.

The purpose of this chapter is to outline a radical behaviorist explanation of long-term correlates of CSA, relying both on more established behavioral paradigms, and on more recent developments within behavior analysis, based on derived relational responding (Barnes & Roche, 1997; Hayes, 1994; Hayes & Hayes, 1992; Hayes & Wilson, 1993; 1994; Sidman & Tailby, 1982). In addition to theoretical consistency, the goal of this analysis is to identify a primary functional commonality across the wide range of long-term effects of CSA. Within this analysis, the role of private events in the maintenance of maladaptive coping by the adult survivor of CSA will be explored, and a recent therapeutic approach, whose principles are consistent with this analysis, will be suggested as a useful treatment for this population.

Prior to reviewing how a behavioral approach can account for the impact of childhood trauma, a brief review of the long-term correlates of CSA outlined in the literature is warranted. A wide range of long-term correlates of childhood sexual abuse have been documented in the literature and periodically summarized in review articles (Browne & Finkelhor, 1986; Beitchman, Zucker, Hood, DaCosta, Akman, & Cassavia, 1992; Polusny & Follette, 1995). For organizational purposes, these various correlates will be subsumed under the headings of private reactions, overt behaviors, and social/interpersonal functioning. This is an *arbitrary* distinction, but may be useful in clarifying subsequent discussions.

Long-Term Correlates of CSA: Private Responses

Several studies have found that, compared to nonabused subjects, CSA survivors experience increased levels of psychological distress and depression (cf. Browne & Finkelhor, 1986; Polusny & Follette, 1995), both within nonclinical (Fromuth & Burkhart, 1989; Briere & Runtz, 1988; Yama, Tovey, & Fogas, 1993) and clinical samples (Pribor & Dinwiddie, 1992).

A number of long-term correlates of CSA include symptoms associated with posttraumatic stress disorder (PTSD). A recent study relying on standardized measures of both CSA and PTSD revealed that within clinical samples most CSA survivors suffer from PTSD. Among help-seeking adult women who reported CSA, 86.7% met criteria for current (97.8% for lifetime) PTSD, compared to only 19.4% of women seeking treatment for relationship distress (Rodriguez et al., 1997). However, PTSD rates were lower among CSA survivors from a community sample who had not experienced penetration during the abuse (Saunders, Villeponteaux, Lipovsky, Kilpatrick, & Veronen, 1992).

A comprehensive discussion of the relationship between the diagnosis of PTSD and a history of CSA is beyond the scope of this chapter; however, PTSD symptoms, such as intrusive memories and persistent increased arousal, have been frequently reported in the CSA literature (Briere & Runtz, 1991). The most often discussed intrusive symptoms are flashbacks—sudden disturbing sensory memories, often including visual, tactile, auditory, or olfactory stimuli experienced during the abuse (Briere, 1992). Flashbacks have been reportedly triggered by sexual interactions, viewing or reading sexual or violent materials, discussions of the abuse, or experiencing other forms of abuse (Briere & Runtz, 1991). Other intrusive symptoms include unwanted thoughts or memories of the abuse, or repetitive nightmares (Briere, 1992). Persistent symptoms of increased arousal include sleep disturbance, poor concentration, and heightened startle response (Briere & Runtz, 1991). Sleep disturbances are more commonly reported by CSA survivors than by nonabused comparison groups (Briere, 1988; Briere, Evans, Runtz, & Wall, 1988). Somatic complaints, which might be indicative of physiological disturbance and hyperarousal (Hoiter et al., 1992), have also been linked to CSA. Both among nonclinical (Briere & Runtz, 1988a) and medical clinical samples (Springs & Friedrich, 1992), CSA female survivors reported higher levels of somatization than nonabused women.

In addition to PTSD-related symptoms, CSA survivors, compared to control groups, appear to experience higher levels of chronic anxiety (e.g., Briere & Runtz,

1988) and to be at a greater risk for developing anxiety disorders in general (cf. Polusny & Follette, 1995). Dissociative symptoms have also been linked to a history of CSA (DiTomasso & Routh, 1993). Although there is some debate about the definition of dissociation (Wagner & Linehan, 1998), Briere (1992), defining dissociation as "a defensive disruption in the normally occurring connections among feelings, thoughts, behavior, and memories, consciously or unconsciously evoked in order to reduce psychological distress" (p. 36), notes that the complex etiology of this behavior appears to be at least partly related to childhood trauma.

As a result of CSA, survivors may develop a number of "cognitive distortions," including, for example, a tendency to "overestimate the amount of danger or adversity in the world, and underestimate their own self-efficacy and self-worth" (Briere, 1992, p. 23). Some studies linked CSA to subsequent guilt, low self-esteem, and self-blame (Jehu, 1988), whereas others found that survivors made more internal attributions of blame for events (Gold, 1986). Interestingly, it appears that these types of "cognitive effects" are more closely linked to psychological abuse, which often coexists with sexual or physical abuse (Briere, 1992). Disturbances of self have also been commonly discussed as a long-term correlate of CSA (e.g., Briere, 1992; Cole & Putnam, 1992). Although there is little empirical validation for this correlate because of the difficulty in measuring the concept, disturbance of self is widely recognized as a problem among CSA survivors (Briere, 1992), and constitutes a diagnostic criterion for borderline personality disorder, itself generally considered a long-term correlate of CSA (Ogata, Silk, Goodrich, Lohr, Westen, & Hill, 1990).

Long-Term Correlates of CSA: Overt Behavior

A number of "behavioral disturbances" have been described as long-term correlates of CSA, such as substance abuse, parasuicidality, and eating disorders. Not only were CSA survivors more likely to report heavy alcohol use than nonabused women (Zierler, Feingold, Laufer, Velentgas, Kantrowitz-Gordon, & Mayer, 1991), but also 75% of treatment-seeking female substance abusers reported a history of CSA (Rohsenow, Corbett, & Devine, 1988). Across several studies, the lifetime prevalence rate for alcohol and drug problems is higher among clinical samples reporting CSA than among non-abused women in treatment, thus suggesting a strong association between substance abuse and CSA (cf. Polusny & Follette, 1995). Women who were sexually abused as children reported significantly more suicidal and self-injurious behavior than nonabused women (Briere & Zaidi, 1989), and a history of self-mutilation was predictive of CSA among women seeking treatment (Briere, 1988). Although the evidence is somewhat mixed, bulimic behaviors, but not other types of eating disordered behaviors, appear to be linked to a history of CSA (Polusny & Follette, 1995).

Long-Term Correlates of CSA: Social and Interpersonal Functioning

Using standardized measures, CSA survivors, compared to nonabused controls, reported greater difficulties with social adjustment (Jackson, Calhoun, Amick, Maddever, & Habif, 1990). Interpersonal functioning, in particular, appears to be a problem for adult survivors, who frequently report considerable distress and dissatisfaction in their relationships (e.g., Briere, 1988; Follette, 1991; Herman, 1992). Both male and female CSA survivors from a community sample reported lower relationship satisfaction than non-abused subjects (Hunter, 1991), and females who had experienced CSA were more likely to be separated or divorced (Russell, 1986).

Additionally, a wide range of issues affecting sexual functioning have been documented (Briere, 1992; Maltz & Holman, 1987). In a clinical sample, 87% of the survivors versus 20% of the controls reported experiencing severe sexual problems (Meiselman, 1978). Similarly, a significantly higher percentage of female survivors reported lower relationship and sexual satisfaction than nonabused women (Waltz, 1993). Some survivors reported less sexual activity due to intrusive symptoms, such as flashbacks, whereas others reported a history of multiple, sequential, brief sexual involvements (Courtois, 1979; Maltz & Holman, 1987).

Several studies have linked CSA with an increased risk for revictimization in adulthood (Briere, 1988; Herman, 1992; Russell, 1986; Wind & Silvern, 1992). When compared to women who were not sexually abused in their childhood, survivors were significantly more likely to experience physical and sexual abuse within their adult relationships (Russell, 1986; Wind & Silvern, 1992). The pairing of relationships with maltreatment may result in either avoidance of intimate relationships altogether or acceptance of aggression in relationships as the norm by survivors (Briere, 1992). The latter perspective may render these women particularly vulnerable to revictimization.

In summary, empirical studies have established a strongly suggested link between CSA and various maladaptive behaviors in adulthood. In view of the correlational nature of these findings, a direct and simple causal relationship between child sexual abuse and these long-term correlates cannot be assumed (Polusny & Follette, 1995). However, the sheer volume of evidence coming from different samples and researchers have led to the conclusion that "it seems clear that untreated trauma arising from abuse in childhood constitutes a major risk factor for a variety of mental health and social problems later in life" (Briere, 1992, p. 76).

The diversity and pervasiveness of such long-term outcomes underscore the need for a consistent framework to explain how a history of childhood sexual trauma leads to the onset and maintenance of a pattern of ineffective responding. Long-term correlates of CSA will first be discussed in terms of classical and operant conditioning, and previous behavioral conceptualizations will be reviewed (Foa, Steketee, & Rothbaum, 1989; Hoier et al., 1992). We will argue that these learning paradigms are not sufficient to account for the long-term correlates of CSA, and a more functional account will be developed based on recent empirical findings in and theoretical postulations from the field of derived relational responding.

Classical Conditioning

Some long-term effects of CSA can be readily explained through classical conditioning. In this type of conditioning process, unconditioned stimuli (UCS) that involve pain, injury, or threats to survival elicit unconditioned responses (UCR) such as increased heartrate, changes in skin conductance, and other autonomic responses. Recently, it has been proposed that an environmental UCS is neither necessary nor sufficient for the conditioning of fear responses in humans; instead, the requirement is that the individual experience a negatively-evaluated abrupt and systemic response, such as panic or alarm, which may not involve pain, injury, or threats to survival (Carter & Barlow, 1995; Forsyth & Eifert, 1997). Among CSA survivors, an originally neutral stimuli, such as a perfume or a time of year, after repeated pairings with pain, injury, or threat (UCS) or after a negatively-evaluated aversive systemic response associated with the sexual abuse, come to elicit conditioned responses (CR) in the form of autonomic arousal, typically fear or anxiety, which are similar to the survivor's response to the sexual abuse (UCR). Conditioned stimuli share some formal property, such as similarity or contiguity, with the abuse itself, and may be external, such as time of the year or a type of lamp shade, or, some have argued, internal, such as self-statements made by the survivor during the abuse or the arousal experienced itself (Hoier et al., 1992).

Classical conditioning accounts of CSA and its associations are relatively easy to follow and understand, even to non-behaviorists. For example, a survivor who as a child heard her perpetrator's footsteps as he walked towards her bedroom in the middle of the night, might, as an adult, report overwhelming anxiety whenever her husband, who is now working nights, walks into their bedroom at odd hours of the night. This situation illustrates how through classical conditioning, footsteps in the middle of the night (originally neutral and then a CS) come to elicit fear and anxiety (CR) through repeated pairings of the sound of footsteps with the childhood sexual abuse (UCS).

In addition to accounting for what survivors call "triggers," this paradigm has been used to explain a variety of PTSD-related long-term outcomes of CSA. Flashbacks being a case in point: "Re-experiencing phenomena appear to be classically conditioned responses rather than functional behaviors that are controlled by their consequences" (Hoier et al., 1992, p. 117). Additionally the PTSD-based increased arousal responses, which are described as components of fear and anxiety, have been said to be initiated by unconditioned stimuli, and eventually, by conditioned stimuli (Hoier et al., 1992). From this perspective, the higher levels of anxiety and increased sleep problems among CSA survivors, compared to control groups, might be viewed as aspects of the unconditioned response, initially elicited by the abuse itself, and later, by a variety of conditioned stimuli, such as the husband's footsteps in the vignette presented above. Some types of sexual difficulties reported by survivors, such as anxiety or pain during sexual relating (Maltz & Holman, 1987), can also be explained through respondent conditioning: sexual relating, as a CS, comes to elicit pain or anxiety similar to that experienced during the abuse.   However appealing respondent conditioning is, many theorists find it insufficient to explain the longevity of the CR, and, therefore, operant conditioning is typically enlisted to account for the maintenance of these effects.

Operant Conditioning and Mowrer's Two-Factor Theory

Mowrer's (1960) two-factor theory, probably the most widely known behavioral account of the effects of trauma and PTSD, combines classical and operant conditioning to explain the onset and maintenance of some of the long-term effects of sexual trauma (e.g., Keane, Zimmerling, & Caddell, 1985; Kilpatrick, Veronen, & Best, 1985). In the context of increased arousal or fear-related responses evoked by conditioned stimuli, the CSA survivor typically responds with an escape/avoidance response. In the above case, the survivor may literally leave the bedroom, withdraw emotionally, dissociate, or have an alcoholic drink before going to bed in order avoid contact with the experience. These literal and metaphorical escape responses preclude the extinction of conditioned responses and further reinforce avoidance behaviors, through the decreased probability of continued aversive stimulation (negative reinforcement). Kilpatrick et al. (1985) also hypothesized that through stimulus generalization and higher-order conditioning a wide number of stimuli, such as thoughts and words associated with the trauma, come to elicit fear and anxiety in the survivor. An alternative explanation for this generalization effect using derived relational responding will be provided later.

In addition to the maintenance of avoidance responses due to negative reinforcement, other long-term consequences CSA may be accounted for by operant principles. For example, in our vignette above, in which the survivor experiences fear in the presence of footsteps, imagine that in the context of a learning history during which voicing one's feelings was followed by punishment, such as withdrawal of warmth on the part of the perpetrator. This survivor may not disclose to her husband the fear and anxiety she is experiencing and may begin to withdraw emotionally from him. This social isolation, in turn, would result in fewer opportunities to contact reinforcers, and, in turn, might lead to depression. While similar processes may account for other outcomes associated with CSA, the applicable clinical scenarios are too numerous to mention. However, for purposes of illustration, let us explore how one long-term correlate of CSA, disturbance of self, may be accounted for by instrumental learning.

Although the definition of "self" constitutes a challenging enterprise, behavioral conceptualizations of the term have been provided (Skinner, 1953, 1974; Kohlenberg & Tsai, 1991). Skinner stated that self pertains to the behavioral repertoire acquired within a particular context, and that "a personality may be tied to a particular type of occasion—when a system of responses is organized around a given discriminative stimulus" (1953, p. 285). This conceptualization seems particularly relevant for CSA survivors. In keeping with Skinner's definition of self, it makes sense that, due to the nature (e.g., secrecy, intimacy) and the aversiveness of the experience (e.g., pain), adult CSA survivors may compartmentalize their experiences during the abuse as a different "self." There are clinical observations which corroborate this hypothesis: survivors appear to experience difficulty incorporating the "self" which endured childhood abuse with their remaining repertoire, as sometimes an adult survivor lapses into the third person ("she" or "her") when referring to herself during abusive experiences.

There is another mechanism through which CSA survivors may come to experience disturbances of self. Skinner stated that awareness of oneself is "of social origin" and, therefore, highly dependent on the contingencies arranged by the verbal community (1974). More recent radical behaviorist explanations of development of a sense of self expanded on this Skinnerian concept (see Chapter 3 of this volume). Kohlenberg & Tsai (1991) postulated that a sense of self is learned through operant conditioning: children's descriptions of initially public and then private events, using "I" statements, are reinforced by caretakers, provided that the environment is a healthy one. One's strength of self, they argued, depends on the degree to which these "I" statements are under the control of private stimuli, such as physical sensations, as opposed to public stimuli, such as other people's desires. Disturbances of self are thought to be more likely to occur in individuals who experienced trauma at an earlier age (Cole & Putnam, 1992; Kohlenberg & Tsai, 1991) or who were subjected to an "invalidating environment" where caretakers were less likely to reinforce consistently and more likely to punish children's communications about their internal experiences, such as thoughts, likes, or dislikes (Wagner & Linehan, 1998).

Derived Relational Responding

Although a great deal of progress has been made in providing behavioral accounts for long-term correlates of CSA, the generalized avoidance noted among CSA survivors and PTSD sufferers does not lend itself very easily to classical or operant conditioning analyses. For example, survivors often find that describing the abuse is in itself aversive, and those suffering from PTSD avoid discussing the abuse altogether (van der Kolk et al., 1996). Often, a great deal of rapport is needed before the survivor "tells her story" (Herman, 1992).

Traditional learning paradigms seem unable to provide adequate explanations for this phenomenon. Although survivors' reluctance to discuss the abuse could be accounted for by a previous history of punishment following report, even survivors who have not previously disclosed about the abuse still find reporting aversive. This effect suggests a *bidirectional* relation between the stimuli, with the words describing the abuse having acquired the stimulus functions of the abuse itself (Hayes & Wilson, 1993; see Chapter 2 in this volume for a detailed discussion of this issue).

Recent findings in the behavior-analytic experimental tradition, reviewed in the previous chapter, provide a model for bi-directional relations (cf. Hayes & Hayes, 1989; 1992). For example, if a language-able child is taught to point to a chair when hearing the word "chair," the child may say the word "chair" given the object itself, without being directly shaped to do so. This type of phenomenon was originally investigated under the rubric of stimulus equivalence (e.g., Sidman & Tailby, 1982) and more recently, Relational Frame Theory (RFT; e.g.,Hayes & Hayes, 1989). Although these concepts have been described comprehensively elsewhere (e.g, Hayes, 1994b), and have been covered in the previous chapter, a very brief summary will be presented below.

Stimulus equivalence (Sidman & Tailby, 1982) has been shown repeatedly among language-able humans, but not with nonverbal organisms (cf. Hayes & Hayes, 1989). Stimulus equivalence is thought to be one instance of derived relational responding (Hayes & Hayes, 1989), one which involves the frame of coordination (similar or the same). However, Hayes and colleagues argue that a more comprehensive account of derived relational responding, Relational Frame Theory (RFT; Hayes & Hayes, 1989) is needed, as relations other than equivalence are also derived, such as "opposite from," "worse than," or "subsequent to." Examples of words participating in frames of opposition are readily available: given "hot," "short," and "good," most readers would probably reply "cold," "tall," and "bad," respectively. In fact, empirical studies show that verbal beings readily derive relations other than equivalence (e.g., Barnes & Roche, 1997; Steele & Hayes, 1991).

RFT (Hayes & Hayes, 1989; 1992) is based on the premise that derived relational responding is a historically established overarching class similar to generalized imitation (Hayes, 1994b). That is, verbally able organisms can come to respond to stimuli not solely based on their formal properties but rather on a history of reinforcement for the application of a particular relational response. RFT theorists propose that humans, through exposure to multiple exemplars, learn to respond to relations among stimuli which are not defined by the relata, but by additional contextual cues ((Hayes, 1994b; Hayes & Hayes, 1989).

Arbitrarily applicable relational responding has three properties: mutual entailment, combinatorial entailment, and transformation of stimulus functions (Hayes, 1994b). In a given context, if X is directly related to Y, then in that context, a derived relation between Y and X is mutually entailed; this is similar to symmetry in stimulus equivalence, except that the derived relation will be based on that which was trained: If the trained relation was "X is greater than Y," then the derived relation will be that "Y is less than X." Individuals who are trained the relation "Men are 'better' than women," will derive the relation that "Women are less than men." Combinatorial entailment, a more general form of transitivity in stimulus equivalence, occurs when, in a given context, if X is directly related to Y in some way, and Y is directly related to Z in some way, then, in that context, a derived relation between X and Z will be mutually entailed. In combinatorial entailment, the derived relation may be more or less specific, depending on the nature of the trained relations. For example, if X is different from Y, and Y is different from Z, the relation between X and Z is unknown. On the other hand, individuals who are trained that "Men are 'better' than women" and "Women are 'better' than children" will derive the relation that "Men are 'better' than children."

The property of arbitrarily applicable relational responding most clearly relevant to clinical phenomena is transformation of stimulus function. In a given context, if there is a mutual relation between X and Y, and X has some additional psychological function, then in a context that selects that function as relevant, the stimulus functions of Y may be transformed consistent with its mutual relation to X. Transfer of stimulus functions has been demonstrated with discriminative, consequential, and respondent stimulus functions (e.g., Barnes, Browne, Smeets, & Roche, 1995; Hayes, Kohlenberg, & Hayes, 1991; and Dougher, Auguston, Markham, Greenway, & Wulfert, 1995). In one recent study, this effect was demonstrated within the realm of sexual arousal (Barnes & Roche, 1997). Subjects were trained to "pick B1, given A1" and "C1, given A1" in the presence of a contextual cue for "same," and to "pick B2, given A2" and "C2, given A2" in the presence of a contextual cue for "opposite." Later, using a stimulus-pairing procedure, sexually arousing and emotionally neutral functions were established for B1 and B2, respectively. Results indicated that most of the subjects who showed significant respondent conditioning (e.g., greater sexual arousal to B1 than B2), also showed transformation of sexual-arousal functions, exhibiting greater sexual arousal to C1 than to C2. This type of preparation may provide a rationale for how survivors come to respond with increased sexual arousal to "unexpected" stimuli, such as the abuse itself.

The importance of equivalence and derived relational responding lies in their noticeable applicability to language phenomenon: "To many behavioral research-ers, . . . the equivalence effect represents an empirical analogue of the symbolic properties of natural language" (Barnes & Roche, 1997, p. 119). Several bits of evidence point in this direction: the derivation of stimulus relations appears to be related to verbal competence (Devany, Hayes, & Nelson, 1986), equivalence procedures have been successfully used to teach some language skills (de Rose, de Souza, Rossito, & de Rose, 1992), and stimulus equivalence has not been unequivo-cally shown among nonhumans (cf. Hayes, 1994b). Indeed, some have proposed that relational frames are a defining characteristic of verbal events, thus re-defining verbal behavior as that type of behavior involving arbitrarily applicable relational responding (Hayes & Hayes, 1989; Hayes & Wilson, 1993).

Relational Frame Theory provides an explanation of why survivors who endured extremely aversive events in childhood find reporting of such events, years later, so aversive. Verbal organisms, within specific contexts, frame events relationally in an arbitrary fashion. Simply put, language is acquired by relating the names of events with the events being named (Hayes & Wilson, 1993). Therefore, when the word "abuse," for example, participates in a frame of coordination or equivalence with the event of child sexual abuse itself (assuming the events are mutually and combinatorially entailed), there is a bidirectional transformation of stimulus functions which leads to the description of the abuse acquiring some (but not all) of the same functions of the abusive experience itself.

There are probably contextual variables, such as emotion and details of the abuse, which could affect the degree to which the functions of the sexual abuse are contacted at the time of the description. For example, it is known that sometimes survivors, particularly those suffering from PTSD, may recount the abuse experi-ence in a detached, rote manner, reporting feeling "numb"; it is unlikely that the functions of the abuse are contacted under these circumstances.

The bidirectionality between words and referents may account for the fact that some PTSD sufferers experience an increase in "PTSD symptoms upon later information about the trauma in the absence of reoccurrence of the trauma" (Foa, Steketee, & Rothbaum, 1989, p. 165). For example, a case has been reported in the literature where a woman who had been raped exhibited only mild levels of distress in response to the rape, until she heard a few months later that her assailant had killed his next victim, at which time her distress increased considerably (Foa et al., 1989). Hayes has made the point that only verbal beings can contact the functions of events that have not yet occurred, such as death, and that this is due to the bidirectional transformation of stimulus functions: it is both the blessing and the curse of "languaging" that it can take us places where we have not been before (Hayes, 1984).

Events, such as a change in the impact of the rape without further trauma, are often accounted for by semantic theories, which focus on the "meaning" attached to particular events (Foa et al., 1989). In this analysis "meaning" is simply the stimulus functions of another event which have come to be contacted. We can speculate, for example, that in the above example, rape and death came to participate in a frame of coordination, and that the functions of the latter, themselves acquired through derived relations, transformed to the former.

In summary, behaviorists have argued that the concepts of classical (pairing of stimuli) and operant (reinforcement and punishment) conditioning cannot readily account for certain aspects of long-term impacts of CSA, particularly the wide generalization of avoidance responses among traumatized individuals across dissimilar situations (Foa et al., 1989) and the maintenance of maladaptive behavior patterns well beyond the duration of the abuse (Hoier et al., 1992). We argue that a relational frames account provides an explanation for both of these factors: the widespread avoidance seen in survivors is likely due to the fact that the functions of the abuse itself have been transformed to a wide variety of stimuli, perhaps formally "dissimilar," which have come to be framed relationally due to arbitrarily applicable relational responding.

What are some of the implications of a conceptualization of CSA correlates in terms of derived relational responding? It has been argued that verbal regulation differs from direct contingency control in terms of indirectness, arbitrariness, and specificity (Hayes & Wilson, 1993). Whereas classical and operant conditioning account for behavioral interactions that are regulated by historical events based on formal properties of stimuli, such as similarity, contiguity, or contingency, verbal regulation can be significantly more indirect, and therefore, the contextual cues regulating derived relational responding may be very subtle, idiosyncratic, or metaphorical (Hayes & Wilson, 1993). For example, CSA adult survivors tend to report difficulties with control within relationships, either by exerting too much control or by being overly dependent on others and feeling out of control (Follette & Pistorello, 1995); this issue is typically traced back to the childhood abuse, during which the survivor, as a child, was unable to have control over her own body. "Control" here has thus taken a metaphorical form: the adult survivor who could not take control over her own body, exercises control over shopping lists, where to go for dinner, and so on. It is similar to the agoraphobic person who cannot "escape" from a marriage and therefore becomes preoccupied with not being able to "escape" from the mall (Hayes, 1994b).

Similarly, because verbal relations are arbitrarily applicable, the stimuli participating in a relational frame may be quite idiosyncratic, with behavioral functions having virtually no connection with the stimuli's formal properties. This means that the variables at work for a particular survivor may be quite different from another's for entirely idiosyncratic reasons. This can also be the case in directly trained relations, albeit less strikingly so. Lastly, specificity indicates that sometimes elaborate and complex verbal formulations, set in place through arbitrarily applicable derived responding, may underlie clinical difficulties. This is often evident when one inquires about why survivors who dress unattractively do so: survivors commonly report having thoughts such as "If I didn't have my short dress on, my dad wouldn't have seen my legs and found me attractive. If he hadn't found me attractive, he would not have abused me." Sometimes, the history can be quite specific and the verbal formulations complex.

As a result of derived stimulus relations, survivors may come to respond to a wide range of otherwise relatively neutral interpersonal events in a fearful or avoidant manner. One such example is the aversive functions some survivors experience when given a compliment of any sort, particularly those of a physical nature. In such a case, for example, the word "pretty" may come to participate in the same equivalence class as "hurt" and "bad," thus acquiring, through derived relations, the same aversive properties as the abuse itself. The survivor, therefore, may start to "avoid" all types of compliments by dressing unattractively, a behavior sometimes reported by survivors (Follette & Pistorello, 1995).

In sum, events are framed through arbitrarily applicable relational responding; events that share no formal properties (such as similarity or contiguity) may come to have similar stimulus functions. Because of the arbitrary applicability of the relational responding, the functions of aversive events may transform to previously neutral stimuli like brushfire, making it more difficult to identify the controlling variables. A recent study showed that "once a pattern of responding had emerged on a matching-to-sample test, it was highly resistant to change by incongruous training phases . . . [suggesting that] simply re-exposing clients to therapeutic strategies that previously failed to change the target behavior may be of little value" (Barnes & Roche, 1997, p. 132). This suggests that when certain derived relations emerge among survivors, such as "I = sad" and "sad = bad," it would be necessary to change the relational frames according to which these functions are transforming.

Rule-Governed Behavior

Another factor that might account for the resiliency of long-term correlates of CSA is that these outcomes might be rule-governed. Sometimes the verbal stimuli participating in relational frames are "contingency-specifying stimuli," or rule-governed behavior (RGB; Skinner, 1969). According to Skinner, "behavior that consists of following rules is inferior to behavior shaped by the contingencies described in the rules" (1977, p. 86). Most sequelae of CSA described by Briere (1992) as due to psychological trauma, such as guilt, shame, or cognitive distortions can be readily explained in terms of RGB. This point was noted by Hoier et al. in discussing the misattributions of cause of trauma among children: "Such cognitive (mis)representations of antecedent-response-consequence relations may underlie the guilt, shame, and low evaluations of self (self-esteem) reported in . . . abuse victims" (1992, p. 130).

Rule Governed Behavior in more recent analyses has been described as "behavior controlled by antecedent verbal stimuli" and the role of rule following has been particularly developed (Hayes & Hayes, 1989). Some rules are followed in the context of a history of reinforcement for following rules (pliance), whereas others are followed due to the correspondence between the rule and the contingencies in the environment (track). Both types of RGB might be at work in maintaining some of these long-term correlates of CSA. A number of such rules may have been stated by the perpetrator (e.g., "If you don't fight, I won't hurt you"or "I will kill you if you tell"). Some were probably followed because, in the context of a patriarchal system, rule following by a female child was repeatedly reinforced, and others were followed due to the correspondence between the rule and the contingencies (e.g., not fighting the perpetrator was followed by a decreased probability of being beaten). However, the maintenance of such rule-governed behavior may have nothing to do with the actual contingencies: "any given instructed rule may or may not accord with reality, that is, it may or may not be an accurate description of natural contingencies . . . the effectiveness of an instructed rule in controlling behavior depends less on its being accurate than on its being believed to be accurate" (Reese, 1989, p.41). This explains why survivors may not disclose the abuse even when the contingencies appear to be have been favorable for disclosure. The resilience of such RGB into adulthood may be explained by the fact that rules instructed by authority figures, who constitute a high percentage of perpetrators, are more reliably followed.

Some rules may have been stated privately (the survivor was the speaker and the listener), rather than publicly by the perpetrator. For example, Briere (1992) suggests that through a sequence of "logical" conclusions the abused child comes to view the abuse as her fault and that she must be "bad" at a core level. The following sequence is illustrative: 1) I [the child] am being hurt by a trusted adult; 2) This must mean that either I am bad or my parent is; 3) Society teaches me that parents are always right, and only hurt you for your own good as a form of punishment for when you are being bad; 4) Therefore, it must be my fault that I am being hurt; I must be bad; 5) Since I am being hurt a lot, I must be very bad. Therefore, in this example, the child may derive the rule that "If I am hurt by a parent, it will be my fault and I will be bad."

The distinction between contingency-shaped and rule-governed behavior is important because the latter is an antecedent verbal stimulus which may change the function of natural contingencies. Laboratory studies show that rule-governed behavior may render the individual's behavior insensitive to direct contingencies control (cf. Reese, 1989). Hayes and colleagues have pointed out that rule-governance is a very handy phenomenon in many respects, but that problems in verbal control tend to occur, such as problems in self-rule formulation, problems in rule-formulation of the group, a failure to follow rules, and excessive rule following (Hayes, Kohlenberg, & Melancon, 1989).

Excessive rule following might be particularly problematic with CSA survivors and may explain the greater vulnerability of survivors to revictimization in adulthood. For example, as a child, the survivor may have derived a rule such as "If I do not react when someone threatens me, I won't be beaten." Perhaps not resisting the perpetrator was the only choice the survivor had as a child, and may well have kept her alive, but adults have access to a much larger repertoire of responses, such as seeking refuge in a shelter or getting a divorce. However, to the extent that the behavior of the adult survivor is under the control of rules, dispensed by established sources (such as a parental figure) and therefore more reliably followed, the survivor's behavior may be insensitive to changes in the environmental contingencies, due to the overpowering effect of previously established rules.

A Functional Commonality

Before proceeding, a brief summary is in order. First, CSA appears to be associated with anxiety, depression, suicidality, and a vast number of other complaints. Second, these complaints can be accounted for entirely by available behavioral principles, when derived relational responding is included. At this point, one may reasonably ask how useful it is for clinicians and researchers to have this knowledge. How can this information be integrated so as to lead to increased prediction and control? Unless these behaviors can be described functionally, not topographically, so as to guide treatment and research in this area, the vast body of research on long-term correlates of CSA remains more informative than useful.

The trauma field has recognized this need and has encouraged the identification of commonalities and differences in the impact of trauma, across different types of traumatic events (Briere, 1992). Interestingly, independent conceptualizations of the effects of trauma, across theoretical boundaries, appear to converge on a similar process: *avoidance*. In different ways, several researchers and theoreticians have voiced the belief that avoidance, not only "behavioral" (meaning within the realm of overt behavior), but also cognitive or emotional avoidance (within the realm of private events), is the primary mechanism of coping with the aftermath of the trauma. Theoreticians further agree that avoidance, initially an adaptive solution, becomes the problem in the long run. It is noteworthy that most accounts also allude to avoidance occuring in the context of negatively-evaluated private events, as illustrated below.

Recently, several behaviors such as dissociation, substance abuse, suicidality, and self-mutilation have been conceptualized as avoidance of abuse-specific memories and affect (Briere, 1992). For instance, the vast majority of a child sexual abuse survivor sample reported engaging in some tension-reducing behavior, such as binging, purging, excessive dieting/exercise, self-mutilating behavior, daily alcohol intoxication, and engaging in compulsive sexual activities (Rodriguez, Ryan, & Foy, 1992). These same researchers found that engaging in more tension-reducing behaviors was associated with higher levels of posttraumatic stress symptoms.

Avoidance has been linked to PTSD in particular. van der Kolk and colleagues (1996) argue that the difference between individuals who experienced CSA but did not develop PTSD and those who did develop PTSD is that the latter became "stuck" in reliving their trauma and came to organize their lives in terms of avoidance of the trauma. The authors go on to say that "Avoidance may take many different forms: keeping away from situations, people, or emotions that remind them of the traumatic event; ingesting alcohol or drugs, which numb awareness of distressing emotional states; or utilizing dissociation to keep unpleasant experiences from conscious awareness" (van der Kolk, McFarlane, van der Hart, 1996, p. 419).

Foa and colleagues, discussing the application of a cognitive-behavioral theory of PTSD, also emphasized that avoidance of negatively-evaluated emotions is a key factor in the maintenance of PTSD symptoms:

Another possible difference between individuals whose PTSD symptoms persist and those for whom they decline may be the degree of avoidance. PTSD individuals for whom anxiety or discomfort carries a high negative valence ("anxiety is bad") will be more likely to avoid confronting situations or images which lead to the experience of anxious feelings. Thus, they are more likely to develop behavioral and cognitive avoidance patterns (Foa, Steketee, & Rothbaum, 1989, p. 171).

Although there is consensus that avoidance is a problem, there are no adequate behavior analytic accounts of why avoidance becomes so pervasive among this population, and why private events in particular should acquire such aversive functions. Most behavior theorists refer to "higher order" conditioning to explain why thoughts, feelings, and words associated with the abuse come to elicit conditioned responses (Kilpatrick et al., 1985), but this concept has had little empirical support. As Hoier et al. (1992) noted "generalization and higher-order learning have been fairly neglected in the research on outcomes of sexual abuse" (p.131). We propose that CSA survivors start avoiding a variety of stimuli, both public and private, not only due to directly trained relations, but also due to derived relations, through the formation of relational frame classes among verbal stimuli, which then come to share similar psychological functions. This would explain the pervasiveness of avoidance among this population, and also why private events come to have similar functions as the abuse itself.

A recent conceptual framework, which is firmly grounded on RFT, also has focused on avoidance as a common function across various long-term correlates of CSA. It was proposed that "experiential avoidance" (referring to both cognitive and emotional avoidance) explains a variety of psychopathological presentations, including presentations frequently comorbid with a history of CSA, such as self-injury, alcoholism, and borderline personality disorder (Hayes, Wilson, Gifford, Follette, & Strosahl, 1996). This analysis is congruent with the view presented here that psychopathology occurs as a by-product of an individual's unwillingness to experience negatively-evaluated private events, such as emotions, memories, thoughts, and behavioral predispositions.

It has been proposed that experiential avoidance "can be characterized as an unwillingness to experience unpleasant internal events such as thoughts and feelings associated with the abuse . . . This unwillingness results in attempts to avoid those stimuli which have been negatively evaluated through a variety of mechanisms, including substance abuse, dissociation, bulimia . . . The avoidance of emotional experiencing is then negatively reinforced by the removal of the acute dysphoric feelings" (Follette, 1994, p. 257). It is noteworthy that experiential avoidance, as so defined, accounts for correlates of CSA under all three subheadings utilized in our initial review of long-term correlates. Survivors may experientially avoid by dissociating, drinking, or withdrawing emotionally from a partner; although the topography differs, the function of the behaviors is the same.

The point of departure between a radical behaviorist approach and other main stream perspectives lies on where the determinants of behavior are to be found (Dougher, 1993; Follette, 1993; Hayes, 1995). More traditional approaches to the treatment of sexual abuse view restructuring or changing thoughts and reducing negatively-evaluated emotions as a necessary step towards behavioral change, as private events are thought to cause undesirable overt behavioral patterns. In these approaches, the goal then becomes to control unwanted private events deliberately, through cognitive restructuring (e.g., Marks, Lovell, Noshirvani, Livanou, & Thrasher, 1997) or thought stopping (as part of Stress Inoculation Training; Kilpatrick, Veronen, & Resick, 1982). Radical behaviorist approaches, albeit recognizing the important role of private events, place the emphasis on in-principle manipulable events (Hayes, 1995).

The RFT analysis outlined above allows us to identify some of the variables which can be manipulated to decrease avoidance, and, more importantly, its deleterious effects. As recently pointed out in the literature (Anderson et al., 1997), when a maladaptive behavior "is clearly under the discriminative control of an observable stimulus, the approach generally taken is not to eliminate the discriminative stimulus or to reduce the frequency of contact with the stimulus, but to manipulate the functional relation such that a stimulus is no longer occasioning the problematic behavior" (p. 173). Recent developments in alcoholism treatment clearly illustrate this principle. Although in the past alcoholics were kept away from any alcoholic cues while in inpatient treatment (Marlatt & Gordon, 1980), recently, planned exposures to the sight and smell of an individual's favorite alcoholic beverage—combined with coping skills training— have been shown to lead to increased abstinence at follow up (Monti, Rohsenow, Rubonis, Niaura, Sirota, Colby, Goddard, & Abrams, 1993). Instead of simply changing the form or frequency of the alcoholic cues, treatment focuses on changing the context in which these cues are encountered, not only through, theoretically, extinction of conditioned responses through a series of nonreinforced exposure trials, but also by expanding one's repertoire of responses.

Insofar as private events are only different from overt events in terms of observability (Skinner, 1953), it makes sense to use the same approach found useful with exteroceptive stimuli with private stimuli. As with exteroceptive cue exposure in alcohol treatment, when private events occasion maladaptive overt behavior, psychological treatment need not involve trying to change, reduce, or eliminate the form or frequency of unwanted private events, but rather to change the context in which these private events occur.

We argue here that the context in which private events, such as sadness or a thought of "I'm bad," come to have discriminative control over overt behavior is inherently verbal. The context that maintains the control of private events over overt behavior includes: (1) excessive literality, such as being unable to distinguish the word "sex" from sex itself, or, within a clinical setting, being unable to experience "I'm bad" as just a thought, rather than an accurate description of the person; (2) the tendency within our culture to reinforce giving verbal reasons, particularly those involving private events, as valid explanations for overt behavior. A child who hits a playmate on the playground is much less likely to be further reprimanded if he says "I hit Johnny because I was mad" than if he says "I don't know why I hit Johnny"—a more likely explanation, perhaps.

In the therapeutic approach stemming from RFT findings, Acceptance and Commitment Therapy (ACT, Hayes, Strosahl, & Wilson, 1999; Walser & Hayes, 1998), it is argued that avoidance of negatively-evaluated emotions or thoughts, which is encouraged and maintained within the social verbal context (such as through reason giving), is a by-product of the "bi-directional transformation of stimulus functions [which is established] through derived relational responding" (Hayes & Wilson, 1994). Thus thoughts or feelings are not viewed as mental events which are avoided (thus assuming a behavior-behavior relationship), but rather are events which through derived stimulus relations come to have similar *functions* as the environmental events belonging to the same relational frame. It is within the context of *this* analysis that we use the term "experiential avoidance."

What are the implications of a derived relational responding analysis for understanding experiential avoidance? The argument follows that (1) If "to describe an event is to contact the stimulus functions of the referent" (Hayes & Wilson, 1993) due to arbitrarily applicable relational responding, and (2) we adopt Skinner's position that private events are only different in that they take place within the skin (1953), then (3) we can assume that as spoken words come to have many of the stimulus functions of their referent, so do events taking place privately, such as thoughts.

For purposes of completion, we will conclude with a brief mention of the clinical implications of the analysis provided in this chapter; however, the interested reader is referred to other publications for comprehensive descriptions of this treatment approach in general (Hayes & Wilson, 1994; Hayes et al., 1999), and as applied to CSA survivors specifically (Follette, 1994; Follette & Pistorello, 1995). In conclusion, if experiential avoidance is primarily a conventional and verbal process, then we should be able to alter this avoidance by altering the social/verbal context in which these verbal processes occur. This social/verbal context is readily manipulable in a way that thoughts and emotions simply are not, since the therapy setting itself forms a small but genuine verbal community. Our therapeutic approach (ACT; Hayes et al., 1999) is based on this insight.

Instead of supporting the view that the cessation of undesirable feelings, thoughts, memories, or emotions is a necessary condition for functioning effectively, our applied theory of psychopathology suggests that we could change both the action of avoidance and the framework which supports the effort of avoidance itself: the literalization of verbal behavior. Our analysis leads us to conclude that pervasive behavior change can occur through **deliteralization**, which can, in part, lead to **acceptance**. This acceptance can function in getting rid of the agenda of control and decreasing experiential avoidance, leading to a more rich and rewarding life for the client (Hayes, 1994a).

References

Alford, B. A., Richards, C. A., & Hanych, J. M. (1995). The causal status of private events. *The Behavior Therapist, 18,* 57-58.

Anderson, C. M., Hawkins, R. P., & Scotti, J. P. (1997). Private events in behavior analysis: Conceptual basis and clinical relevance. *Behavior Therapy, 28,* 157-179.

Barnes, D., & Roche, B. (1997). Relational frame theory and the experimental analysis of human sexuality. *Applied and Preventive Psychology, 6,* 117-135.

Barnes, D., Browne, M., Smeets, P. M., & Roche, B. (1995). A transfer of functions and a conditional transfer of functions through equivalence relations in three to six year old children. *Psychological Record, 45,* 405-430.

Beitchman, J. E., Zucker, K. J., Hood, J. E., DaCosta, G. A., Akman, D., & Cassavia, E. (1992). A review of the long-term effects of child sexual abuse. *Child Abuse and Neglect, 16,* 101-118.

Briere, J. N. (1988). The long-term clinical correlates of childhood sexual victimization. *Annals of the New York Academy of Sciences, 528,* 327-334.

Briere, J. N. (1992). *Child abuse trauma: Theory and treatment of the lasting effects.* Newbury Park, CA: SAGE Publications.

Briere, J. N., Evans, D., Runtz, M., & Wall, T. (1988). Symptomatology in men who were molested as children: A comparison study. *American Journal of Orthopsychiatry, 58,* 457-461.

Briere, J., & Runtz, M. (1989). The Trauma Symptom Checklist: Early data on a new scale. *Journal of Interpersonal Violence, 4,* 151-163.

Briere, J. N., & Runtz, M. (1991). The long-term effects of sexual abuse: A review and synthesis. In J. Briere (Ed.), *Treating victims of child sexual abuse.* San Francisco: Jossey-Bass Inc.

Briere, J. N., & Zaidi, L. Y. (1989). Sexual abuse histories and sequelae in female psychiatric emergency room patients. *American Journal of Psychiatry, 146* (12), 1602-1606.

Browne, A., & Finkelhor, D. (1986) Impact of child sexual abuse: A review of the research. *Psychological Bulletin, 99,* 66-77.

Carter, M. M., & Barlow, D. H. (1995). Learned alarms: The origins of panic. In W. O'Donohue & L. Krasner (Eds.), *Theories of behavior therapy: Exploring behavior change* (pp. 209-228). Washington, DC: American Psychological Association.

Christensen, A., Jacobson, N. S., & Babcock, J. C. (1995). Integrative behavioral couple therapy. In N. S. Jacobson & A. S. Gurman (Eds.), *Clinical handbook of couple therapy* (pp. 31-64). New York: Guilford Press.

Cole, P.M., & Putnam, F. W. (1992). Effect of incest on self and social functioning: A developmental psychopathology perspective. *Journal of Consulting and Counseling Psychology, 60,* 174-184.

Courtois, C. A. (1979). The incest experience and its aftermath. *Victimology: An International Journal, 4,* 337-347.

Cummings, C., Gordon, J. P., & Marlatt, G. A. (1980). Relapse: Strategies of prevention and prediction. In W. R. Miller (Ed.), *The addictive behaviors: Treatment of alcoholism, drug abuse, smoking, and obesity.* Oxford, U. K.: Pergamon Press.

de Rose, J. C., de Souza, D. G., Rossito, A. L., & de Rose, T. M. S. (1992). Stimulus equivalence and generalization in reading after matching-to-sample by exclusion. In S. C. Hayes & L. J. Hayes (Eds.), *Understanding verbal relations* (pp. 69-82). Reno, NV: Context Press.

Devaney, J. M., Hayes, S. C., & Nelson, R. O. (1986). Equivalence class formation in language-able and language disabled children. *Journal of the Experimental Analysis of Behavior, 46,* 243-257.

DiTomasso, M. J., & Routh, D. K. (1993). Recall of abuse in childhood and three measures of dissociation. *Child Abuse & Neglect, 17,* 477-485.

Dougher, M. J. (1993). On the advantages and implications of a radical behavioral treatment of private events. *The Behavior Therapist, 16,* 204-206.

Dougher, M. J., Auguston, E., Markham, M. R., Greenway, D. E., & Wulfert, E. (1994). The transfer of respondent eliciting and extinction functions through stimulus equivalence classes. *Journal of Experimental Analysis of Behavior, 62,* 331-352.

Foa, E. B., Steketee, G., & Rothbaum, B. O. (1989). Behavioral/cognitive conceptualizations of posttraumatic stress disorder. *Behavior Therapy, 20,* 155-176.

Follette, V. M. (1991). Marital therapy for sexual abuse survivors. In J. Briere (Ed.), *Treating victims of child sexual abuse.* San Francisco: Jossey-Bass.

Follette, V. M. (1994). Acceptance and commitment in the treatment of incest survivors: A contextual approach. In S. C. Hayes, N. S. Jacobson, V. M. Follette, & M. Dougher (Eds.), *Acceptance and change: Content and context in psychotherapy.* Reno, NV: Context Press.

Follette, W. C. (1993). Private events–The straw-person argument against radical behaviorism. *The Behavior Therapist, 16,* 204.

Follette, W. C. (1995). The last visitation of private events (1995). *The Behavior Therapist, 18,* 57.

Follette, V. M., & Pistorello, J. (1995). Couples therapy. In Y. D. Yalom (Series Ed.) & C. Classen (Vol. Ed.), *Treating women molested in childhood* (pp. 129-161). San Francisco: Jossey-Bass.

Forsyth, J. P. & Eifert, G. H. (1996). Systematic alarms in fear conditioning: A reappraisal of what is being conditioned. *Behavior Therapy, 27,* 441-462.

Fromuth, M. E., & Burkhart, B. R. (1989). Long-term psychological correlates of childhood sexual abuse in two samples of college men. *Child Abuse & Neglect, 13,* 533-542.

Gold, E. R. (1986). Long-term effects of sexual victimization in childhood: An attributional approach. *Journal of Consulting and Clinical Psychology, 54,* 471-475.

Harter, S., Alexander, P. C., & Neimeyer, R. A. (1988). Long-term effects of incestuous child abuse in college women: Social adjustment, social cognition, and family characteristics. *Journal of Consulting and Clinical Psychology, 56,* 5-8.

Hayes, S. C. (1984). Making sense of spirituality. *Behaviorism, 12,* 99-110.

Hayes, S. C. (1991). A relational control theory of stimulus equivalence. In L. J. Hayes & P. N. Chase (Eds.), *Dialogues on verbal behavior: Proceedings on the first international institute on verbal relations.* Reno, NV: Context Press.

Hayes, S. C. (1994a). Content, context, and types of psychological acceptance. In S. C. Hayes, N. S. Jacobson, V. M. Follette, & M. J. Dougher (Eds.), *Acceptance and change: Content and context in psychotherapy* (pp. 13-32) Reno, NV: Context Press.

Hayes, S. C. (1994b). Relational frame theory as a behavioral approach to verbal events. In S. C. Hayes, L. J. Hayes, M. Sato, and K. Ono (Eds.), *Behavior analysis of language and cognition.* Reno, NV: Context Press.

Hayes, S. C. (1995). Why cognitions are not causes. *The Behavior Therapist, 18,* 59-60.

Hayes, S. C., & Hayes, L. J. (1989). The verbal action of the listener as a basis for rule-governance. In S. C. Hayes (Ed.), Rule-governed behavior: Cognition, contingencies, and instructional control (pp. 153-190). New York: Plenum.

Hayes, S.C. & Hayes, L. J. (1992). Verbal relations and the evolution of behavior analysis. *American Psychologist, 47,* 1383-1395.

Hayes, S. C., Jacobson, N. S., Follette, V. M., & Dougher, M. J. (Eds.). (1994). *Acceptance and change: Content and Context in Psychotherapy.* Reno, NV: Context Press.

Hayes, S. C., Kohlenberg, B. S., & Hayes, L. J. (1991). The transfer of specific and general consequential functions through simple and conditional equivalence relations. *Journal of the Experimental Analysis of Behavior, 56,* 119-137.

Hayes, S. C., Kohlenberg, F. B., & Melancon, S. M. (1989). Avoiding and altering rule-control as a strategy of clinical intervention. In S. C. Hayes *Rule-governed behavior, cognition, contingencies, and instructional control* (pp. 359-385). New York: Plenum.

Hayes, S. C., Strosahl, K., D. & Wilson, K. G. (1999). *Acceptance and Commitment Therapy: An experiential approach to behavior change.* New York: Guilford Press.

Hayes, S.C. & Wilson, K.G. (1993). Some applied implications of contemporary behavior-analytic account of verbal events. *The Behavior Analyst, 16,* 283-301.

Hayes, S.C. & Wilson, K.G. (1994). Acceptance and Commitment Therapy: Altering the verbal support for experiential avoidance. *The Behavior Analyst, 17,* 289-303.

Hayes, S. C., Wilson, K., Gifford, E., Follette, V. M., & Strosahl, K. (1996). Experiential avoidance and behavioral disorders: A functional dimensional approach to diagnosis and treatment. *Journal of Consulting and Clinical Psychology, 64,* 1152-1168.

Herman, J. L. (1992). *Trauma and recovery: The aftermath of violence – from domestic violence to political terror.* New York: Harper Collins.

Hoier, T. S., Shawchuck, C. R., Palotta, G. M., Freeman, T., Inderbitzen-Pisaruk, H., MacMillan, V. M., Malinosky-Rummell, R., & Greene, A. L. (1992). The impact of sexual abuse: A cognitive-behavioral model. In W. T. O'Donohue & J. H. Greer, *The sexual abuse of children, Vol. 1: Theory and research, Volume 2: Clinical issues* (pp. 101-142). Hillsdale, NJ: Lawrence Erlbaum Associates.

Hunter, J. A. (1991). A comparison of the psychosocial maladjustment of adult males and females sexually molested as children. *Journal of Interpersonal Violence, 6,* 205-217.

Jackson, J. L., Calhoun, K. S., Amick, A. A., Maddever, H. M., & Habif, V. L. (1990). Young adult women who report childhood intrafamilial sexual abuse: Subsequent adjustment. *Archives of Sexual Behavior, 19,* 211-221.

Keane, T. M., Zimmerling, R. T., & Caddell, J. M. (1985). A behavioral formulation of post-traumatic stress disorder in Vietnam veterans. *The Behavior Therapist, 8,* 9-12.

Kilpatrick, D. G., Veronen, L. J., & Best, C. L. (1985). Factors predicting psychological distress among rape victims. In C. R. Figley (Ed.), Trauma and its wake. New York: Brunner/Mazel.

Kohlenberg, R. J., & Tsai, M. (1991). Functional Analytic Psychotherapy: Creating intense and curative therapeutic relationships. New York: Plenum Press.

Linehan, M. M. (1993). *Cognitive-behavioral treatment of borderline personality disorder.* New York: Guilford Press, Inc.

Maltz, W., & Holman, B. (1987). *Incest and sexuality: A guide to understanding and healing.* Lexington, Massachusetts: Lexington Books.

Marks, I., Lovell, K., Norshirvani, H., Livanou, M., & Thrasher, S. (1997). *Exposure and cognitive restructuring alone and combined in PTSD: A controlled study.* Manuscript in preparation.

Meadows, E. A., & Foa, E. B. (1998). Intrusion, arousal, and avoidance: Sexual trauma survivors. In V. M. Follette, J. I. Ruzek, & F. R. Abueg (Eds.), *Cognitive-Behavioral Therapies for Trauma* (pp. 100-123). New York: Guilford Press.

Meiselman, K. (1978). *Incest: A psychological study of causes and effects with treatment recommendations.* San Francisco: Jossey-Bass.

Monti, P.M., Rohsenow, D.J., Rubonis, A.V., Niaura, R.S., Sirota, A.D., Colby, S.M., Goddard, P., and Abrams, D.B. (1993). Cue exposure with coping skills treatment for male alcoholics: A preliminary investigation. *Journal of Consulting and Clinical Psychology, 61,* 1011-1019.

Mowrer, O. H. (1960). *Learning theory and behavior.* New York: Wiley.

Ogata, S. N., Silk, K. R., Goodrich, S., Lohr, N. E., Westen, D., & Hill, E. M. (1990). Childhood sexual and physical abuse in adult patients with borderline personality disorder. *American Journal of Psychiatry, 147,* 1008-1013.

Pribor, E. F., & Dinwiddie, S. H. (1992). Psychiatric correlates of incest in childhood. *American Journal of Psychiatry, 149,* 52-56.

Polusny, M., & Follette, V. M. (1995). Long-term correlates of child sexual abuse: Theory and review of the empirical literature. *Applied and Preventive Psychology, 4,* 143-166.

Reese, H. W. (1989). Rules and rule-governance: Cognitive and behavioristic views. In S. C. Hayes (Ed.), Rule-governed behavior: Cognition, contingencies, and instructional control (pp. 3-84). New York: Plenum.

Resick, P. A., & Schnicke, M. K. (1992). Cognitive processing therapy for sexual assault victims. *Journal of Consulting and Clinical Psychology, 60,* 748-756.

Rodriguez, N., Ryan, S. W., & Foy, D. W. (1992). *Tension reduction and PTSD: Adult survivors of sexual abuse.* Paper presented at the annual meeting of the International Society for Traumatic Stress Studies, Los Angeles.

Rodriguez, N., Ryan, S. W., Kemp, H. V., & Foy, D. W. (1997). Posttraumatic stress disorder in adult female survivors of childhood sexual abuse: A comparison study. *Journal of Consulting and Clinical Psychology, 65,* 53-59.

Rohsenow, D. J., Corbett, R., & Devine, D. (1988). Molested as children: A hidden contribution to substance abuse? *Journal of Substance Abuse Treatment, 5,* 13-18.

Russell, D. E. H. (1986). *The secret trauma: Incest in the lives of girls and women.* New York: Basic Books, Inc.

Saunders, B. E., Villeponteaux, L. A., Lipovsky, J. A., Kilpatrick, D. G., & Veronen, L. J. (1992). Child sexual assault as a risk factor for mental health disorders among women: A community sample. *Journal of Interpersonal Violence, 7,* 189-204.

Skinner, B. F. (1953). *Science and human behavior.* New York: Free Press.

Skinner, B. F. (1969). Behaviorism at fifty. In A. C. Catania & S. Harnard (Eds.), *The selection of behavior: The operant behaviorism of B. F. Skinner: Comments and consequences* (pp. 278-381). New York, NY: Cambridge Press.

Skinner, B. F. (1974). *About behaviorism.* New York: Knopf.

Sidman, M., & Tailby, W. (1982). Conditional discriminations versus matching to sample: An extension of the testing paradigm. *Journal of the Experimental Analysis of Behavior, 37,* 5-22.

Steele, D., & Hayes, S. C. (1991). Stimulus equivalence and arbitrarily applicable relational responding. *Journal of the Experimental Analysis of Behavior, 56,* 519-555.

van der Kolk, B. McFarlane, A. C., & Weisaeth, L. (1996). Traumatic stress: The effects of overwhelming experience on mind, body, an society. New York: Guilford Press.

van der Kolk, B. A., A., Perry, J. C., & Herman, J. L. (1991). Childhood origins of self-destructive behavior. *American Journal of Psychiatry, 148,* 1665-1671.

Vander-Mey, B. J. (1992). Theories of incest. In W. T. O'Donohue & J. H. Geer, *The sexual abuse of children, Vol. 1: Theory and research, Volume 2: Clinical issues* (pp. 204-260). Hillsdale, NJ: Lawrence Erlbaum Associates.

Vaughan, M. (1989). Rule-governed behavior in behavior analysis: A theoretical and experimental history. In S. C. Hayes (Ed.), *Rule-governed behavior: Cognition, contingencies, and instructional control* (pp. 97-118). New York: Plenum.

Wagner, A. W., & Linehan, M. M. (1998). Dissociative Behavior. In V. M. Follette, J. I. Ruzek, & F. R. Abueg (Eds.) *Cognitive-Behavioral Therapies for Trauma* (pp. 191-225). New York: Guilford Press.

Walser, R. D., & Hayes, S. C. (1998). Acceptance and trauma survivors: Applied issues and problems. In V. M. Follette, J. I. Ruzek, & F. R. Abueg (Eds.) *Cognitive-Behavioral Therapies for Trauma* (pp. 256-277). New York: Guilford Press.

Waltz, J. (1993). *The long-term effects of childhood sexual abuse on women's relationships with partners.* Unpublished doctoral dissertation, University of Washington, Seattle.

Wegner, D. M. (1989). *White bears and other unwanted thoughts.* New York: Guilford Press.

Wind, T. W., & Silvern, L. (1992). Type and extent of child abuse as predictors of adult functioning. *Journal of Family Violence, 7,* 261-281.

Wyatt, G. E., & Newcomb, M. (1990). Internal and external mediators of women's sexual abuse in childhood. *Journal of Consulting and Clinical Psychology, 58*(6), 758-767.

Wyatt, G. E., Newcomb, M. D., & Riederle, M. H. (1993). *Sexual abuse and consensual sex: Women's developmental patterns and outcomes.* Newbury Park, CA: Sage.

Yama, M. F., Tovey, S. L., & Fogas, B. S. (1993). Childhood family environment and sexual abuse as predictors of anxiety and depression in adult women. *American Journal of Orthopsychiatry, 63,* 136-141.

Zettle, R. D., & Hayes, S. C. (1986). Dysfunctional control by client verbal behavior: The context of reason giving. *The Analysis of Verbal Behavior, 4,* 30-38.

Zierler, S., Feingold, L., Laufer, D., Velentgas, P., Kantrowitz-Gordon, I., & Mayer, K. (1991). Adult survivors of childhood sexual abuse and subsequent risk for HIV infection. *American Journal of Public Health, 81,* 572-575.

Chapter 5

Functional Alternatives to Traditional Assessment and Diagnosis

William C. Follette
Amy E. Naugle
Peter J. N. Linnerooth
University of Nevada

In order to appreciate functional assessment, one must understand what exactly it seeks to achieve, and how it differs from other assessment approaches. In this chapter we focus primarily on functional case conceptualization. Functional case conceptualization has as its goal the assessment and conceptualization of clinically relevant problem behaviors, adequately understood in their historical context, for the purpose of identifying a treatment intervention that will produce the desired change. Thus, one of the standards against which functional case conceptualization is measured is whether it leads to a particular intervention you would not have envisioned had you not done such an assessment. If this or any other kind of assessment does not lead one to do a different intervention, it can have no treatment utility (Hayes, Nelson, & Jarret, 1987) and could not withstand any kind of cost-benefit analysis. Assessment, in and of itself, is merely data. Functional assessment, or functional case conceptualization, is the process of linking assessment data to a specific treatment plan.

While one cannot easily characterize more traditional forms of assessment, they might be said to have three goals (Barrios, 1988). The first is to aid in the diagnosis or classification of clinical problems. For example, one might give a structured interview in order to make the diagnosis of depression. Second, traditional assessment seeks to identify the etiology of a problem. Perhaps an assessment procedure can give some clue as to the original source of a current problem, such as a history of childhood sexual abuse leading to current sexual dysfunction. Third, traditional assessment is designed to assist in providing a prognosis. For example, a score on a particular measure of psychopathology may lead one to conclude that a particular client will not return to an appreciably higher level of functioning. These goals are largely descriptive.

In contrast, functional assessment has four goals: 1) to identify target behaviors and the conditions that maintain the behaviors; 2) to aid in selecting an appropriate intervention; 3) to provide a means to monitor treatment progress; and 4) to aid in the evaluation of the effectiveness of an intervention.

Thus far we have used the term functional assessment or functional case conceptualization. One may notice the similarity between what we have described thus far and what has been termed behavioral assessment by others. In fact, functional assessment and *behavioral* assessment mean the same thing, but are not interchangeable with the term *behavior* assessment. Engaging in behavior assessment merely constitutes the counting of behavior. One can see elements of this tradition in DSM-IV (American Psychiatric Association, 1994), where one can be diagnosed as having had a major depressive episode if he or she is observed to have had five or more predefined symptoms during the same two-week period (e.g., First, Frances, Widiger, Pincus, & Davis, 1992). While behavior assessment in the DSM tradition focuses merely on the number of symptoms, behavioral or functional assessment identifies under what circumstances these depressive behaviors are most likely to occur and what happens when they do. We use the term functional assessment throughout this chapter to emphasize our interest in the function of behavior rather then merely its form or topography.

An Overview of the Assumptions of Functional Assessment

This section outlines some of the basic assumptions upon which a functional assessment rests. Appreciating the implications of these assumptions will help one understand the differences between traditional and functional assessment.

Distinction between Topography and Function

The primary tenet of functional analysis is that behavior is understood according to its function, or what purpose it serves, rather than by its formal features (Hayes, Follette, & Follette, 1995). The function of behavior is understood by examining the relevant controlling variables of an objectively defined behavior, including the antecedents, consequences, and the conditions under which the behavior most often occurs. Understanding behavior in terms of its function rather then merely its form or topography is essential for an adequate assessment. In an obvious example, it is useful to distinguish between clearing one's throat because one has a sore throat versus clearing one's throat because one is anxious. The form of the throat clearing is clearly identical, yet the function is very different in these two cases.

As an example with clinical relevance, consider the case where a client cries during therapy. The mere fact that he or she cries is not particularly informative. Is the client crying because he or she is sad? Is the client crying because he or she is relieved? Is the client crying because he or she wishes the therapist to stop pursuing a particular line of inquiry? Is the client crying for sympathy? Until one understands what the function of the crying is, one has no idea what to do with the observation that the client is crying. When one understands what exactly gave rise to the crying, and what changes in the environment are associated with decreases or increases in the crying, one has done a functional assessment of the crying and could presumably affect its occurrence if one so chose.

Functional Classes

So far we have been talking about isolated behaviors. However, continuing to amplify on the distinction between topography and function, in a functional analysis individual behaviors or stimuli are often considered to be members of larger functional classes. Many seemingly unrelated behaviors may come to be understood as members of one particular response class. Response classes are hypothetical groupings of behaviors that all share the same function even though the topography of the individual behaviors in a particular class might appear quite different (Malott, Whaley, & Malott, 1996; Sturmey, 1996). All that is necessary for two or more behaviors to be elements in a response class is that the behaviors have a similar function on the environment.

Let us again consider the case where we observe that a client cries frequently during therapy. After a careful analysis we may conclude that the client cries whenever the therapist tries to elicit some trust from the client. When the therapist backs off from seeking trust from the client, the crying decreases. In this case we have the beginnings of a functional understanding of the crying. After considerable work in therapy, the therapist notices that the client's crying has dropped to a reasonable level. Concurrently, however, the client becomes increasingly angry during therapy. Upon closer examination, the therapist realizes that the client's anger is functioning in the same way that the crying functioned previously. That is, when the therapist seeks trust from the client, the client becomes angry concerning some issue. Anger and crying are conceptualized as members of the same response class because they both function to disrupt the therapist's efforts to build trust in the relationship. It could be that if the therapist then addressed the anger issue, the client might subsequently arrive late for therapy sessions, all in the service of moderating the degree of trust the client is asked to demonstrate in therapy. The reader is asked to note, however, that this is not the same as a hydraulic model of behavior where blocking one behavior causes the emergence of another because of some intrapsychic bottling of energy. The notion of a response class simply implies that there are multiple ways in which a client can achieve a particular goal. In the case of moderating trust, the client can cry, become angry, arrive late for therapy sessions, or exhibit any of a number of other behaviors that might function to keep some distance between the client and the therapist.

There is simply an efficiency to be gained by thinking in terms of the major functions that behaviors can serve for a client rather than understanding each behavior in isolation from all others. Identifying common functions that different behaviors may accomplish for a client can simplify the understanding of any new behaviors that a therapist might see.

Just as behaviors may be elements of larger response classes, it is possible to think of different stimulus situations as being members of a common stimulus class. For a client who has a history of failed relationships, it may be that all social relationships are seen as potentially hurtful. In such an instance, the client may be incorrectly discriminating that everyone is dangerous rather than allowing that some people are dangerous, others are not, and that it would be useful to recognize the difference.

Etiology and Topography

At this point it is perhaps obvious that a particular historical antecedent or etiologic event may result in very different behavioral topographies depending primarily upon one's history and what happens to a person subsequent to the etiologic event. For example, in a case where a young, recently engaged woman loses her fiancé in an automobile accident, one cannot predict how the woman would respond simply by knowing that her fiancee died. It could be that the woman would mourn and then at some point reengage in social contact with other men. Alternatively, she could try to distract herself from her grief by using alcohol or engaging in a series of short-term, superficial relationships. Which of these or any other behaviors she emits must be understood in the entire context of her history. Likewise, there is no behavior that can result from one and only one antecedent event. It is an egregious error to say, for example, that a 25-year old woman's fear of the dark is a definitive sign that the woman was sexually abused as a child. This is not to say that some behaviors might not be probabilistically more related to some antecedents than others or that some antecedents don't lead to some outcomes being more likely than others. We are emphasizing here the fact that the link between antecedents and behaviors is complex and multiply determined.

Sign versus Sample

To gain a functional understanding of a particular problem, we perform a functional analysis in order to identify and understand the controlling variables. Certain forms of traditional assessment have assumed that when we observe a behavior it is a sign of some underlying problem other than the behavior itself (Goldfried & Kent, 1972; Livingston, 1977). For example, one might think that when one observes self-mutilation, it is not the self-mutilation itself that is important, but rather that this behavior is a sign of underlying, inner directed rage or loathing. In a functional assessment it is assumed that the behavior in question is a sample of a basic class of problems that share a similar function for the client. In this case we would be interested in understanding the self-mutilation and any functionally related behaviors for their own sake. When does it occur? How do people respond when it does? Are there other behaviors that perform the same function? This difference, understanding behavior as being a sample of the problem rather than a sign of some other underlying condition, is an important characteristic of functional assessment.

Unit of Analysis

Another important assumption of functional assessment or a functional analysis is that the unit of study is the whole person interacting in and with a particular environmental context. That is, one cannot understand a person's behavior in isolation from the conditions under which it first occurred and under which it currently functions. For example, consider two children receiving corrective feedback from an athletic coach. Imagine that one of the children has a history of being chronically criticized and berated at home. Imagine a second child who has a history of being encouraged to try new behaviors and supported when they do not work well. One who adopts a functional analytic perspective realizes that the experience each of these children is having while receiving feedback from the coach is vastly different given their individual histories. Thus, a functional assessment occurs at a psychological level and does not consider behavior as merely movement through time and space.

The Process of a Functional Analysis

Recall that the desired outcome from a functional assessment is an analysis that has treatment utility. Ideally, a good functional analysis yields a good treatment outcome. With this in mind, two related key features characterize a functional analysis. First, a functional analysis is iterative. This means that one must cycle through the process of assessment as often as necessary in order to arrive at an analysis that leads to a useful intervention. The second key feature is that the functional analytic process is self-correcting. One cycles through the process until one gets the desired clinical outcome. A schematic of the process is shown in figure 1.

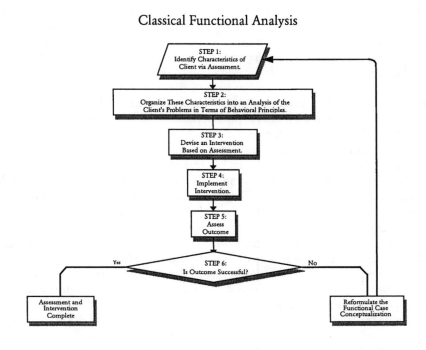

Figure 1: Schematic representation of a classical functional analysis

Step 1 in this process would be familiar to most clinicians. At this point the task is to identify the client's presenting problems and place them into some sort of hierarchy of clinical importance. In addition to a problem list, an evaluation of the client's assets and liabilities is made. Assets may include such features as functional social support, personal attributes including financial resources and attractiveness, diversity in sources of social reinforcement and robust health. Liabilities could entail such things as limited social opportunities, various disabilities, financial constraints and legal problems.

The unique features of functional analysis become apparent in Step 2. Here the functional analyst produces an analysis of the client's problems in terms of *behavioral principles*. A functional analysis has its roots in behavioral learning theory and relies on principles of operant and classical conditioning to understand the function of behavior. It is the application of behavioral principles that leads to the derivation of an intervention strategy as shown in Step 3. Once a principle-based intervention has been formulated, it is then implemented in Step 4. While not indicated directly in Figure 1, the assessment of outcome shown in Step 5 occurs continuously throughout treatment. For simplicity, step 6 indicates that the results from the assessment shown in Step 5 are judged for adequacy. If the treatment outcome based on a functional assessment was successful, assessment and intervention are complete. If, however, the assessment indicates that problems identified in Step 1 have not been adequately resolved, the functional analyst assumes that the analysis is incorrect or inadequate. This perspective differs from an interpretation of treatment failure that is cast in terms of constructs such as resistance on the part of the client. Indeed it is often the case that functional conceptualizations are fluid and become increasingly sophisticated as time goes by. It is neither surprising nor threatening to the behavior analyst to find that the initial assessment based on limited information was not adequate. What is important is that when a successful outcome has not been achieved the process iterates. Successive iterations are usually more time efficient because the assessment is based on much greater familiarity with the client, his or her situation, and assets.

One of the approaches that makes this process easier has been called the constructional approach (Goldiamond, 1974; Goldiamond, 1975; Hawkins, 1986). Using this approach, at the end of Step 1, the functional analyst states in observable terms the target or outcome to be established or constructed by the end of a successful intervention. This process serves two goals. First it forces the analyst to identify a behavioral repertoire that will serve the client well by the end of therapy. This repertoire should be readily observable and not refer to solely internal states. Second, a well-specified end point facilitates the assessment of outcome at Step 6. In addition to specifying the desired outcome, the analyst is required to give a description of the entering repertoire the client possesses that is relevant to achieving the final target behavior. This directs the attention of the assessor to the positive attributes the client may bring to the situation rather than focusing only on the client's deficits. In the constructive approach, functional assessment requires the specification and use of change procedures that will expand the client's entering repertoire so as to produce the desired outcome through steps of successive approximation. This approach frames the intervention process as positively as possible for both the therapist and the client. Finally the assessment procedure must identify natural maintaining variables that can be used to bring about and sustain change, rather than invoking arbitrary or extrinsic consequences (Ferster, 1967). The purpose of this requirement is to ensure that the reinforcers used to initiate change in the therapy setting are the same reinforcers the client will encounter in the real world, thereby ensuring that treatment gains produced in any intervention will be maintained in the natural environment.

When one begins a functional assessment the obvious first question is "what kinds of things should I attend to?" While there is no precise answer to this question, Haynes and O'Brien (1990) have suggested focusing on variables that are important, controllable, and causally related to the client's presenting problems. By important, Haynes and O'Brien mean that the variable in question explains a significant portion of the variability in the presenting problem. For example, one might wish to increase self-reported marital satisfaction for a couple. Functional analysis might indicate that a slight gain would result from the husband spending less time watching TV, while a large gain would accrue if the husband spent more time talking about emotional content in the relationship. By Haynes and O'Brien's criteria in this case the assessment ought to favor trying to manipulate how the couple talks with each other.

The second criterion Haynes and O'Brien used to identify important variables in a functional analysis is whether the variable of interest is, in principle, controllable. This is a particularly interesting guideline because it can conflict with topics that are of interest to both the therapist and the client. For example, historical variables often do not meet this criterion. In a functional analysis it is not useful to know only that someone has been sexually abused as a child. Those events occurred in the past and those facts cannot be changed and are therefore uncontrollable in the way Haynes and O'Brien mean control. Naturally, both clients and therapists tend to ascribe causal status to such vivid historical events. The criterion of controllability does not exclude the exploration of such events. For an historical event to be important in a functional analysis, however, the assessment must focus on how that history manifests itself in the present. It is not sufficient to say that a history of childhood sexual abuse is the reason why a particular person does not sustain close personal relationships. Rather one would need to identify how this history interferes with relationships in the present. This requirement may lead one to assess whether a client has a difficult time responding to intimacy or developing trust. Such hypotheses may derive from knowledge of childhood sexual abuse, but it is the response to intimacy and trusting behavior in the present that can be controlled and are hence the object of study in a functional analysis. Thus, historical variables can be important if they lead one to identify important contemporary, controllable variables. Otherwise the mere knowledge of historical facts does not constitute a sufficient functional analysis.

The third guideline for identifying which variables to attend to in a functional analysis is that they should be causal. Haynes and O'Brien's notion of causality is practical and simple. For a variable to be causal in a functional analysis it must covary with the problem behavior. This means that upon manipulation of the proposed causal variable, the target behavior must change as well. Haynes and O'Brien are not using the term causal in a strict philosophy of science sense. It is not important whether there is a direct causal path between one variable and another or whether change is mediated via a third variable. The important feature of causality is that when we change one variable the other reliably changes in turn. Their second requirement for causality derives from the need to understand how to bring about behavior change. Here, for a variable to be considered causal, changes in the causal variable must precede changes in the targeted problem. In summary, when deciding which variables on which to focus in a functional analysis, one should give priority to those that are important, controllable, and causal.

Organizing the Analysis Using Behavioral Principles

Functional assessment is done in order to devise an intervention that will bring about the desired behavior change. There is a strong link between assessment and intervention. Functional analysis applies behavioral principles to understand the maintenance and modification of observed problem behaviors. So in order to conduct a useful behavior analysis one must be well versed in the application of behavioral principles. It is the application of behavioral principles to a particular case in order to devise an intervention strategy that occurs during Steps 2 and 3 of the functional analysis.

There is no clear road map to follow in order to guide you through a thoughtful functional analysis. However, an understanding of behavioral principles can help organize the search for functionally important variables and planning an intervention strategy. Therefore, the remainder of this section outlines some basic behavioral principles and describes how they may appear clinically. A more complete description of learning principles can be found in many other sources (e.g., Kimble & Catania, 1992; Malott et al., 1996; Michael, 1993).

As background it will be useful to review a diagram of the operant paradigm since it organizes how we present some of the following material (see Figure 2).

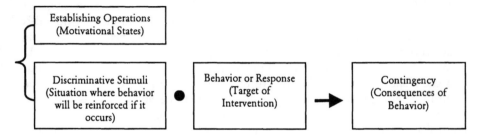

Figure 2: Schematic of Operant Behavior

The leftmost portion of this schematic diagram describes the environmental conditions in which a behavior may occur. The two bracketed boxes are the establishing operations and the discriminative stimuli. The bracket indicates that these two conditions occur and must be evaluated simultaneously. The next box to the right indicates the behavior being studied. In clinical settings this is typically the problem or target behavior that is the focus of intervention. Notice that between the discriminative stimuli box and the response box is a dot. The dot represents a probability function and indicates that in a given circumstance there is a probability that a behavior will follow. Next comes an arrow linking the behavior to some contingency in the environment. The nature of that contingency will determine whether or not the behavior in question is more or less likely to be emitted under the same or similar stimulus conditions.

Antecedents and Stimulus Control

As environmental conditions change, so do behaviors. Antecedents are environmental stimuli that precede the behavior as indicated in figure 2. Antecedents are generally referred to as discriminative stimuli. Discriminative stimuli are environmental events that set the occasion for when a particular response is likely to be reinforced. Generally, a discriminative stimulus occurs in relative temporal proximity to the behavior. However, antecedent conditions that exert control over the behavior can often be complicated (e.g., occur some time before the behavior). Stimulus control is an operation that determines and signals the conditions under which behavior is likely to be reinforced. Consider a simple, non-clinical example. Law enforcement officials use stimulus control strategies by placing signs that detect and display your current speed along sections of road where they are trying to control the speed of drivers. The signs (and the police cruiser a little further down the road!) act as discriminative stimuli signaling that a particular contingency is in force. These stimuli comprise an occasion for drivers' behavior of checking and adjusting their current speed to avoid the aversive consequence of a speeding ticket.

Contingencies of Reinforcement

Reinforcing stimuli are those stimuli that follow a behavior and increase the probability of its occurrence. Positive reinforcement is the delivery of a stimulus that strengthens behavior and increases the probability of occurrence. Effective parenting, for example, often involves implementing both arbitrary and natural reinforcers in order to increase the probability of a child's desirable behavior. We give allowances when children tidy their rooms and comment on how pleased we are to see siblings playing together harmoniously. Both monetary rewards and compliments may serve as reinforcers, if they indeed influence the occurrence of the behavior we are trying to shape.

Negative reinforcement also strengthens behavior that it is contingent upon, but involves the removal of an aversive stimulus. Both escape from aversive stimulation and avoidance of aversive events are examples of negative reinforcement. In some cases assertive behavior may be negatively reinforced. For example, imagine driving in a car with an acquaintance that lights up a cigarette. The presence of smoke within the close confines of the automobile is particularly aversive to you. You politely ask the passenger to extinguish the cigarette, a request with which he or she complies. The removal of the aversive condition is thus said to negatively reinforce your assertive behavior.

Punishment, on the other hand, decreases the probability of occurrence of a behavior through the delivery of an aversive stimulus. Using a parenting example once again, one might consequate a very young child's behavior of reaching for a hot stove with a loud, stern "No!" In this example, the child's reaching behavior is punished by the parent's harsh verbalization and the probability of the child reaching for the hot stove in the future is decreased.

In addition to specifying the contingencies that maintain problematic behavior, an adequate functional analysis should also identify the environmental contingencies that have not supported more effective behavior (Sturmey, 1996). It is possible that effective or desirable behavior was never learned, that such behavior was never adequately reinforced, or that punishing contingencies diminished the strength of the behavior. In simple terms, this means that a person may not have a sufficiently developed behavioral repertoire to take advantage of opportunities that could lead to important personal benefits.

Establishing Operations

Establishing or motivational operations differ from stimulus control operations (Michael, 1982; Michael, 1993). As stated earlier, discriminative stimuli are those stimuli that directly precede the reinforcement contingent on a particular response. Establishing stimuli are the environmental conditions such as deprivation, satiation, aversive stimulation, or other physiological processes that establish a discriminative stimulus as an occasion for reinforcement or punishment. One can think of establishing operations as those conditions that produce a motivational state. Establishing stimuli can change the relative value of the reinforcing or punishing stimulus.

Alcohol or drug intoxication is one example of an establishing operation that is relevant to clinical populations (Wulfert, Greenway, & Dougher, 1996). The level of intoxication by alcohol or other illicit substances may alter the effectiveness of a reinforcer. One example of this is illustrated by the question regarding whether or not concurrent pharmacological and psychological interventions for anxiety are an effective combination. Exposure-based interventions may have diminished effectiveness when combined with anxiolytic medications. Such interventions are based on the assumption that repeated or prolonged exposure to the conditions that evoke the fear or anxiety will result in a reduction in anxiety. The classical conditioning aspect of exposure-based interventions assumes that the reduction in anxiety is directly related to the level of response that is generated during the exposure exercises (Falls, 1998). Therefore, reducing anxiety with medication does not allow for a maximal fear response under the exposure conditions.

The Role of Private Events

Within contemporary behavior analysis private events such as thoughts, feelings, and physiological responses are legitimate subject matter and can be understood just as any overt behavior. That is, in conducting a functional analysis we examine private events according to their functions or by examining the relevant controlling variables. For example, a cognitive therapist may select a client's negative thoughts as the target for intervention (i.e., "I am a complete failure"). From a functional analytic perspective we come to understand the function or purpose of such a thought by examining the environmental variables that control that thought. What are the antecedents under which the thought occurs? What are the contingencies of reinforcement that maintain such a thought?

Functional Domains of Clinical Problems

We have given an elementary overview of some of the behavioral principles that may be useful in analyzing the problem behavior of clients. To help better organize these ideas, let us consider a few specific examples. The following list of functional domains is adapted from the examples of clinical problems and interventions outlined by Hayes, Follette, & Follette (1995). We will revisit be antecedent, behavior, and consequent domains pointing out different ways in which one may think about how a clinical problem could be understood from a variety of perspectives.

Antecedents

Lack of appropriate antecedents. Consider a client who presents for treatment saying that he or she feels disconnected from the people around them. In doing the functional analysis you identify no apparent social skills or communication deficits. This may lead one to look at the client's social milieu and discover that he or she has no real peers in the environment. This means there are no or a few occasions when the client would have an opportunity to emit behaviors that would enhance intimacy and have those behaviors be reinforced. Without this careful analysis of antecedent conditions one might mistakenly work with this client on his or her skills repertoire intensely to no avail. The appropriate intervention, revealed by careful functional analytic investigation, would be to facilitate the client's discovery of and participation in environments where peer-to-peer contact is more likely to occur.

Lack of discriminative control. There are some occasions where a client's behavior may occur and be appropriate in some contexts, but prove maladaptive in others. In these cases the client does not recognize the exact conditions under which behavior of a certain class will lead to a useful outcome rather than one that is less desirable. For instance, a client may demonstrate many positive interpersonal attributes that would make him or her a desirable partner. However such a client might present for therapy complaining that he or she cannot develop and sustain close personal relationships. A functional analysis of the client's social behavior reveals that he or she can successfully begin relationships, but on the 3rd date he or she says something like, "I love you for all eternity and want to raise my children with you." Here the behavior, though impassioned, would not be a problem had it been emitted when the relationship was significantly farther along. In this case, however, the client did not discriminate the precise stimulus conditions under which his or her expression of affection would be responded to favorably. The unfortunate consequence of this heartfelt but inappropriately timed assertion might be to frighten or otherwise put off the prospective partner leading to a premature termination of the relationship.

Inappropriate discriminative control. There are some behaviors that are not appropriate under any set of stimulus conditions even though they may consistently affect the environment in a way that is desirable for the client. In the case of a developmentally delayed child, behaviors such as head banging or physical assault of caregivers might function to terminate some aversive event. For example, infliction of harm on self or others might allow the child to escape from training in a difficult self-care skill. In this case it would be much more useful for the client to be shaped to discriminate the context of self-care activities as an opportunity to emit a functionally equivalent, but less destructive, behavior such as a simple verbal request for assistance or for a brief respite from training.

Consequences

Lack of appropriate consequences. It is sometimes the case that people develop maladaptive behaviors because the environment simply does not support more useful responses. For example, in a family where the parents are completely intertwined with one another to the exclusion of being able to psychologically attend to a child, that child might initially engage in appropriate social behavior only to have that behavior go unnoticed. In such cases a functional analyst could anticipate that the appropriate behavior would decrease to some low baseline level, and eventually be replaced by more dramatic, maladaptive behaviors that effectively secured the attention of parents. The decrease in prosocial behavior in this example is a direct function of a lack of appropriate consequences.

Competing consequential control. The real world is a complex place. Any given behavior may be determined and refined by a variety of competing influences. Many kinds of behavior develop under one set of conditions, but later become influenced by a variety of others. In these cases behavior is not easy to predict because it is sometimes difficult to identify the exact source of the contingencies that are maintaining the behavior. Children, for example, often develop a perfectly reasonable social and interpersonal repertoire when they are young. People in the environment who share a common value primarily control this repertoire. Parents, grandparents, and preschool teachers all shape similar behavior about cooperative play, responsibility, respecting others, and sharing. As children reach adolescence, however, others who do not share the same values may become a significant influence upon the social behavior of this individual. Peers, for example, may shape less responsible, more hedonistic behavior. As time with peers increases and time with parents decreases, behavior that was under the control of parental influences may subsequently come under the control of peer influences. In such a situation, the adolescent's social repertoire may substantially change, much to parents' confusion and distress. Other examples of competing consequential control need not even involve socially mediated reinforcement. For example dieting is a clear instance where eating behavior is clearly subject to competing contingencies. Prudent eating behavior may be under the control of better fitting clothes while the tendency to let a diet lapse is controlled by the immediate gratification of the taste of a particularly desirable food. It is often the case that when two competing contingencies influence behavior, all else being equal, the more immediate contingency is likely to be more potent.

Inappropriate consequential control. For some individuals behaviors are maintained by reinforcing stimuli that are simply not appropriate. An obvious example is the instance where sexual behavior with a child is reinforcing to an adult as in the case of pedophilia. Once an inappropriate reinforcer is identified the task would be to engineer the environment to restrict access to the inappropriate reinforcer or to increase the response cost of emitting the inappropriate behavior.

Behavior

Behavioral excesses. When one actually conducts a functional case conceptualization, the initial focus is on the behavior the client identifies as problematic. One way to gain an understanding of the behavior is to determine whether the behavior is occurring too often or with too much intensity. Such behaviors might usefully be considered behavioral excesses. Keep in mind that when we speak of behavior we are implicitly referring to response classes rather than specific, individual behaviors. The task is to identify the classes of behaviors that occur too frequently and then strengthen alternative behaviors that will function more usefully for the client.

Behavioral deficits. The complement to behavioral excesses is the identification of behavioral deficits. A client may alternatively have deficits in assertion skills, may be deficient in perspective taking, or have difficulty expressing emotion or experiencing intimacy. Whether a client's problems in living are conceptualized as behavioral excesses or behavioral deficits often depends on the perspective the functional analyst takes. One could identify the same behavioral repertoire as including an excessive degree of self focused talk or turn the analysis around and say the person is deficient at allowing others to speak. The question of which analysis is correct depends upon which one yields a more useful intervention plan.

Interfering behaviors. Sometimes it is useful to identify behaviors that interfere with a client's potential to emit other, more useful behaviors that are already present in the repertoire. A functional analysis may reveal that a client is not being as socially successful as one might anticipate given the client's apparent interpersonal assets. During a role playing assessment or an in vivo observation, a client might be observed to have a tendency to fill in the end of sentences during conversations with others. Besides being annoying, and perhaps therefore being considered a behavioral excess, this behavior interferes with the client being an effective listener and pleasant social partner. The distinction between interfering behaviors and behavioral excesses is that the interfering behaviors prevent the client from emitting the more useful alternative behaviors. This circumstance must be illuminated and dealt with before alternative behaviors can be established at a useful level. Behavioral excesses on the other hand can, in principle, be replaced by more useful behaviors using the constructional approach to describe earlier.

Applying the Analysis to the Self

Kanfer and Grimm (1977) have taken each of the domains described above and recast the assessment issues in terms of how a client might have problems self-regulating various aspects of his or her life. Though most of these assessment issues can be derived from the larger domains of which they are a set, we present them individually because they may serve as a useful heuristic when trying to conduct a functional analysis.

Deficits in self-regulation. Kanfer and Grimm have described eight areas of assessment that may be useful to consider. Although one can probably account for each of the following specific deficits under the more general category of behavioral deficits, the specific examples of what to assess may be useful.

1. Inadequate knowledge base for guiding behavioral choices. We will soon deal with this topic from the perspective of the rule governance of behavior. For now, however, we can cast this analysis as a deficit on the part of an individual in being able to describe the relationship between a particular environmental situation and the anticipated outcome of any behavioral choice the person might make. In simple terms, a person manifesting this deficit does not know what to do in a particular situation in order to produce a particular outcome.

2. Skills deficits. In this case the client fails to engage in acceptable social behavior because of specific skills deficits. This category is simply a particular subcategory of behavioral deficits.

3. Deficits in self-directing skills. In this case the person exhibits an inability to supplement or counter immediate environmental influences in order to regulate one's own behavior. Individuals who present with problems of impulse control or who seem to be distracted by short-term reinforcers rather than perhaps more important long-term reinforcers might be considered to have deficits in self-directing skills.

4. Deficits in self-reinforcement. There many aspects of life where the actual supporting contingencies are far removed from behavior in the moment. In these cases an individual must supply their own more immediate reinforcement for appropriate behavior. For example a student must keep current on his or her studies even though tests (the externally mediated contingency) may occur only once every several weeks. To succeed in academics, the student must learn to structure their environment such that daily studying behavior is reinforced.

5. Deficits in self-monitoring. In order to correctly predict outcomes it is necessary to monitor one's own behavior. Self-monitoring can be thought of in two ways. First, one can monitor his or her behavior, as it is occurring, in order to determine if it is of reasonable form. If one were monitoring their behavior and the

social situation, one might first make sure he or she were making reasonable eye contact, reflectively listening, engaging in appropriate humor for the context, etc. The second, more important, part of self-monitoring requires that one assesses the actual impact his or her behavior is having on those around them. That is, one must also effectively monitor whether or not the behavior one emits actually has the desired effect. If a client can accurately monitor both what she does and whether it works, it is likely she will be socially successful.

6. Self control. This assessment requires one to evaluate the degree to which her client can alter their responses in a conflict situation. When a client is involved in a conflict situation, the goal of winning might become the predominant motivating factor controlling behavior. When this occurs to the extent that it prevents client behavior change in the service of more useful goals, self control may become a target for behavior change.

7. Deficits in the range of reinforcers. This category of problems may better fall under the section on consequences. There is some utility, however, in assisting the client in accepting responsibility for ensuring that their life contains a variety of behaviors that are satisfying. Clients may present for therapy when some central aspect of their lives has been disrupted. This may occur, for example, within the context of a close relationship, a job, or some important change in health status. The greatest amount of psychological distress will be observed when a person has historically "placed all her eggs in one basket" and that basket gets overturned. If a particular client has derived most of his social pleasure from a single relationship, then when that relationship is disturbed social isolation and depression are common. For a client who has taken pride and derived reinforcement from her business acumen to the extent that "she is what she does," psychological distress following job loss will almost certainly ensue. Assessing the range of reinforcement available to clients can form an important aspect of any functional assessment. The clinician's task would be to identify when a client is vulnerable to having a high portion of reinforcers dependent upon a single aspect of their life.

8. Skills deficits in cognitive or motor behaviors necessary to meet the demands of daily living. It is important to assess whether someone has the capability to emit the behaviors that are necessary in order to find life satisfying (reinforcing). At the simplest level, there may be obvious cognitive or physical limitations that make it difficult for a client to cope with the basic demands of his or her life. A more complex case occurs when people set goals for themselves that they cannot possibly meet. When these demands are self-imposed, assessment must focus on whether someone is appropriately setting challenging goals or goals that are clearly beyond their grasp.

Self-referential behavioral excesses.

1. Excessive anxiety resulting from conditioned inappropriate fear of objects or events. When one observes anxiety or fear as the primary presenting problem, it is useful to assess whether this is a classically conditioned response that could be successfully treated with an exposure-based intervention.

2. Excessive self-monitoring. It is possible for one to exhibit excessive self-observational activity. In such a case, the individual will overly attend to their own behavior and therefore inhibit performance. Hoberman and Lewinsohn (1985) have suggested that this may lead to negative self-evaluations. Readers who have participated in competitive athletics may recognize that causing an opponent to self-monitor a complex behavior is part of the fine art of gamesmanship. Imagine that you are playing golf in a final round of an important tournament. Just before you tee off your opponent casually says to you, "I really admire the way you accomplish that subtle weight transfer during your backswing." If that observation induces one to overly self-monitor, it will surely interfere with the formerly "natural" production of complex motor behavior. The same phenomenon can be seen in clients who are overly introspective or are socially anxious.

Inappropriate self-generated stimulus control.

1. Self-labeling. Assessment around self-labeling practices concerns itself with identifying self-descriptions that function as cues for behaviors leading to negative outcomes. The topography of such behavior may be obvious, such as when a client states "I'm not a worthwhile person." Besides functioning as a self-fulfilling prophecy, this verbal behavior may function as a discriminative stimulus to avoid new social relationships. If proclaimed publicly, the client's self-generated label, whether accurate or not may narrow what others pay attention to and negatively affect new social interactions. For example, it is sometimes useful to teach clients not to prematurely reveal aspects of their history that function as negative self-labels for themselves or others. While it may not be desirable to teach clients to be secretive about aspect of their past, it is generally good to teach them to not start conversations with phrases such as, "Hi, I'm Bob. I'm an alcoholic."

2. Covert behaviors that serve to cue inappropriate behavior. Covert behaviors include symbolic activity that function as stimuli that signal stress or danger. If during the course of functional assessment a client exhibits avoidance behavior that makes little sense to the observing clinician, it may be useful to investigate whether the client is having a private response to some stimulus features of the situation that indicate it is somehow aversive. Consider a case where you have been working with a client with the goal of increasing their social interactions. On several occasions, the client has described upcoming opportunities for dates but subsequently reports that "something came up" and they didn't go out on the date. At this point, one might generate and test the hypothesis that the client is engaging in some private behavior that functions to make the dating situation seem dangerous (see Hayes, 1994).

3. Faulty discrimination of internal cues. A common problem confronting many clients is an inability to properly label internal states or feelings and communicate these to others. This likely stems from the presence of one of two problems. The first is that the client may have no clear sense how to respond emotionally to the people around them. One may see glimpses of this problem in the therapy setting when you ask a client how they felt about some interaction. If the client exhibits a high rate of responding "I don't know" or if they almost exclusively use the same verbal

label, such as "fine" to describe their feelings, this may cue the assessor to evaluate the sophistication of the client's repertoire for labeling feelings. The second consequence of having an inadequate repertoire to discriminate and label internal cues is that it is difficult for a client to tell others about the impact others are having on the client. This makes it difficult for people in the client's environment to be properly responsive to their needs. One common context in which one can see instances of this problem is parent-adolescent interaction. Here the adolescent replies, "I don't know", or "I don't care" to most requests for information by the parent. While there may be other functions for these responses, one effect is that it becomes difficult for either the adolescent or the parent to understand how to improve the relationship.

Rule-Governed Behavior

One unique thing about verbal organisms, that is, people, is that they can describe some of the contingencies that control their behavior. These descriptions of contingencies can come to function as rules for individual. The degree to which rules function in a useful way usually involves a trade-off. When an individual encounters a new situation they may recognize aspects of it as similar to familiar situations and assume that they know what behaviors will lead to what contingencies. Such a prediction regarding the relationship between behavior and contingencies is a rule. When these predictions are entirely correct, one can apply an existing repertoire to the new situation without having to "start from scratch." There is an obvious efficiency to this accurate, rule-governed behavior. One does not have to treat every new situation as if it were entirely novel. In reality, however, there exist unique elements to almost all situations. By attending to rules a person may fail to notice and respond to the truly novel aspects of situations in ways that would lead to better outcomes. In addition, there is experimental evidence that once a rule that describes a particular contingency is formed, it is difficult to modify that rule when the contingencies actually do change (Hayes, Brownstein, Zettle, Rosenfarb, & Korn, 1986). Though rules can be efficient for individuals, rules can also be a source of clinical problems.

Poor rule generation. Rules are only useful to the degree that they accurately describe the relationship between behavior and outcome. One source of many clinical problems may be that an individual does not construct rules that accurately describe this relationship. For example, after a client has experienced the end of a close relationship, the client may generate a rule such as, "all relationships lead to painful endings, therefore to protect myself I will never be in another relationship." Such a rule is clearly not correct and, if followed, will limit or even preclude significant new sources of interpersonal reinforcement.

Difficulties with pliance. The term *pliance* comes from the word compliance and describes a particular kind of rule-governed behavior where the behavior itself is under the control of socially mediated consequences. If someone emits a behavior that corresponds to a rule, and others then reinforce that behavior, the rule is said to function as a ply. For example, if a friend said, "When you ask for a raise, be assertive and don't back down," and one exhibited such behavior to conform to the friend's advice, one would be demonstrating pliance. If one intentionally did not follow the advice, this would be an example of counterpliance. Pliance is rule following and as such, is shaped by the consequences of following rules as well as the natural consequences for a particular behavior in a given circumstance. That is to say, under some conditions it is reinforcing simply to follow rules. Rule following per se may prove a sufficient consequence to maintain a behavior. Under other conditions rule following behavior may be maintained only if it leads to a useful environmental consequence.

In a functional analysis one may observe instances of weak pliance. Weak pliance is a clinical problem when one does not adequately adhere to rule governed behaviors. The clinical result can be that the client contacts aversive consequences that could otherwise be avoided had he or she followed a rule. A simple example occurs when a child fails to follow his or her parents' rule "Wear your raincoat, it is pouring outside."

One can also observe the opposite problem, termed excessive pliance. Excessive pliance means that an individual overly attends to rules or conventions, sometimes appearing oblivious to the actual consequences of their behavior. The result is that the individual appears rigid and insensitive. Excessive pliance can be easily observed in ambiguous social situations, that is, in those circumstances where one cannot readily predicted the outcome of certain behaviors and therefore reverts to some implicit or explicit rule. Anyone who has done clinical supervision has seen instances of excessive pliance on the part of beginning therapists. In a supervision session the supervisor may suggest, "In the next session you should get a relationship history from your client." In the next session, however, the client opens with the statement, "I have been feeling really badly, and I don't know if I can take it any longer." Beginning therapists, exhibiting excessive pliance are likely to respond with, "I see . . . can you tell me about the first important relationship you ever had?" Here, the task is to teach individuals to recognize when attending to rules will be useful versus situations in which they must attend to changing environmental conditions that demand behavioral flexibility.

Weak tracking. Tracking refers to the behavior of following a rule. Tracking is under the control of the apparent relationship between the rule and how the world seems to work. One might be told, "To do well in school, you must make sure that you understand the assignments, and then do your homework." If one followed this rule because there was an apparent correspondence between the rule and how the world seems to work, it would be an instance of tracking. Weak tracking would be a failure to follow rules that, in fact, do correspond to how the world works. For the purposes of this discussion, we won't distinguish between when someone tries to follow the rule but fails to detect a deviation from when one does not recognize the correspondence between the rule and the contingency. In clinical practice this distinction may be important.

Functional Classification and Treatment Utility

The point of doing a functional assessment is to understand clinical problems using behavioral principles that have been empirically derived and studied in the laboratory. There is a science of human behavior that can be brought to bear to direct us in our clinical activities once we have a functional understanding of a client's problems. It is the task of the applied clinical scientist to understand clinically relevant behavior using empirically derived principles. In general we assume that clinical problems are the result of an individual acting in a context that establishes and maintains dysfunctional behaviors. Dysfunctional behaviors are those that, in the long run, will serve a person less well than other, more useful, behavioral alternatives. Clinically problematic or dysfunctional behaviors are not abnormal in the sense that they cannot be understood using behavioral principles. In most instances clinicians can readily see how maladaptive behaviors might initially have come into existence. It is not hard to understand, for example, how a woman with a history of childhood sexual abuse and subsequent revictimization would come to exhibit mistrust of males, have difficulty clearly expressing emotions, or experience problems in sexually intimate situations. One can readily understand how these behaviors would develop and even be adaptive initially. Clinical problems arise, however, when a person with this history fails to recognize that not all situations or relationships are abusive. The clinical task may then be to teach the client to discriminate dangerous from safe potential partners, and how to clearly recognize and communicate their feelings and preferences. As this example illustrates, the use of the term "abnormal" is useless within a functional analysis. The term would appropriately be applied only to those cases where a client does not behave according to known operant or respondent principles.

There have been several critiques of the current system of classification of mental disorders described in DSM-IV (e.g., Follette & Houts, 1996). While an in depth discussion of these criticisms is beyond the scope of this chapter, two concerns are particularly relevant to the clinician trying to bring about behavior change will be briefly discussed. The first problem with DSM-IV is that making a diagnosis tells us little about what to do clinically. That is, there is little treatment utility to be gained from the process of applying a DSM-IV label to a particular client. The second problem with DSM-IV is that clinical problems are seen in terms of disorder to the exclusion of any consideration of what might constitute psychological health or well being. The apparent goal of DSM-IV is to get rid of the disorder. The goal of functional analysis is to provide the clinician with a case conceptualization that will not only allow him or her to decrease a client's maladaptive behaviors, but to also identify and shape maximally effective ways for the client to interact with the environment to promote psychological well-being.

Treatment Utility of Assessment

Earlier we outlined how a functional analysis can help to identify problems. The very nature of the functional analysis implies that once one has conducted the assessment, one knows what should be changed to improve clinical functioning. For example, a functional assessment might indicate that a client who reports depressed affect has difficulty identifying situations where his or her naturally occurring behaviors are likely to be reinforced. It then follows that the treatment program should increase the client's recognition of such instances. The act of functional assessment prescribes treatment and thus makes the assessment itself valid and useful. Recall, also, that functional assessment is an iterative and self-correcting process. If the initial functional assessment is incorrect, then treatment is not likely to be successful and the clinician will loop back through the process to refine the analysis and alter treatment.

There are situations in which the assessment process will have no apparent treatment utility. Treatment utility of assessment can be demonstrated only when the assessment information leads one to make a particular treatment alteration for the benefit of the client. Thus there are conditions where a functional assessment cannot demonstrate treatment utility, and cannot be justified.

Standardized treatment packages based on topography. If one works in an environment where the form and method of treatment depends only on the presence of a diagnosis based on certain manifest symptoms without regard to their origins or functions, then a functional assessment cannot show treatment utility. This is generally the case in environments where a DSM diagnosis is used to choose a treatment package. If one makes a diagnosis of major depression using DSM-IV criteria and then always chooses to use a particular cognitive therapy manual, then making the diagnosis itself is the assessment and treatment is automatic. There can be no additional advantage to doing a functional assessment because treatment would not be changed regardless of any additional understanding one may gain concerning the problem. Unless standard treatment packages allow for modifications based on new information, there is no way that treatment utility can become apparent.

Common causes. Functional assessment occurs in a clinical context where both the client and the therapist want to make efficient use of time and resources. Thus, if a particular clinical problem results from a common etiology a very large proportion of the time, and responds to a particular treatment a very large proportion of the time, then it makes no economic sense to conduct a functional assessment unless the initial treatment fails.

An obvious clinical example is in the treatment of simple phobias. If a client presents with a fear of a specific stimulus object, e.g., a fear of a dog, the presumption of most behavior therapists is that the fear originated as a classically conditioned response that is maintained in the present by the negative reinforcement that follows avoidance of the phobic object – the dog (Mowrer, 1939). Other possibilities could exist for the acquisition and maintenance of the fear, but the initial assumptions lead to a treatment (desensitization) that is effective such a high proportion of the time as to not justify the additional time and cost of an in depth functional assessment. If, however, treatment fails, then a functional analysis is warranted. The point of this example is that some problems have either a common etiology or set of maintaining factors. In such cases we can efficiently assume that we know the functional cause of the problem, and can therefore initiate treatment without further analysis.

Inflective treatment technology. There are instances of clinical problems where even if we know the functional cause of a problem (at least descriptively), we don't know how to reliably alter the problem. For example, a pedophilic client has a clear problem with being under the control of inappropriate reinforcers, i.e., he or she finds sexual activity with children reinforcing in spite of societal mores to the contrary. We understand some aspect of the problem, but we thus far have no reliable treatment technology to alter the reinforcing properties of children for a pedophile. In this case, the treatment utility of assessment cannot be demonstrated since we do not have a treatment that will alter these reinforcing properties. We can partially treat the problem by increasing the discomfort of the pedophile through covert sensitization. Alternatively we might use response prevention (imprisonment). Finally, we might make use of antecedent stimulus control strategies by teaching the pedophile to interrupt the behavioral chain that leads up to putting themselves in the position of being near children in an unsafe manner. None of these techniques, however, alters the basic problem. There is not an effective strategy for changing the inappropriate reinforcers that function for pedophilia at this time. Thus, the treatment utility of assessment cannot be demonstrated when there is no technology for changing the identified cause. This example does illustrate, of course, that conducting a functional analysis that identifies the problem can still do much to highlight areas in need of additional research. This outcome itself is valuable, but is a different issue than demonstrating actual treatment utility.

Combination treatment programs. The general tendency in modern treatment development programs seems to be to devise programs that use a wide number of techniques to address the most common assumed causes of a particular problem. Sometime later there may be an effort to conduct dismantling studies that identify the primary active ingredient or element of therapy (Kazdin, 1998, pg. 142). For the present, however, many therapies use multiple techniques in hope of including something that will be effective for a broad population of people with a particular topography of problem. If a treatment program presents many technical manipulations of variables, then presumably sooner or later the treatment will hit on the right cause. If this were true, then there would be little opportunity for additional treatment utility of assessment to become apparent.

There are two obvious problems to this approach. First, there is an inherent inefficiency in treatment programs that are designed to treat all common causes versus the actual cause of a problem for a particular client. For example, in the case of depression a treatment package might be designed to both increase behaviors and hence access to reinforcers and also address inappropriate rule-governed behavior. Part of therapy is wasted in this case if the primary cause of the depression is lack of reinforcement secondary to low activity levels. If low activity levels were the primary problem, then therapy could be made more effective by an idiographic assessment that led to the targeting of only the primary problem. Increased effectiveness could be gained, in this example, from the economic benefits of a shorter, focused therapy. Further, spending additional therapy time strengthening the behavior activation component of therapy, ignoring the incorrectly assumed rule-governed cause of the problem might attain a larger effect size.

Using multicomponent packaged treatments has some advantages in that it is likely that the therapy may be at least partially effective for many individuals and requires no assessment. Assessment costs resources. The trade-off comes when treatment turns out to be less effective than it might otherwise have been. Staying with the depression example, Biglan (1985) has found that some depression observed in women occurs because it is negatively reinforced by the reduction of spousal abuse when the woman emits depressed behaviors. The depression can be understood as an adaptive control strategy in such cases. A treatment package for depression is not likely to be effective in these cases unless it anticipates this less commonly targeted function of depressive behavior.

To be fair to treatment packages for problems that combine several components, it is often the case that multiple factors operate to maintain a clinical problem regardless of the conditions that originally led to the occurrence of the problem. Thus, "pure" forms of single cause problems may be rare enough that the cost-effectiveness of a functional assessment may be difficult to demonstrate.

The desire to do treatment matching has been around for a long time. Treatment matching is at the heart of Gordon Paul's (1967) now classic question: "What treatment, by whom, is most effective for this individual with that specific problem, and under which set of circumstances?"

Functional analysis makes use of known behavioral science principles to try to answer that question so that we can maximize treatment outcomes and efficiency in service delivery.

Limitations of Functional Assessment

Given the long behavioral tradition behind functional analysis and functional assessment, why hasn't it become a staple of psychological assessment? There are several legitimate reasons. In cases where the treatment utility of assessment is difficult to demonstrate, there is a real issue of whether functional assessment practices can pass the test of demonstrating cost-effectiveness in the era of managed health care. If it is to do so, then several technical problems must be addressed. First, though functional assessment is clear founded on strong behavioral principles, advocates of functional analysis have not satisfactorily addressed important methodological problems. One important problem that still exists is that of how to reliably perform a functional analysis. In a classic chapter on functional diagnosis, Kanfer and Salsow (1969) described the elements of a functional analysis. The reader of their chapter is struck by its thoroughness, daunted by its scope, and frustrated by its lack of methodological specificity. We have described many domains that may be relevant to the development and maintenance of clinical problems. At present, we lack both a clearly defined rationale for the identification of which areas should be assessed first and for deciding when one has adequately surveyed a broad enough domain to begin forming a case conceptualization that has treatment utility.

In fact, it is unclear how to reliably combine assessment information into a coherent case conceptualization. Behavior analysts have generally ignored the problems of reliability of procedural issues in functional diagnosis, instead finding comfort in the tradition of idiographic assessment practices. Idiographic assessment emphasizes the fact that assessment and conceptualization should be tailored to an analysis of a particular individual in a particular context using assessment practices that are presumed to be most appropriate for the circumstances. In the earlier years of functional analysis this made some sense. If a clinician were treating severe head-banging in an autistic child, counting the behavior was simple and issues of reliability could perhaps have been assumed to be relatively unimportant. Likewise, when observation and intervention took place in highly controlled institutional settings, access to all the controlling variables was more readily available than in the case of higher functioning, outpatient populations. As functional assessment expands to include a broader class of problems in less controlled contexts, the issue of reliability can no longer be ignored.

Finally, there is no specific strategy defined for moving from assessment data to a treatment plan. As we have argued previously, in some ways the treatment plan follows logically from the functional case conceptualization. For example, if one identifies that depressed mood is the result of insufficient contingent reinforcement by noting the covariation between social activity and low mood, then the treatment is to increase response contingent reinforcement. However, current treatment literature is not often organized to link functional assessment to the corresponding treatment. While it is obvious from the functional assessment what to do, it is not always clear how to do it.

Hayes and Follette (1992a) have described some of these problems elsewhere and suggested possible solutions, but to date tests of these solutions have not been conducted. Elsewhere, on the question of how to efficiently and reliably survey what domains to assess when we conduct our functional analysis, Hayes and Follette (1992b) have suggested that it might be possible to identify replicable functional assessment procedures by using formal, specified decision algorithms. Once these algorithms have been specified, it would be possible to test them against one another to see which yields better outcomes in terms of both effectiveness and efficiency. How to develop such algorithms is still an open question. We have also suggested the use of expert systems based on how those who teach and conduct functional analyses structure them in their own settings. The tricky question, however, is determining exactly what constitutes a clinically significantly better outcome when comparing two interventions based on competing functional analytic strategies.

An alternative approach that may be more practical and familiar is to reorganize clinical problems in terms of functional diagnostic categories rather than topographical categories, as is the case in DSM-IV. The diagnostic categories are based on behavioral principles, while the assessment would be partially functional and partially topographical. For example, Hayes and Follette (1993) described a "emotional avoidance disorder" where topography and function are both implied. In this example, a client exhibits a behavioral class, avoiding strong emotions that are maintained by the behavioral principle of negative reinforcement. There could even be variations on the functional category where in one case the problem is caused by the emotional behavior being punished, thereby leading to aversive consequences that a client would seek to avoid in the future. In another case the problem could be caused by a client responding to a broad variety of verbally mediated stimuli that lead to strong affective arousal that is experienced as aversive. Treatment in one case would focus on altering the punishing properties of the environment while treatment in the second case would attempt to change the stimulus functions of verbal stimuli. Classification would depend on identifying the topographies that likely make up a response class (emotional avoidance), and then evaluate the possible causal factors that elicit or maintain the behavior (see Hayes, Wilson, Gifford, Follette, & Stroshahl, 1996).

The success of a functional classification system depends partly on the ability of the clinician to manipulate the suspected stimuli that maintain the problematic behavior. As a practical matter the immediate success of such a system depends on at least some treatment utility. Thus, the initial functional categories could consist of problems where a technology exists to affect change in the relevant variables. For example, one might work out the taxonomy of various behavioral deficit disorders before embarking on disorders of establishing operations (i.e., motivational deficits) because in the latter case there is not a well establish technology for altering motivational factors in outpatient clients.

Psychological Health

The behavior analytic tradition has generally not viewed clinical behavior problems as evidence of an underlying personal flaw or pathological condition. Behaviors are understood to be the result of particular learning histories and changing the histories and the current environment are where the interventions focus. The purpose of doing an assessment and intervention is to understand the clinical situation well enough to modify the context sufficiently for a person to function optimally. This stands in contrast to the model of mental disorders represented by DSM-IV. In DSM-IV clinical interventions are primarily for the purpose of making someone disease free. There is nothing in the philosophy behind the DSM that would lead a clinician to do more than remove symptoms, since once symptoms are removed, a person no longer meets criterion for a diagnosis.

However, a functional case conceptualization should yield an intervention strategy that offers substantially more to a client than merely reducing distress. If one were to conduct a thorough analysis of a client's history, environment and behavioral repertoire, it should follow that one would seek to optimize functioning in all domains without emphasizing pathology or disease states (Follette, 1997; Follette, Bach, & Follette, 1993). The goal would be to teach clients to effectively manipulate their environments to lead to maximal levels of reinforcement and the broadest possible range of potential reinforcers without encroaching on the rights of others. One planning a functionally based intervention would seek to teach a client to be willing to experience life without fear of fear. An intervention would teach client to come under the control of self-identified reinforcers that would lead to optimal experiences of freedom and control. The client would emerge with an understanding of how to anticipate consequences and influence those elements of his or her environment that will lead to good health related behaviors. While learning to do a functional case conceptualization and intervention requires diligence, creativity, and work, the potential benefits for therapist and client alike are well worth the effort.

References

American Psychiatric Association. (1994). *Diagnostic and statistical manual of mental disorders*. (4th ed.). Washington, DC: American Psychiatric Association.

Barrios, B. A. (1988). On the changing nature of behavioral assessment. In A. S. Bellack & M. Hersen (Eds.), *Behavioral assessment: A practical handbook*. Elmsford, NY: Pergamon Press, Inc.

Biglan, A., Hops, H., Sherman, L., Friedman, L. S., Arthur, J., & Osteen, V. (1985). Problem-solving interactions of depressed women and their husbands. *Behavior Therapy, 16*, 431-451.

Falls, W. A. (1998). Extinction: A review of theory and the evidence suggesting that memories are not erased with nonreinforcement. In W. T. O'Donohue (Ed.), *Learning and behavior therapy*. Boston: Allyn & Bacon, Inc.

Ferster, C. B. (1967). Arbitrary and natural reinforcement. *The Psychological Record, 22*, 1-16.

First, M. B., Frances, A., Widiger, T. A., Pincus, H. A., & Davis, W. W. (1992). DSM-IV and behavioral assessment. *Behavioral Assessment, 14*, 297-306.

Follette, W. C. (1997). A behavioral analytic conceptualization of personality disorders: A response to Clark, Livesley, and Morey. *Journal of Personality Disorders, 11*(3), 232-241.

Follette, W. C., Bach, P. A., & Follette, V. M. (1993). A behavior analytic view of psychological health. *The Behavior Analyst, 16*, 303-316.

Follette, W. C., & Houts, A. C. (1996). Models of scientific progress and the role of theory in taxonomy development: A case study of the DSM. *Journal of Consulting and Clinical Psychology, 64*(6), 1120-1132.

Goldfried, M. R., & Kent, R. N. (1972). Traditional versus behavioral personality assessment: A comparison of methodological and theoretical assumptions. *Psychological Bulletin, 77*, 409-420.

Goldiamond, I. (1974). Toward a constructional approach to social problems: Ethical and constitutional issues raised by applied behavior analysis. *Behaviorism, 2*, 1-85.

Goldiamond, I. (1975). Insider-outsider problems: A constructional approach. *Rehabilitation Psychology, 22,* 103-116.

Hawkins, R. P. (1986). Selection of target behaviors. In R. O. Nelson & S. C. Hayes (Eds.), *Conceptual foundations of behavioral assessment* (pp. 331-385). New York: Guilford.

Hayes, S. C. (1994). Relational Frame Theory: A functional approach to verbal events. In S. C. Hayes & L. J. Hayes (Eds.), *Behavior analysis of language and cognition* (pp. 9-30). Reno, NV: Context Press.

Hayes, S. C., Brownstein, A. J., Zettle, R. D., Rosenfarb, I., & Korn, Z. (1986). Rule-governed behavior and sensitivity to changing consequences of responding. *Journal of the Experimental Analysis of Behavior, 45,* 237-256.

Hayes, S. C., & Follette, W. C. (1992a). Behavioral assessment in the DSM era. *Behavioral Assessment, 14,* 293-295.

Hayes, S. C., & Follette, W. C. (1992b). Can functional analysis provide a substitute for syndromal classification? *Behavioral Assessment, 14,* 345-365.

Hayes, S. C., & Follette, W. C. (1993). The challenge faced by behavioral assessment. *European Journal of Psychological Assessment, 9*(3), 182-188.

Hayes, S. C., Follette, W. C., & Follette, V. M. (1995). Behavior therapy: A contextual approach. In A. S. Gurman & S. B. Messer (Eds.), *Essential psychotherapies: Theory and practice.* New York: Guilford.

Hayes, S. C., Nelson, R. O., & Jarret, R. (1987). Treatment utility of assessment: A functional approach to evaluating quality of assessment. *American Psychologist, 42,* 963-974.

Hayes, S. C., Wilson, K. G., Gifford, E. V., Follette, V. M., & Stroshahl, K. (1996). Experiential avoidance and behavioral disorders: A functional dimensional approach to diagnosis and treatment. *Journal of Consulting and Clinical Psychology, 64*(6), 1152-1168.

Haynes, S. N., & O'Brien, W. H. (1990). Functional analysis in behavior therapy. *Clinical Psychology Review, 10,* 649-668.

Hoberman, H. M., & Lewinsohn, P. M. (1985). The behavioral treatment of depression. In E. E. Beckham & W. R. Leber (Eds.), *Handbook of depression: Treatment, assessment, and research* (pp. 39-81). Homewood, IL: The Dorsey Press.

Kanfer, F. H., & Grimm, L. G. (1977). Behavioral analysis: Selecting target behaviors in the interview. *Behavior Modification, 1,* 7-28.

Kanfer, F. H., & Saslow, G. (1969). Behavioral diagnosis. In C. M. Franks (Ed.), *Behavior therapy: Appraisal and status* (pp. 417-444). New York: McGraw-Hill.

Kazdin, A. E. (1998). Research design in clinical psychology (3rd ed.). Boston: Allyn and Bacon.

Kimble, G. A., & Catania, A. C. (1992). Learning. In S. Koch & D. E. O'Leary (Eds.), *A century of psychology as science* (pp. 284-335). Washington, D. C.: American Psychological Association.

Livingston, S. A. (1977). Psychometric techniques for criterion-referenced testing and behavioral assessment. In J. D. Cone & R. P. Hawkins (Eds.), *Behavioral assessment: New directions in clinical psychology* (pp. 308-329). New York: Brunner/ Mazel.

Malott, R. W., Whaley, D. L., & Malott, M. E. (1996). *Elementary principles of behavior*. (2nd ed.). Englewood Cliffs, New Jersey: Prentice-Hall.

Michael, J. (1982). Distinguishing between discriminative and motivational functions of stimuli. *Journal of the Experimental Analysis of Behavior, 37*, 149-155.

Michael, J. L. (1993). *Concepts and principles of behavior analysis*. Kalamazoo, MI: Society for the Advancement of Behavior Analysis.

Mowrer, O. H. (1939). A stimulus-response analysis of anxiety and its role as a reinforcing agent. *Psychological Review, 46*, 553-565.

Paul, G. (1967). Strategy of outcome research in psychotherapy. *Journal of Consulting and Clinical Psychology, 31*, 109-118.

Sturmey, P. (1996). *Functional analysis in clinical psychology*. New York: John Wiley & Sons.

Wulfert, E., Greenway, D. E., & Dougher, M. J. (1996). A logical functional analysis of reinforcement-based disorders: Alcoholism and pedophilia. *Journal of Consulting and Clinical Psychology, 64*(6), 1140-1151.

Chapter 6

Behavior Analysis and Depression

Madelon Y. Bolling
Robert J. Kohlenberg
Chauncey R. Parker
University of Washington

Behavior analysis is relatively new on the adult outpatient treatment scene (Dougher & Hackbert, 1994; Ferster, 1973; Kohlenberg & Tsai, 1991; Kohlenberg, Tsai & Dougher, 1993; Moss & Boren, 1972). But here we are, jumping into matters of treatment for specific disorders even though we don't consider syndromal classification to have sufficient treatment utility to justify its use (Hayes & Follette, 1992). Strictly speaking, it makes little difference to us whether there "is" or "is not" a depressive syndrome. At the very least it is practical to be able to speak in a common language provided by the nearly universal acceptance of syndromal classification these days.

Depression as Adaptive

A peculiarity of behavioral analysis as an approach is the tendency to see all behavior as adaptive, that is, as serving a function that has furthered survival in the individual's life (Cordova & Kohlenberg, 1994; Follette, Bach & Follette, 1993; Kohlenberg & Tsai, 1991). Granted, survival thus won may be uncomfortable for the individual or for those around her/him. Nonetheless it is useful to be aware that the person in front of us is doing the best she/he can to survive under the circumstances, and that survival behavior is contingency-shaped and therefore likely to be largely an unconscious process.

Identified features of the depressive syndrome are all in the spectrum of a withdrawal from contact with the world and the consequences of activity. The primary symptoms, sad mood or anhedonia, are respondents, the physical correlates of withdrawal, shift in reinforcement schedule or removal of reinforcers from the environment. Sleep and appetite disturbances and inability to think or concentrate are part of a biological response pattern that Schmale (1973) identified as the conservation-withdrawal response to excesses or deficits of stimulation. Cognitive symptoms such as low self-esteem, hopelessness, or helplessness are related to this response, according to Schmale, and we add that these may be either effects or maintainers of the individual's problems.

Behaviorally, the overall effect of a depressive withdrawal is deprivation. Deprivation states (such as hunger or lack of sleep) prepare one to respond to different contingencies than may have been operative prior to withdrawal. For example, I (myb) would not name dill pickles among my favorite foods. Nonetheless, once after recovering from a period of fever, aches and vomiting, I came across a dill pickle in the refrigerator as I looked for something to eat. It was the first food I'd had for three or four days, and the effect was utterly ambrosial. Similarly, a person who has lost social reinforcers through death, disability or disaffection is prepared by isolation and withdrawal (deprivation states) to re-establish social contacts (obtain reinforcers) in different ways and with new people, even with those who would not have been considered adequate companions, prior to the loss.

When the conservation-withdrawal response occurs in reaction to an excess of stimuli, an overwhelming combination of stressors, the eventual effect is similar, a recalibration towards the world of stimuli following a period of deprivation. In this case, one maintains contact only with manageable portions of the environment, successfully ignoring the massive input from unmanageable situations due to the vastly reduced physical and mental resources available to the depressed person. Even suicidality, the most extreme and dreaded marker of depression, has its roots in a life-sustaining behavioral process: escape or avoidance of aversive experience (Hayes, 1992). Be that as it may, we still have before us the matter of the therapeutic treatment of people who come to us complaining of their depression.

Building on Existing Knowledge

Behavior analysts can benefit from the experiences of other, non-behavioral clinicians and researchers who have had extensive therapeutic contact with depressed clients. The work of Aaron T. Beck and colleagues is a leading example (Beck, Rush, Shaw, & Emery, 1979). His cognitive therapy is probably the most widely researched effective psychological procedure for the treatment of depression. This presents a dilemma for the behavior analyst. On the one hand, according to cognitive therapists, cognitive concepts are mental events or entities that cause depression. To behavior analysts, this means that the cognitive approach is subject to all the practical and theoretical problems and inconsistencies that should render it useless. On the other hand, it is the cognitive therapist who has developed an effective treatment based on these mentalistic notions (cf. Reitman & Drabman, 1997). Our position is that these concepts, as problematic as they may be, are ultimately based on direct observation and have evolved through treatment outcome studies.

Thus we feel that behavior analytic approaches can benefit from the experience of cognitive therapists. In turn, behavior analysis can be of benefit to cognitive therapists by 1) helping to clarify the phenomena and interventions used by cognitive therapists; 2) resolving inconsistencies that cognitive therapists themselves admit to (Hollon & Kriss, 1984); and 3) pointing to methods for improving the effectiveness of the interventions (see Kohlenberg & Tsai, 1991, pp. 97-123, for a more detailed discussion). Kohlenberg and Tsai have done such an analysis for cognitive therapy in general and have shown how a behavioral analysis of cognitive therapy can both clarify and improve the treatment.

A behavior-analytic view of the *ABC* (*A*ntecedent event; *B*elief; *C*onsequent behavior or feeling) model of the thought-behavior relationship is central to our analysis of cognitive therapy for depression (Kohlenberg and Tsai, 1991; 1994a; 1994b; Kohlenberg, Tsai & Kohlenberg, 1996). In a nutshell, we view cognitions as private verbal behavior that may contribute extensively, partially, or not at all to subsequent behavior (Kohlenberg, Tsai & Dougher, 1993). Although this approach to the relationship of prior verbal behavior and subsequent clinical problems accommodates cognitive therapy techniques, it also extends the analysis to clients who are viewed as resistant to treatment guided by the traditional cognitive model. For example, clients who do not experience a connection between their thoughts and depression, or those who may not have any thoughts that precede mood changes, are not easily accommodated by the cognitive model. Instead, they are subjected to the questionable therapeutic intervention of being told that they need further cognitive therapy because they do not believe their thoughts sufficiently (Beck et al., 1979, p. 302-303). This is inherently questionable because it involves punishment and engenders all of the counter-therapeutic features of aversive stimuli. When we consider both thoughts and subsequent behavior (including mood) from a behavior-analytic stance, however, the quest is not for the proper degree of belief but for environmental variables that have produced this particular behavior-behavior relationship, or lack thereof (Coyne, 1982; Dougher, Augustson, Markham, Greenway, & Wulfert, 1994; Hayes & Brownstein, 1986). We will now build on our earlier work with a behavioral analysis of the processes cognitive theorists identify as specific to depression.

Beck's Cognitive Triad

The core of the cognitive therapy (CT) theory of depression is the cognitive triad. According to Beck, Rush, Shaw, & Emery (1979), the triad consists of a negative view of self, world, and future, which in turn comprises the psychological substrate that predisposes a person to depression. The cognitive model considers all the signs and symptoms of the depressive syndrome to be the result of the activation of these negative cognitive patterns (Beck et al., 1979, p. 11).

Accordingly, we will examine 1) a negative view of self; 2) a negative view of the world; 3) a negative view of the future; and 4) the activation of these negative cognitive patterns. Behavior analysts view the triad as repertoires of behavior, and have two questions to answer about this model: 1) What kinds of experiences (history) could produce these repertoires? And 2) once present, how could these lead to depression?

A functional analysis of the repertoires described by the cognitive triad points to environmental variables that lead to and maintain these three cognitive patterns. The functional analytic concept of cognition is based on an analysis of verbal behavior, specifically, "tacts" (descriptions) and "mands" (demands or requests), based on Skinner's *Verbal Behavior* (1957). A functional analysis of the activation of these negative patterns in turn points to environmental variables that may evoke repertoires of negative thinking. From there, we will consider the relation of these repertoires to other symptoms of the depressive syndrome.

Negative View of Self

Beck et al. (1979) say, first, that the depressed person "sees himself as defective, inadequate, diseased or deprived," and "tends to attribute his unpleasant experiences to a psychological, moral, or physical defect in himself (p.11)." Second, once these judgments are made, the person goes on to underestimate and criticize himself because of these defects. (Despite Beck's unvarying use of the masculine pronoun, he does maintain that the causes of depression are the same in women as in men.)

First of all, how might a person come to tact him/herself as "defective"? A defect is the lack of something necessary or desirable (*American Heritage Dictionary*, 1978). A chair with a broken leg is called "defective" because it cannot function as intended: Nobody can safely sit on it. A period-piece chair or fine antique with modern replacement parts may be called defective because it no longer functions as a representative of its historical period, even though one may safely sit on it. In both of these cases, the "defective" item does not meet a standard or fulfill a requirement. This overlaps almost exactly with the meaning of "inadequate": not adequate, sufficient, able or capable. Similarly, "diseased" refers to lack of health or soundness, to not being free from defect, decay or damage. "Deprived," on the other hand, refers to having had something taken away or denied. Presumably, the deprivation is of some material, quality or capacity that is required in order to meet a standard or fulfill a requirement. Defective, inadequate, diseased and deprived all refer to lack, in the sense of not meeting an expectation or standard, or not fulfilling a requirement.

How does one come to perceive such lack in oneself? A project may be left unfinished, or an attempt to do something may fail, perhaps repeatedly. Accordingly, if one does not meet expectations (whether one's own or others'), it is perfectly appropriate, given that "defective" may mean "not meeting a standard," to tact oneself as defective in that sense. The problem is then acting as though this "defect" were a permanent, irreparable feature of one's being. This is the behavioral equivalent of "belief": to act in accordance with, in this case, a statement. (See the section on schemas, below.)

When other people react to one's performance as substandard, it is usually experienced as aversive. The respondent aspect of aversive experience is a bodily state of some kind that we learn to tact variously as "a bad mood," bummed-out, blue or perhaps angry. Cognitive researchers have said that the depressed person tacts himself as defective, and then tends to attribute his unpleasant experiences to the defect (Beck et al., 1979, p. 11) so identified. The simplest case might work like this: In the process of moving the refrigerator, I scratch the new flooring in the kitchen. I notice this, and say, "Well, I can't believe it! I'm *such a klutz*." My friend asks, "Why are you looking so glum?" I answer, "I'm such a *klutz*! Can't even move the refrigerator right." What is it that makes a person stay stuck in identifying the unchanging "defect" as causal?

This is clearly an instance of being out of contact with functional aspects of the situation. One of the useful features of cognitive treatment strategies is that searching for alternative explanations of situations helps (though inadvertently) to put depressed persons in contact with those functional aspects of their lives. But how does a person come to be out of contact with them in the first place?

Persons so afflicted may be responding to their particular histories of experiences that suggest the irreparable nature and finality of defectiveness (1). For example, they may have developed a repertoire for discarding and/or destroying chairs with broken legs. Then, when they self-tact, "I am defective," . . . this is the end. As such, it would be a rule-governed behavior (Hayes, 1989).

Identifying a defect as causal, final and irreparable may also be a response shaped by past contingencies, wherein for example, an authority figure refused to deal further with the person in question the moment a substandard performance or characteristic was noted. As individuals are developing, their sense of self is created through interaction with the social world. Skinner (1974) said, "It is only when a person's private world becomes important to others that it is made important to him" (p.35). In patterns of self-description we can in fact perceive just which aspects of an individual have been important to (made salient by) others in her/his history.

Perhaps it was a mother who promptly stopped helping a child with a cooking project (fixing a family dinner) when the child "clumsily" dropped an egg on the floor, so the child was left to fix dinner unaided, and the result was a disaster that was further ridiculed. Or perhaps a ballet teacher, citing a child's emerging chunky body shape at age 12, refuses to give lessons any more (regardless of this child's love of dance), on the grounds that nobody built like that will get anywhere in the ballet world. Having the good will and attention of this authority figure was important to the individual, and it was withdrawn as a consequence of his or her "defective" behavior or undesirable characteristics. These substandard behaviors or characteristics were given more weight by the primary others in his/her history than were the behaviors or characteristics that did meet standards, in this context. Negative views of self and concomitant loss of contact with current consequences are a result.

Being out of touch with current contingencies may also be a combination of both rule-governed behavior and contingency-shaped behavior. Thus when a person does not attend parties, in accordance with the rule, "It's no use to go to parties: People will only ignore or insult me, anyway," it is negatively reinforced by the avoidance of such insult and positively reinforced by the soothing responses of friends, "But everyone likes you!"

In addressing the first segment of the cognitive triad, then, we note that the sense of self is a function of social interaction, and that a negative view of self is fundamental to the negative cognitive triad. It follows that interaction in the therapeutic relationship has the potential of shaping contingencies that affect the self-tacting of the client with an immediacy that may be missing in standard cognitive therapy (Callaghan, Naugle, & Follette, 1996; Follette, Naugle, & Callaghan, 1996).

Automatic thoughts. According to CT, a negative view of self manifests primarily as automatic thoughts, though these may also be spoken aloud. We understand automatic thoughts as "thinking," or covert verbal behaving, the making of private self-statements that we call "tacting to self." Thus, self-talk (whether spoken aloud or not) such as, "I am terrible, hopeless, worthless, crazy, useless, stupid, ugly, incompetent, disgusting," etc., is a salient behavioral manifestation of the first element of the cognitive triad.

The list of adjectives above is fairly typical both of depressed persons' self-descriptions and of observers strongly objecting to, judging or criticizing a person's behavior. Neither negative self-tacting nor the original form of authoritarian disapproval is usually pure descriptive tacting. That is, judgmental words such as, "You're a stupid fool," most likely function primarily as disguised mands (Kohlenberg & Tsai, 1991), statements in the form of descriptions (tacts) but maintained by their effect on others (mands). When directed at another, these words show disapproval or dislike of a person or his/her actions. They are the verbal equivalent of a slap in the face. The effect is punitive, decreasing the likelihood of recurrence of prior behavior. It may also increase the likelihood of the recipient's future compliance with the speaker's wishes, to prevent the recurrence of the speaker's displeasure.

Describing one's own behavior is usually a form or style of self-labeling learned early in life from people in authority positions. Children don't automatically do this, but if, for instance, negative tacting of the child's person occurs frequently as a form of parental rejection, the child may learn that anticipating the rejection by saying it out loud first will preclude rejection or punishment coming directly from the parent, which is likely to be more aversive than negative self-tacting. Such behavior is maintained by this negative reinforcement. In addition it may be positively reinforced by expressions of sympathy, soothing, positive descriptions of the child's person ("Oh no, Jen, you're a good little girl, you're the best little girl a mommy could have"), etc.

Because in the past, negative self-tacting may have prevented a parent or caretaker from saying similar words, and/or from further punishing or rejecting the child, the self-directed negative tact in the present may be the functional equivalent of, "Please don't reject (hurt, criticize) me," and/or, "Comfort me!" and it must have been successful in order to have these functions in the present. Thus it is a disguised mand, having functioned as a mand even though it is in the form of a tact (Kohlenberg & Tsai, 1991). There is a fairly strong probability, therefore, that the first element of the cognitive triad may be understood behaviorally as a history of aversive control leading to a repertoire of disguised manding.

Negative View of Experiences

The second element of the depressive cognitive triad is the tendency to interpret experiences negatively. Cognitive theorists note that the depressed person sees the world as demanding beyond human capacity, or as presenting insurmountable barriers to life goals. Interactions with people and things are interpreted in terms of defeat or deprivation (Beck et al., 1979). Beck says that these are "negative misinterpretations" of situations, on the grounds that more plausible and positive interpretations are obvious and available to a person who is not depressed. What might be the cause of this discrepancy between the verbal behaviors of depressed and non-depressed people?

On stimulus, interpretation and context. Even though phenomena of depressed persons tending to view situations negatively are of interest to us as behavior analysts, the theoretical differences between cognitive therapy and behavior analysis are nowhere more salient than in this area. Here, the radical behaviorist believes that reality is unknowable independent of perceiving. Perceiving, in turn, is a behavior shaped by the individual's experiences from birth to the present. Thus, when a behavior analyst uses the term "situation," also known as "stimulus," she or he means "discriminative stimulus," which by assumption is holistic and idiosyncratic in nature, depending on the individual's history. Meanwhile, the cognitive therapist may accept the notion of a fixed, knowable reality and use the term "stimulus" or "situation" to speak of a real object or particular configuration of objects in the environment.

From this viewpoint, there is a serious problem with the term "stimulus." The problem is that different organisms perceive the "same" stimulus in different ways. The resolution to this problem requires that the organism actively construe the stimulus. This construction is based on the individual history of experience. In the heat of argument, both the behavior analyst and the cognitive therapist may go away missing the point that entirely different "stimuli" are being discussed. The discriminative stimulus includes context, both internal and external, that is, the individual history of experience with such a configuration, which stands in contrast to stimulus as discrete, objectively existent, and identifiable by public agreement.

Thus, the behavior analyst is immediately aware that the "same" objective situation actually exists in two different contexts for any two individuals. Cognitive theory deals with this state of affairs by positing schemas, stable cognitive patterns that form the basis for the individual's interpretations of situations. What the behavior analyst terms "context" here, indicating the individual's reinforcement history as it construes the situation, is split by cognitive theorists into consistent cognitive patterns on the one hand, and an objective situation on the other. Although Beck et al. (1979) do recognize that every individual, sick or well, "selectively attends to specific stimuli, combines them in a pattern, and conceptualizes the situation" (p.12), they maintain that some schemas are appropriate and others inappropriate, some functional and some dysfunctional.

Context, then, is what determines the meaning (that is, the function) of any interaction with people or things. A unique history of experience constitutes the larger context for each person in any given situation. This invisible context of past experience is the source of differing interpretations of current situations. It is somewhat misleading therefore to call some of these "mis-" interpretations, and others "correct" interpretations. An interpretation is just an interpretation, and must be understood as a product of the individual's reinforcement history, something that is part and parcel of each of us.

Furthermore, the pathological process identified by cognitive theorists as idiosyncratic schemas becoming more active, being evoked by wider ranges of stimuli less logically related to them (Beck et al., p. 13), points to the behavioral process of generalization. This, and the notion that the patient thus "loses much of his voluntary control over his thinking processes" (Beck et al., p. 13), indicates contingency-shaped behavior to the behavior analyst even as it points out an assumption of the cognitivist, namely, that logic and voluntary control are the operative factors in emotional health.

Negative tact as mand and maintainer. Interpretation, again, is accessible as verbal behavior in the second leg of the cognitive triad, this time in the act of describing (or *tacting*) the world, that is, one's interactions with people and things, in a negative way. For example, if I were given plain mustard on my deli sandwich rather than Dijon style mustard, I might interpret this as evidence that the proprietors don't think Asians can tell the difference, or that I am not a valued customer, and they're trying to get rid of me. Perhaps the fact is they ran out of Dijon style mustard. But interpreting the situation as a function of discrimination against me, averts the possibility of receiving social rejection unexpectedly, with its associated experience of pain. This "misinterpretation" is the result of my history of receiving an unexpected rejection (in the form of a racial slur) by a shopkeeper when I complained about a product. This was painful enough that in similar situations of disappointment, I don't return defective items or question how an order has been filled. As a result, no proprietor has made snide remarks about me or my judgment: The behavior is negatively reinforced by precluding a possible repetition of the old aversive experience.

To a certain extent, negative interpretations of the world serve to perpetuate negative experiences through the effect of such communications on other people (Beck et al., 1979; Coyne, 1976a, 1976b). Such negative interpretations are maintained not only by initial avoidance of rejection, but also by the positive soothing attentions of others anxious to assure one that things are really OK, that one is acceptable and even likable. This style of behaving may even bring on anticipated rejection where it would not have occurred otherwise, a dreadful kind of self-fulfilling prophecy. For example, the deli owner on a bad day may make a remark about "certain surly customers" when she observes me scuttling away with a frown on my face. As Coyne (1976b) pointed out, however, even the soothers subtly betray an annoyance with a person who remains consistently negative in outlook. This is not lost on the subject of their attentions: Contact with this contingency further confirms her/his perception that she/he is disliked, producing further withdrawal or surliness, etc.

Another function of the second element. This second element of the cognitive triad is somewhat more complex than the first. A persistently negative description of experiences of the world may have a number of functions and sources in an individual's life. A history of negative experiences, as above, may play a part, certainly—but a negative view of the world may also show up in a person who has had an objectively idyllic or privileged and protected life. The clinician needs to determine just what is being tacted or emitted as a disguised mand. Although the content of the words points to "the world," any experience of the world is always by means of the sensorium, and necessarily includes qualities pertaining to the individual's state at the moment, her or his feelings. A depressed person's persistently negative description of the world may actually be an acceptable way of explaining persistent negative (aversive, uncomfortable) feelings, physical states that are contingency-shaped while the actual contingencies operating still lie outside the individual's current verbal awareness. This corresponds to Kohlenberg and Tsai's (1991, 1994a) analysis of the *ABC* model wherein an antecedent directly elicits an aversive mood, which then is explained verbally (the *ACB* version).

There is a strong cultural tendency to provide socially acceptable verbal explanations for our behavior (Hayes, Wilson, Gifford, Follette & Strosahl, 1996; Zettle & Hayes, 1986). People seek any plausible cause to satisfy the demand to "know why" they behave as they do, and often offer feelings and thoughts as (circular) causal explanations, or idiosyncratic interpretations of external events. Thus, "bad" (aversive and socially unacceptable) feelings manifesting in tears, anger or sad expressions may be satisfactorily explained by "bad" things happening to us. Such explanations, even when they refer to external circumstances, rarely tact the actual causes of behavior, which are likely to be contingency-shaped and may not be available to verbal description. Furthermore, these explanations may be perceived as distortions by a third party who no more understands the origins of my behavior than I do, but they satisfy social demands both public and private. For example in the deli scenario above, if a friend came along and asked, "Why are you so long-faced?" I might say, "Oh, those guys hate Asians..." The friend may know full well that the shop keeper's in-laws are beloved and Chinese. But she inquires into the event, offers support and tries to persuade me that things are not as bad as I imagine. Thus a negative view of the world may consist at least partially of disguised mands once again, something like, "I have a legitimate reason to feel what I feel: Please do not reject me. Really, you ought to help, sympathize, support me."

The second element of the cognitive triad, a negative view of the world, or a tendency to interpret experiences negatively, may be seen behaviorally as functioning to avoid or preclude aversive experiences, or to explain behavior correlated with aversive private experiences in order to mand soothing attention from others. In any case, this cognitive pattern is often more usefully interpreted as disguised manding in the form of tacts not congruent with those of significant others in the client's social surrounds.

Negative View of the Future

The third element of the cognitive triad is a negative view of the future, such that a person anticipates continued suffering, hardship, frustration, deprivation and failure. Beck et al. (1979) observed that the depressed person exaggerates the difficulties of undertaking a task and minimizes the possibility of undertaking corrective action. Is this negative view a causal factor in depression or not (Coyne, 1982; Dougher, 1995, 1997)? One behavior correlated with a negative view of the future is a withdrawal from action. But there is no guarantee that the negative view or explanation for lack of action is actually its cause, although the possibility exists, providing that the person is extremely rule-governed. For example, such a person might say, "It's no use going to parties. People will just insult and ignore me anyway," and act on this premise even though they have never attended parties. Not attending parties is under the control of the rule in this case: It is a statement of situation and consequences. This is the paradigm *A-B-C* configuration, wherein a cognition is actually producing subsequent behavior, nonattendance of parties. This cognition may also contribute to negative mood due to contact with the unavailability of positive interpersonal interactions in this person's experience (Augustson, & Dougher, 1997; Dougher, Augustson, Markham, Greenway, & Wulfert, 1994).

In addition, one who, for instance, dwells on the difficulties of undertaking a task to demonstrate its impossibility, may also be offering an explanation for her or his lack of action, manding sympathy and encouragement rather than condemnation. The controlling variable(s) may be a combination of a history of aversive control (avoidance of inevitable criticism and rejection), lack of reinforcement, inadequate schedule of reinforcement, physical exhaustion, a narrow range of stimulus control, or any number of historically based deficits having their own chains of causes.

Activation of Negative Cognitive Patterns

Cognitive researchers have not emphasized the process of activation of the cognitive triad. Rather, they seem to have dealt primarily with phenomena of negative cognitions as predictors of depression (e.g., Zuroff, Igreja, & Mongrain, 1990), and with correlations between stressful events and depressive reactions mediated by negative cognitions (e.g., Hammen & Mayol, 1982; Overholser, 1996; Robins, Block, & Peselow, 1990). Miranda and Persons (1988; Miranda, Persons, & Byers, 1990; Miranda, 1992) have found the presence of negative thinking only when the subject is in a negative mood state, and that people with a history of depression report more rigid global negative thinking following stressful life events than people who had no history of depression.

A critical question is, supposing a person has a history of aversive control and has developed a repertoire of avoidance strategies, some in the form of negative cognitive patterns such as those above: Why are the huge numbers of depressed people not depressed all the time? Not everyone suffers from "double depression," or episodes of major depression superimposed on long term underlying dysthymia. How could someone who had developed a repertoire of negative cognitive patterns, or verbal behaviors, sometimes have normal un-depressed periods in her/his life, prior to therapy? Why is it that not everyone who shows dysfunctional thought patterns goes on to develop depression (Lewinsohn, Steinmetz, Larson, & Franklin, 1981)? What accounts for the episodic nature of depression if repertoires of negative verbal behaviors maintain it? Do these repertoires appear and disappear?

The theory is that a stressful event comes along, and then everything changes, at least for people with a history of depression (Miranda, 1992). The cognitive triad of negative views of self, world and future is activated and begins self-perpetuating interactions with the negative mood that it creates. This triad of negative cognitive patterns lurks, ready to be activated, at all times. But not every stressful negative event will lead to depression (Brown, Bifulco, & Harris, 1987; Hammen & Mayol, 1982), hence not every stressful event activates the triad.

To the behavior analyst, such a situation indicates a history of multiple reinforcement schedules, and that the change in response (activation of the negative verbal repertoires) is signaled or under stimulus control. For example, the presence of one discriminative stimulus, say, a significant other in a particular mood in a public place, signals a repertoire of helpful, cheerful, optimistic behaviors in the individual under study, even in the case of a stressful event, such as a car accident. On the other hand, the presence of another discriminative stimulus, which may be the same mood in the same significant other but in a private place, may signal a repertoire of withdrawal, pessimism, avoidance, essentially the "depressive" syndrome. This helps to account for the frustratingly idiosyncratic nature of responses to various classes of stressful events (Brown, Bifulco, & Harris, 1987; Hammen & Mayol, 1982; Overholser, 1996).

We have proposed possible functional analyses of the cognitive triad and its activation by tracing verbal behavior to the environmental or contextual variables that may evoke repertoires of negative thinking. In accord with sophisticated forms of cognitive theory, functional analysis reveals that negative cognitions have a variety of functions, but that they are not necessarily causal. In this regard, cognitive theorists consider all the symptoms of the depressive syndrome to be due to the consequences of maladaptive negative cognitive patterns or structures underlying the more readily accessible cognitive products (Hollon & Kriss, 1984) that we understand as verbal behaviors.

Schemas

We have been considering the cognitive triad, negative thoughts of self, world, and future. While it is true that cognitive therapists have developed various strategies to change such thoughts, these readily-accessible verbal behaviors are not themselves considered to cause depression. Hollon and Kriss (1984) and others (Beck, 1984; Safran, Vallis, Segal, & Shaw, 1986) suggest that any clinical interventions that only effect change at this level are guilty of merely treating symptoms. Rather, underlying organizational entities or cognitive structures are hypothesized to play an active role in processing information, and to be the ultimate therapeutically active causal factor in depression, (Hollon & Kriss, 1984; Kohlenberg & Tsai, 1994a) although organic factors are certainly taken into consideration as well. Such structures or schemas, when activated, are thought to cause the negative verbal behavior of the cognitive triad to appear, and ultimately are responsible for the rest of the depressive syndrome as well.

As described by Hollon and Kriss, schemas are inaccessible, non-behavioral entities operating at an unconscious level. Hence their content cannot be known directly but must be inferred from the more superficial automatic thoughts and underlying assumptions that are readily accessible. In accord with a behavior-analytic view, cognitive theorists propose that negative concepts of self, world and future, structured as schemas, are based on early experiences (Beck et al., p. 16; Hollon & Kriss, 1984). These theorists further propose that the underlying negative constructs (schemas) are latent until activated by specific types of situation to which the individual is particularly sensitive due to the nature of this underlying cognitive organization (Miranda, 1992; Persons & Miranda, 1995).

Behavior analysis clarifies this somewhat by understanding underlying cognitive structures or schemas as contingency-shaped behaviors (Kohlenberg & Tsai, 1991, 1994a; Kohlenberg, Tsai & Kohlenberg, 1996). Contingency-shaped behaviors may be changed through experience with contingencies, rather than through talk about contingencies, except in those cases where the contingency-shaped behavior is rule-governance itself, verbal behavior which in turn is ultimately contingency-shaped. The changing of schemas has been called the "holy grail" of cognitive therapy (Zuroff, 1992, p.274), an unattainable mystery. But behavior analysts are comfortable dealing with contingency-shaped behavior. The process of ferreting out controlling variables and shaping new behavior, while never easy, is our stock in trade.

Treatment: A Behavior-Analytic Enhancement of Cognitive Therapy

The main steps in cognitive therapy for depression are (1) providing the cognitive hypothesis as a rationale to clients, (2) training in self-monitoring, and (3) training in identifying cognitions, evaluating beliefs, and exploring underlying assumptions and schemas (Beck et al., 1979).

Kohlenberg and Tsai have applied features of their functional analytic psychotherapy (FAP) to the cognitive therapy model (Kohlenberg & Tsai, 1991, 1994a, 1994b; Kohlenberg, Tsai & Kohlenberg, 1996). The main steps in the FAP-enhanced cognitive therapy (FECT) for depression are (1) providing a behavior-analytically enhanced version of the rationale, (1a) observing in-session behavior to determine variables affecting the behavior-behavior relationship of thinking and speaking to subsequent operant and respondent "depressed" client behaviors, (2) training the client in self-monitoring, focusing especially on in-session thinking, as a means to contacting the functional aspects of one's behavior, and (3) working with contingency-shaped behavioral patterns by shaping desired client behaviors through the natural contingencies of interpersonal behavior in the therapist-client interaction.

The Importance of the Therapeutic Relationship in FAP and FECT

Regardless of the particulars of a sufferer's reinforcement history, the depression she or he suffers is typically in relation with other people. Even a purely organically caused depression involves other people, inasmuch as the expression of negative affect has a noticeable effect on others, in such a way that it tends to isolate the sufferer even more, which only helps maintain the depressive state of affairs (Beck et al., 1979; Coyne, 1976b). Furthermore, as we have said, if the sense of self is a function of social interaction and a contingently shaped negative view of self is fundamental to the negative cognitive triad (which predisposes one to depression), interaction in the therapeutic relationship has the potential of directly shaping the contingencies that affect the self-tacting and self-experience of the client.

Thus FAP relies on an involved, emotional, nonmanipulative, client-therapist relationship as the vehicle of change. A therapy environment is constructed in which the client's daily life problems can occur in the session and be changed by the naturally reinforcing reactions of the therapist. The emotional responses of the client indicate that he or she is in touch with clinically relevant behavior; the emotional responses of the therapist are potentially similar to those in the community and can thus facilitate natural reinforcement during the session.

Rationale

In parallel with the practice of cognitive therapists, we offer relevant explanations of client problems near the beginning of a course of therapy. First, we offer a broader rationale based on Zeiss & Jones' (1983) formulation, "Whatever is keeping you from getting the life satisfactions that could eliminate your depression will be the target of our treatment" (p. 198). Then we continue to mention various possible cognitive factors, interpersonal skills, avoidance, and various historical factors and the in-session focus. The classic cognitive *A-B-C* model may be presented first, on grounds that it has an intuitive appeal for many people, and that it is desirable for clients and their concepts of depression to feel included in the process (Addis & Jacobson, 1996).

At this point (and at all subsequent points where e.g., homework assignments are consistent with this rationale), it is vital that the therapist attend to client reactions, and take seriously any tendency to disagree with the model. It may be that as the client attempts to monitor thinking and mood, client and therapist will become aware of discrepancies between her/his experience and the *A-B-C* model. This is the time to elaborate on the behavior-analytically expanded rationale for why a person becomes depressed, and what may be done about it.

Although it is possible for a client with a mood that they do not perceive as related to their thinking to improve when given an *A-B-C* interpretation, less favorable outcomes are also possible. This is especially true for clients who grew up in dysfunctional families where they were abused, neglected, negated, or otherwise punished for expressing their feelings. Children who are repeatedly told, either directly or indirectly, that "there's no reason for you to feel or think that way" mistrust their feelings and are unsure of who they are (cf. remarks on the sense of self, above). Suggesting to such clients that their beliefs are dysfunctional or irrational can replay the contingencies associated with the invalidation and alienation they experienced while growing up. Such clients may drop out of treatment if they feel invalidated.

For example, in the case of a client who intellectually "knows" she/he is not worthless but does not accept this on an emotional level, the FECT rationale offered would be that "knowing" is not always sufficient to produce change, and that actual experience is required to change the effects of history. Therapy would then focus on what kinds of experience are needed, how they might be obtained in daily life, and how the client-therapist relationship might be relevant to this process.

Although a functional analysis is consistent with the cognitive therapy position that thinking can precede actions, we regard the thought-behavior relationship always as a behavior-behavior relationship. When thoughts are considered as behavior, the therapist is led to consider the various environmental origins of the thinking behaviors involved and the arbitrary nature of their connection to other behavior as well as to pay attention to the ongoing contingencies of reinforcement in their development and modification.

A Focus on the Here and Now: Self-Monitoring In Session

The client's behavior will be most subject to change if it occurs close in time and place to relevant contingencies and stimulus control. Thus, whenever possible, we recommend focusing on thinking, believing, and other relevant behaviors that occur during the session, in response to present context. This focus engenders an in-vivo self-monitoring that leads eventually to client contact with actual controlling variables in her/his behavior.

Opportunities to shape more adaptive verbal behaviors directly frequently occur as the client's dysfunctional thinking is brought into the client-therapist relationship. For example, a client who apologizes for bringing up a certain topic, saying, "I hate to bother you with this, it's so trivial, but I can't seem to get it out of my head," is manifesting a view of her unimportance in the context of the therapeutic relationship at least as important to the process as the topic itself.

With the notable exception of Safran and colleagues (Safran, 1990a, 1990b; Safran, McMain, Crocker, & Murray, 1990; Safran & Segal, 1990; also Young, 1994), cognitive therapists usually focus on behavior occurring elsewhere, thereby avoiding or preventing therapeutic opportunities provided by the therapist-client interaction. For example, in a discussion of "technical problems" in doing cognitive therapy for depression, Beck et al. (1979) raised the problem of a client who says, "You are more interested in doing research than in helping me." First, Beck wisely pointed out that even if nothing is said, a client who is in a clinical research project may be secretly harboring such thoughts. However, the reason such thoughts occur, according to Beck, is that depressed clients may be distorting what the therapist does. He then suggested that the therapist inquire if any such notions are present and put these worries to rest. According to Beck, if possible, the therapist should avoid such problems in the first place by anticipating their occurrence and giving complete explanations to the client.

Our functional analysis of that situation would be somewhat different. A depressed client who feels unimportant to the therapist highlights the fact that the therapy situation could be evoking the same problem that the client experiences with others (for example, not acting important and not asking for what she wants). This would not be viewed as a technical problem to be disposed of but as a situation that provides an important therapeutic opportunity. Also, it would not be assumed that the client is distorting, just that the therapist and the client are contacting different aspects of the situation. It is even possible that the research is more important to the therapist than the client is, and in that sense, the client would not be "distorting." The notion that the client might be secretly harboring such ideas rather than telling the therapist suggests the clinical problem of the client not being direct, open, or assertive during the session.

Although Beck's theory may, in general, lead the cognitive therapist to overlook situations of interest according to functional analysis, he recognized that certain therapist-client interactions can provide therapeutic opportunity. For example, in discussing ways to strengthen collaboration, he pointed out that a client may react to a homework assignment as a test of self-worth and that the therapist should use this as an opportunity to correct faulty cognitions. Beck, however, gave no special significance to the fact that the therapeutic work focused on behavior as it is occurring. Instead, he viewed it as having the same effects as dealing with a cognition that occurs elsewhere. Jacobson (1989), on the other hand, discussed the importance of focusing on behavior during the session when doing Beck's cognitive therapy. Furthermore, he suggested that this factor be incorporated into the conceptual underpinnings of cognitive therapy for depression.

Work With Contingency-Shaped Behavioral Patterns

Use direct cognitive manipulation with caution. We define direct cognitive manipulation as therapist behaviors that involve appeals to reason or logical arguments, hence, primarily rule-giving. Clients may resonate to the theory that cognition mediates their problems, so direct cognitive manipulations can sometimes be beneficial even if the problems are mainly A-C types, directly elicited by events or situations.

When clients respond to rules by changing their cognitions, these changes are rule-governed behavior. This process can benefit the client for several reasons. First, beliefs contribute, at least to some degree, to many client problems even if contingencies are the primary factor. Direct cognitive manipulations would then be helpful, particularly if the client was also exposed to contingencies for improved behavior.

Second, linear and logical thinkers who interpret their directly elicited, A-C problems according to the ABC hypothesis may benefit because these individuals have learned to be consistent. That is, they grew up in environments where "practicing what you preach" was highly valued and "saying one thing and doing another" was not. Inclination exists for this type of client to act in accordance with instructed "beliefs." The strength of such inclinations, however, is generally weak and is dependent on how much emphasis was placed on consistency in the client's subculture.

Third, direct cognitive manipulation can help with *A-C* problems through engendering covert contingencies and rules. For example, an unintended effect of rationally convincing clients to hold a certain belief is that it involves a therapist demand or description implying that if the clients behave as told they will get better (a rule). If the clients do behave differently, and this new way of behaving is naturally reinforced, the clients improve. For example, Beck et al. (1979) encouraged clients to act against their assumptions because it is "the most powerful way to change it" (p. 264). Although Beck preferred to view this intervention as changing a cognition (an assumption), it can also be seen as the therapist issuing a rule and the client following a rule that results in exposing the client's behavior to contingencies that directly strengthen the improved behavior. This emphasis on building in new behavior is consistent with a functional analysis.

When the client changes to please the therapist, however, the danger is that natural reinforcers in the client's daily life will not maintain these improvements when therapy ends. Since direct cognitive manipulations involve instructions on how to think or behave and make explicit demands for improvements, it is difficult to avoid pleasing the therapist. A notable exception is the use in Beck et al. (1979) of the Socratic method and "hypothesis testing," which we view as ingenious ways of reducing motivation to please the therapist and of bringing clients into contact with natural reinforcers.

When appeals to reason are not successful, they are treated differently by behavior analysts than by cognitive therapists. The latter might raise additional arguments as to why the client's thoughts are incorrect. But getting a client to change a belief through reason is not guaranteed to have a favorable result because it is unclear what behavior, other than verbal behavior, has been changed.

When a client changes a belief statement because of a therapist's logical arguments, the meaning of the statement changes. Before the therapeutic intervention, the belief described past experiences or indicated the likelihood of certain actions. After the client's belief is changed due to the therapist's logical arguments, it is no longer derived from experience but is instead a response made to please the therapist or to conform to the rules of logic. It is therefore not surprising that many clients who have been "convinced" to change their beliefs subsequently do not change their behavior in the problem situation. Such "failures" are usually accompanied by explanations such as, "I believe it intellectually, but I do not accept it on an emotional level." From a functional analytic standpoint, this inconsistency is not perplexing since there is no reason to expect anything else. Strategies to deal with such inconsistencies would be to accept them and to identify variables that account for behaviors, such as espousing belief *X* and acting consistent with belief *Y*, trying to be consistent, or trying to please the therapist by being rational.

Examples From a FECT Case

The following example of FECT treatment of a depressed person illustrates the immediacy of the therapeutic relationship and its potential for altering a negative self-concept that is deeply ingrained. These portions of verbatim transcript were selected from the third author's work with MC, a healthy, attractive, and articulate Caucasian female in her late twenties. She came to therapy asking for help with her depression and for her concerns about how she interacts with others. Feelings and thoughts of being ugly, not good enough, and a failure often plagued her. She recoiled from seeing herself in a mirror. A central theme of therapy was working on her "self hatred" and general negativity in thoughts and feelings about herself, corresponding to the first element of the cognitive triad. In accordance with our analysis, MC reports an extensive history of aversive control. Her mother was very critical and abusive throughout MC's childhood, a pattern that still continued at the time that MC entered therapy.

In the following example, the therapist had asked MC to try writing out an autobiographical outline or timeline. He explicitly said that anything MC could do was fine, even a rough draft of an outline. If she wanted to write more, that would be fine too.

MC is unvaryingly self-critical about not writing enough, even though there were no requirements of length in the therapist's request. Clearly, she is out of contact with the contingencies of the current situation. The therapist senses that this is functionally similar to problem interactions in other areas of her life. In this excerpt the therapist addresses the effect of the self-deprecating behavior on him and checks to see if MC is aware that her self-criticism affects other parts of her life.

1. T: OK . . . OK . . . Um, anything else that comes to mind? [MC: Um, um, no] I wonder if you had any thoughts or feelings about coming into session today? (Here, the therapist is eliciting thoughts and feelings about therapy and the therapeutic relationship, bringing the focus of therapy onto the session itself.)

1a. MC: I don't know. I just wish I could've written more. (MC's "I don't know" indicates unwillingness or inability to contact private responses to the situation.)

2. T: You wish you could've written more? (Therapist inquires into the immediate self-criticism or tacting of inadequacy, probing further to determine whether this is under public or private control.)

2a. MC: Yeah, like, a lot of it I feel like I can't remember, like, junior high school, I can only remember a few things. (Reason-giving, attributing the supposed shortcoming to a memory deficit.)

3. T: What do you mean, you wish you had written more? (Continued probe for public or private control over the perception of lack.)

3a. MC: Oh, I just wish I hadn't—well, some things, I think I'd have, like, tons to write about, but I wish I had written more, but I didn't.

4. T: I see. I wondered if you were feeling that I might have a reaction to you having not written more. (Probing for possible interpersonal function of the descrip-

tion of shortcoming; bringing the interaction explicitly into the here and now of the relationship.)

4a. MC: To not have written more? [T: Yeah] Probably. (MC admits, tentatively, that she is concerned about the therapist's reaction.)

5. T: I wonder when you're thinking about, you know, me, and you having not written enough about that. Was there a sense of having not done that well enough? (Therapist probes for enduring interpersonal behavioral pattern around performance, not specifying either cognition or feeling, but leaving it ambiguous with "sense.")

5a. MC: Yeah, I just kinda felt like I failed. I chose to go hiking instead. (MC tacts "failure," following work on the assignment, even though the assignment was without standards for judgment. She further reports leaving the situation, which may be an avoidance move, or it may be a positive move toward self-assertion and away from public control of her actions, or "people-pleasing.")

In the next excerpt, the therapist pursues this topic and describes the paradoxical position he is now experiencing as a result of MC's self-critical report on the assignment he had given her. By reflecting on his own reaction to the situation, the therapist models both in-vivo self-monitoring and the open (not publicly-controlled) reporting of private experience and verbal behaviors (feelings and thoughts).

Furthermore, he probes for the presence of a pervasive or generalized pattern of behavior, tacted as "I never do well enough." This is distinctly in the realm of phenomena that cognitive therapists understand as cognitive structures, as it is ordinarily outside of verbal awareness and gives rise to a variety of automatic responses or cognitive products, which in turn seem to be out of synch with current consequences.

1. T: Well, um, I noticed, OK, I'm gonna mention something I'm thinking of and then we'll come back to some other things. [MC: OK] But, I notice feeling like I'm in kind of a jam with the autobiography thing. Cuz, I'm wondering, in a way it has become another opportunity for you to do something not well enough. Does that make any sense?

1a. MC: Yeah, but everything's like that. (MC tacts the pervasiveness of the pattern. Such a way of constructing reality signals the possibility of long-standing contingency-shaped behavior that has generalized.)

2. T: And, I remember—how I remember presenting it, is like, anything you can do, anything you're willing to do, it's completely in your court how you do that. I don't have a standard. I'm not going to grade it. I'm not going to expect—I don't have expectations. You didn't have to do anything. You could've just written [your name] on it and said, "That's all I feel like doing. I'm not into this." (Therapist presents actual contingencies again, in an attempt to shape her response here in session. The immediacy is palpable.)

2a. MC: Yeah, but that's not fair. (Hints at a way the basic construct has been elaborated in her life.)

3. T: And, when I say I feel like I'm in a jam, by saying that, I saw yet another thing for you to not do right. I don't know if you can follow that. I might have to

clarify that. (Modeling reporting private responses.)

3a. MC: No, I follow it, but I don't think . . . (Tries to avoid by mollifying.)

4. T: But, by saying, you know, something about you feeling like you didn't do it right, well, that's not doing it right maybe. Do you see the Catch-22 sort of? (Blocks avoidance and again presents actual consequences in the form of his response to MC's self-criticism.) [MC: Yeah.] OK. So, what do you mean it's not fair? (Probing for elaboration of the construct, actually asking client to tact consequences she has experienced in the past, in order to determine the function of her problematic behavior.)

4a. MC: Well, it's not, I mean, cuz, you wouldn't feel like you're in a jam cuz anytime you ask me to do anything, that's my fault or problem if I feel like I didn't do it right. It's not your fault. [T: mm hm] You didn't, like, you told me it was just whatever I wanted to write and I guess I just put in my mind that I wanted to, like, write a book, you know. And instead, it's like . . . (Approximately, "If anything goes wrong, it's my fault...")

5. T: OK. I guess what I want to put out there is that there was no right way to do that [MC: Yeah.], and you have, in a sense, if you, if you have a way to do it that would not be a failure, which I don't know if there is such a thing for you right now. I would hope that that might become the case. Um, I might, you know, it's almost like I started getting afraid, I won't let this affect me too much, I think, but the conundrum I get in, the jam I get in is, like, gosh, I can't put anything out there without you feeling like you're a failure and haven't done it well enough. So, anything I would do—ask you to do, would bring some uncomfortable feelings up for you. (Modeling self-disclosure of in-vivo private experience, a form of self-monitoring.)

5a. MC: Yeah, but that's not your fault. (Reiterating part of the construct, possibly functioning as a disguised mand, "Please don't feel bad.")

6. T: I'm not, I'm not saying it is. It's just kind of confusing for me. [MC: Mmm, I'm sorry.] It's just uncomfortable to, um, have everything—and here's this other Catch-22 emerging, too, and now you're sorry about that, and if I point that out, you'd be sorry about being sorry. (Offering a description of how MC's immediate behavior is functioning in the relationship.)

6a. MC: I'm really sorry! (This clinically-relevant behavior is evoked once again.)

Here it is evident that MC is powerfully caught in her experience of not having done well enough, first with the autobiography and now in her interaction with the therapist. The therapist attempts to break the continuity of this experience and contact current contingencies by having MC notice and observe what is happening between the two of them. But she is unable to distance herself from the situation, and reacts stereo-typically (for her) by apologizing, in effect taking the blame for the therapist's discomfort. Although this high strength problematic behavior is pervasive, we do not yet know what its actual function may have been in the client's past.

Next, the therapist attempts to have MC detach herself from the situation enough to be able to perceive the actual effects of her behavior:

1. T: OK, so, let me back away from this. What, if we were to be able to step aside and listen and watch what was happening—in fact, we could. We could watch the tape. Um, what would we be seeing and saying about this interaction? Can you imagine it that way? I wonder if you can imagine it that way. Can you pull aside and slide up into the camera there?

1a. MC: What do you mean, like, when you said . . .

2. T: What, what would you say if we watched this observation, if we were just person X and Y watching this interaction. I wonder if you can kinda rewind and watch this again, so to speak. What would you notice? What would you see is happening between these two people?

2a. MC: That anything I did would make you feel bad, because I would feel like a failure, and then you'd feel like you couldn't ask me to do anything.

3. T: OK. And then I'd feel like I couldn't ask you to do anything. So, what does that do to our relationship? (Asks her to describe current consequences.)

3a. MC: I don't know. You'd probably avoid me. Like, "Oh, I can't ask her to do anything."

4. T: Yeah. I think if I was watching it, what would it be like? I just realized that I wasn't pulling out of it and observing it. I'm still stuck in my experience of it. (Therapist again models immediate reporting of private experience, this time describing a shortcoming of his own.)

4. (cont'd) T: It seems like, that the person in this chair would start to feel really cautious and careful about putting anything out there. And it seems like it might kind of slow down or hamper the interaction in a way, kind of impair the interaction in a way. It could. There's something else on my mind I'm not bringing up about this. I'm wondering how much this sort of thing goes on with other people in your life? (Therapist probes for a relationship to daily-life experiences, hinting that MC's behavior may bring about similar reactions in others, possibly contributing to the difficulties she originally brought to therapy. The query is as non-blaming as possible.)

4a. MC: I, I guess I always thought it was just me. I didn't worry about what they thought. [T: mm hm] I mean, I worried if they thought I was a failure. (Again, she construes everything to be her fault, unaware that her taking the blame had any effect on others. The original, probably self-protective function remains undisclosed.)

5. T: Right, right. I mean, cuz what's happening with people that like you and care about you and want to be a peer, a mutual, a friend, you know, a compatriot, a companion, and it feels like the relationship gets tilted in a way by that, and they, I don't know, they start to be careful with you, I don't know. Do you think that goes on with others in your life? Or does it make sense?

5a. MC: Yeah. Probably, I'm that way with people I'm really close to. [T: mm hm] But usually, like most of my friends, like, I usually try really hard to be whatever someone asks from me. I always gotta, like, stretch myself really thin, like if someone asks me to do something for them, I'll make sure I do that, even though I'm supposed to do something else, too. (Describes her people-pleasing pattern in daily life, and notes that with very close relationships, she also tends to be self-disparaging rather than simply ingratiating.)

6. T: So, it sounds like it would be hard to be—to feel like a balanced friendship or companionship.

6a. MC: Yeah, I have a really hard time, like, saying no to my friends, like if they need something. [T: mm hm] Like, I'll go, "OK, I'll come over. Don't worry." Cuz, I don't want to fail them. (Interesting description of "disappointment" as "failure.")

7. T: Right. OK, I'm gonna leave this specific topic right now. And I want to let you know that my feeling about what you do with that autobiography is great. Anything at all, anything at all that you do with that is great. (Reemphasizing current contingencies in further attempt to shape MC's behavior.) [MC: OK] And it already sounds like you've noticed some interesting and maybe useful things by doing that. Does that sound accurate? (Reinforcement of self-monitoring.) [MC: Yeah.] That, that is the whole reason. It's not for me at all. I mean, it may be useful for me, but if something productive comes of it for you, that's why we're here. [MC: True.] What are you feeling right now? What are you thinking? (Request for in-vivo self-monitoring.)

7a. MC: I don't know. (High-strength problematic response possibly indicating public control and uncertainty about cues.)

7a. (cont'd) MC: Just like, I don't want to say the word 'forget', but, like, I feel like I kinda don't realize, sometimes, that I'm here for me, or whatever, and [T: mm hm] I don't know. (Client tacts function of therapy, and immediately retracts, possibly looking for cues from the therapist that would indicate validation or disagreement.)

8. T: What's your reaction to that, what do you feel? (Again asks for private experience.)

8a. MC: Just like, I don't know. Just like, I feel, like, I feel like I have something for me, and I feel like, I don't know what the word is. I'm not, like, shy, but kinda . . . [T: Sheepish?] Yeah, kind of. (Not wanting to contradict, agreeing: The tentative "kind of" may indicate a first approximation of private control over this tact.)

9. T: That's weird, cuz, you can see it but can't express it. You know, like you don't deserve it?

9a. MC: Yeah, kind of. Maybe that's it. (Possibly another approximation of private control.)

10. T: I hope if there's a more accurate way you can think of saying it. (Therapist shows interest in MC's actual, unqualified characterization of her private experience—further shaping.)

10a. MC: No, that's actually a pretty accurate way of saying. You know, cuz a lot of times I feel like I don't deserve stuff. (Here's a clear statement of what the cognitive therapists might call an underlying assumption. But whether the clarity thus shaped by the therapist's persistent probing indicates that "being undeserving" is the actual experience, or whether MC is making an affirmative statement to please the therapist, is not yet certain. More patient exposure to non-punitive contingencies will have to happen in future sessions.)

These excerpts illustrate the ongoing assessment of functional relationships, the therapist's task implied by the expanded rationale given above. Second, they show the therapist focusing on the here and now, encouraging the client to self-monitor by modeling as well as by direct request. And finally, they show the therapist beginning to shape a deeply ingrained contingency-shaped client behavioral pattern through the natural consequences of interpersonal behavior within the therapeutic relationship.

In Conclusion

In this chapter we have cast a behavior-analytic eye on negative thinking patterns that cognitive therapists have identified as underlying and maintaining the depressive syndrome. The most clinically-relevant of these is the schema, a deeply ingrained negative belief, which, being a non-behavioral entity in CT theory, is reputed to be difficult to work with. In offering our view of the schema as contingency-shaped behavior, however, we have proposed and demonstrated briefly an approach to therapeutic work with this most elusive aspect of human behavior.

These are perilous times for the psychosocial treatment of depression. Widespread increase in the use of medications, the ease of dispensing and the relative mildness of side-effects, not to mention the role of insurance companies in advocating a quick fix, all serve to cast doubts on the usefulness of talk therapy. There are people for whom antidepressants seem to be an ideal response to their problems. It is difficult to convince third-party payers that a longish series of psychotherapy sessions presents any advantage over a simple prescription.

Skinner (1983) once asked, "Can behavior analysis save psychology?" The question was never more pertinent. Depressive patterns of behavior may reassert themselves when people stop taking medications, which after all are not intended to be used for the lifetime of the individual. We believe that working directly to change problematic contingency-shaped behaviors by appropriate new shaping within the therapeutic relationship offers a more powerful initial intervention and a hope of long-term effectiveness that even medications cannot offer. Determining the appropriateness of a therapeutic intervention means tailoring it for the individual, something that functional analysis enables us to approach with confidence. Thus we propose that in the long run, clinical behavior analysis may indeed save clinical psychology.

Footnote

(1) Throughout, our examples are simplified for the sake of illustration: The analyses of function represent a possible, not an exhaustive, selection of ways that behavior adapts to circumstance.

References

Addis, M. E., & Jacobson, N. S. (1996). Reasons for depression and the process and outcome of cognitive-behavioral psychotherapies. *Journal of Consulting and Clinical Psychology, 64*(6), 1417-1424.

Augustson, E. M., & Dougher, M. J. (1997). The transfer of avoidance evoking functions through stimulus equivalence classes. *Journal of Behavior Therapy & Experimental Psychiatry, 28*(3), 181-191.

Beck, A. T., Rush, A. J., Shaw, B. F., & Emery, G. (1979). *Cognitive therapy of depression.* New York: Guilford Press.

Brown, G. W., Bifulco, A., & Harris, T. O. (1987). Life events, vulnerability and onset of depression: Some refinements. *British Journal of Psychiatry, 150*, 30-42.

Callaghan, G. M., Naugle, A. E., & Follette, W. C. (1996). Useful construction of the client-therapist relationship. *Psychotherapy, 33*(3), 381-390.

Cordova, J. V., & Kohlenberg, R. J. (1994). Acceptance and the therapeutic relationship. In S. C. Hayes, N. S. Jacobson, V. M. Follette, & M. J. Dougher (Eds.), *Acceptance and change* (125-142). Reno, NV: Context Press.

Coyne, J. C. (1976a). Toward an interactional description of depression. *Psychiatry, 39*, 28-40.

Coyne, J. C. (1976b). Depression and the response of others. *Journal of Abnormal Psychology, 85* (2), 186-193.

Coyne, J. C. (1982). A critique of cognitions as causal entities with particular reference to depression. *Cognitive Therapy and Research, 6* (1), 3-13.

Dougher, M. J. (1995). A bigger picture: Cause and cognition in relation to differing scientific frameworks. *Journal of Behavior Therapy & Experimental Psychiatry, 26* (3), 215-219.

Dougher, M. J. (1997). Cognitive concepts, behavior analysis, and behavior therapy. *Journal of Behavior Therapy & Experimental Psychiatry, 28* (1), 65-70.

Dougher, M. J., Augustson, E., Markham, M. R., Greenway, D. E., & Wulfert, E. (1994). The transfer of respondent eliciting and extinction functions through stimulus equivalence classes. *Journal of the Experimental Analysis of Behavior, 62* (3), 331-351.

Dougher, M. J., & Hackbert, L. (1994). A behavior-analytic account of depression and a case report using acceptance-based procedures. *The Behavior Analyst, 17*(2), 321-334.

Ferster, C. B. (1973). A functional analysis of depression. *American Psychologist, 28,* 857-870.

Follette, W. C., Bach, P. A., & Follette, V. M. (1993). A Behavior-analytic view of psychological health. *The Behavior Analyst, 16* (2), 303-316.

Follette, W. C., Naugle, A. E., Callaghan, G. M. (1996). A Radical behavioral understanding of the therapeutic relationship in effecting change. *Behavior Therapy, 27*, 623-641.

Hammen, C., & Mayol, A. (1982). Depression and cognitive characteristics of stressful life-event types. *Journal of Abnormal Psychology, 91* (3), 165-174.

Hayes, S. C. (Ed.) (1989). *Rule-governed behavior: Cognition, contingencies and instructional control.* NY: Plenum Press.

Hayes, S. C. (1992). Verbal relations, time, and suicide. In Hayes, S. C., & Hayes, L. J. (Eds.), *Understanding verbal relations,* (109-118). Reno, NV: Context Press.

Hayes, S. C., & Brownstein, A. J. (1986). Mentalism, behavior-behavior relations, and a behavior-analytic view of the purposes of science. *The Behavior Analyst, 9* (2), 175-190.

Hayes, S. C., & Follette, W. C. (1992). Can functional analysis provide a substitute for syndromal classification? *Behavioral Assessment, 14,* 345-365.

Hayes, S. C., Wilson, K. G., Gifford, E. V., Follette, V. M., & Strohsahl, K. (1996). Experiential avoidance and behavioral disorders: A functional dimensional approach to diagnosis and treatment. *Journal of Consulting and Clinical Psychology, 64* (6), 1152-1168.

Hollon, S. D., & Kriss, M. R. (1984). Cognitive factors in clinical research and practice. *Clinical Psychology Review, 4,* 35-76.

Jacobson, N. S. (1989). The therapist-client relationship in cognitive behavior therapy: Implications for treating depression. *Journal of Cognitive Psychotherapy, 3,* 85-96.

Kohlenberg, R. J., & Tsai, M. (1991). *Functional analytic psychotherapy.* New York: Plenum Press.

Kohlenberg, R. J., & Tsai, M. (1994a). Improving cognitive therapy for depression with functional analytic psychotherapy: Theory and case study. *The Behavior Analyst, 17* (2), 305-319.

Kohlenberg, R. J., & Tsai, M. (1994b). Functional analytic psychotherapy: A radical behavioral approach to treatment and integration. *Journal of Psychotherapy Integration, 4* (3), 175-201.

Kohlenberg, R. J., Tsai, M., & Dougher, M. J. (1993). The dimensions of clinical behavior analysis. *The Behavior Analyst, 16*(2), 271-282.

Kohlenberg, R. J., Tsai, M., & Kohlenberg, B. S. (1996). Functional analysis in behavior therapy. In M. Hersen, R. M. Eisler, & P. M. Miller (Eds.), *Progress in behavior modification,* (Volume 30). New York: Brooks/Cole Publishing.

Lewinsohn, P. M., Steinmetz, J. L., Larson, D. W., & Franklin, J. (1981). Depression-related cognitions: Antecedent or consequence? *Journal of Abnormal Psychology, 90,* 213-219.

Miranda, J. (1992). Dysfunctional thinking is activated by stressful life events. *Cognitive Therapy and Research, 16,* 473-483.

Miranda, J., & Persons, J. B. (1988). Dysfunctional attitudes are mood-state dependent. *Journal of Abnormal Psychology, 97* (1), 76-79.

Miranda, J., Persons, J. B., & Byers, C. N. (1990). Endorsement of dysfunctional beliefs depends on current mood state. *Journal of Abnormal Psychology, 99* (3), 237-241.

Morris, W. (Ed.). (1978). *The American heritage dictionary of the English language* (New college edition). Boston: Houghton Mifflin.

Moss, R. G., & Boren, J. H. (1972). Depression as a model for behavioral analysis. *Comprehensive Psychiatry, 13* (6), 581-590.

Overholser, J. C. (1996). Cognitive-behavioral treatment of depression, part VII: Coping with precipitating events. *Journal of Contemporary Psychotherapy, 26* (4), 337-360.

Persons, J. B., & Miranda, J. (1995). The search for mode-specific effects of cognitive and other therapies: A methodological suggestion. *Psychotherapy Research, 5* (2), 102-112.

Reitman, D, & Drabman, R. S. (1997). The value of recognizing our differences and promoting healthy competition: The cognitive behavioral debate. *Behavior Therapy, 28,* 419-429.

Robins, C. J., Block, P., & Peselow, E. D. (1990). Cognition and life events in major depression: A test of the mediation and interaction hypotheses. *Cognitive Therapy and Research, 14* (3), 299-313.

Safran, J. D. (1990a). Towards a refinement of cognitive therapy in light of interpersonal theory: I. Theory. *Clinical Psychology Review, 10,* 87-105.

Safran, J. D. (1990b). Towards a refinement of cognitive therapy in light of interpersonal theory: II. Practice. *Clinical Psychology Review, 10,* 107-121.

Safran, J. D., McMain, S., Crocker, P., & Murray, P. (1990). Therapeutic alliance rupture as a therapy event for empirical investigation. *Psychotherapy: Theory, Research and Practice, 27,* 154-165.

Safran, J. D., & Segal, Z. V. (1990). *Interpersonal process in cognitive therapy.* New York: Basic Books.

Safran, J. D., Vallis, T. M., Segal, Z. V., & Shaw, B. F. (1986). Assessment of core cognitive processes in cognitive therapy. *Cognitive Therapy and Research, 10* (5), 509-526.

Schmale, A. H. (1973). Adaptive role of depression in health and disease. In Scott, J. P., & Senay, E. C., (Eds.), *Separation and depression: Clinical and research aspects,* (pp. 187-214). (Publication No. 94) Washington, DC: American Association for the Advancement of Science.

Skinner, B. F. (1957, 1992). *Verbal behavior.* Acton, MA: Copley Publishing.

Skinner, B. F. (1974). *About behaviorism.* New York: Vintage Books.

Skinner, B. F. (1983). Can the experimental analysis of behavior rescue psychology? *The Behavior Analyst, 6* (1), 9-17.

Young, J. E. (1994). *Cognitive therapy for personality disorders: A schema-focused approach* (Rev. ed.). Sarasota, FL: Professional Resource Press.

Zeiss, A. M., & Jones, S. (1983). Behavioral treatment of depression: Examining treatment failures. In E. B. Foa and P. M. G. Emmelkamp (Eds.), *Failures in behavior therapy* (pp. 197-216). New York: Wiley.

Zettle, R. D., & Hayes, S. C. (1986). Dysfunctional control by client verbal behavior: The context of reason-giving. *The Analysis of Verbal Behavior, 4,* 30-38.

Zuroff, D. C. (1992). New directions for cognitive models of depression. *Psychological Inquiry, 3*, 274-277.

Zuroff, D. C., Igreja, I., & Mongrain, M. (1990). Dysfunctional attitudes, dependency, and self-criticism as predictors of depressive mood states: A 12-month longitudinal study. *Cognitive Therapy and Research, 14* (3), 315-326.

Chapter 7

A Process-Oriented Behavioral Approach to the Etiology, Maintenance, and Treatment of Anxiety-Related Disorders

John P. Forsyth
University at Albany, State University of New York

Over the last 30 years, behavior therapy has led the development of empirically derived and time-limited psychological interventions to assist those suffering from anxiety and fear-related problems. Yet, all is not well. Despite such developments, we are still far from producing overwhelming success rates in terms of long-term recovery and prevention of relapse. Indeed, many time-limited cognitive-behavioral interventions for anxiety-related disorders appear to produce equally time-limited treatment gains (Foa & Kozak, 1996). And, despite numerous theoretical and conceptual advances in understanding the etiology and maintenance of anxiety-related disorders, we still lack agreement on the critical variables that may be involved, and do not yet agree on how best to approach the problem (Rapee, 1996). The result has been a growing literature of conflicting and unrelated findings, numerous disagreements and controversies, and a proliferation of disorder specific mini-theories and models that implicate so many different hypothetical and real variables and processes that it is difficult to make any meaningful sense out of them (e.g., Barlow, 1988; Beck & Emery, 1985; Lang, 1985, 1993). This is somewhat ironic given that the anxiety disorders represent one of the more homogeneous diagnostic categories. Finally, despite refinements in our current nosological diagnostic system (*Diagnostic and Statistical Manual of Mental Disorders-IV*; American Psychiatric Association, 1994)—a system that has become more atheoretical, symptom based, and categorical in nature—we are still undecided about how best to classify and assess problems in living that are grouped under the anxiety disorders, with diagnostic reliability often taking precedence over validity (Brown, 1996). What is certain is that anxiety and fear-related problems are ubiquitous in human affairs and often represent the main concerns of clients seeking outpatient psychotherapy. What is more uncertain is whether cognitive-behavior therapists are addressing the real problem of anxiety and fear in the most parsimonious way.

Most chapters on the anxiety disorders describe etiological, theoretical, and treatment differences for each anxiety disorder consistent with the *Diagnostic and*

Statistical Manual of Mental Disorders-IV (DSM-IV); a system that classifies disorders and anxiety subtypes based on symptoms defined topographically and structurally, not functionally or dimensionally. Using the DSM system as a bedrock for conceptual and treatment development is problematic for a number of reasons, not the least of which is that it tells us little about processes involved in how one comes to have the symptoms that they do, and how those symptoms and associated problems in living can be effectively influenced in therapy. Indeed, it has become customary, if not mandatory, for behavior therapists to approach an analysis of the anxiety disorders as discrete diagnostic entities, with each having its own separate etiologies, and assessment and treatment strategies. As a result, the bigger picture is lost and readers of standard chapters and texts on the anxiety disorders can be easily left with the false impression that the anxiety disorders are more different than they really are. Clearly, there is considerable overlap across the anxiety disorders. Such overlap, in turn, suggests that common behavioral processes may be operative in how such problems develop, how they are maintained, and how they may be best treated. Perhaps if we were to come to grips with the common processes involved in how anxiety-related problems develop and are maintained, we might be in a more powerful position to produce longer lasting behavior change with our treatments and alleviate a wider range of human suffering. This is the more general aim of the present chapter.

In this chapter, a radically different behavioral approach is offered, one that attempts to elucidate core processes and functional similarities amongst the presumably "different" anxiety disorders, with an eye toward describing how such processes may be involved in producing more lasting behavior change and better treatment outcome. To set a context for the discussion, the first part of the chapter begins with an integrative overview of behavioral conceptualizations of the etiology and maintenance of anxious and fearful behavior, with particular emphasis on the role of verbal behavior and language and its relation to bodily events and private experiences. In so doing, attention is devoted to contemporary contextual approaches, and more specifically to the contexts of controllability, avoidance, and acceptance. The remainder of the chapter builds upon the theory-driven functional approach to understanding etiology, and extends this approach to treatment. In so doing, the role of nonacceptance, and particularly inflexible and rigid avoidance and control-based strategies, is highlighted and contrasted with more acceptance-based interventions. Finally, a different method to classify, assess, and treat anxiety problems is presented using dimensional and functional criteria based on common behavioral processes (Forsyth & Eifert, 1998). Such an approach was once the hallmark of good behavior therapy, and still remains the hallmark of behavior analysis, and its growing applied branch known as clinical behavior analysis.

Before proceeding, I would like to challenge the reader to put aside for a moment some of the following commonly held assumptions about anxiety: (a) that anxiety exists as something to be discovered rather than what a person does; (b) that anxiety is the cause of human suffering and life problems; and (c) that our task as therapists is to help clients "get rid of," "control," or "eliminate," faulty feelings or thoughts associated with anxiety and fear which are typically viewed as *the* problem from both the client's and therapist's perspective. In place of these assumptions, I offer a different view of anxiety and fear and its treatment, and hence psychological health.

Adaptive and Nonadaptive Dimensions of Anxiety and Fear: An Overview

Emotions, and particularly anxiety and fear, have captured the attention of much of applied psychology, and for good reasons. They are pervasive and fundamental emotional events; they can serve adaptive functions across species by mobilizing organisms to take action in response to real threat or danger. They can also pervade almost every aspect of one's existence by occurring immediately and without warning, and in the absence of real threat or danger. They can also become in a very literal sense defining of who we are (e.g., "I'm anxious," "I'm obsessive-compulsive," or "I'm a nervous wreck"), and they can, as a consequence, interfere with our ability to behave effectively and adaptively such as holding a job, having meaningful interpersonal relationships, caring for oneself and others, etc. When we speak of the anxiety disorders, we are not speaking of the experience of anxiety and fear in the adaptive sense, or as a normal emergency response to immediate or impending real threat or danger. Rather, persons suffering from such disorders share in common the nonadaptive experience of anxiety and fear in the *absence* of real threat or danger, and often to such a degree that it interferes with important areas of life functioning. Herein lies the crux of the problem, and answers to the following three questions may bear directly on therapeutic attempts at a solution: (a) what circumstances move someone from a normal and adaptive experience of anxiety and fear, to a nonadaptive or disordered experience of anxiety and fear? (b) is anxiety and fear the source or cause of suffering and clients' inability to behave effectively? and, (c) is the therapeutic solution to teach and help clients to reduce, eliminate, or better control such emotional experiences, or is there another way? In the sections to follow, each of these questions will be addressed in the context of a theory driven processes-oriented contextual approach to etiology and treatment.

Understanding the Etiology of Anxiety-Related Disorders

What is the Fundamental Problem

Most etiologic accounts of the anxiety disorders more of less start with the DSM-IV diagnostic typologies and work backwards. For example, we may start with the diagnostic criteria for panic disorder, and then attempt to provide an account of how such symptoms develop. In this case, the symptoms represent the problem and the phenomena to be explained, and numerous processes and mechanisms have been offered to explain the symptoms (e.g., Barlow, 1988; see McNally, 1990, for a review). From various theoretical perspectives, similar strategies have been applied to each of the 12 anxiety disorders described in the DSM-IV. Unfortunately, many elements of these theoretical models are one step removed from a working analysis and are not subject to direct influence in therapy (e.g., genetics, biological vulnerability, psychological vulnerability, thoughts, and the feelings themselves). This has left cognitive-behavior therapists in a somewhat weakened position because we cannot influence the underlying mechanisms directly. We can only influence the context directly, and, thereby, what a client thinks and feels.

A somewhat different approach would be to identify contextual factors with clear treatment implications in relation to core behavioral processes that may, either in whole or in part, lead to the more general problem of anxiety and fear, and particularly instances when such processes lead to suffering and life problems (Hayes, Wilson, Gifford, Follette, & Strosahl, 1996). With anxiety, for example, it is generally agreed that we are talking about a negatively evaluated neurobiological response that is relatively chronic or long-lived. Anxiety is also usually thought of as anxious apprehension about future events, in contrast to more immediate responses to real or imagined impending threat. Fear, on the other hand, is also a negatively evaluated neurobiological response, but unlike an anxious response, it is typically abrupt and occurs quickly in response to real or imagined threat. Thus, with both anxiety and fear we are talking about a negatively evaluated response; a response that is otherwise considered adaptive in many instances. Even laboratory animals can be shown to exhibit topographically similar responses, usually due to a history of some form of aversive conditioning. Yet, there is one main difference between infrahuman and human responses in this regard that is, indeed, fundamental. As Hayes and colleagues (1996) have pointed out, animals can be taught to respond discriminatively to their own responses (e.g., physical effects of a chemical substance) and can be taught to report when they have experienced an aversive event such as being shocked (Hayes et al., 1996). Yet, it is not aversive for an animal to report an aversive event, whereas for humans the labeling and reporting of an aversive environmental or bodily event may be aversive. This difference between animal and human learning is based, in large part, on humans' capacity for language and the verbal functions and meaning ascribed to emotional experience.

It is hard to imagine any emotional experience, whether adaptive or not, in the absence of verbal behavior. It is also equally hard to imagine any one of the anxiety disorders in the absence of humans responding to their own responses or environmental events in an effort to control, reduce, eliminate, escape, or avoid them. To illustrate with a somewhat absurd example, suppose that we lived in a world where all people experienced the following events chronically: racing heart, dizziness, breathlessness, and a great deal of perspiration. Let's also assume that such physical events were the rule, not the exception. Most of us then, would go about our daily activities sweating, breathing hard, being dizzy at times, and would likely carry extra clothes with us or perhaps wear none at all. Would such physical events be of any concern, or a reason to seek help? My guess is that they would not. In this *Panic World*, they would instead represent normal and normative events. In fact, what may be problematic is an instance where a person stopped breathing hard, or ceased perspiring profusely on a regular basis. In fact, in may be the case that in such instances, a person may be led to seek help from a physician or a psychologist to find ways to increase their heart rate or sweat gland activity. What may be even more "maladaptive" in such a world is for a person to attempt to reduce, eliminate, or control such physical events.

It is hard for us to imagine such a world, but doing so illustrates a point, namely, that how we feel and how we respond to what we feel is, in large part, a function of how we learn what it means to feel a given way. Direct contact with aversive events, in the absence of a verbal community, will not provide us with this information; though the effects of the aversive event, such as pain resulting from being bitten, may be quite real. We share one thing in common with the "maladaptive" inhabitants of *Panic World* in that we also try to eliminate, control, reduce, or avoid experiencing negative emotions such as anxiety, fear, and depression. Such attempts, in this view, are the more fundamental problem behind what we call the anxiety disorders.

Clients with post-traumatic stress disorder, for example, respond to a variety of events that are otherwise unwanted (e.g., physical sensations, reminders of the trauma, memories), and the effects of those events (i.e., flashbacks, dissociation, numbing, increased arousal, tension, disrupted interpersonal and occupational functioning), in an attempt not to have or experience them. Similarly, persons with specific phobias often "rationally" acknowledge that they should not be afraid, but yet still respond to verbal and nonverbal reminders of the phobic stimulus as something that they would otherwise not want to experience. Persons with panic disorder likewise respond to their own benign bodily events as indicative of threat or danger, and often do everything they can to not experience such events, including agoraphobic avoidance, and the use of anxiolytics and controlled substances. Persons suffering from social phobias and generalized anxiety disorder also demonstrate an unwillingness to experience what are otherwise normal physical and psychological emotional reactions; though such persons may endure anxiety-evoking situations with great distress. The same is true of persons with obsessive compulsive disorder, where the issue shifts to unwanted thoughts and needless rituals. Thus, all the anxiety disorders share at least one fundamental thread in common; namely, persons do not like how they think and feel and engage in behaviors to reduce, control, or avoid such private experiences. The paradox, however, is that persons can never truly escape from or avoid their bodies or their psychological experience. The person who panics in a mall and escapes outside, takes their responses, thoughts, and emotional experiences with them.

The question now is what circumstances lead humans to respond to their own responses and what role (if any) do such behaviors play in the development and maintenance of anxiety-related disorders? To answer this question in a manner that has some treatment utility, we need to step outside the skin of emotional experience for a moment and consider two related issues: First, how do aversive stimulus and response functions become related to verbal and nonverbal events, and secondly, what circumstances lead humans to respond to such responses in a manner that results in psychological suffering and life problems.

Early Conditioning Views and Controversies:
Anxiety and Fear in Total Isolation

Historically, learning or conditioning has been at the core of behavioral explanations of the etiology of fear and anxiety-related disorders. According to this view, fear and anxiety are considered responses to otherwise innocuous environmental and bodily stimuli that are acquired via some form of aversive conditioning, most often Pavlovian or respondent conditioning (Rachman, 1977, 1991; Wolpe, 1958). For a time, conditioning views had great appeal and led to the development of several efficacious treatments for anxiety disorders, based largely on in vivo and imaginal extinction and exposure paradigms (e.g., Eysenck, 1987; Wolpe, 1958). These techniques were firmly rooted in the conditioning theories of Hull (1943), Pavlov (1927), Skinner (1938), and Watson (1930) and emphasized the role of observable processes while minimizing the role of cognitive mediation. It was not long, however, before many questioned the viability of this model as a comprehensive account of how one learns to be afraid or anxious.

Although a variety of criticisms were launched, the most damaging criticisms were derived from clinical observation suggesting that direct traumatic conditioning is often the exception, not the rule (Lazarus, 1984). That is, across most of the anxiety disorders, finding a traumatic event to account for etiology—with the exception of posttraumatic stress disorder (PTSD) which is defined, in part, by the occurrence of a identifiable trauma or conditioning event—is unusual, if not rare (Menzies & Clarke, 1995; Mineka & Zinbarg, 1996). Even in cases where exposure to trauma or extreme stress can be identified, it is not uncommon to find that many persons still emerge psychologically unscathed. Such findings, though largely based on retrospective self-report, were sufficient in leading many to view the respondent conditioning paradigm as limited, unidimensional, and lacking in complexity to account for the multifaceted ways that people can become fearful and anxious (see Forsyth & Eifert, 1996a, 1996b, for reviews and reconceptualizations).

We now know, however, that respondent conditioning is considerably more complex than previously thought or described (Mineka & Zinbarg, 1996). In humans, for example, respondent conditioning processes can be established with either a respondent or operant preparation (Schlinger & Blakely, 1994; Staats & Eifert, 1990). Further, such processes are often heavily dependent on language. Thus, if I punish acting out behavior in my child by spanking (an aversive event), and the probability of the child's behavior decreases in the future in similar circumstances, the spanking can be said to function technically as a punisher. Now, suppose I see the child acting out and say "If you don't stop I am going to give you a spanking." Here, the word spanking is no longer a neutral word, and will likely evoke aversive responses in the child, and quite likely fear, because the word spanking has acquired aversive psychological functions in the past. That is, spanking is not only an event, but it is also an event that can be named and experienced without necessarily contacting the contingencies directly. Similar effects with language have been demonstrated reliably in experimental conditioning studies using both respondent (semantic conditioning) and operant (equivalence) preparations (see Forsyth & Eifert, 1996a, for a review). Semantic conditioning has shown how emotional functions can be acquired via directly or higher-order relations with emotion-eliciting events, whereas equivalence has expanded this view to account for the transfer of numerous functions that need not be trained directly. With equivalence, for example, it appears that once humans learn that certain members of a class of verbal and nonverbal events belong together (i.e., they are functionally equivalent), simply applying a new psychological function to one member of the class can result in that function transferring to all members of the class without direct pairings. This effect has been demonstrated in several studies with respondent fear evoking, avoidance, and extinction-related functions (see Augustson & Dougher, 1997; Dougher, Augustson, Markham, Greenway, & Wulfurt, 1994; Dougher & Markham, 1994). Such verbal processes are frequently overlooked by critics of respondent conditioning, in part, because of a somewhat narrow and limited view of respondent learning processes as being equivalent to respondent preparations involving pairings between nonverbal neutral stimuli (NSs) and nonverbal unconditioned stimuli (UCSs).

Equally overlooked is the importance of the response in relation to verbal and nonverbal objects or events in such learning, and other critical dimensions of the response such as intensity and duration. Instead, the tendency has been to define clinical fear onset in terms of being able to document relations that conform to laboratory fear conditioning preparations. Thus, failing to find specific instances of previous NS-UCS pairings has been taken to mean that fear or anxiety must have been acquired via some other nonassociative process (e.g., Menzies & Clarke, 1995). Stated somewhat differently, conditioning preparations are equivalent to aversive learning processes, and the failure to attribute aversive learning to a conditioning preparation means that learning processes are not involved.

From either an experimenter's or clinician's perspective, it makes sense to talk about identifiable and manipulable UCSs in relation to objects or events in the environment as evidence of conditioning processes. From this perspective, traumatic or painful environmental UCSs serve as conditioning events. From the research participant's or client's perspective, the conditioning event may not be UCS per se, but the effects of the UCS in producing untoward psychological and biological responses. Eysenck (1987) made a similar observation, noting that humans experience the psychological effects of aversive events (UCSs), not the UCSs themselves. It is those psychological effects, or more accurately the aversive response and stimulus functions, that serve as the basis for establishing and altering the functions of other verbal and nonverbal events in the environment and those occurring within the skin. In other words, the bodily response is the conditioning event and what serves as the basis for the transfer of aversive functions to verbal and nonverbal events (Forsyth & Eifert, 1996b).

This view may help explain cases of fear onset in the absence of an identifiable environmental conditioning event. In such cases, the conditioning event may consist of an aversive, negatively evaluated neurobiological response similar to a panic attack. To date, two experimental studies from our laboratory suggest that panic-like responses, induced by breathing high concentrations of carbon-dioxide enriched air (UCS), can function as conditioning events (see Forsyth & Eifert, in press). Although preliminary, it also appears that the magnitude of fear condition-ing and resistance to extinction is largely mediated by the intensity of the UCR, not the intensity of the UCS (see also Forsyth, Daleiden, & Chorpita, 1998, for a study demonstrating the importance of response intensity in fear onset over UCS intensity). This emerging body of research suggests documenting the onset and maintenance of anxiety-related problems should focus on the frequency, intensity, and duration of untoward bodily responses as events that can serve to establish and maintain fearful and anxious behavior to a variety of bodily and environmental cues and circumstances. Such aversive response functions, whether established via respondent or operant contingencies, can be flexibly applied and modified depending on the context or circumstances that serve to establish and modify them.

To summarize, much of the controversy and confusion over the place of conditioning in fear onset has been the result of disagreements over what consti-tutes a conditioning event, and what exactly is being conditioned. Disagreements have also been due, in part, to the tendency to equate experimental conditioning preparations with clinical processes. However, making a distinction between preparation and process may be useful in directing attention to the complexity of respondent and operant learning and by focusing our attention on the salient processes involved. Experimentally it is important to be able to identify and influence the stimuli and the relation between them to establish process, but clinically it is not. By the time clients enter therapy, there are often a host of multiple operant and respondent circumstances that have, either in whole or in part, led to significant life problems. Attempting, therefore, to isolate any one preparation as responsible for anxiety or fear would seem difficult, if not impossible, in most clinical cases given the difficulties in reliably accounting for important etiological variables that may have contributed to the current presenting problem(s). Further, we should not expect clients to be accurate in reporting what caused their fear or anxiety, for we know that humans are often poor in accounting for the subtle and often complex circumstances that control their behavior. Salient processes, and the psychological effects of past and present circumstances, are immediately available and often serve as intervention targets in therapy; a point I will return to again shortly.

Contemporary Views: Anxiety and Fear in Context

In recent years, behavior therapists have rediscovered the importance of context to explain the development and maintenance of anxiety-related disorders (see Mineka & Zinbarg, 1996, for a review). Such contexts include, but are not limited to, past experiential history with unpredictable and uncontrollable life events, current stressful life events, and verbal behavior. Recognizing the impor-tance of context is critical in explaining the rich complexity of human emotional behavior, and how relevant processes from one's past can be potentiated or depotentiated in the present. To illustrate, suppose we pair a shock with a square in the presence of a blue light, but in the presence of a green light shock is never paired with the square. The likely result of this training is that the square will evoke some type of fear response in the presence of the blue light but not in the presence of the green light. Both humans and animals can learn such straightforward conditional discriminations, and it would be difficult to imagine instances of learning where relations were invariably fixed once established and not modifiable by a given set of circumstances. Taking a more clinically-relevant example, it is not uncommon for clients who suffer from panic attacks to report that their attacks are less severe in the context of a clinic or a research laboratory; however, in the context of being alone, those very same events are often experienced as quite severe and disruptive. In both circumstances, the physical events felt in the "attack" may be quite similar, but the meaning and application of a particular relational response to those felt events is quite different. Context, therefore, seems critical not only in the establishment of emotional behavior, but also in how such behavior manifests and functions, and how it can be influenced in therapy. Of interest to the present discussion, are those contextual processes that can be modified and influenced in therapy, and particularly the role of language and verbal functions in relation to emotional experience, and how such verbal behavior can interfere with effective action and contribute to human suffering.

Toward a Process-Oriented Account of Etiology and Maintenance

The Language Hypothesis and the Meaning of Anxiety and Fear

Much of what we call human emotional experience is intimately intertwined with language and verbal behavior. As indicated, it is difficult to imagine a psychological experience of emotion such as love, joy, hate, fear, or anxiety without language and a verbal community that repeatedly questions its members about how they feel and how their feelings and thoughts relate to how they behave. Such words, however, are more than just fear-eliciting stimuli, for they have come to mean something to us as a result of our unique social-verbal experiences. Although an important subset of the human emotional experience of anxiety and fear may be influenced by direct contact with aversive events (e.g., direct traumatic conditioning), much of this experience appears to be influenced indirectly via verbal-symbolic experiences.

Language is important because it can provide humans with emotional experiences without actual contact with the physical stimuli or events that ordinarily elicit those responses (Staats & Eifert, 1990). In this sense, language and verbal communication can often be adaptive in helping us predict our own behavior and that of others as well as in avoiding direct contact with contingencies that might otherwise cause significant harm or even death. There is also a darker side to language, for the very same processes that lead to adaptive functioning can also interfere with adaptive functioning (Hayes & Wilson, 1993). For example, responding to a fast beating heart with "I'm going crazy and dying" is not the same thing as the actual experience of going crazy and dying. Indeed, such statements are quite common among persons with panic disorder, and yet most have never contacted the actual experience of craziness or death. Similarly, thinking about a past traumatic event, is not the same thing as physically being back in the context of the trauma where there was real threat and danger; a distinction which, by the way, is often extremely difficult for persons suffering from posttraumatic stress disorder to make.

The only way to account for the establishment of such functions and how they are learned is to address the meaning of verbal-emotional events in the psychological sense and not in the literal sense. Yet, it is very difficult to avoid getting trapped in the literal content of client verbalizations as if what clients say is, in fact, what is going on psychologically (e.g., "I can't fly in planes *because* I am anxious," or "I can't speak in front of a group *because* I will panic"). Everyday language also underscores the difference between feelings and behavior, and laypersons commonly give feelings some causal role in their actions. For example, we speak of being "gripped" by fear, "overcome" by anger, "paralyzed" by anxiety, and "haunted" by remorse. Such locutions carry a very powerful message, that being, my actions are not my actions and the I who is me was temporarily taken over by some*thing* else that is not me (Forsyth, 1998). Such expressions represent emotions as things that happen to us, which are for the most part outside our personal control. As Averill (1980) notes, "[i]t is as though emotions were alien forces which 'overcome' and 'possess' and individual" (p. 151). Such reasons sound quite reasonable at first glance, and direct attention to the feeling as the cause of the client's inability to behave effectively. This view also makes intuitive sense if one views "what one thinks" in relation to "what one experiences or feels" as the problem. What follows from this view, however, is that to change the problem, one must change either how one thinks or how one feels.

Not surprisingly, mainstream cognitive-behavioral treatments often view dysfunctional thoughts and feelings as the problem, and attempt to help clients to eliminate, control, or reduce them (e.g., Barlow, 1988; Beck & Emery, 1985). Such treatments also maintain, either explicitly or implicitly, that to live a happy and successful life one must experience good feelings and thoughts and that bad or aversive ones are not healthy and are the cause of human suffering. By explicitly targeting these "unhealthy" private events in therapy, many behavior therapists are also assuming that the thoughts or feelings are the source of the problem. Otherwise, it would make no sense to target them for change (cf. Forsyth & Eifert, in press). Yet, there is little clinical or experimental evidence to support the conclusion that it is necessary to change what a client thinks to produce a positive therapeutic outcome in most persons suffering from anxiety-related disorders. Such research is notoriously difficult to do, for in order to show that changing a thought or feeling was necessary for a change in behavior, we would have to be able to influence the thought or feeling apart from other behaviors and circumstances that might also be influencing the thought or feeling. A somewhat different strategy would be to attempt to influence the context of the feelings directly, and hence the thought-feeling relation.

A clinical behavior analytic approach to the psychological meaning of verbal events entails different assumptions and strategies than those used within mainstream behavior therapy. Most notably, verbal relations are contextually sensitive and functionally defined (Hayes & Wilson, 1993). Thus, the meaning of anxiety in a psychological sense represents a complex act of relating largely arbitrary verbal-symbolic events with other events and psychological functions in and within a context. The context, therefore, is crucial in determining the kinds of verbal-emotive relations and behaviors that may occur. Further, thoughts and feelings are not viewed as causes of suffering or as obstacles to change (Hayes & Wilson, 1994). Rather, such private events are viewed as behaviors that are learned, shaped, and influenced by the often subtle circumstances which give rise to them. What follows from this perspective is the assumption that just as there is "knowing what to do" so to there is "knowing what to feel." Both involve verbal understanding of some activity and the relation between them and the circumstances that can either potentiate or depotentiate such relations.

This brings us to one of the more unique and important features of the language of feeling, that is, its referential or relational quality (Forsyth & Eifert, 1996a). Words such as anxious or afraid either explicitly or implicitly establish relations with other events such as "I am anxious or afraid of...something, some event, or someone (including the self). To say, "anxious," "afraid," or even "depressed" without some relational referent would strip these words of their meaning (i.e., their functions). The relational quality of emotional language, in turn, can only be identified by certain descriptions. These descriptions are often tied to occurrences of behavior and events with a variety of stimulus functions (e.g., eliciting, evocative, reinforcing, punishing) and meanings (e.g., good, bad, unpleasant, painful). In turn, people often describe their emotional experiences metaphorically in ways that others can understand (e.g., "When I feel anxious it's like a knife going though my chest" or "When I'm depressed...I feel empty"). Such metaphorical extensions have no real counterpart inside the person. Instead they function to communicate the meaning of emotional experience by identifying and relating events with known stimulus functions. One consequence of such actions, however, is that the metaphor can come to mean, in a very literal sense, what is actually going on psychologically (Hayes & Wilson, 1994).

Although this topic is exceedingly complex, the main point to be made here is that one cannot know what it means to feel X without first understanding what it is to feel X. To do this, however, requires verbal specification of what is felt (either privately or overtly) in order for it to be labeled and experienced as such. For instance, even saying "I have a feeling" as vague as it may seem, meets this requirement. This is not to imply that the process cannot occur without awareness, for there is sufficient evidence that verbal and nonverbal learning can occur without immediate awareness (e.g., Öhman & Soares, 1993, 1994). Rather, the main issue is that the concept of emotion is, by definition, related to meaning and function. Nothing about the form of central nervous system responses (e.g., increased heart rate or electrodermal activity) requires them to stand for a particular emotional description or experience such as fear, despite years of research attempting to show just that (Averill, 1980; Barlow, 1988). Similarly, nothing inherent in the formal properties of words denoting emotional experience (e.g., anxiety, fear, anguish, terror, joy) requires it to stand in relation to a particular bodily or environmental referent. Indeed, depending on the cultural context, a variety of emotions may be fashioned from the same biological system. Conversely, elements from several different biological systems may be involved in the psychological experience of a single emotion. For the most part, however, biology only sets limits upon the social construction of emotional experience (Averill, 1980). Instead, the stimuli and events placed in a relation and the nature of that relation are determined by the social-verbal community without regard for the formal properties of the stimuli involved (Hayes & Hayes, 1989). In other words, the relation between the "language of anxiety and fear" and the "feeling of anxiety and fear" is arbitrary in the sense that we use certain words, and not others, to convey emotional experience, and more importantly perhaps, what it means to feel a given way.

Relational Responding to Verbal-Derived Events as a Core Problem

As outlined, anxious and fearful responses are quite adaptive under normal circumstances in preparing humans to take immediate life preserving action. In circumstances where we are faced with immediate or possible future threat or danger, we do not normally ask ourselves "why we felt afraid or anxious." We act first, and then ask questions later. The situation is different when considering persons suffering from anxiety-related disorders in that such persons often respond to the stimulus functions of their responses and environmental events, and fail to act effectively as a result. That is, given what is otherwise a normal emotional response, persons with anxiety disorders respond to their responses in an effort to eliminate, control, or avoid them in some way. Again, it is difficult to imagine a "disordered" experience of fear or anxiety in the absence of avoidance and control-based strategies. For example, a person with obsessive compulsive disorder may often try not to think about yelling profanities aloud during a church service, whereas a person with posttraumatic stress disorder may attempt to avoid thinking about the original trauma and circumstances that are functionally equivalent to the original traumatic event.

Yet, there is now sufficient evidence from the thought suppression literature that such strategies are largely ineffective and may even serve to make the unwanted thought and related emotional experience occur with more frequency, especially in contexts where being able to control the thought and feeling is most desired (Hayes et al., 1996; Lavy & van den Hout, 1990). For instance, attempts not to think about yelling profanities is itself a thought about profanities. To the extent that profanities is also associated with a variety of negative functions, the thought itself my bring about the very experience that is otherwise unwanted and when it is most unwanted, such as during a church service. Panic disorder is also another good example of a strategy of responding to one's own responses as if the responses themselves were the problem. Indeed, across all the anxiety disorders, we can find evidence of person's unwillingness to experience unwanted thoughts and feelings, and the use of such avoidance strategies as reasons for suffering and an inability to life a happy and meaningful life. This is not to diminish the reality of the suffering experienced by persons with any one of the anxiety disorders. Rather, what I am suggesting is that such persons are literally trapped in a pattern of avoidance and control that is largely ineffective as a solution to their suffering precisely because their experience of suffering is psychological and experiential and cannot be effectively avoided or controlled (see Hayes, 1994).

Here, I do not wish to imply that avoidance and control of thoughts, feelings, and emotional experience is uniformly pathogenic. In fact, in many circumstances, it may be the failure of emotional inhibition and control that is problematic. Uninhibited outbursts of anger and rage is one example of an instance where some degree of emotional regulation is desirable, especially for others that may bear the cost of such unfettered expression. Yet, there is a growing body of evidence suggesting that emotional experience can by inhibited and controlled only to a point. Gross and Levenson (1997), for example, found that attempts to suppress either positive or negative emotions does not provide relief from the psychological experience of that emotion. In fact, just the opposite occurs; the emotion becomes stronger and more salient, and results in increases in activation of the sympathetic nervous system. Further, their research suggests that hiding or suppressing one's emotions is unlikely to help one feel better, and that battles to fight one's psychology may result in more psychopathology and suffering.

Such findings, although preliminary, appear quite applicable to persons suffering from anxiety-related disorders. In such cases, it is not necessarily the emotional inhibition that is the problem, but emotional inhibition that is chronic, inflexible, and insensitive to circumstances in the environment. In particular, it appears that inhibition of unwanted emotional experience, when applied in contexts that demand or evoke emotional experience and its expression, is the likely culprit. Such inhibitory strategies, in turn, can result in impaired cognitive processing, limited ability to engage in effective and meaningful action, decreased contact with reinforcing consequences, and significant social and interpersonal suffering.

Attempts, therefore, to teach clients to become better suppressors or avoiders of their unwanted thoughts and fearful or anxious feelings is unlikely to work as a lasting solution, for this is what many persons with anxiety-related problems are already attempting to do by the time they enter therapy. Further, targeting the unwanted thought or feeling in therapy is also likely to result in only short term gains, in part, because the implication is that such private events are the problem, and when they occur again (and they will likely occur again), they should be controlled or else more problems may result. Moreover, such strategies also imply that psychological health occurs only at one end of the emotional spectrum (i.e., positive thoughts and feelings), and that negative emotional experience is problematic and the cause of life problems. Yet, we do not live in a world where people only experience good thoughts and feelings (Hayes, 1994). Indeed, what makes us human is our capacity to experience a wide range of emotional experience, and to adapt and behave effectively despite what we may think or feel.

In the remaining sections, I describe a functional and process-oriented approach to assessment and treatment that builds on the preceding analysis that may assist behavior therapists in producing more lasting and meaningful behavior change in their clients presenting with anxiety and fear-related disorders.

Cognitive-Behavioral Treatments for Anxiety Disorders: Moving Beyond Symptom Alleviation

As indicated, many clients who eventually seek treatment for anxiety-related complaints come to therapy for one main reason: they do not like how they think or feel. If this were the whole story, then it would make complete sense to help clients change how they think or feel. But there is usually more to the problem than the feeling or thought. Many clients not only dislike how they feel, but they also dislike the disruptive consequences of their feelings on their ability to live a happy and successful life. In many cases, fear and anxiety are disruptive precisely because client's respond inflexibly and rigidly to their own responses in an effort to control or avoid experiencing them. Further, many anxious and fearful clients often use their unwanted feelings and thoughts as good reasons for not behaving effectively. The consequences of such strategies, however, severely interfere with and restrict other important areas of the person's life which, in turn, further compounds the problem. In fact, many behavior problems occur when ineffective *verbal* behavior gets in the way of effective action. If this is the case, then what can be done about it?

Mainstream Cognitive-Behavioral Interventions: Symptom Mastery and Control as a Path Toward Psychological Health

Most empirically-derived cognitive-behavior therapies for the anxiety disorders view a client's symptoms as the problem, and with the therapeutic solution being to help clients to either master, control, or to alleviate their symptoms as a means to achieve psychological health (e.g., Barlow, Rapee, & Brown, 1992). Often this is achieved, or at least initiated, by getting clients to confront feared objects or aversive bodily events in a safe therapeutic context, which is believed to facilitate corrective emotional learning and fear reduction. A variety of techniques are believed to facilitate this process, including direct exteroceptive or interoceptive in vivo exposure, imaginal exposure, thought stopping, response prevention, flooding, systematic desensitization, worry control and decatastrophizing, cognitive restructuring, systematic desensitization, guided imagery, breathing retraining, and progressive muscle relation, to name a few. Such techniques, in turn, have a more general objective; namely, to get clients to experience unpleasant thoughts and feelings that they have otherwise avoided, and to learn how to reduce or control them in the future. Many of these and other-related techniques have been shown to be quite efficacious, at least in the short term, in producing symptom reduction and relief for most clients most of the time. Not surprisingly, therefore, many empirically-derived treatments for anxiety disorders include such techniques as components of comprehensive treatment manuals developed for many of the DSM anxiety disorders: panic disorder (e.g., Mastery of Your Anxiety and Panic, 2nd ed.; Barlow & Craske, 1994), specific phobias (e.g., Mastery of Your Specific Phobia; Antony, Craske, & Barlow, 1995), obsessive-compulsive disorder (Mastery of Obsessive-Compulsive Disorder; Foa & Kozak, 1997), and generalized anxiety disorder (Mastery of Your Anxiety and Worry; Craske, Barlow, & O'Leary, 1992), to name a few.

The word "mastery," as contained in the titles of such manuals is not accidental, but descriptive of the underlying philosophy and approach of such treatments. For in most cases, the aim of the techniques outlined in manualized treatments is to assist clients in becoming better at controlling (i.e., mastering) their thoughts and emotional experiences (i.e., the symptoms) by giving clients more and "better" control and avoidance strategies, or by replacing "dysfunctional" thoughts and feelings with more "functional" thoughts and feelings. As such, most of these and other similar manualized treatments for anxiety-related disorders are symptom-based and disorder grounded, not process-based and contextually grounded. In other words, the techniques and manuals devised to address disorders and symptoms overlook process in favor of symptom mastery and control. Matching treatments to disorders and symptoms, however, is somewhat antithetical to the original aims and goals of behavior therapy. That is, matching treatments to disorders or symptoms is a structural, topographic, and normative approach; it yields little information that is useful to the individual case; it fosters treatments that are eliminative, not constructive; and, it contributes little to a scientific understanding of the principles, processes, and mechanisms that contribute to the presenting symptoms and psychological suffering. There is also every reason to believe that most clients may not need all components of a treatment manual to improve. Thus, some degree of idiographic tailoring of treatment is often necessary and desirable; though some have argued that individualized treatment does not outperform more standardized treatment packages (see Eifert, Schulte, Zvolensky, Lejuez, & Lau, 1997). The question, however, is whether more could be done in such treatments to move beyond simple symptom alleviation to more lasting improvement and functioning

Moving Beyond Symptom Alleviation Toward More Fundamental Behavior Change

Perhaps it goes without saying that clients can present with the same symptoms for entirely different reasons, and that DSM-IV diagnostic categories can be produced via many different processes. With the anxiety disorders, we are not only talking about symptoms, but symptoms that are actively struggled with, avoided, or often controlled unsuccessfully in some way. Such patterns of control and avoidance are often ingrained by the time clients enter into therapy. Indeed, the fact that most clients are unwilling and often reluctant to engage in exposure exercises is quite informative in many respects, and is perhaps even diagnostic of this more fundamental problem. In such exercises, we are asking clients to directly experience psychological events that they have been struggling to control, reduce, or avoid in some way.

There is also every indication to believe that exposure will not be effective if clients avoid experiencing or otherwise struggle with their thoughts and feelings during exposure. In fact, when this happens, it can often have the undesired effect of increasing the very events that are being targeted for corrective emotional change in treatment, and thereby further solidifying negative verbal-emotive functions with other behaviors. There is also compelling evidence that fear or anxiety extinction is not necessary as a precursor of avoidance response extinction (Rachman, 1985, for a review and critical evaluation). Fear reduction, therefore, is not a necessary condition for change, but dealing with avoidance behavior is necessary. If our treatment techniques fail to address the more fundamental struggle to avoid experiencing negative thoughts and emotions, and if clients continue to believe that such private experiences are the causes and reasons for life suffering, then those very same techniques will play into the very system of control and avoidance that clients believe is the solution to their problems.

Thus, with most mainstream cognitive-behavioral interventions, we are, in effect, teaching clients that (a) their thoughts and feelings are the cause of their suffering and life problems; (b) that in order to live a happy and successful life they need to become better at mastering (i.e., controlling or reducing) unwanted thoughts and feelings; (c) we are going to give our clients new techniques to accomplish better control of their private experiences for anxiety-related problems; and (d) if and when they are better at controlling their thoughts and feelings, they will then become better at living a happy and productive life. A somewhat different strategy may be to address the struggle to control and avoid unwanted thoughts and feelings directly, and hence the problem of unwanted thoughts and feelings.

Altering the Struggle to Control and Avoid as a Fundamental Process in Treatment

Throughout this chapter, I have argued that many persons with anxiety-related disorders dislike how they think and feel, and engage in a variety of deliberate and automatic strategies to avoid or control such private experiences. Most of this behavior seems to be governed by the view by clients that "if I were only able to think and feel differently, then I might be able to behave differently." The corollary of this perspective is that my thoughts and feelings are the cause of my problems. We are all Westernized into this view, and much of our psychological establishment similarly accepts private experiences as causes and reasons for suffering (cf. Hayes, 1994). We do not generally believe that persons can behave effectively despite what they may think or feel. Yet, this is often what needs to happen for persons with anxiety-related problems to get better. As indicated, exposure-based interventions are one direct means to achieve this end; altering the struggle to control and avoid is another. This latter alternative, one that is different from emotional control techniques in cognitive-behavior therapy, is at the core of clinical behavior analytic strategies and has been referred to as psychological acceptance.

Emotional and experiential acceptance as a fundamental process. The notion of acceptance is not new to psychology, but it has been gaining more widespread attention in recent years (see Hayes, Jacobson, Follette, & Dougher, 1994, for a detailed conceptual and technical analysis of the varieties of psychological acceptance as well as its relevance in treating a variety of problems in living). Although the concept of acceptance is, at times, difficult to operationalize and pin down, it can be described more generally as a person's willingness to experience thoughts and feelings fully and without any attempt to control or avoid them. In the realm of psychological experience, this involves a willingness to experience events fully and without defense for what they are and not what we say they are. More technically, acceptance involves contacting the direct or automatic stimulus functions of events without (a) acting to reduce or manipulate those functions and (b) acting because of their derived verbal functions (cf. Hayes, 1994).

By definition, the problems categorized under the anxiety disorders, all share the feature of nonacceptance (i.e., avoidance and control), and often to such an extent that it is rigidly and inflexibly applied to the point of leading to diminished contact with the world and one's own psychological experiences. Thus, with relatively new acceptance based behavior-analytic strategies, an attempt is made to alter the struggle of control and avoidance itself, often verbally, with the goal of getting clients to behave despite what they think or feel. According to this perspective, thoughts and feelings are not viewed as the causes of suffering or as the obstacles to change. Rather, it is a person's avoidance and control-based strategies, when applied to the realm of private experience, that is problematic. Put simply, it is the person's change agenda, or view that they need to be something other than they are, that is the problem. This change agenda, in turn, represents the "context" or "system" in which the client operates; a system that, by the time a client seeks help in therapy, is largely ineffective as a solution. With acceptance-based strategies, an attempt is made to undermine clients' existing patterns of control and avoidance, and the verbally-derived stimulus functions of such relations, by establishing a new verbal context in therapy. The goal of such interventions, therefore, is not to get the client to think and feel differently, but rather to think and to feel what is there to be thought and felt, and to behave effectively. Paradoxical and experiential exercises represent one useful way of achieving this goal, but other techniques are also used.

Undermining experiential avoidance and control via paradoxical directives and experiential exercises. At a conceptual level, paradoxical techniques place both the symptoms and explanations in a different context, one in which they lose their original function and meaning. Clinically, paradoxical techniques commonly take the form of verbal injunctions (e.g., "I want you to change by staying the same") and symptom prescriptions (e.g., "Hmm, it sounds as though you are having about 4-5 panic attacks weekly...Now, what I would like you to do is to have 5-10 panic attacks weekly, but not fewer...Can you do that for me?") that, if taken literally, are nonsensical and contrary to what clients expect from therapy and what they have learned needs to be done to resolve their problems. Paradoxical techniques, when used explicitly and judiciously, can weaken and modify existing relational or functional equivalence classes without necessarily changing their form or frequency (e.g., reason giving, control over private events, and avoidance of painful feelings). Further, such techniques, when used in the context of acceptance, create a therapeutic double-bind by implying that the only way to change is to remain unchanged (cf. Hayes & Wilson, 1994).

Paradoxical interventions also rely on the patients' conceptualizations of their problems and their attempts at solving these problems. As Nardone and Watzlawick (1993) suggest, "clinical experience has shown that, ironically, it is often the patient's very attempts to solve the problem that, in fact, maintains it. The attempted solution becomes the true problem" (p. 51). For example, "anxiety" and "fear" cease to be mere words, but represent a series of other involuntary events (i.e., symptoms) and consequences of what it means to have anxiety (e.g., "I'm dying, "I'm going crazy" or "I'll humiliate myself"). Clients who then view anxiety or fear as bad and as something to be avoided, in turn, engage in a variety of strategies to solve the problem such as cognitive avoidance, overt behavioral avoidance, distraction, medications, use of controlled substances, and deliberate thought and emotional suppression. The result, however, is often not the elimination of anxiety or fear, but more of the same, and diminished contact with other meaningful activities. Paradoxical techniques undermine this preexisting system of verbal constructions and reactions regarding reality by breaking the cycle of repetitive behavior that forms the "attempted solution" (cf. Nardone & Watzlawick, 1993).

To illustrate, we saw a woman in our clinic who had been struggling unsuccessfully to control her worry and physical tension. Initially she viewed her worry, physical tension, and nervousness as the main problem in her life and the reason why she could not be happy and do the things she previously enjoyed doing. She was, however, an avid baker. Over the course of therapy, the therapist used the client's baking activities to undermine her struggle to control and avoid by directly challenging her in session.

Therapist: "You said that you love to bake and that you are quite good at it."

Client: "Oh yes, I'm quite a good baker."

Therapist: "You also said that your worry and tension has been getting in the way of several meaningful activities in your life"

Client: "Yes...It has been brutal...I wish I could get rid of it and move on with my life"

Therapist: "From the sounds of it, I bet that your worry and anxiety must keep you from baking too...Also, I'd bet, given what you've said, that if I made you really anxious and worried you couldn't bake a thing"

Client: "Like hell!...Nothing can keep me from baking when I want to"

Therapist: "I see...so you can bake despite what you think and feel, but somehow you can't do other things because of how you think and feel...Is that true?"

Client: "Well...uh...not really"

From this point on in therapy, our client began to see her former solutions to her problems as problems in themselves (Hayes & Wilson, 1994), and eventually committed herself to behaving despite her thoughts and feelings. A variety of experiential exercises, such as in vivo and imaginal exposure, were included to facilitate this process. Such exercises were used to help our client more fully experience her thoughts and feelings for what they are. In so doing, such exercises also likely had the indirect effect of changing the evocative aversive functions of such events and, more importantly perhaps, her responses to them. As she said to us during a six month follow-up visit, "I used to cross bridges before I got to them, now I don't cross those bridges until there is a real bridge to cross...Then, I just deal with it and move on."

Some final thoughts and implications for acceptance-based approaches with anxiety-related disorders. Acceptance-based strategies appear to offer an alternative approach to psychological health and well-being that is quite different from most mainstream cognitive-behavioral interventions for the anxiety-disorders. Foremost, it redirects attention away from symptom alleviation as a goal and problem in itself to the context of the symptoms (both public and private) and the circumstances that contribute to and maintain such symptoms. Therapy, and particularly the actions of therapists and clients in session, are viewed as one important context that can be directly influenced, not the client's thoughts or feelings.

The acceptance-based contextual approach is also unique in that it is process-focused, idiographic and functional, not mechanistic, structural, or symptom-focused. When viewed within the framework of acceptance, most anxiety-related disorders represent verbally-derived and largely ineffective strategies of control and avoidance that interfere with effective action. As long as such strategies are in place and misapplied in areas where they are ineffective (i.e., with thoughts and feelings), any targeting of symptoms in therapy will also likely be ineffective in the long run. Thus, to produce better long term outcome and greater functioning, it appears that greater attention should be devoted to influencing more entrenched and ineffective patterns of behavioral control and avoidance of negative thoughts and emotions as part of more comprehensive treatments for anxiety-related disorders.

Obviously, acceptance-based interventions appear to stand in opposition to more established mainstream cognitive-behavioral interventions for the anxiety-disorders. It remains to be seen, however, whether both treatment strategies are effective via different processes, or whether both operate on similar core processes, but through different means. Further, it would be interesting to see whether current "mastery-based" manualized treatments for the anxiety disorders can be reframed into "acceptance-based" approaches. I suspect that they can, especially if "mastery" is placed in the context of mastering one's capacity to experience more fully what is there to be felt and thought. The educational components of existing manualized treatments for the anxiety disorders often provide a useful starting point for clients by describing how anxiety, fear, and worry are normal and adaptive experiences. Unfortunately, most of the existing techniques and strategies that follow suggest otherwise. It is here where acceptance-based strategies offer intriguing and promising alternatives to psychological health and the alleviation of human suffering.

Future Directions for Process-Oriented Psychological Interventions

Based on the preceding analysis, there is some indication that certain symptom-based first-order cognitive-behavioral treatments may not be the most efficacious approach in producing comprehensive and long-lasting behavior change. In this last section, therefore, I briefly outline several recommendations for assessment and treatment development based on a functional process-oriented approach that may lead to better long-term outcome.

Need for Triage and Idiographic Process-Oriented Assessment

Aside from the diagnostic criteria outlined in the DSM-IV, we do not have any other means for classifying and assessing persons with anxiety disorders, apart from categorizing them based on symptoms arranged topographically and disorders subdivided categorically. Perhaps a different way to classify disorders of anxiety more functionally would be to arrange the presenting problems around certain relational dimensions. For instance, all anxiety disorders can be placed along at least three functional dimensions: (a) *origin of the feared or anxiety arousing stimulus* (e.g., internal or bodily vs. external or environmental); (b) *stimulus specificity* (general vs. specific); and (c) *the nature of the negatively evaluated psychophysiological responses* (abrupt and immediate vs. chronic and sustained). According to this dimensional perspective (Forsyth & Eifert, 1998), panic disorder can be understood as involving an abrupt psychophysiological responses to a general class of internal physical sensations, whereas specific phobias and PTSD would represent abrupt psychophysiological responses to either specific or more generalized classes of environmental events. Similarly, obsessive-compulsive disorder might be understood as a chronic psychophysiological response to a general class of internal events (i.e., thoughts), whereas generalized anxiety disorder is often represented as a chronic psychophysiological responses to a general class of external (situations) and internal (thoughts) events. Within this framework, anxiety disorders are understood as involving relations among events; events that can be viewed as having both verbal and nonverbal stimulus and response functions which can be established and modified in subtle and complex ways as a function of contextual factors. This type of process and theory-driven approach, where treatments are matched to classes of environment-behavior relations defined functionally, stands in stark contrast to the overwhelming trend to match treatments to various diagnostic labels (Eifert, 1996). This trend has had the deleterious effect of moving behavior therapists further away from performing careful functional-idiographic assessments and treatments by relating basic behavioral principles and theory with the practice of behavior therapy.

Need to Address Psychological Vulnerability

Although the preceding dimensional-relational scheme may be helpful in identifying problematic relational responses and perhaps differentiating problems based on the nature and phenomenology of such relational responses, it is not sufficient to establish what we call the disorders of anxiety. As indicated, such relations, in and of themselves, and the psychological effects of such relations (e.g., the experience of fear or anxiety), are not necessarily problematic if one can still lead a happy and productive life. Given that the response and associated symptoms are insufficient in accounting for the development of anxiety related disorders, it would seem important to also address psychological vulnerability factors.

A variety of psychological vulnerability factors have been proposed to explain the shift from a normal experience of anxiety and fear to a disordered experience of anxiety and fear (e.g., genetics and temperament, uncontrollability, unpredictability, anxious apprehension, cognitive threat biases and catastrophic misinterpretations, fear networks, fear of fear, anxiety sensitivity, to name a few). In the present view, it is suggested that one of the core vulnerability factors that has been overlooked is the rigid and inflexible application of control-based strategies in an attempt to alter and avoid the verbal and nonverbal stimulus functions entailed in a particular class of relational responses. For instance, try to imagine the role of anxious apprehension in the absence a more general strategy of control and avoidance. It is difficult to do, precisely because anxious apprehension entails the assumption that something out there in the future is threatening and must be avoided or controlled. Otherwise, there would be nothing to anxiously apprehend. Similarly, imagine the role of a fear network in the absence of a person attempting to control and avoid the psychological effects evoked by activation of such a network. Likewise, consider what would become of "fear of fear" (a somewhat circular and nebulous construct) in the absence of attempts to struggle or avoid the physical and psychological experience of fear itself. It is likely that we would be left with the ubiquitous phenomena of "nonclinical panic" (Barlow, 1988; Antony & Barlow, 1996) and otherwise adaptive experiences of anxious and fearful emotional behavior. Uncontrollability and unpredictability as vulnerabilities also seem to derive meaning only with the context of rigid attempts to control or avoid. Because such attempts are largely ineffective in the realm of private experience, the consequence will likely be a greater sense of uncontrollability and unpredictability, with even more attempts to control and avoid, and so on in a vicious cycle (Barlow, 1988). Assessing controllability may, however, be quite useful as a means to address the rigidity of a client's more general repertoire of ineffective strategies, in addition to the use of exposure-based experiential exercises designed to evoke relevant problematic avoidance and control-based strategies in session.

Need to Address the Context of Such Relations

To date, mainstream behavioral treatments, and especially those of the manualized type, pay far to little attention to the context of client problems, and too much attention to the alleviation of symptoms. I suspect that this is one reason why many persons with anxiety disorders relapse after time-limited treatments. As suggested here, one relevant context to address is clients' struggle to control and avoid their psychological experiences. An equally relevant context to address is the rigidity and inflexibility of clients' control and avoidance strategies, as well as the extent to which clients use thoughts and feelings as reasons for not behaving effectively. Context is also important for another reason. That is, the goal of treatment is often the alleviation of suffering and effective action beyond the therapeutic setting. It does no good for improvement to occur only within the confines of the treatment setting. To arrange for more lasting improvement beyond the treatment setting, however, requires both the therapist and client to address a variety of verbal and experiential circumstances that may later evoke relevant features of clients' repertoires that brought them into therapy in the first place. In other words, the better we are at evoking and shaping feeling and its expression in session, and to the extent that such circumstances parallel what is happening the real world, the better we will be in fostering more generalized positive outcome (see Kohlenberg & Tsai, 1991).

Need for Theory-Driven and Process-Oriented Manualization

Increasingly, cognitive-behavioral interventions are finding their way into diagnosis-driven manualized treatments for each of the 12 anxiety-related disorders. Despite such efforts, there is still insufficient attention to theory and process in such manuals, with the overriding concern being symptom reduction and alleviation. Further, there is every indication that not every client with a given problem will need all components of a given manual to improve, and that many clients do not fit neatly into pure diagnostic groups for which the manuals were designed. Clearly, clinical practice dictates a more flexible process-oriented individualized approach to manualized treatments than is suggested by proponents and developers of treatment manuals. To date, however, treatment manuals for the anxiety-related disorders do not contain mention of how clinicians might match relevant components of such manuals to target salient behavioral processes in a given client. Rather, the approach has been more akin to casting a wider therapeutic net by hitting the client over the head with numerous techniques such that most clients with a given DSM diagnosis are bound to show some symptom reduction. What cannot be addressed as readily with such an approach is why a given client, with a given set of presenting problems, improved or failed to do so. Increasing the long-term efficacy, cost-effectiveness, and clinical relevance of such manuals would seem to require decision based rules that illustrate what techniques may be useful to target what behavioral processes in a given client. Some relevant, but overlooked, processes might include (a) verbally-derived learning; (b) contextual factors that potentiate or depotentiate aspects of a client's history, and especially those related to feeling and its expression; and (c) the rigidity and inflexibility of a client's reason giving, control, and avoidance-based strategies concerning private experiences. As suggested here, it is likely that attempts to first address and weaken such processes in relation to aversive bodily and environmental stimulus functions might pave the way for more lasting and profound behavior change that goes beyond immediate symptom alleviation. In turn, such an individualized process-oriented approach may help explain some of the collateral and quantum changes that often occur in client's behavior as a result of treatment. In any event, clinical and experimental research that bears directly on process issues is sorely needed.

Need to Move Beyond the 50 Minute Solution

Much of the psychological establishment still follows the tradition of attempting to alleviate human suffering within the constraints of the 50 minute therapeutic hour (Hayes, 1997b). Managed care has added further constraints in terms of the number of such 50 minute hours that are reimbursable. So, we are left with little time to alleviate what are often extensive and ingrained patterns of ineffective behavior. This is further compounded by the somewhat artificial caps placed on many manualized treatments for anxiety-related disorders, many of which are said to take only 12-15 weeks. It is somewhat ironic that we maintain, on the one hand, that psychological suffering is largely a function of complex and often chronic patterns of behavior and experience, and on the other, that somehow we can reverse the effects of such histories of ineffective action by creating new and more powerful histories within a limited time frame. If our goal is to produce lasting change in our clients as a result of our interventions, then at least two possibilities exist: (a) create more powerful treatment interventions designed to target fundamental core processes responsible for the maintenance of anxiety-related disorders and suffering and (b) attempt to expand our view of the treatment process beyond caps on number of sessions. Regarding (a), more could be done to advance our treatments beyond simple symptom alleviation and/or elimination, and several of the ideas expressed in this chapter suggest how such developments might proceed. The second possibility (b) suggests that we should reconsider whether it makes sense to continue with arbitrary caps on number treatment sessions and time spent in each treatment session. Behavior therapy has long prided itself on being able to provide time-limited efficacious interventions for a wide range of problems. For some problems, time limited interventions seem to be enough, for other more complex and chronic life problems, however, more treatment may be needed and often is required. Perhaps a programmed approach to treatment may offer a solution to more intractable and chronic problems. In such an approach, length of therapy sessions and number of sessions would be a function of the content and extent of problems, not a matter of economic convention (Chorpita, 1997). According to this view, clients might be encouraged to enroll in a program of treatment, much like a course, a pay a flat fee for the program, thus removing the immediate negative incentives for paying for treatment on a session-by-session basis. Such a program, therefore, would not be constrained by 50 minute hours or caps on the number of treatment sessions. Rather, it would include more comprehensive and tailor made experiences that address unique areas of concern for a given client. In the case of panic disorder, for example, such a program may include education about emotion and its expression, individualized treatment that addresses control and nonacceptance issues, group or individual experiential exercises that attempt to evoke feeling and its expression (e.g., interoceptive exposure), skill building groups, and those that may address spiritual, marital, and interpersonal areas. Improvement in such a program would be gauged, in part, by symptom alleviation, but more importantly by effective action across other areas of life functioning. We are currently in the process of developing such a program, and plan to also include periodic booster sessions and wellness checks as an integral part, not simply as an index of whether treatment produced lasting improvement or a "cure."

Conclusions

Throughout this chapter, I have attempted to describe what appear to be fundamental process that cut across the seemingly different anxiety disorders. In so doing, I have eschewed discussion of the disorders individually, and have instead attempted to address what makes a disordered experience of anxiety and fear "disordered" in the first place. As suggested here, some of the relevant but overlooked psychological processes appear to center of rigid and inflexible control and avoidance-based strategies when applied to unwanted thoughts or emotional experiences. Stip away such strategies, and it is difficult to imagine any one of the DSM anxiety disorders. It is equally difficult to imagine the relevance of psychological vulnerability factors (e.g., conditioning, anxiety sensitivity, anxious apprehension, negative evaluations) in the absence of persons responding to their own responses and the evocative functions of events in the environment in an effort to control and avoid them. According to this view, it is not the anxiety and fear, nor the negative and unwanted thoughts, that are necessarily problematic in themselves. Rather, the central problem is how one responds to such responses, and particularly the consequences of such actions in restricting the flexibility and adaptability of a person's behavior across other valued and meaningful areas of life functioning; a view that seems quite different from most mainstream symptom and syndromal-based cognitive-behavioral interventions.

With acceptance, therefore, we have an exciting and somewhat counterintuitive view of psychological health and human suffering. In recent years, several new clinical behavior analytic psychotherapies have been developed in the context of acceptance and change as a fundamental process, not in the context of disorders of syndromes as a fundamental problem (e.g., Acceptance and Commitment Therapy; Hayes & Wilson, 1994; Functional Analytic Psychotherapy; Kohlenberg & Tsai, 1991; Integrative Behavioral Couple Therapy; Koerner, Jacobson, & Christensen, 1994). Such interventions, in turn, provide both a context and a set of common behavioral processes to understand the etiology, assessment, and treatment of anxiety-related disorders that moves well beyond symptom alleviation. Further, such approaches suggest what needs to be done in therapy to alleviate human suffering and what can be done to prevent psychological suffering in the future. In both cases, it seems critical to develop contexts that promote experiencing thoughts and feelings more fully for what they are, and behaving effectively as a result. When considering the anxiety disorders, therefore, this involves clients giving up the struggle to avoid, escape, or control private events evoked by aversive stimuli, and the use of private events are reasons for not doing. Unfortunately, we are all taught to do just the opposite with unwanted thoughts and feelings, and some more so than others. Perhaps as we rethink what psychological health means in the coming years, we may be better positioned to develop more powerful and comprehensive treatments to alleviate a wider range of human suffering. To do so, however, will require more attention to process, function, and context, and a willingness on the part of scientists and practitioners to change our change agendas.

References

American Psychiatric Association (1994). *The Diagnostic and statistical manual of mental disorders (4th ed.)*. Washington, DC: Author.

Antony, M. M., & Barlow, D. H. (1996). Emotion theory as a framework for explaining panic attacks and panic disorder. In R. M. Rapee (Ed.), *Current controversies in the anxiety disorders* (pp. 55-76). New York: Guilford.

Antony, M. M., Craske, M. G., & Barlow, D. H. (1995). *Mastery of your specific phobia*. San Antonio: The Psychological Corporation.

Augustson, E. M, & Dougher, M. J. (1997). The transfer of avoidance evoking functions through stimulus equivalence classes. *Journal of Behavior Therapy and Experimental Psychiatry, 28*, 181-191.

Averill, J. R. (1980). The emotions. In E. Staub (Ed.), *Personality: Basic aspects and current research* (pp. 134-199). Englewood Cliffs, NJ: Prentice-Hall.

Barlow, D. H. (1988). *Anxiety and its disorders: The nature and treatment of anxiety and panic*. New York: Guilford.

Barlow, D. H., & Craske, M. G. (1994). *Mastery of your anxiety and panic (2nd ed.)*. *(MAP II)*. San Antonio: The Psychological Corporation.

Barlow, D. H., Rapee, R. M., & Brown, T. B. (1992). Behavioral treatment of generalized anxiety disorder. *Behavior Therapy, 23*, 529-550.

Beck, A. T., & Emery, G. (1985). *Anxiety disorders and phobias: A cognitive perspective*. New York: Basic Books.

Brown, T. A. (1996). Validity of the DSM-III-R and DSM-IV classification systems for anxiety disorders. In R. M. Rapee (Ed.), *Current controversies in the anxiety disorders* (pp. 21-45). New York: Guilford.

Chorpita, B. F. (1997). Since the operant chamber: Is behavior therapy still thinking in boxes? *Behavior Therapy, 28*, 577-583.

Craske, M. G., Barlow, D. H., & O'Leary, T. (1992). *Mastery of your anxiety and worry*. San Antonio: The Psychological Corporation.

Dougher, M. J., Augustson, E., Markham, M. R., Greenway, D. E., & Wulfurt, E. (1994). The transfer of respondent eliciting and extinction functions through stimulus equivalence classes. *Journal of the Experimental Analysis of Behavior, 62*, 331-352.

Dougher, M. J., & Markham, M. R. (1994). Stimulus equivalence, functional equivalence, and the transfer of function. In S. C. Hayes, L. J. Hayes, M. Sato, & K. Ono (Eds.), *Behavior analysis of language and cognition* (pp. 71-90). Reno, NV: Context Press.

Eifert, G. H. (1996). More theory-driven and less diagnosis-based behavior therapy. *Journal of Behavior Therapy and Experimental Psychiatry, 27*, 75-86.

Eifert, G. H., Schulte, D., Zvolensky, M. J., Lejuez, C. W., & Lau, A. W. (1997). Manualized behavior therapy: Merits and challenges. *Behavior Therapy, 28*, 499-507.

Eysenck, H. J. (1987). Behavior therapy. In H. J. Eysenck & I. Martin (Eds.), *Theoretical foundations of behavior therapy* (pp. 3-34). New York: Plenum.

Foa, E. B., & Kozak, M. J. (1996). Obsessive-compulsive disorder. In C. Lindemann (Ed.), *Handbook of the treatment of anxiety disorders (2nd ed.)*, (pp. 137-171). Northvale, NJ: Jason Aronson.

Foa, E. B., & Kozak, M. J. (1997). *Mastery of obsessive-compulsive disorder.* San Antonio: The Psychological Corporation.

Forsyth, J. P. (1998). Emotion: Important causal influences, epiphenomena, or collateral by-products of behavior. *Manuscript Under Review.*

Forsyth, J. P., Daleiden, E., & Chorpita, B. F. (1998). Response primacy in fear conditioning: Disentangling the relative contributions of UCS vs. UCR intensity. *Manuscript Under Review.*

Forsyth, J. P., & Eifert, G. H. (in press). Response intensity in content-specific fear conditioning comparing 20% vs. 13% carbon dioxide enriched air as unconditioned stimuli. *Journal of Abnormal Psychology 107*, 291-304.

Forsyth, J. P., & Eifert, G. H. (1998). Phobic anxiety and panic: An integrative account of their origin and treatment. In J. J. Plaud & G. H. Eifert (Eds.), *From behavior theory to behavior therapy* (pp. 38-67). Needham Heights, MA: Allyn & Bacon.

Forsyth, J. P., & Eifert, G. H. (1996a). The language of feeling and the feeling of anxiety: Contributions of the behaviorisms toward understanding the function-altering effects of language. *The Psychological Record, 46*, 607-649.

Forsyth, J. P., & Eifert, G. H. (1996b). Systemic alarms and fear conditioning–I: A reappraisal of what is being conditioned. *Behavior Therapy, 27*, 441-462.

Gross, J. J., & Levenson, R. W. (1997). Hiding feelings: The acute effects of inhibiting negative and positive emotion. *Journal of Abnormal Psychology, 106*, 95-103.

Hayes, S. C. (1994). Content, context, and the types of psychological acceptance. In S. C. Hayes, N. S. Jacobson, V. M. Follette, & M. J. Dougher (Eds.), *Acceptance and change: Content and context in psychotherapy* (pp. 13-32). Reno, NV: Context Press.

Hayes, S. C. (1997). Technology, theory, and the alleviation of human suffering: We still have such a long way to go. *Behavior Therapy, 28*, 517-525.

Hayes, S. C., & Hayes, L. J. (1989). The verbal action of the listener as a basis for rule-governance. In S.C. Hayes (Ed.), *Rule-governed behavior* (pp. 153-190). New York: Plenum.

Hayes, S. C., & Wilson, K. G. (1993). Some applied implications of a contemporary behavior analytic account of verbal events. *The Behavior Analyst, 16*, 283-301.

Hayes, S. C., & Wilson, K. G. (1994). Acceptance and commitment therapy: Altering the verbal support for experiential avoidance. *The Behavior Analyst, 17,* 289-303.

Hayes, S. C., Wilson, K. G., Gifford, E. V., Follette, V. M., & Strosahl, K. (1996). Experiential avoidance and behavioral disorders: A functional dimensional approach to diagnosis and treatment. *Journal of Consulting and Clinical Psychology, 64,* 1152-1168.

Hull, C. L. (1943). *Principles of behavior.* New York: Appleton-Century-Crofts.

Koerner, K., Jacobson, N. S., & Christensen, A. (1994). Emotional acceptance in integrative behavioral couple therapy. In S. C. Hayes, N. S. Jacobson, V. M. Follette, & M. J. Dougher (Eds.), *Acceptance and change: Content and context in psychotherapy* (pp. 109-118). Reno, NV: Context Press.

Kohlenberg, R. J., Tsai, M. (1991). *Functional analytic psychotherapy: Creating intense and curative relationships.* New York: Plenum.

Lang, P. J. (1985). The cognitive psychophysiology of emotion: Fear and anxiety. In H. Tuma & J. Maser (Eds.), *Anxiety and the anxiety disorders.* Hillsdale, NJ: Erlbaum.

Lang, P. J. (1993). The network model of emotion: Motivational connections. In R. S. Wyer & T. K. Srull (Eds.), *Perspectives on anger and emotion: Advances in social cognition* (Vol 6, pp. 109-133). Hillsdale, NJ: Erlbaum.

Lavy, E. H., & van den Hout, M. A. (1990). Thought suppression induces intrusions. *Behavioural Psychotherapy, 18,* 251-258.

Lazarus, A. (1984). On the primacy of cognition. *American Psychologist, 39,* 124-129.

McNally, R. J. (1990). Psychological approaches to panic disorder: A review. *Psychological Bulletin, 108,* 403-419.

Menzies, R. G., & Clarke, J. C. (1995). The etiology of phobias: A nonassociative account. *Clinical Psychology Review, 15,* 23-48.

Mineka, S., & Zinbarg, R. (1996). Conditioning and ethological models of anxiety disorders: Stress-in-dynamic context anxiety models. In D. A. Hope (Ed.), *Perspectives on anxiety, panic, and fear: Vol. 43 of the Nebraska Symposium on Motivation* (pp. 135-210). Lincoln, NB: University of Nebraska Press.

Nardone, G., & Watzlawick (1993). Clinical practice, processes, and procedures. In G. Nardone & P. Watzlawick (Eds.), *The art of change* (pp. 45-72). San Francisco: Jossey-Bass.

Öhman, A., & Soares, J. J. F. (1993). On the automatic nature of phobic fear: Conditioned electrodermal responses to masked fear-relevant stimuli. *Journal of Abnormal Psychology, 102,* 121-132.

Öhman, A., & Soares, J. J. F. (1994). "Unconscious anxiety": Phobic responses to masked stimuli. *Journal of Abnormal Psychology, 103,* 231-240.

Pavlov, I. P. (1927). *Conditioned reflexes: An investigation of the activity of the cerebral cortex.* New York: Dover.

Rachman, S. (1977). The conditioning theory of fear acquisition. *Behaviour Research and Therapy, 15,* 375-387.

Rachman, S. (1985). The treatment of anxiety disorders: A critique of the implications for psychopathology. In A. H. Tuma & J. Maser (Eds.), *Anxiety and the anxiety disorders* (pp. 453-461). Hillsdale, NJ: Erlbaum.

Rachman, S. (1991). Neo-conditioning and the classical theory of fear acquisition. *Clinical Psychology Review, 11*, 155-173.

Rapee, R. M. (Ed.) (1996). *Current controversies in the anxiety disorders.* New York: Guilford.

Schlinger, H. D., & Blakely, E. (1994). A descriptive taxonomy of environmental operations and its implications for behavior analysis. *The Behavior Analyst, 17*, 43-57.

Staats, A. W., & Eifert, G. H. (1990). The paradigmatic behaviorism theory of emotions: Basis for unification. *Clinical Psychology Review, 10*, 539-566.

Watson, J. B. (1930). *Behaviorism.* New York: Norton.

Wolpe, J. (1958). *Psychotherapy by reciprocal inhibition.* Stanford, CA: Stanford University Press.

Chapter 8

Marital Problems

Sara Berns
Neil Jacobson
University of Washington
Andrew Christensen
University of California, Los Angeles

When a relationship transitions from loving and happy, to stressful and painful, the psychological and physical effects on each member can be devastating. There is growing evidence that relationship distress can lead to a host of psychological difficulties (Gotlib & McCabe, 1990), as well as physical problems (Burman & Margolin, 1992). As the profound impact of marital problems becomes more and more evident, researchers and clinicians have striven to develop models of distress and treatment. The result of these efforts is a constantly expanding body of literature consisting of theoretical speculation and empirical work on couples therapy. Of all the proposed models of relationship distress in the literature, the most widely investigated treatment for couple problems has been Traditional Behavioral Couple Therapy (TBCT) (Hahlweg & Markman, 1988).

Based on social-exchange theories and operant learning principles, TBCT posits a link between marital satisfaction and the ratio of positive to negative behaviors exchanged by couples at home. When an imbalance occurs, and more aversive than pleasurable behaviors are exchanged, the marriage is likely to be unsatisfying and unstable (Gottman, 1993). Behavior exchange interventions are aimed at instigating positive exchanges through the use of homework assignments presented by the therapist (Jacobson & Margolin, 1979). Altering the positive exchange of behaviors provides some expeditious relief from the distress caused by specific, current problems. Although increasing positive exchanges may produce rapid change, the change can be transient. Longer-lasting changes are produced through the use of communication and problem-solving techniques. In essence, the partners learn to be their own therapists, applying skills to future arguments as they occur. Using skills to negotiate change in their relationships, couples learn how to bring about the changes in effective, noncoercive, ways.

TBCT has been shown to be an effective treatment for marital discord (Baucom & Hoffman, 1986; Gurman, Kniskern, & Pinsoff, 1986; Jacobson, 1978, 1984; Jacobson & Addis, 1993). To be more specific, there have been approximately two-dozen clinical trials showing TBCT to be more effective than various kinds of control groups (Jacobson & Addis 1993). With the number of research efforts showing positive changes in relationship discord, TBCT is the closest the field has to an established, proven therapy. In follow-ups covering up to two years, relationship quality has been shown to improve for almost two thirds of couples presenting for TBCT (Jacobson, Schmaling, & Holtzworth-Munroe, 1987). However, this leaves one-third of the couples as treatment failures. Additionally, of the couples that responded to therapy, about 30% relapse during a two-year period, most between the first and second year. Instead of solely focusing on the "successful" couples, Christensen and Jacobson sought to determine what factors are at play with the "unsuccessful" couples (Christensen & Jacobson, in press; Christensen, Jacobson, & Babcock, 1995; Jacobson, 1992; Jacobson & Christensen, 1996). They sought to answer the questions: What factors underlie the treatment failures, and how can we use knowledge of those factors to improve the efficacy of our treatments?

Using the results of empirical works on predictors of treatment response, Jacobson and his colleagues searched for an underlying factor that rendered TBCT incomplete for a proportion of the couples (Jacobson, Follette, & Pagel, 1986). A review of treatment response research revealed that successful couples were less severely distressed (Baucom & Hoffman, 1986), younger (Baucom & Hoffman, 1986), more emotionally engaged (Hahlweg, Schindler, Revenstorf, & Brangelmann, 1984), and less polarized on basic issues (Jacobson et al., 1986). When all of these factors are combined, the result is a couple that can collaborate, accommodate to each other, and handle the give and take of relationships. Younger couples have not yet been stuck in a rut of ineffective communication, and are thus more willing to compromise. The "chemistry" of emotionally engaged couples keeps them interacting with one another instead of avoiding conflict. Finally, less distressed and more compatible couples can work together on their problems, facing the problems from similar viewpoints.

Why is TBCT successful for couples who can compromise and accommodate, but not for couples that are unable to do so? The behavior exchange homework assignments and communication and problem-solving techniques of TBCT *require* a couple to compromise and accommodate. With change as the ultimate goal, couples must be able to work together effectively to make the changes come about. For the couples who cannot or will not work together to induce change, TBCT has little to offer. Even couples who can collaborate can't always make the desired changes, and sometimes trying to do so makes the problem even more unchangeable. Partners become even more entrenched in their position, becoming increasingly polarized in their attempts to unify. For example, as partners try to discuss their differences in parenting practices, they may find themselves feeling even stronger about their own views on how parenting should be handled. Instead of moving towards a resolution, they have moved even farther away. It became apparent that for a couple to strengthen their relationship, they would have to give up on some of their struggles to change one another. Clearly a successful model of treatment for marital distress was needed that could integrate the change techniques of TBCT with techniques for giving up on change as the ultimate goal.

The desire for a more comprehensive and effective treatment led Andrew Christensen and Neil Jacobson to develop a new, more complete approach: Integrative Behavioral Couples Therapy (IBCT) (Christensen & Jacobson, in press; Christensen et al., 1995; Jacobson, 1992; Jacobson & Christensen, 1996). The change strategies of TBCT were combined with newer techniques that promote acceptance of unresolvable problems. Within this integrative approach, problems can become vehicles for intimacy, instead of destructive, polarizing forces. The struggle for change can be replaced with a journey toward closeness and understanding. Although the notion of acceptance is not new to the field of psychotherapy, it is a marked departure from the traditional focus on change in behavioral approaches. In keeping with traditional behavioral approaches is an emphasis on the procedures necessary to a goal, instead of vague conceptualizations of an end product. Therefore IBCT provides a delineation of change strategies along with a clear description of procedures designed to promote and foster acceptance.

It is important to note that acceptance is not equated with resignation in our approach. Acceptance has two important components that distinguish it from grudgingly giving in to the status quo. First, instead of viewing problems as things that have to be eradicated, our integrative approach attempts to convert them into vehicles for intimacy. Under this paradigm relationships can thrive because of their problems and conflict areas, rather than in spite of them. The second dimension of acceptance involves both partners letting go of the struggle to change one another. They can achieve this goal by experiencing the differences between them as tolerable, and therefore giving up the effort to mold their partners into idealized images of husband or wife. Problems, which before could not be handled through direct efforts, can change themselves once this contextual shift occurs.

Theoretical and Methodological Underpinnings

The response to IBCT in the research community has been favorable, although some have suggested that the union of change and acceptance deviates from the basic tenets of behaviorism (Gurman, 1991; Johnson & Greenberg, 1991; Snyder & Wills, 1991). In actuality, IBCT represents a return to behavioral roots. Through a renewed emphasis on functional analysis, IBCT has restored the behavior analytic tradition in couples therapy. The functional analysis allows for the identification of the unique factors between partners and external to their relationship that inevitably affect its course. When we consider the unique history of both partners as they learned to behave in intimate relationships, the combination of these unique histories, and the variety of specific environmental contingencies affecting them in their current relationship, the picture becomes quite complex. Nevertheless, a systematic, ideographic approach to dealing with couples has long been missing from TBCT, and we have restored it.

TBCT had become rigid, applying the same basic strategies to all distressed couples regardless of individual history and current environmental contingencies.

IBCT tailors the treatment program to the unique characteristics of particular couples. Rather than emphasizing the form or topography of behavior, IBCT looks to the function that a behavior serves for a particular couple. For example, initiating sex with a partner may be seen topographically as an attempt to increase intimacy. For one couple, initiating sex may very well serve that function. However, for another couple, initiation of sex by one partner may be an act of control or dominance. Although the acts may be topographically similar, they serve very different functions for each couple. Failing to look at the individual differences in each couple will cause the therapist to overlook a great deal of relevant and useful information.

For most couples there exists a set of topographically different behaviors that all serve a similar function. These sets of behaviors are called "response classes", and awareness of their existence provides the therapist with a greater ability to foster generalization of treatment gains. Through the strengthening of one behavior in a response class, other behaviors in the class are concomitantly strengthened. For example, a therapist might discover that a wife engages in a variety of topographically different behaviors related to controlling the couple's free time. In the therapy session the therapist might reinforce the wife for listening supportively and not shooting down ideas proposed by the husband on how they should spend the weekend. Because the behaviors in the session are similar to her time-controlling behaviors outside of therapy, decreasing them in the session can automatically decrease them at home.

In the transition from TBCT to IBCT an important behavioral distinction was brought into the forefront for closer scrutiny. The distinction is between arbitrary and natural reinforcement (Ferster, 1967; Skinner, 1974). When a wife is instructed by her therapist to cook exquisite dinners for her husband in exchange for his acts of self-disclosure, he is being given a reinforcer that does not stem naturally from the transaction between them. The reinforcer is contrived. Although these arbitrary reinforcers may increase the frequency of the behavior while the instruction is in place to apply them, when the instruction ends (i.e. therapy is over), the behavior is likely to extinguish. If the reinforcement is reliant on anything else outside of the very act of engaging in the behavior, the behavior will undoubtedly decrease in frequency once the outside force is gone. TBCT relied too strongly on arbitrary reinforcers, failing to pay close attention to natural contingencies. Natural reinforcement, in contrast, takes advantages of just such contingencies. Instead of being reinforced with nice dinners, the husband in the above example may find that self-disclosure leads to more positive and intimate interactions with his wife. Through contacting the naturally reinforcing events inherent in the task of self-disclosure he is more likely to continue to self-disclose in the future. Arbitrary and natural reinforcers both increase the frequency of the behavior they follow, but only natural reinforcement is likely to lead to generalization outside of the therapy session. With the realization that the arbitrary vs. natural reinforcement distinction is important for treatment success and maintenance, therapists are strongly urged to utilize natural reinforcers whenever possible.

Another important distinction in IBCT is between contingency-shaped and rule-governed behavior (Skinner, 1966). In BCT, couples engaged in a variety of experiences simply because they were instructed to do so by the therapist. In other words, the reinforcement was for rule-following, not for any natural consequences related to the rule. Consider a wife instructed by the therapist to help more around the house. She will be reinforced for compliance, but ultimately the therapist hopes that natural contingencies will take over to maintain the behavior. The behavior may only continue if the wife either begins to appreciate a cleaner house herself, or enjoys the compliments given to her by her husband for helping out. By engaging in a behavior because of the verbal contingencies placed on her by the therapist, the wife above would be exhibiting "rule-governed" behavior.

Although rule-governed and contingency-shaped behavior may appear to be topographically similar, they can have quite different effects. Initiating sexual interactions because one is instructed to do so, as opposed to doing so out of passion and desire, will inevitably feel different to both the initiator and the recipient. In addition to different effects, rule-governed behavior is less likely to generalize outside of the treatment setting (Hayes, 1989). Contingency-shaped behavior, on the other hand, is directly strengthened by the natural contingencies present in the environment. Without directly contacting the contingencies, the shaping of durable behaviors is unlikely to occur.

We eventually realized that many of the communication skills in TBCT were never bringing clients into contact with natural reinforcers, and were thus prone to extinction. For enduring treatment gains IBCT was designed to promote direct contact with natural contingencies. Acceptance work, described later in the chapter, is about utilizing natural contingencies.

Case Formulation

Making the transition from a blaming, accusatory stance to a willingness to accept a partner takes time. For couples to make the transition they need a framework for viewing their relationship, their partner, and themselves in a new light. This "new light" is the case formulation, perhaps the most important component of IBCT. The assessment period is aimed at contributing to the development of the formulation and each of its components. Once developed, however, the formulation is far from a packaged, finished product. Instead it is constantly under construction as the therapist and couple interact and learn more about their individual history and experiences.

The first component of the formulation, the theme, describes a characteristic pattern of interactions that underlies each conflict for a particular couple. In a sense, the theme can be thought of as the script that defines each partner's role and the intentions or functions of their behaviors. The role each partner plays is made up of a set of behaviors that all serve a similar function (defined earlier as a "response class"). Although the exact features of a theme vary from couple to couple, there are certain themes that seem to constantly reappear in therapy. Perhaps the most common theme presented by couples in therapy is the "closeness-distance" theme (Jacobson, 1989). In these interactions one partner's role involves wanting more closeness and intimacy, and the other partner's role involves wanting more distance and independence.

An interesting aspect of themes is that they are based on differences between the two partners. The role a partner plays in a relationship theme is invariably at one end of a behavioral spectrum, with his/her partner at the other end. Whereas one partner might define an ideal relationship as one filled with intimacy and closeness, the other partner might define an ideal relationship very differently. The gap between the two ends of the spectrum is precisely their major incompatibility. Instead of being defined as a difference in viewpoints, the gap is seen as an intolerable situation that both partners want to eradicate. Each partner comes to believe that in order for the marriage to be viable they must pull the other person towards their end of the spectrum and eliminate the gap at all costs. However, through the process of IBCT, couples learn that differences are not always gaps that must be eliminated. Differences are to be expected, can be experienced without pain, and are at times even desirable.

Identification of relationship themes serves several important functions in the development of a formulation. First, because behaviors in a response class serve similar functions, a shift in one behavior often results in shifts in other behaviors. The interconnectedness of the behaviors allows for a reduced need to change every behavior in the class. Second, determining a relationship theme provides the couple and the therapist with a way of discussing interpersonal conflict without needing to describe each and every interaction in behavioral detail. Delineating every possible argument is time consuming, and probably impossible. Once a theme is identified, viewing subsequent arguments as manifestations of the theme decreases the time spent on peripheral details.

The "polarization process" is the second component of the formulation, and can be a direct outcome of the roles each partner plays in the relationship theme. As each partner attempts to close the gap between them, the paradoxical result is a broadening of that very gap. Each partner thinks, "If I could just make him stop being that way, and see my point of view, we'd be so much happier." The other person becomes the problem that must be solved. However, when someone's well-entrenched beliefs and patterns of behaving are threatened, the natural tendency is to become even more entrenched, to "stand one's ground." The more entrenched both partners become in their own beliefs, the more disturbing and distressing their partner's behaviors seem. Just as pulling a stubborn dog's leash harder and harder only makes him dig his claws into the ground with greater fervor, trying to change someone can often make them vehemently resistant.

The third part of the formulation, the "mutual trap," is the outcome of polarization. As the efforts to change a partner become obviously futile, each person is bound to feel trapped and helpless. Both partners have tried everything they know of to make the other person see their point of view, and not only has nothing worked, but the situation has worsened. They are caught in a mutual trap, and every effort to close the gap only widens it further. Although both partners feel the strain and frustration of the trap, it is rarely discussed. Instead, each partner experiences the trap privately, unaware that the other person is undergoing the same experience.

When couples shift their focus from the theme to the polarization process, and the roles they play in that process, they begin to see their positions as simply different, not weird or inherently problematic. They join together in their frustration over being caught in the mutual trap, and find compassion and empathy for the other person's experience. The formulation combines the concepts of the theme, polarization process, and mutual trap to provide a new context for couples to view their relationship. With help from their therapist, a couple learns that their conflicts reflect a theme, and that their efforts to change the other may be leading to greater polarization. The mere awareness of this processes can interrupt them and change the impact they have on the relationship.

Overview and Structure of IBCT

A young couple committed to staying together that shares a similar definition of a good relationship is likely to enter therapy with the collaborative set necessary for success with traditional behavior change techniques. However, couples of this sort are in the minority. Years of clinical experience as well as our own pilot data indicate that the prerequisites for success with acceptance work are practically nonexistent. With most couples we strongly encourage therapists to begin with acceptance work.

The decision to begin with acceptance work (Christensen & Jacobson, in press) may be better understood by underscoring the distinction between rule-governed and contingency-based behavior. Both Behavior Exchange (BE) and Communication/Problem-Solving Training (CPT) are rule-governed procedures, and changes which they induce are unlikely to generalize to the home environment unless they come under the control of natural contingencies. In contrast, acceptance strategies are contingency-shaped, relying on shifts in context which naturally reinforce satisfaction-increasing behaviors. Generalization becomes automatic with acceptance work, as the contextual shifts make it highly probable that the behaviors will spread to the home environment, and become enduring.

For some couples, once acceptance work has taken hold, BE and CPT strategies are not necessary even later in therapy. The increased acceptance may result in no longer wanting the changes initially requested; or the changes may come about by themselves, as a consequence of acceptance work. If the decision to continue forward with BE and CPT strategies is made, the work will proceed more smoothly once acceptance has been promoted. Acceptance work enhances the ability to collaborate, accommodate, and compromise, making BE and CPT more straightforward and effective. The ease with which these strategies are implemented also serves as a form of feedback to the therapist that the acceptance work did what it was supposed to do.

Strategies to Promote Emotional Acceptance between Partners

When couples enter therapy, partners often believe that if the other person would "come around" to his/her point of view, the relationship could improve.

Strategies to promote emotional acceptance help the partners experience their problems in a new way. To help eliminate the need for the other to change, and promote acceptance, the IBCT therapist uses three main strategies: (1) acceptance through empathic joining around the problem, (2) acceptance through detachment from the problem, and (3) acceptance through tolerance building.

Empathic Joining Around the Problem

Consider a couple, Susan and Michael, in which Michael believes in saving money and making financial plans for the future, and Susan endorses being spontaneous with money, and living for today rather than planning for tomorrow. In light of the pain and frustration caused by this fundamental difference, Susan may experience Michael as boring, unromantic, or stingy. Similarly, Michael may experience Susan as immature, irresponsible, or pathologically controlling. The prognosis for acceptance is not good if partners are experiencing each other in this light.

The major tactic in empathic joining is the therapist's reformulation of the problem and each partner's negative behaviors. The purpose of reformulating is to soften the impact of negative behavior. For example, instead of "pathological" behavior, a problem might be seen as an example of common differences that divide people. Instead of "dysfunctional" strategies to deal with the behaviors, the strategies used are reformulated as understandable, and perhaps even inevitable results of the emotional reaction to the behaviors. The emphasis is on the pain felt by each partner; pain that is only exacerbated by their current attempts to assuage it. We attempt to take the "accusation" out of the pain, because pain plus accusation equals relationship discord, whereas pain minus accusation equals acceptance.

The initial formulation is often early in therapy. For example, in providing feedback to Susan and Michael about their theme, the therapist might say:

"A major problem that I see the two of you having comes from a difference in views on spending money. You, Susan, live for today, while you, Michael, prepare for tomorrow. Both positions are reasonable. This is a common difference between people, but it gets the two of you in trouble because of an unpleasant sequence of actions that gets set in motion when you try to deal with this difference. It probably started with the disappointment each of you felt when you discovered that the other person didn't want the kind of lifestyle that you thought you both wanted. In reaction to that disappointment, at some point, Susan, you become more spontaneous and less interested in planning for the future. You, Michael, grew to believe even more strongly in the importance of preparing for tomorrow. But the problem doesn't end with a difference in lifestyle preference. Michael, you become nervous about the difference in views, so you try even harder to make financial plans. However, when you approach Susan you are already nervous and tense because you are anticipating the negative cycle that often happens. Susan, you sense this tension and feel controlled and pressured. Michael, the more planning you desire, the

more spontaneity Susan fights for. You both end up feeling like you got
less than you even started with."
If the formulation is presented as non-blaming, and it accurately characterizes the
couple, they are likely to agree with it. However, agreeing with the formulation is
only the beginning. The couple will need to see their problems and strategies for
handling their problems in this new light many more times before they can move
substantially toward greater acceptance of each other.

Working on the way couples talk about their problems, the language they use,
is a major part of empathic joining. At the expressive level, the language of
acceptance focuses on personal feelings and experience, as opposed to what the
other partner has done or said. To prompt such expressions, we may ask a partner,
"Susan, you have described some of the things you think are going on with Michael
when he gets depressed. I'm wondering what is going on inside of you." Although
topographically similar to the therapeutic admonition to use "I statements", IBCT
therapist are concerned more with the content of the expression than the actual
syntax. Without a focus on content, a partner may use an "I statement" as a mask
for a "you statement" (e.g., "I feel like you are trying to dominate me").

We encourage clients to focus on "softening" their expressions. "Hard"
disclosures present the disclosing partner as accusing, invulnerable, and controlling
(e.g. "I will not let you get away with dominating me"). The listening partner is likely
to feel defensive, and may counterattack by listing the partner's faults or weaknesses.
"Soft" disclosures, on the other hand, reveal a partner's vulnerability within the
relationship. They can include such emotions as fear, sadness, hurt, insecurity, and
love (e.g. "I get so scared when I think of being alone"). Instead of becoming
defensive, the listening partner will be more likely to empathize and understand. By
the time a couple seeks therapy, hard disclosures dominate their repertoire. Blaming
and accusation are well ingrained, and tend to be the most immediate responses
when in the midst of a negative interaction. Although these disclosures are no less
accurate expressions of the internal state of the speaker than a soft disclosure, they
are likely to be followed by similarly hard expressions from the listener.

Because soft expressions do not come naturally to many couples, the therapist
may need to make suggestions. Based on the assumption that there are soft
counterparts to most hard disclosures, the therapist may reframe a partner's
expression of anger and annoyance by saying, "I wonder, Michael, if your anger at
Susan might come from an understandable fear of losing her, of being alone."
Consistent with the functional analytic approach of IBCT, there are no set rules for
what is a "hard" disclosure, and what is "soft." This may vary from couple to couple;
therefore reformulations that have a softening impact must be determined ideo-
graphically.

It is not necessary for couples to eliminate all uses of hard disclosures from their
communication. However, if the therapist consistently reformulates and prompts
in the ways described above, acceptance can occur in the absence of consistent soft
disclosures by the clients. The therapist's perspective can become part of the clients'
learning histories, influencing the impact of the problem on their relationship.

Whether the speaker comes up with a soft disclosure on his/her own, or the therapist prompts the disclosure, the effect on both partners can be profound. The recovery period after an argument may be more brief. They may learn to discuss their problem in a non-blaming manner. And finally, they may realize and come to accept the inevitability of conflicts within any relationship.

There are four types of incidents that tend to be the focus of the therapeutic interactions:

1. A general discussion of the basic differences between them and the resultant interaction pattern
2. Discussion of an upcoming event that may trigger the problem
3. Discussion of a recent negative event during which the problem occurred
4. Discussion of a recent positive event in which they handled the problem better

The general discussion serves the purposes of promoting a view of the problem as arising from *differences* between the partners, and providing a more sympathetic context for understanding those differences. A discussion regarding personal history, current environmental pressures, and gender-related differences may help elucidate the understandable ways that each partner behaves. For example, Michael was raised in a relatively poor family, whereas Susan's family rarely worried about money. These family-of-origin differences may very well play a part in their current differences regarding spending money. Susan's job requires her to schedule out every hour of her day, whereas Michael's job allows for flexibility. When they come home from work, they each need an escape from the environment they came from, and this desire exacerbates their differences in views regarding spontaneity vs. planning. Instead of conducting an extensive analysis of the possible underlying differences between the spouses, the IBCT therapist relies on available information to underscore and reframe the differences that arise from human experience. During the general discussion an emphasis is also placed on the "themes" or "dances" that the couple tend to engage in. The therapist helps the couple reformulate these themes in terms of the understandable reactions and counterreactions to the differences in each partner.

General discussions of basic differences are necessary. But equally important are discussions of particular incidents. When a couple can anticipate an upcoming problematic incident, discussing the anticipated reactions can help develop an understanding and acceptance of those reactions, and possibly provide some resilience to help prevent negative escalation. For example, Michael is considering the possibility of putting a large sum of money into retirement funds. Even before informing Susan of the investment plan, Michael is already tense and frustrated, anticipating Susan's unwillingness to put away money for the future. He may have even "role-played" the entire interaction in his head before ever bringing it up, and once he does, it is likely to be in a way that results in defensiveness from Susan (e.g. "I know you probably won't want to do it anyway, but I'm thinking of putting money away"). A nonblaming discussion of each partner's anticipated reactions can do much to promote acceptance.

Negative interactions will often occur between sessions. If the couple can generate a recent problem-related interaction that went well for them, the therapist should seize this opportunity to reinforce the partners for their respective actions. For example, suppose Michael's family had come for a visit the past weekend, and Susan willingly and happily spent the day with them on Saturday. A discussion of the event in more depth reveals that Susan was appreciative of the space Michael had given her a few days before, and this eased her unwillingness to accommodate to Michael's pressures for intimacy. In addition to giving the therapist an opportunity to reinforce Susan's willingness to accommodate, discussion of positive interactions helps the couple prepare for problem-related interactions that are not quite as successful. These "slip-ups" are inevitable, and there is no better time to discuss them than in the context of successful interactions. After the discussion of a positive interaction, we commonly inquire "When this comes up again, what will you do if does not go as well?" The mere asking of the question emphasizes the inevitability of slip-ups, and the ability to avoid demoralization when these slip-ups occur.

Particularly in the beginning of therapy, the couple may be hard-pressed to come up with any problem-related interaction that ended successfully. If the focus must remain on negative interactions, the IBCT therapist narrows in on the beginning stages of the argument, even pre-incident material, rather than the heated, emotion-laden middle and end of the argument. Once an argument has already gotten fully underway, the blaming and accusations overpower any possibly understandable behaviors that may have predated the actual argument. The partners may feel as if they have already hit "rewind" and "play" on their "argument recorder", replaying the same sequences of anger and frustration they have gone through so many times before. However, if the focus remains on the initial stages of the argument, the therapist can more easily promote acceptance through reframing each partner's understandable behaviors and reactions in a nonblaming, softening way.

Emotional Acceptance through Unified Detachment

By engendering empathy and compassion in each member through counteracting blame, empathic joining around the problem promotes acceptance. Our second strategy, emotional acceptance through unified detachment, promotes acceptance in a slightly different manner. Couples learn how to discuss their problems in a detached, descriptive manner, rather than focus on soft emotional expression. In an intellectual analysis of the sequence of events that lead to conflict and the patterns of conflict that emerge, the therapist avoids any evaluative analysis that puts one partner in a position of culpability for the couple's problems. Instead of the problem being a "you", the problem becomes an "it". By making the problem an "it", the relationship changes from adversarial to two people fighting a common enemy, or handling a cross they both must bear. The couple can share the problem, commiserate about it, and without blaming one another. Like empathic joining, unified detachment can be used throughout a general discussion of the problem, a discussion of an upcoming event that may trigger the problem, discussion of a recent positive event relevant to the problem, and discussion of a recent negative incident relevant to the problem.

When not used in a manner that may demean or embarrass either partner, humor or metaphor can be used to aid detachment and distance from the problem. Consider, for example, Elizabeth and Howard, who have a problem with planning weekend activities. Early in the week, Elizabeth becomes anxious about being able to organize all of their plans for the weekend. When she feels that Howard is not doing his fair share of helping her organize she becomes even more anxious and eager to sit down and plan. In response, Howard avoids interacting with Elizabeth, hoping that he won't have to face the ordeal of trying to coordinate their plans. If a discussion of this interaction pattern could be humorously characterized as the "Eager Elizabeth and Hideaway Howard syndrome", the couple could use this label to maintain enough distance from their problem to begin to notice the roles they are each playing.

Although presented as a separate strategy from empathic joining around the problem, unified detachment and empathic joining are often mixed. For example, a therapist can encourage partners to discuss their own behaviors in a unified, detached manner, and then focus on the soft side of their emotional reactions. If they are unable to use such detached language during the argument (e.g. "This sure feels like a return of the Eager Elizabeth and Hideaway Howard syndrome"), then at the very least they are encouraged to use non-accusatory language after the argument has subsided, when they talk about the accusatory language they used in the heat of the argument.

There are several exercises that help couples detach from their problem, and view the problem as an "it". One exercise involves bringing in a fourth chair to the therapy room, and designating that chair as where the "it" resides. The therapist might say, "Let's put the problem in the chair and talk about it. But whenever you refer to it, talk about it as an 'it' sitting in this chair." When at home, instead of putting the "it" in the chair, the couple can designate the chair as for the therapist. The use of the "imaginary therapist" may enable clients to speak more freely, telling the "therapist" things they have difficulty saying to the face of their partners. Instead of directly blaming and accusing each other, this exercise helps them to use descriptive language in explaining blaming and accusing feelings and thoughts.

Although acceptance strategies are presented separately from change strategies in this chapter, it should be noted that acceptance work often facilities changes. As couples detach from their self-defeating strategies, the solutions can emerge spontaneously. The acceptance work can actually pave the way towards change. For example, when Jason and Chris stopped arguing over how Jason needed to start being more responsible with money, and instead descriptively discussed the difficulties Jason has with money in general, they became closer and Jason ultimately started becoming more responsible.

Emotional Acceptance through Tolerance Building

If it were not for the fact that relationship problems can cause so much pain for each partner, acceptance might come more naturally and spontaneously to all couples. Elimination of all relationship pain is an unrealistic goal, but diminishing the pain is a possibility for most couples. One way to diminish the pain of conflicts is to increase people's tolerance for their partner's behaviors. Promoting tolerance involves techniques designed to expose partners to conflicts in a safe environment where their partners aversive behaviors can be more easily tolerated. Whereas the first two acceptance strategies, empathic joining and unified detachment, result in intimacy because of the problem rather than in spite of it, tolerance building has a more modest goal. Unpleasant behaviors will become less so, the consequences of the arguments will be less catastrophic, and the ability to cope with conflict will increase. Partners give up the struggle to change one another, and instead try to experience each other's negative behaviors in a context that promotes acceptance. Here are examples of four strategies that attempt to achieve that contextual shift.

Highlighting the Positive Features of Negative Behavior

The ability to tolerate a partner's aversive behaviors can be increased if the positive features of these behaviors can be accented. Those familiar with strategic therapy may recognize this strategy as "positive connotation". However, highlighting positive features in the context of IBCT differs from positive connotation in two important ways.

First, IBCT does not attempt to highlight positive features to the exclusion of all negative features. Instead of a wholesale reframing of the problem into a positive light, IBCT continues to acknowledge the negative features. For most couples, a completely positive reframe will lack credibility. Second, we are careful to only delineate positive aspects that truly exist for the couple. For example, if an IBCT therapist understood Hillary's put-downs of Richard's job to reflect her anger at Richard and her desire to hurt him, her put-downs would not be reframed as positive efforts to help Richard. Instead, we might search for the soft emotions that underlie the put-downs, such as her own hurt, or her view that put-downs are the only way to get emotion out of Richard. For this couple, instead of an arbitrary strategic reformulation to promote tolerance, the therapist looks for positive features that resonate with the couple.

When negative behavior can be framed in terms of characteristics that originally attracted or still attract the partner, the strategy of pointing out the positive in the negative is made easier. For example, assume that Hillary's attraction to Richard included his spontaneous nature. On a moment's notice he'd pack his bags and take a week long journey. Whereas other men were boring and predictable, Richard was exciting and dangerous, in the good sense of the word. He encouraged her to become more spontaneous herself, often whisking her away for surprise weekends. When discussing the current problem of Richard's unwillingness to make financial plans for their future, we might emphasize the difference between

Richard and the other men Hillary had dated previously. For example, we might say
to Hillary:

> "Early on you appreciated Richard's spontaneity, and the way he led an
> unpredictable lifestyle. I know that now you wish he would settle down a
> little bit more and make plans for the future, and it upsets you when he
> won't. Although sometimes you still appreciate the surprises Richard can
> bring to the relationship, right now you are mainly feeling the negative side
> of this, that you have to always be the responsible one."

Sometimes the partners may not provide enough information to allow the
therapist to interpret the negative behaviors as at least partly positive. In these
situations, the therapist can point to a general benefit of differences between
people: differences create a balance in a relationship, allowing it to function more
smoothly. For example, if Richard were to be as plan-oriented as Hillary is, their
relationship might lack some of the fun it now has. Or, if Hillary were to be as
spontaneous as Richard is, they would probably run out of money pretty quickly.
Framing the differences in this manner can facilitate both acceptance and change.
The partners will begin to notice that both have important characteristics to
maintain the relationship, it's just that these characteristics have been taken to
extremes. Partners can begin to accept the differences, as well as strive to "tone
down" their side of the difference to help close the gap a little further.

Role-Playing Negative Behavior During the Therapy Session

Traditional behavioral couple therapy has utilized role-playing to teach
couples communications skills within the session that can be used outside of the
session. These skills emphasize more effective ways of communicating one's
desires, without explicitly trying to change these desires. IBCT takes this one step
further by accepting not only the couple's divergent needs but also their sometimes
ineffective ways of communicating those needs. No matter how effective Robin and
Aaron become at signaling each other, there will inevitably be times when they
forget to use the skills they learned. Slip-ups will occur, and accepting the
inevitability of slip-ups will help prevent the exasperation that is likely to be felt by
both partners. Instead of attempting to prevent slip-ups, we help couples prepare
for them.

Based on this rationale, the IBCT therapist will ask the couple to rehearse a slip-
up in the session. During the interaction, the therapist will actively help the couple
discuss the feelings that arise during the role-play, as well as the feelings that might
arise if the interaction were to occur at home. The therapist puts these feelings into
a sympathetic context by emphasizing how understandable they are. For example,
after role-playing a scene in which Robin attacks Aaron for not being affectionate,
the therapist might comment to Robin that she is experiencing the lack of physical
affection in the relationship as neglect. Under those conditions, it is hard for her
not to attack him for being uncaring, because he doesn't seem to act in caring ways.
The therapist will also point out that to Aaron, the attack feels unjustified. He feels
like he's been just going about his daily business. If Robin had asked for some more

affection, he probably would have been happy to give it. But now, after being attacked his feelings are hurt too.

The goal of this exercise is to let couples experience likely scenarios in the absence of destructive forces that muddle each person's abilities to recognize their own thoughts and emotions. Having been desensitized to these situations, they are more able to face the situations with greater acceptance in the future.

Faked Incidents of Negative Behavior at Home

Another strategy designed to increase tolerance to negative behaviors is to have couples fake instances of these behaviors at home. In other words, partners are instructed to engage in these behaviors at times when they are not particularly inclined to do so. For example, Jamie will be asked to purposefully react strongly when Mitch comes home a little late from work. She will plan to act this way, and will pretend to be upset even though she isn't at the moment.

Rather than waiting until a negative interaction occurs, and then debriefing afterwards, IBCT therapists instruct partners to fake the behaviors so that the faker can more clearly see his/her partner's pain. During a real negative interaction, the strong emotional component to arguments tends to override this ability.

Because the instruction to fake negative behavior is given in front of both spouses, a shadow of doubt is cast upon future arguments. When Jamie becomes irate because Mitch isn't home right on time, he won't be sure whether this anger is a spontaneous example of the problem, or a directive from the therapist. Whereas in a normal argument Mitch's stereotypical responses are likely to take over, knowledge of the possibility that Jamie is faking could break this cycle. Jamie will be more likely to empathize with Mitch and understand the bind that he is in which is the source of his defensiveness. The mere knowledge that the partner might be faking changes the function of the negative behavior, thus affecting the impact is it likely to have.

It is quite possible that decreases in the likelihood of the negative behavior may occur as well. However, this is a bonus of the intervention, but not the goal. As with all other tolerance-building interventions described, the goal is decrease the pain that can be felt during negative interactions. The rationale for the assignment is greater desensitization, as well as acceptance of the inevitability of negative behaviors.

Emotional Acceptance through Greater Self-care

Even within couples whose partners ardently strive to meet one another's needs, it is unlikely that all of a person's needs can be met at all times. Increasing each partner's self-reliance is one way of building tolerance and fostering acceptance.

When a partner is unwilling or simply unable to fulfill the needs of the other, a likely response is to passively fume over the partner's inadequacies, or blame the partner for the discontent. However, if needs can be met through other means, engaging in one of those negative behaviors is less likely. The therapist helps partners explore other options for need fulfillment, without giving them the impression that this will absolve them from trying to satisfy their partners when they are capable of doing so. The therapist must be aware that alternative options for need fulfillment will likely be viewed as less ideal. If the attention of the exercise is placed on building a closer relationship, the self-care techniques are more likely to be favorably received.

Even when partners do not utilize the methods of need satisfaction discussed in the therapy discussion, the mere discussion of the importance of autonomy and personal responsibility will likely promote acceptance. For example, even if Jamie doesn't use her own resources to deal with her loneliness when Mitch spends a lot of time on the computer (e.g. exercise, play piano, call a friend), the discussion of alternatives for need fulfillment might help make Mitch's lateness less painful. If she does utilize these methods, the discussion of the incident that follows will likely be less painful, as Jamie has had time to process the interaction.

In the midst of an argument, when the polarization process begins to rear its ugly head, partners are likely to feel vulnerable and in need of self-care. When Jamie accuses Mitch of caring more about his work than his family, something his previous wife also accused him of, he becomes particularly upset. With his strong emotion overriding his ability to use "good communication" skills, he is bound to polarize the situation further by accusing Jamie of being oversensitive and controlling. The cycle becomes more painful as Jamie polarizes further, trying harder to make him listen. It is at these difficult times that spouses may need to rely on self-care behaviors to ameliorate the pain. Common means to achieve this goal include leaving the situation, seeking solace from others, or acting assertively to alter the situation. For example, in the face of Jamie's accusations, Mitch could leave the room, talk to a friend for solace, or assertively inform Jamie that he can not tolerate attacks on his character.

The self-protection strategy used must take the other partner into account. The wrong strategy could actually serve to increase polarization. For example, Mitch leaving the house may make Jamie even more furious, and she may try to chase after him. Because all partners respond differently to the actions of their significant others, the ideographic approach of IBCT must be taken seriously. As with other tolerance building strategies, promoting self-care highlights the likelihood of future arguments, and helps prepare the couple to deal with the anxiety that can arise when slip-ups do occur.

Strategies for Promoting Change

Behavior Exchange (BE) Strategies

BE strategies are direct efforts to identify and change the frequency with which certain behaviors are reinforced and punished. These strategies help couples take advantage of their abilities to please one another by increasing the proportion of positive interactions occurring within the relationship. These strategies primarily use tasks presented by the therapist for completion at home. In TBCT, BE strategies are usually implemented first. However, because the success of BE depends on a couple's ability to collaborate and accommodate to one another, BE as a first intervention is successful only in mildly distressed couples. More distressed couples, or couples whose commitment to the relationship are low, are not successful at using the strategies. Implementing change strategies with couples who do not have the collaborative set necessary to bring about the change only brings about rapid relapse for many couples (Jacobson, 1984). Therefore, within IBCT, acceptance work usually precedes BE.

For most couples, whether or not they are entering therapy, their ability to please one another can dwindle. Perhaps their sexual encounters are less exciting than they used to be, or they just don't seem to enjoy their common interests as much as they did in the past. Some couples take steps to overcome this phenomenon without the aid of a therapist, by discovering creative ways to please one another, or developing new and common interests. Some couples, however, believe that dwindling pleasure is simply part of being married, and resign to the fact that there is nothing that can be done. Many couples who decide to come to therapy present with dissatisfaction in the amount of pleasing behaviors, and an inability to counteract it. Known as "reinforcement erosion" (Jacobson & Margolin, 1979), this phenomenon is directly tackled with BE strategies.

BE strategies help couples overcome reinforcement erosion in three main ways. First, BE strategies emphasize the necessity of putting work, time, and effort into a relationship. Like any other endeavor, relationships need nourishment to survive and flourish. Whereas previous to learning these strategies a couple might cling to the hope that love will carry them through, after learning them they have the tools to carry themselves through. Second, BE techniques provide the partners with the ability to monitor their relationship on a day-to-day basis. In order to increase the quality of a relationship, it is necessary to be able to accurately assess its state, and where it needs improvement. Finally, once a couple learns where in their day-to-day interactions they need improvement, BE strategies provide them with the skills to counteract reinforcement erosion.

In TBCT, both members of a couple are asked to generate lists of behaviors they want from their partners. In contrast, a prototypical BE task in IBCT begins with an assignment for each partner to independently generate a list of their own behaviors that might improve the relationship for their partners. Without any input from the recipient at all, each partner tries to determine which of his/her behaviors, when altered in frequency, could increase the satisfaction of the recipient. The assignment keeps the focus on the role each partner plays in determining the success of the relationship, instead of focusing on the ways each spouse fails to do so.

If the couple completes this homework assignment, they will return to the next therapy session with their finished wish lists. The purpose of this session is to clarify the items on the list, without the aid of the receiving partner. Even if the receiving partner thinks a suggestion is silly or inappropriate, that partner is asked to show no indication. As the giver reads each item on the list, the therapist helps ensure that each item is clearly operationalized. For example, if a wife were to write, "My husband would like it if I was more affectionate", the therapist helps her clarify what she specifically means by "affectionate". Does it mean to hug more often? Does it mean to be more interested in sex? This procedure occurs with each item on the list, while the receiving partner sits quietly and listens. Because the receiver is not providing input, the therapist can help enhance a list by suggesting behaviors that the spouse has brought up previously but may have forgotten to include on the list.

The couples are then assigned to enhance each other's relationship satisfaction. From the generated list, each person chooses a behavior that is expected to increase the other's satisfaction. Partners must be instructed to choose behaviors that will not be self-defeating because of their high cost. Although a high cost behavior might be pleasurable to the recipient, the unpleasantness felt by the giver is likely to be self-defeating. This task of increasing the ratio of positive to negative behaviors has long been a part of behavior exchange procedures. However, choosing to have each person list what the other person would want has several advantages. First, the giver is more likely to engage in a behavior that he/she has chosen, rather than one that has been asked for by the partner. Choosing from a list of possible behaviors to accelerate or decelerate enhances a sense of control. Second, a behavior chosen without input from the partner is more likely to be well received. If a wife thinks, "he is only doing that because I made him, not because he really wants to", she is less likely to be pleased by the behavior. Instead, if the husband chooses the behavior on his own, it will be viewed as more giving and positive.

If the couple returns to the therapy session feeling more satisfied than the previous week, the therapist encourages each spouse to describe what behaviors were chosen from the lists, and which of these behaviors were noticed by the recipient. Additionally, each spouse is asked if the change in behavior seemed to result in increased satisfaction by the partner. Another important piece of information is how "costly" it was for the giver to engage in the chosen behavior. For example, Larry initiated sex more often with Penny, even though he was lacking in sexual desire. Although Penny responded positively, Larry knew that it was not something he could continue doing over the subsequent weeks. On the other side of the coin, Penny spent more time on the weekends with Larry, even though she thought it might be an incredible burden. After engaging in the behavior, she realized she could do so quite effortlessly, and she actually enjoyed doing so.

After discussing which behaviors increased partner satisfaction and which did not, the partners have the opportunity to examine each other's lists and give input. Each item on the list is designated as a "keeper," a "minor but still pleasing" behavior, or "off the mark." Instead of instructing which behaviors should be tried next, this input arms each partner with more information about what pleases the other. Each person also has the opportunity to suggest behaviors to be added to the lists. The same assignment as the previous week is reassigned, and this time each partner has enough information to choose behaviors that will likely have a maximum reinforcing impact.

Some couples do not have success in the first week of trying to please their partners. For some, this simply means they did not comply with the task. Aside from the therapist's failure to assign the task in a clear and easy to understand manner, failure to comply usually means that the task should never had been assigned in the first place. These situations imply that previous acceptance work did not sufficiently promote the ability to collaborate and compromise. For the couples that tried to comply, but did not get good results, it may be that the behaviors chosen simply were not behaviors that would increase the partner's satisfaction. Once the task is reassigned with input from the recipient, this problem is likely to be alleviated.

Communication and Problem-Solving Training

Communication and Problem-Solving Training (CPT) teaches couples skills towards solving future problems that inevitably arise. In contrast to BE, CPT does not focus on presenting problems, or short-term changes in the ratio of positive to negative behaviors. Instead, couples learn how to become their own therapists, enabling them to resolve their own problems in the future. These skills are taught for resolving conflict, not as a means of expression or general communication. Although the expression of feelings is involved in resolving conflict, additional skills are needed to help couples identify their goals when a conflict arises, and create a permissive atmosphere about a range of goals. Problem-solving is a structured interaction designed to resolve a particular dispute, not a spontaneous discussion.

When CPT becomes the focus of therapy, the partner must have direct access to the target behaviors. Examples include engaging in a shared activity, not spending as much money, or doing more housework. However, a behavior such as "lack of sexual desire" is a poor candidate for problem-solving, as it is not under the same amount of voluntary control. Unfortunately, CPT is limited by the fact that many important areas in a relationship, such as love, trust, and self-esteem cannot be defined by instrumental behaviors. Another limiting factor to CPT is that it requires compromise. Decisions with only two possible solutions (e.g. to quit or not quit a job) do not make the brainstorming, negotiation, and cost-benefit analysis of problem-solving possible.

Because problem-solving is a structured interaction, it is only appropriate for certain settings. The heat of an argument is not the place for this interaction. Emotions are too strong, particularly negative emotions, to engage in the negotiation of problem-solving. Instead, the couple should chose a place and a time to problem-solve, preferably at a time when distractions are at a minimum. They should allow enough time to work through the stages of problem-solving for one problem at a time (60 minutes should be the maximum). Attempting to problem-solve more than one problem is too exhausting, and may make the interaction too aversive.

For problem-solving to be successful, each partner must make some short-term sacrifices for the sake of the relationship as a whole. Because many couples come into therapy bound in rigid power struggles, the willingness to make such sacrifices is likely to be nonexistent. It is understandable that after years of struggling with little reinforcement for change, many couples resist making the necessary changes. However, if CPT is proceeded by a focus on promoting acceptance, the couple is much more likely to be able to collaborate and bring the focus away from the individual to the level of the relationship. By reducing blame for negative behavior, and making the behavior more tolerable, the acceptance work allows each partner to come in contact with the natural reinforcement that results from working towards a healthy relationship. The partners are not expected to change all of their behaviors, but to have a focus towards the long-term benefits of change rather than its immediate costs.

There are two distinct phases of problem-solving: problem definition and problem solving. During the problem definition stage, the couple comes up with a clear, specific statement of the problem, without attempting to generate possible solutions. Similarly, during the problem solving phase, the couple attempts to generate possible solutions without backtracking into the problem definition stage. For many couples, communication during such interactions has a history of being chaotic and ambiguous. Keeping the phases distinct provides the structure necessary to make problem-solving efficient.

Stage 1: Problem Definition

There are five rules to follow during the problem definition stage. First, when stating a problem each partner should try to begin with something positive. It is extremely difficult to hear problem statements without becoming defensive, and starting with a positive remark helps prevent this response. An example of a problem statement with a positive beginning is: "I really love seeing you when you come home from work. Because of this it makes me angry when you come home late." Without the positive beginning, the listener is likely to feel attacked. Instead, phrasing the statement with an expression of love in the beginning reminds the listener that care and appreciation exist even through the distress.

The second rule of problem definition is to be specific when defining a problem. Instead of using general statements such as, "you aren't affectionate to me any more", the problem should be described in a way that the listener can identify specific words and actions that bring about the feelings, and the situations in which the problem occurs. There are two ways that couples tend to avoid specificity when defining their problems. One way is by using derogatory adjectives or nouns such as "you are lazy". In addition to being vague, such name-calling will undoubtedly leave the listener feeling defensive. Couples who find it difficult to remove such labels from their speech are probably not ready for CPT, and need to focus more on acceptance work. Another way couples avoid specificity is by using overgeneralizations such as "you're *always* late." Similar to the effects of derogatory adjectives, the listener feels attacked and unsure of the exact situations when the behavior really does occur.

The third rule to problem definition is to share the emotionally upsetting impact of the behavior. For example, a partner might say, "I feel hurt and frightened when you go away for the weekend without telling me where you're going." When such discomfort is disclosed, the listener is more likely to be sympathetic and understanding of the request for change.

The fourth rule to problem-solving is to be brief when defining problems. By overanalyzing the causes of problems, or spending too much time trying to come up with examples of the problem's occurrence, or arguing over nit-picky details, couples are likely to spend an excessive amounts of unproductive time. Although doing all of the above has a place in therapy, its place is not during the definition phase of problem-solving. This is not to say that couples shouldn't try to understand the reasons for the occurrence or non-occurrence of the problem. Clarification is valuable, but unsolicited diatribes on every past misdeed are not.

All the parts are now in place for presenting a well-defined problem: a positive statement, a clear description of the undesirable behavior, a specification of the situations in which the problem occurs, and the emotional effects of the problem. An example of a well-stated problem is: "I think you are a wonderful mother and really have good ideas about how to raise the children, but when you don't discipline them for failing to do their chores I get very angry at you." With a well-defined problem clearly put forth, both the speaker and the listener must acknowledge a role in creating and maintaining the problem. Instead of casting blame, both partners need to accept responsibility or at least acknowledge that the other partner is upset and something will need to change.

Stage 2: Problem Solving

Once a clear definition of the problem has been stated, the first rule to problem solving is to focus on solutions. The discussion should be on the future, on eliminating the problem, not on discussions of the past. The best technique towards achieving this goal is brainstorming. During brainstorming, possible solutions are proposed without a discussion of whether or not they are feasible. No matter how absurd the solution may seem, the couple should write down the solutions as they come to mind. Brainstorming keeps the focus of the interaction on the future, and because no solution is eliminated, each partner feels less inhibited to come up with ideas.

The next step in problem solving is to discuss the pros and cons of proposed solutions. One at a time, each solution on the list is discussed. If the solution is not tossed out for being absurd, the couple considers whether adopting the solution would contribute to resolving the problem. If so, the benefits and costs of adopting the solution are discussed. Once these have been weighed, the couple must decide whether to eliminate the solution from the list, include it, or defer a decision until the other solutions have been discussed.

The final stage in problem solution is to combine the possible solutions to reach an agreement. The final change agreement should be specific, should clearly state what each spouse is going to do differently, should not be open to interpretation, and should be recorded in writing. An example of a change agreement might be: "Each day when Nora and Kevin get home, before dinner Nora will speak with Kevin about the events of her day. Kevin will sit and listen to her talk without engaging in other activities". The behavior change agreement should always include mutuality and compromise. In other words, the solution should involve change on the part of both partners. Partners are more willing to change if both people change, and mutual change agreements allow the complainant to aid the other partner in the behavior change, providing feedback on success. Finally, when a partner has a complaint, it is frequently the case that a change in his/her behavior could increase the chances of the other partner changing his/her behavior. Although both spouses might be willing to compromise, some changes are too drastic to occur all at once. A good solution is to start with a request that may be less than what is ideally wanted, but is still a step in the right direction. Instead of asking for what is ideally wanted, the partners first ask for what they are willing to settle for. Later the request may increase, or the requesting partner may find that the amount of change that has already occurred is acceptable.

Once the final agreement has been written up, both partners should check to make sure that the decision is satisfactory, and that the solution will really address the problem. When the couple has had the opportunity to fulfill the agreement, it should be checked at a future date to make sure it is still working. If it is not, the agreement should be renegotiated through brainstorming new ideas or reevaluating the original solutions.

There are some general guidelines that apply to both problem definition and problem solving. First, the couple should make sure to discuss only one problem at a time. Bringing in additional problems, or "side-tracking", only increases the difficulty of problem-solving. Additionally, each partner should paraphrase the other partner's remarks and then check to make sure the paraphrase was accurate. Such summary statements help clarify and improve communication by forcing each partner to listen more carefully, making sure each partner clearly understands what the other is saying, and preventing the listeners from interrupting. A third guideline is to only talk about observable behaviors. In other words, each partner should avoid mind-reading by making such statements as, "I know that when you come home late it's because of all the built-up anger you have inside." Such statements are likely to make the listener defensive, and do not aid in making the behavioral request more clear and specific. Finally, couples should try to be neutral rather than negative. For problem-solving to be successful, attempts to put down or humiliate must be replaced with collaboration.

Training Methods

The behavioral skills paradigm used to teach CPT consists of instructions, behavior rehearsal, feedback and continued practice until mastery, practice at home, and fading therapist control.

Instruction in CPT is a combination of discussion with the therapist and the reading of certain materials that delineate CPT skills. The readings used are typically the first three chapters of Gottman, Notarius, Gonso, & Markman (1976), as well as a manual developed by Christensen & Jacobson (in press). Once couples understand the readings and the skills described, they begin practicing the skills within the therapy session. As the couple continues practicing the skills, the therapist provides feedback, and the couple incorporates this feedback into their continued practice. Once mastery has been achieved within the therapy session, the couple is instructed to practice at home. Over time, the therapist fades control by becoming less directive, and the couples eventually learn how to have their own conflict resolutions sessions at home.

General Applicability of Treatment

In this era of managed care, treatments are becoming more streamlined to accommodate the decrease in number of sessions allowed. Therapists and researchers have begun to adjust their intervention strategies to the time allotted to them. For therapists interested in conducting IBCT, we have some recommendations for how to proceed under the current health-care conditions.

First, therapists should keep in mind that some couples may have the ability to pay out of pocket for the therapy once the insurance coverage runs out. For these couples, two options are presented. The first option is to contract for only those sessions they are covered for, using a truncated version of IBCT. At the last session their progress is evaluated, and if more sessions are necessary, and they are able to continue, they can pay out of pocket for those remaining sessions. A related option is to do IBCT in its complete form until the insurance runs out. At the end of the allotted number of sessions, the therapy stops and the therapist evaluates whether further sessions are necessary. Both of these situations call into question the ideal number of sessions for IBCT. In our research, the protocol allowed couples up to 25 sessions. However, the number of sessions varied from 13 to 25. In clinical practice, although most couples are seen for an average of 20 sessions, some couples have been successfully treated in as few as 5 sessions. In some cases it might be possible to request extensions in the number of sessions allowed. This requires a persuasive argument, usually containing three factors: 1) Evidence that therapy has reaped some benefits, 2) indications that future therapy would reap further benefits, and 3) empirical validation for the treatment. Perhaps an even more persuasive argument is that of prevention: There is evidence to support that it is easier to prevent marital problems than do deal with them after the fact (cf. Jacobson & Addis, 1993).

Second, despite a decrease in the number of sessions, therapists should not be tempted to drop the acceptance work. It might appear that the quick behavior change sometimes found in BE might override the necessity of promoting acceptance. However, such changes are likely to be short-lived (Jacobson, 1984). Instead, a focus on acceptance work during the limited number of sessions is more likely to make the changes long-lasting.

A third consideration in streamlining treatment is to condense the assessment process. Through the use of questionnaires, the therapist can have a working formulation prior to the first session. The first session then becomes a combination of discussing assessment questions as well as the feedback session, without the individual sessions. The emphasis would remain on delineating a formulation, with less time spent on relationship history and family of origin. If the questionnaires are well utilized, and the first session remains focused on the formulation, the therapist can present the formulation to the couple by the end of the first session.

Another consideration when restricted in terms of the number of sessions is to schedule more time than usual between sessions. Instead of meeting once a week, the couple can meet once every other week, every three weeks, or even once a month. If the couple is focusing on BE or CPT strategies, more tasks can be assigned between sessions, with brief phone calls by the therapist to make sure that the tasks are being completed. If the focus of therapy is promoting acceptance, the delay between sessions gives the couple more time to integrate the formulation into their daily interactions. Because more slip-ups are likely to occur during a longer period between sessions, the delay allows the therapist the opportunity to assess whether tolerance-building strategies are having the desired effect.

Because more progress tends to be made in acceptance work when there are incidents to discuss, another option for dealing with fewer sessions is to schedule sessions at the time incidents occur, rather than according to specified time intervals. The opportunity to "strike while the iron is hot" can be seized, and the session can focus on the polarization that is likely to be occurring, and how to soften anger and frustration.

Outcome

We have recently completed a federally funded pilot study comparing IBCT to TBCT. Twenty couples were randomly assigned to one of the two treatments and completed 20 weeks of therapy. All couples were seen at the Center for Clinical Research, Jacobson's laboratory at the University of Washington. Five therapists from the community were trained in both approaches, with half of the cases being supervised by Jacobson, and the other half by Christensen. Four of the therapists were licensed psychologists, while the fifth graduated with a master's degree from a training program in marital and family therapy. All of the videotaped therapy sessions were viewed by supervisors and monitored for adherence and competence by trained and expert raters.

In order to clearly show the superiority of IBCT over TBCT, we had to ensure that therapists could keep each of the two treatments distinct. Our data shows that therapists did indeed administer separate protocols for IBCT and TBCT (Eldridge, 1995). We hypothesized that both TBCT and IBCT would include behavior change techniques, though TBCT would contain more. The results supported these hypotheses, with results indicating that behavior change techniques were found in IBCT and TBCT, but were used more often in TBCT. We also predicted that IBCT would contain more acceptance work than TBCT. Analyses revealed that acceptance work was used often in IBCT, and very little in TBCT (Eldridge, 1995).

Perhaps most importantly, our outcome analyses showed that IBCT couples reported significantly more relationship satisfaction than TBCT couples. Furthermore, whereas 50% of the TBCT couples showed significant improvement, virtually every couple that completed IBCT showed clinically significant improvement, with a vast majority recovering to the point that they were no longer distinguishable from happily married couples on measures of marital satisfaction. These improvements were maintained at a 6-month follow-up. Interestingly, both husbands and wives in the IBCT condition reported more positive behavior changes in their partners than TBCT couples. This supports the theory that acceptance interventions can often be important vehicles for change.

Conclusion

In this chapter we have presented the latest developments in the evolution of the treatment of marital discord. Based on a concern for those couples for whom TBCT was unable to help, the development of IBCT has led to a freedom from the traditional constraints of behavior change. The integration of strategies designed to promote change with those designed to promote acceptance offers an important and needed step forward in helping couples in distress.

Dedication

I would like to dedicate this chapter to my advisor, mentor, and dear friend Neil Jacobson, who passed away on June 2, 1999. Many people know of his enormous intellectual and creative contributions to the field of marital therapy. However, Neil was much more than an intellectual force. He was also a kind, generous, funny, loving man who cared deeply for his family, friends, and students. He will be greatly missed. -SB

References

Baucom, D. H. & Hoffman, J. A. (1986). The effectiveness of marital therapy: current status and applications to the clinical setting. In N. S. Jacobson (Ed.), *Clinical handbook of marital therapy* (pp. 597-620). New York: Guilford.

Burman, B. & Margolin, G. (1992). Analysis of the association between marital relationships and health problems: an international perspective. *Psychological Bulletin, 112,* 39-63.

Christensen, A. & Jacobson, N. S. (in press) *When lovers make war.* New York: Guilford.

Christensen, A., Jacobson, N. S., and Babcock, J. C. (1995). Integrative behavioral couple therapy. In N. S. Jacobson & A. S. Gurman (Eds.), *Clinical handbook of couples therapy* (pp. 31-64). New York: Guilford.

Eldridge, K.E. (1995). Treatment integrity in Traditional Behavioral Couple Therapy and Integrative Behavioral Couple Therapy. Unpublished master's thesis, University of California Los Angeles, Los Angeles, CA.

Ferster, C. B. (1967). Arbitrary and natural reinforcement. *Psychological Record, 22,* 1-16.

Gotlib, I. H. & McCabe, S. B. (1990). Marriage and psychopathology. In F. D. Fincham & T. N. Bradbury (Eds.) *The psychology of marriage: basic issues and applications.* New York: Guilford.

Gottman, J. M. (1993). The roles of conflict engagement, escalation, and avoidance in marital interaction: a longitudinal view of five types of couples. *Journal of Consulting and Clinical Psychology, 61,* 6-15.

Gottman, J., Notarius, C., Gonso, J., & Markman, H. (1976). *A couple's guide to communication.* Champaign, IL: Research Press.

Gurman, A. S. (1991). Back to the future, ahead to the past: is marital therapy going in circles? *Journal of Family Psychology, 4,* 402-406.

Gurman, A. S., Kniskern, D. P., & Pinsof, W. M. (1986). Research on the process and outcome of marital and family therapy. In S. L. Garfield & A. E. Bergin (Eds.) *Handbook of psychotherapy and behavior change* (pp. 565-624). New York: Wiley.

Hahlweg, K. & Markman, H. J. (1988). Effectiveness of behavioral marital therapy: empirical status of behavioral techniques in preventing and alleviating marital distress. *Journal of Consulting and Clinical Psychology, 56,* 440-447.

Hahlweg, K., Schindler, L., Revenstorf, D., & Brangelmann, J.C. (1984). The Munich marital therapy study. In K. Hahlweg & N. S. Jacobson (Eds.) *Marital interaction: Analysis and modification* (pp. 3-26). New York: Guilford.

Hayes, S. C. (1989). *Rule-governed behavior: Cognition, contingencies, and instructional control.* New York: Plenum Press.

Jacobson, N. S. (1978). Specific and nonspecific factors in the effectiveness of a behavioral approach to the treatment of marital discord. *Journal of Consulting and Clinical Psychology, 46,* 442-452.

Jacobson, N. S. (1984). A component analysis of behavioral marital therapy: the relative effectiveness of behavior exchange and problem solving training. *Journal of Consulting and Clinical Psychology, 52,* 295-305.

Jacobson, N. S. (1989). The politics of intimacy. *The Behavior Therapist, 12,* 29-32.

Jacobson, N. S. (1992). Behavioral couple therapy: A new beginning. *Behavior Therapy, 23,* 493-506.

Jacobson, N. S. and Addis, M. E. (1993). Research on couples and couple therapy: what do we know? Where are we going? *Journal of Consulting and Clinical Psychology, 61,* 85-93.

Jacobson, N. S. & Christensen, A. (1996). *Integrative couple therapy: Promoting acceptance and change.* New York: W.W. Norton.

Jacobson, N. S. & Margolin, G. (1979). *Marital therapy: Strategies based on social learning and behavior exchange principles.* New York: Brunner/Mazel.

Jacobson, N. S., Follette, W. C., & Pagel, M. (1986). Predicting who will benefit from behavioral marital therapy. *Journal of Consulting and Clinical Psychology, 54,* 518-522.

Jacobson, N. S., Schmaling, K. B., & Holtzworth-Munroe, A. (1987). Component analysis of behavioral marital therapy: Two-year follow-up and prediction of relapse. *Journal of Marital and Family Therapy, 13,* 187-195.

Johnson, S. M. & Greenberg, L. S. (1991). The emotionally focused approach to problems in adult attachment. In N. S. Jacobson & A. S. Gurman (Eds.) *Clinical handbook of couple therapy* (pp. 121-141). New York: Guilford.

Skinner, B. F. (1966). *The behavior of organisms: An experimental analysis.* Englewood Cliffs, NJ: Prentice Hall.

Skinner, B. F. (1974). *About behaviorism.* New York: Knopf.

Snyder, D. K. & Wills, R. M. (1991). Facilitating change in marital therapy and research. *Journal of Family Psychology, 4,* 426-435.

Chapter 9

CRA: The Community Reinforcement Approach for Treating Alcohol Problems

Jane Ellen Smith
Robert J. Meyers
University of New Mexico
and the Center for Alcohol, Substance Abuse
and Addictions, University of New Mexico

Overview

The Community Reinforcement Approach (CRA) is a broad spectrum behavioral program for treating substance abuse problems. It is based on the belief that environmental contingencies can play a powerful role in encouraging or discouraging drinking or drug-using behavior. Consequently, it utilizes social, recreational, familial, and vocational reinforcers to assist clients in the recovery process. Its goal is to rearrange various aspects of an individual's "community" such that a sober lifestyle is more rewarding than one involving alcohol and drugs.

Three recent meta-analytic reviews ranked CRA as one of the most efficacious and cost-effective alcohol treatments. Holder, Longabaugh, Miller, and Rubonis (1991) defined efficacy by a weighted evidence index. This value was based on whether an intervention had shown superior results to another program on a drinking-related measure at some point during the follow-up period. The cost of program implementation was estimated from national and regional data. In their rank ordering of 33 treatments, CRA was placed fifth. A second meta-analysis (Miller, et al., 1995) utilized cumulative evidence scores based on ratings of the methodological quality of each study. CRA was positioned fourth in this ranking. Finally, the meta-analysis by Finney and Monahan (1995) introduced an adjusted effectiveness index. This took into consideration the probability that a study would yield a significant treatment effect, as determined by such factors as the number of tests conducted, the sample size, and the strength of the comparison treatments used. This time CRA moved into the top position in the ranking.

CRA Procedures

The components of the CRA program are presented next. The assessment and treatment planning techniques are utilized with all clients, but only those skills training procedures deemed necessary for addressing a client's particular behavioral deficits are introduced clinically.

CRA Functional Analyses

Although a functional analysis is a standard part of most behavior analytic treatments, it is still a relatively rare tool as far as substance abuse programs. Within the alcohol field, most inpatient and many outpatient centers continue to be built around the concept of denial, and the belief that denial is handled most capably through confrontation. So the typical message received by clients upon entering treatment is, "You're an alcoholic and you can never drink again." CRA therapists believe that not only is this an ineffectual way to establish rapport, but it is an attitude that makes assumptions about or simply ignores the role that the drinking is serving. Knowledge of the context in which the drinking is occurring is vital for the CRA program, and consequently a functional analysis is the first order of business.

One of the unique features of the CRA functional analysis is that both drinking and non-drinking behaviors are examined routinely, since each is believed to be maintained by contingencies of reinforcement. For the drinking (or drug-using) behavior, many CRA therapists gather the relevant information about antecedents and consequences through a semi-structured interview, while utilizing one of the available charts (see Figure 1).

The first goal in conducting the functional analysis for drinking behavior is to identify the client's triggers for alcohol use, so that the establishing operations are readily apparent. The CRA therapist begins this discussion by asking the client to describe a fairly common drinking scenario. Questions are posed until both the external and internal triggers for drinking are clearly outlined. The former are environmental factors, such as people, places, and times frequently associated with alcohol use. For example, a client might report that he tends to drink on the two evenings that he works overtime. The other critical external antecedents include leaving the office on those nights with a heavy-drinking colleague, and stopping with this friend at a favorite pub with the expressed intention of "just getting some dinner." The therapist labels this environmental context as a high-risk situation for the client, and moves on to an exploration of internal triggers. These are the thoughts, physical sensations, and emotions that set the stage for the drinking episode. In other words, the therapists does not assume that the mere presence of a drinking companion is sufficient to trigger the use of alcohol, but that other factors contribute. Imagine, for example, that this client reports feeling physically exhausted and emotionally stressed on these same occasions when he works overtime. His thoughts are along the line of, "I need to relax" and "I deserve a little bit of fun after working so hard today." As is often the case, this client engages in both Type P and Type N drinking; the former implying that the drinking is positively reinforcing (i.e. for relaxation and fun) and the latter indicating that it also is negatively reinforcing (i.e. it alleviates stress) (Wulfert, Greenway, & Dougher, 1996). The CRA therapist accepts the client's thoughts and feelings that are

CRA FUNCTIONAL ANALYSIS FOR DRINKING BEHAVIOR (INITIAL ASSESSMENT)

External Triggers	Internal Triggers	Drinking Behavior	Short-Term Positive Consequences	Long-Term Negative Consequences
1. Who are you usually with when you drink?	1. What are you usually thinking about right before you drink?	1. What do you usually drink?	1. What do you like about drinking with _____? (who)	1. What are the negative results of your drinking in each of these areas: a) Interpersonal:
			2. What do you like about drinking _____? (where)	b) Physical:
2. Where do you usually drink?	2. What are you usually feeling physically right before you drink?	2. How much do you usually drink?	3. What do you like about drinking _____? (when)	c) Emotional:
			4. What are some of the pleasant thoughts you have while you are drinking?	d) Legal:
3. When do you usually drink?	3. What are you usually feeling emotionally right before you drink?	3. Over how long a period of time do you usually drink?	5. What are some of the pleasant physical feelings you have while you are drinking?	e) Job:
				f) Financial:
			6. What are some of the pleasant emotional feelings you have while you are drinking?	g) Other:

Figure 1. CRA Functional Analysis for Drinking Behavior (Initial Assessment). Source: From Clinical guide to alcohol treatment: The community reinforcement approach (pp. 34-35) by R. J. Meyers & J. E. Smith, 1995, New York: Guilford Press. Copyright 1995 by Guilford Press. Adapted by permission.

associated with excessive drinking, and explains how therapy will focus on finding healthier options for relaxing and having fun after a stressful day at work.

The middle segment of the CRA functional analysis entails gathering basic quantity and frequency information about the drinking behavior. The severity of the alcohol problem often can be gleaned from this, and progress can be monitored by referring back to this data throughout treatment. The final part of the CRA functional analysis examines the consequences of the drinking behavior. The short-term positive experiences are explored first, since these are the factors that are maintaining the behavior. The goal is to acknowledge the function of the drinking, and eventually to work toward finding alternate routes to those same outcomes, or to modify a series of behaviors so that the outcomes are no longer needed. In the case of the client who reportedly stops at a pub to relax, have fun, and alleviate stress, it is first important to verify that these are, in fact, the normal consequences of the drinking, and to investigate whether there are others. It would not be unusual, for example, for the client to add that some of his enjoyment stems from the fact that he often runs into one or two female "admirers" there. The CRA functional analysis for drinking chart is designed to elicit this and additional important information, since it asks not only about the pleasant aspects associated with the external drinking environment, but it also inquires about the thoughts and feeling prompted by the alcohol. It would be useful to know, for example, whether the client is also saying to himself at the pub, "Wow, that woman seems interested in me. I'm going to be brave and ask her out." With prompting the therapist may learn that the client's self-esteem typically is enhanced in these situations, and that he feels confident enough to be socially assertive.

In summary, a host of factors are maintaining the client's drinking in this particular environment. In order for the client to be able to eliminate his excessive drinking, he will need to have other avenues for increasing self-esteem, feeling socially assertive, relaxing, and alleviating stress. The solution may involve a combination of approaches, such as helping the client find enjoyable non-drinking social activities, teaching him social skills, helping him develop new ways to relax, or decreasing his job stress in the first place. But given that a certain amount of time is required to build new behavioral repertoires, it is necessary to focus part of the initial functional analysis on the long-term negative consequences of the drinking. In this manner a clear connection is made between the problematic drinking and its cost to the client.

The long-term negative consequences column on the CRA chart serves as a reminder to the therapist to inquire about several basic areas in which drinking is likely to have had a negative impact: interpersonal, physical, emotional, legal, job, and financial. Although the client may be painfully aware of some of these connections already, additional consequences often are discovered during the interview. Furthermore, the CRA therapist finds it useful to have a list of negative consequences that can be referred to in later sessions. So assume the client states that the only downside to his drinking is the DWI that brought him into treatment (legal area). With some discussion the client may also report that he does not function quite as well at work on the days he has a hangover (job area), and that he spends a lot of money on alcohol (financial area). The therapist may pursue the matter further by asking whether the client is satisfied with his relationships with women that typically begin in an intoxicated state at a bar (interpersonal area), or whether his health has suffered as a result of his habit of "drinking" his dinners (physical area). The CRA therapist does not inquire about these problems in an effort to shame the client, but instead to gain information about the individual's reinforcers.

The second type of CRA functional analysis is for pleasurable non-drinking behaviors (see Figure 2). One purpose of this exercise is to highlight the fact that the client already is engaging in enjoyable activities that do not involve alcohol. Eventually the therapist will encourage the client to increase the frequency of participation in these or other pleasurable, alcohol-free activities. But in order to set the stage to do this, the functional analysis is needed to outline both the common precursors for this behavior as well as some of the unfavorable consequences. Since in this situation the goal will be to increase the chances that this behavior will occur, the therapist will teach the client to recognize these triggers and to respond more regularly to them with a healthy behavior. Also, the therapist later will teach problem-solving skills in an effort to reduce any of the minimally negative consequences associated with the mostly pleasurable activities.

Clients usually react enthusiastically to the notion of focusing on ways to increase the positive activities in their lives. To begin with, over the years most drinkers have had innumerable people, including therapists, dwelling on all of the enjoyable, alcohol-related things that they should *stop* doing. So it comes as a surprise to have a therapist explain how it is equally important to introduce pleasant activities that can compete with and replace drinking behaviors. With this in mind, the therapist invites the client to select one pleasurable, non-drinking activity that already is in his or her behavioral repertoire, and then to describe the external and internal triggers that set the stage for the behavior (see Figure 2). Assume that the client introduced earlier wants to examine his weekend gardening for his pleasurable activity. If the therapist determines that the gardening competes with weekend drinking, then a functional analysis would be completed for it. Regardless, it would still be necessary for the client to also identify an activity that could compete with the weeknight drinking.

Imagine that the client says he periodically enjoys participating in an ongoing coed volleyball league that has weeknight games. Since the client indicates that volleyball conceivably could compete with drinking, a functional analysis is completed to determine whether it appears to offer some of the same reinforcers as drinking. In examining the external triggers, the therapist learns that the client's team members do not tend to drink together. Also, the games are played in a gym that is relatively close to the client's workplace, and they frequently are scheduled for later in the evening on the days that the client works overtime. The therapist elects to continue with this particular activity, since it does not place the client in a high-risk situation, it seems feasible, and it is available during a high-risk time. In exploring the internal triggers for playing volleyball, the therapist listens for signs

CRA FUNCTIONAL ANALYSIS FOR NON-DRINKING BEHAVIOR (_____)
(behavior/activity)

External Triggers	Internal Triggers	Non-drinking Behavior	Short-Term Negative Consequences	Long-Term Positive Consequences
1. Who are you usually with when you ____? (behavior/activity)	1. What are you usually thinking about right before you ____?	1. What is the non-drinking behavior/activity?	1. What do you dislike about ____ (behavior/activity) with ____ ? (who)	1. What are the positive results of ____ (behavior/activity) in each of these areas: a) Interpersonal:
	2. What are you usually feeling physically right before you ____?	2. How often do you usually ____?	2. What do you dislike about ____ (behavior/activity) ____ ? (where)	b) Physical:
2. Where do you usually ____?	3. What are you usually feeling emotionally right before you ____?	3. How long does ____ usually last?	3. What do you dislike about ____ (behavior/activity) ____ ? (when)	c) Emotional:
			4. What are some of the unpleasant thoughts you usually have while you are ____ ?	d) Legal:
3. When do you usually ____?			5. What are some of the unpleasant physical feelings you usually have while you are ____ ?	e) Job:
			6. What are some of the unpleasant emotional feelings you usually have while you are ____ ?	f) Financial:
				g) Other:

Figure 2. CRA Functional Analysis for Non-drinking Behavior.

Source: From Clinical guide to alcohol treatment: The community reinforcement approach (pp. 38-39) by R. J. Meyers & J. E. Smith, 1995, New York: Guilford Press. Copyright 1995 by Guilford Press. Adapted by permission.

that can be turned into cues to select volleyball over drinking. For example, assume the client states that typically before playing volleyball he is thinking about how he needs the exercise and that he is anxious to see his friends. The therapist may ask him to focus on the fitness thoughts, since attention to the social aspects could steer him toward the pub instead. Additionally, the therapist would listen for any ambivalent feelings that may precede the volleyball decision, and which consequently could act as a deterrent. So if the client reports that sometimes he almost talks himself out of a sporting activity because he feels too tired, the therapist might introduce problem-solving to address the reasons for the fatigue in the first place, or to devise a plan for motivating the client to play despite feeling tired.

The column for describing the non-drinking behavior frequently has been completed already at this point in the functional analysis, and so the therapist moves to the short-term negative consequences. Not surprisingly, many pleasurable activities have some aversive components that, at times, interfere with the decision to select that activity. The functional analysis helps sort out these various factors by specifically inquiring about the client's negative thoughts and feelings both during and immediately following the behavior of interest. Suppose, for example, the client reports that he dislikes playing with one team member, due to his highly competitive spirit and sarcastic remarks. The therapist would determine the threat posed by this other player as far as dissuading the client from selecting volleyball as his evening activity. A reasonable degree of threat would call for problem-solving. Suppose the client also mentions the fatigue factor again, particularly after the 9 P.M. games. The therapist might first ask the client to monitor his tiredness for a week, to see if it is more pronounced on the days after he has been out drinking. If so, the tiredness automatically will be addressed once the drinking is reduced. If one of the short-term negative feelings is disappointment related to making an unfavorable impression on a female member of another team, the therapist would investigate whether the problem could best be handled through social skills training, or perhaps by scheduling some additional non-drinking coed social occasions.

As far as identifying the long-term positive consequences for the non-drinking behavior, the same categories are presented as for the drinking chart. In this situation the therapist takes note of the client's reinforcers, so that they can be incorporated into subsequent sessions and presented as reasons to pursue a healthier life-style. The therapist does not shy away from suggesting other possible reinforcing aspects of the behavior, since activities that are seen as rewarding in many different areas of the client's life will probably be good candidates for behaviors that compete with drinking. So assume the client reports that an interpersonal benefit of the volleyball games is that he enjoys the friendships that have resulted. Eventually the client may be asked to consider planning additional recreational activities with some of these individuals, particularly if they are nondrinkers. The client may also be encouraged to think about the types of friends or romantic partners who complement his long-term relationship goals: those who are intoxicated at a bar, or those who are playing a sport together.

Although functional analyses for drinking and non-drinking behaviors are always completed at the beginning of CRA treatment, they are referred to throughout the program and new ones are introduced as needed. Some therapists elect to send copies of the charts home with clients to serve as reminders of high-risk situations and their warning signals, or in the case of the non-drinking charts, to prompt them to select behaviors that compete with drinking.

Sobriety Sampling

CRA can be used with individuals having goals of either abstinence or moderate drinking. Regardless, the initial stages of the program are identical, since at least a limited period of abstinence at the start of treatment is deemed essential for all. This works to increase nonalcoholic behaviors, thereby enhancing the relevant consequences as reinforcers (Dougher & Hackbert, 1994). Some of the specific advantages of a "time-out" from drinking include:

1. It allows the client to experience the sensation of being sober on a daily basis. After a short time this usually focuses attention automatically on positive changes in cognitive, emotional, and physical symptoms.
2. It disrupts old habits that involve drinking and gives the client the opportunity to substitute new coping behaviors.
3. It is viewed by family members as a commitment to change, which in turn elicits their support.
4. It affords the client some practice in setting and achieving manageable goals, which then works to enhance self-esteem and confidence.
5. In the event that the client experiences difficulty in maintaining sobriety during this monitored period, it provides valuable information regarding troublesome areas.

CRA therapists typically present much of this information to new clients as they discuss the notion of sampling sobriety for a limited time period. Clients tend to be much more receptive to this message than to the traditional one of never being able to drink again, particularly if they do not think they even have a drinking problem. Sobriety Sampling operates on the assumption that one can more successfully hook individuals into treatment by not overwhelming them with rigid rules and frightening expectations. Once in treatment, the belief is that a marked increase in the density of reinforcement for the client will accompany sobriety, thereby keeping the client invested in therapy.

Once a client agrees to sample sobriety, a reasonable period of time must be selected. The therapist should first suggest a relatively lengthy period, such as 90 days, knowing fully that this will leave plenty of room for negotiation downward. The suggestion should be backed with the rationale that the first 90 days appears to be the time during which most relapses occur (Marlatt, 1980). The majority of clients report that they are unwilling or unable to make a 90-day commitment. The

CRA therapist does not interpret this as resistance, but instead simply works with the client to select a shorter time period that appears challenging yet obtainable. Whenever possible, the client's reinforcers are introduced to provide an added incentive. For example, assume a drinker has reported on her functional analysis that one of the negative interpersonal consequences associated with her alcohol use is that her daughter does not like to spend time with her in public. One specific instance is the daughter stating that she is uncomfortable having her mom attend her dance recitals when she has been drinking. The therapist would inquire about any upcoming social functions with the daughter, and would point out, if applicable, that 30 days of sobriety would take the mom through her daughter's next recital.

Whether the negotiated period for sobriety is 3 or 30 days, the therapist will need to help the client devise a plan for accomplishing this at least until the necessary skills can be taught. Typically the therapist refers to the client's triggers on the functional analysis, and assists in identifying behaviors that compete with drinking in those high-risk situations. Problem-solving training is often introduced at this point as well. Finally, sessions are scheduled several times per week during this stage in therapy, so that the client will have the opportunity to quickly learn the skills needed to honor the sobriety commitment. Assuming that a client reaches the negotiated sobriety goal, the therapist typically discusses the advantages of sampling sobriety for an additional limited period. The many reinforcers already received by the client for being abstinent are reviewed.

Monitored Disulfiram

Some clients appear unable to achieve a period of abstinence early in treatment, despite their desire to do so. For these individuals, the addition of disulfiram to their treatment program may be indicated. Disulfiram (Antabuse) is a medication that acts as a deterrent to drinking, since the ingestion of any alcohol while taking disulfiram causes an aversive chemical reaction. Depending on a number of factors, the individual will react anywhere on a continuum from feeling mildly sick, to requiring emergency medical attention. So disulfiram tends to be an extremely effective punisher, but obviously only if individuals agree to take it in the first place, and then only as long as they remain on it.

Individuals who appear to be good candidates for disulfiram are presented with its pros and cons. The advantages include:

1. A reduction in "slips" that result from impulsive drinking.
2. A decrease in complicated, agonizing daily decisions about drinking, because there is only one decision to make each day: whether or not to take the pill.
3. An increase in family trust and a decrease in family worry.
4. An increase in the ability to address many drinking triggers at once.
5. An increase in opportunities for positive reinforcement, since at the very least the client will be praised daily by the monitor who is administering the disulfiram.

If the client agrees to take disulfiram it must first be cleared by a physician. Then a monitor must be identified. This individual is a concerned family member or friend who is available to administer the disulfiram to the client daily. The monitor is invited to a therapy session so that he or she can be trained to communicate with the client during the daily disulfiram administration in a manner that is positively reinforcing. For example, the monitor might be taught to hand the disulfiram to the drinker and say, "Thank you for taking your disulfiram again. It shows me how serious you are about stopping drinking. I know it must be hard to do." The client would be instructed to reply in a supportive manner as well. But since this type of conversation is not typically a natural one, it would be rehearsed several times during the session and feedback would be provided. The client and monitor would then be asked to select a time and place to take the disulfiram daily, so as to establish a routine (see Meyers & Smith, 1995, pp. 72-73 for a complete description).

Clients do not usually remain on disulfiram for more than a few months. This is sufficient time to teach most problem drinkers the necessary skills to support a non-drinking life-style. Additionally, the density of reinforcement usually increases during this alcohol-free period, as family, friends, and bosses respond positively to the behavior changes in the drinker. This, in turn, supports continued sobriety.

CRA Treatment Plan

Two instruments form the basis of CRA's behavioral treatment plan: The Happiness Scale and the Goals of Counseling form. The former is a one-page questionnaire that inquires about an individual's current level of happiness in 10 categories: drinking, job/educational progress, money management, social life, personal habits, marriage/family relationships, legal issues, emotional life, communication, and general happiness. The client circles a number from 1 (completely unhappy) to 10 (completely happy) for each category. The Happiness Scale provides a precounseling baseline of dissatisfaction across a number of problem areas, and subsequent administrations of it serve as evaluations of progress. Clients typically react positively to completing this form, as it illustrates that the therapy will focus on other important areas of their lives in addition to the substance use.

Once problem areas are identified, the next step entails devising behavioral goals. The Goals of Counseling form provides a useful framework for this exercise, as it includes the same 10 categories listed on the Happiness Scale. As with most behavioral plans, both the goals and the strategies for obtaining them are specified in brief and measurable terms. Also, an emphasis is placed on stating goals in a positive manner; namely, what the client *will* do, as opposed to what he or she will *not* do anymore. Experience shows that clients usually know what they should stop doing, but they often are unaware of how to replace the behavior. Given that this manner of speaking does not come naturally, the therapist spends time shaping the verbal behavior. For example, assume a client wishes to work on communication with his teenage daughter. A common first attempt at stating a goal might be, "I want to stop arguing with my daughter all the time." The therapist would reinforce the client's efforts in general, and the fact that the goal was worded briefly. Guidance would be provided to redefine the goal in positive, measurable terms, such as, "I will excuse myself and leave the room for a minute if I catch myself starting to yell at my daughter." A companion goal might be, "I will compliment my daughter once a day."

Specific strategies for achieving the goals must be identified next. Depending on the individual's skills, several steps may need to be outlined. For instance, the client may require assistance both in generating a list of potential compliments for his daughter, and in determining appropriate times to deliver them. He may also need to analyze the sequence of behaviors that results in an argument, so that he is aware of the precursors to his own outbursts of anger. He can then be taught to recognize these antecedents as signals to respond differently (e.g. leave the room). Additional options for responding would be developed in later sessions using problem-solving.

The CRA treatment plan is similar to the functional analysis inasmuch as it is referred to and modified throughout treatment. Not only do clients' goals change as therapy progresses, but the strategies available to them for achieving the goals diversify as clients acquire additional behavioral skills.

Behavioral Skills Training

An essential component of the CRA program involves identifying areas of behavioral skill deficits, and then providing training to enhance those skills. Therapists often proceed by returning to the functional analysis to review the role served by the drinking. For those situations in which the drinking is maintained by positive reinforcement, the therapist would ascertain whether the client has the behavioral repertoire to obtain positive reinforcement through healthier means. For example, if the drinking is experienced as pleasant because it provides an opportunity to socialize with friends, then the therapist would assess whether the client possesses the communication skills to meet new, non-drinking friends. In the event that the client is already reasonably socially skillful, but is uncertain how to find non-drinking friends, problem-solving training would be indicated instead. Finally, if the client is willing to seek new social outlets, but his or her unassertive style is a risk factor for joining in and drinking if alcohol is offered, then drink-refusal training would be introduced. For cases in which the drinking is maintained by negative reinforcement, such as decreasing stress and anxiety, the therapist would determine whether the client needed problem-solving training to assist in generating other feasible options for alleviating stress.

In terms of *communication skills training*, there are many excellent options available. The CRA program relies on a basic approach that offers seven guidelines for improving conversations, particularly those that involve discussions of problems. They were selected because they offer a precise communication in a manner that minimizes a defensive reaction from the listener. The steps are:

1. Be brief.
2. Be positive.

3. Use specific (quantifiable) terms.
4. Label your feelings.
5. Give an understanding statement.
6. Accept partial responsibility.
7. Offer to help.

The therapist points out that the first three steps were already taught as part of learning how to formulate clear goals and strategies for the treatment plan. Steps 4 and 5 are seen as working together, since one is a comment about the client's feelings, while the understanding statement introduces empathy. Clients are asked to make a partial responsibility statement as a way of showing acceptance for some role in creating the problem, and offering to help is viewed as a positive first step toward devising a solution. Clients sometimes express resentment when asked to practice the last two steps if they believe that they are, in fact, not at all responsible for the problem. The therapist reminds these clients that communication can only be effective if the other person listens to it, and that the last two steps play an important role in facilitating this.

Behavioral rehearsal and modeling are important parts of communication skills training. Assume a client's first attempt at asking his wife to stop inquiring about where he is going every time he leaves the room is, "Please stop following me everywhere. It's annoying. I told you I wasn't drinking anymore." The therapist would reinforce the client for being brief and for labeling his feelings, and then would model an improved conversation that incorporated additional steps. The conversation eventually would approximate the following: "Honey, I can see why you're worried about me (understanding statement), because I haven't always been totally honest with you in the past (partial responsibility). But it bothers me when you follow me into the kitchen and garage (feelings; specific terms). Is there something I can do now (offer to help), so that you're comfortable, even when you can't always see what I'm up to?" (positive terms).

Although most clients improve dramatically throughout the training process, some still are only able to incorporate a few of the steps into their conversations. These clients are verbally rewarded nonetheless for their efforts, and are informed that the use of even just 1-2 new steps is seen as an improvement over previous communications. Generalization of skills into the real world is monitored.

The second area of focus within CRA's behavioral skills program is *problem-solving training*. A modified version of D'Zurilla and Goldfried's (1971) approach is utilized. The purpose of the procedure is to teach clients a structured format for addressing problems in any area. The steps are as follows:

1. Define the problem. The client verbalizes the problem, and the therapist helps modify it so that it is stated clearly and in very specific terms.
2. Brainstorm possible solutions. The client is encouraged to generate a list of potential solutions to the problem. The therapist ensures that none of the ideas will be criticized; that no suggestion will be considered too odd or wild. All of the suggestions are written down for

the client to see on a blackboard or tablet. Usually at least 10 suggestions are expected, and so the therapist may need to assist by offering a few ideas.

3. Eliminate undesired solutions. The client is instructed simply to cross out any solutions that he or she is not interested in trying in the upcoming week. Explanations for eliminating the different suggestions are not expected.

4. Select one potential solution. The client is asked to examine the remaining solutions, to select one, and to agree to trying it prior to the next session.

5. Generate possible obstacles. The client is asked to consider potential obstacles in the upcoming week that might interfere with carrying out the selected solution. Common examples may be given: forgetting, becoming too busy.

6. Devise a plan for each obstacle. The client is instructed to devise a specific plan for addressing each obstacle. If this proves impossible to do, the client is asked to select a different solution.

7. Evaluate the effectiveness of the solution. At the next session the therapist checks with the client to ascertain whether the solution was attempted, and if so, how well it worked. Frequently the solution needs to be modified somewhat for the next week, and sometimes a new solution is decided upon instead.

Problem-solving training is an excellent mechanism for teaching independence. To facilitate its application to real-life issues as they occur, the therapist should utilize problem-solving during sessions whenever a current problem is raised by the client. For instance, if a client arrives 20 minutes late for a session and explains that he is having trouble getting a ride, the therapist should introduce the problem-solving procedure to generate a solution to the transportation problem.

The third part of CRA's behavioral skills training is *drink (or drug) refusal*. There are several components to this program, with the first involving the enlistment of social support. Clients are asked to inform family members and close friends that they are no longer drinking, and that they would appreciate their loved ones' support. The belief is that if a client's "community" reinforces non-drinking behavior, then the client is more likely to continue engaging in it. The second component of drink-refusal training entails reviewing high-risk drinking situations. The triggers identified on the functional analysis can be referred to here, but additionally the client should be asked to generate a list of the 5-10 most common scenarios in which a slip is possible. Depending on the situation, the client may be advised to avoid it altogether, or to assertively refuse alcohol if offered.

Teaching a client how to refuse alcohol in an assertive manner is the third component of drink-refusal training. The CRA method for this is drawn from the work of Monti, Abrams, Kadden, and Cooney (1989). Several options for turning down alcohol are presented, and the client is asked to rehearse these repeatedly in role-plays. The basic options include:

1. Saying, "No, thanks."
2. Suggesting alternatives.
3. Changing the subject.
4. Confronting the aggressor.

The "just say no" option is discussed because many clients believe that they owe individuals an explanation for refusing alcohol. Turning down a drink feels abnormal to them, and they think that others will perceive it that way also. There are a variety of ways to handle this, perhaps the simplest being to have them agree to try it for a week, and to report the consequences in the next session. Option #2 is another type of verbal behavior that is foreign to most problem drinkers. So they are taught, for example, to say, "Actually, I'd love a strong cup of coffee instead." The third suggestion, which involves raising a new topic, is a distraction technique. The client might practice saying, "No, thanks. I really don't feel like having a beer tonight. Hey, did you see that last Bulls' game? Jordon was unbelievable!"

The final option is reserved for cases in which the client is being pressured to drink despite having executed options #1-3 already. An example of it is, "I have told you several times that I do not want a drink tonight, and yet you keep pressuring me. Why is it so important to you that I drink?" Regardless of the option selected, clients are taught to pay close attention to their tone of voice and body language when they deliver these messages, since assertive words can be overlooked in the context of an unassertive presentation.

Job Skills

A major part of most people's "community" is their job environment, and consequently it is an important potential source of reinforcement. This may come in the form of stimulating challenges, praise from supervisors, enhanced self-esteem, pleasant social interactions with coworkers, and financial rewards (basic salary and raises). A steady job also competes with drinking and serves as a deterrent because of the structure it introduces into a day.

CRA's job counseling program consists of three parts: getting a job, keeping a job, and enhancing job satisfaction. For unemployed clients, initial training is based largely on Azrin and Besalel's *Job Club Counselor's Manual* (1980). This excellent workbook outlines the necessary steps for obtaining a job, and includes such topics as: developing a resume, completing job applications, generating and tracking job leads, telephone skills training, and interview rehearsal. Extensive monitoring of job-seeking behaviors is built into the process, in part so that therapists are able to make behavioral contracts with clients and reinforce signs of progress. Importantly, the relative risk of certain jobs for promoting drinking always is considered.

Obtaining a job is often the easy step for clients. Time should be devoted to analyzing the sequence of events that typically has resulted in the client being fired or quitting in the past. Many of these may be alcohol or drug related, but others may be due to anger management difficulties. In the latter case, both communication skills and problem-solving training might be useful.

Finally, therapists should not assume that the employment topic can be ignored simply because a client already has a job. The Happiness Scale asks specifically about job satisfaction, and consequently it provides an avenue for determining whether the client finds his or her job reinforcing. Again, CRA works to enhance the level of satisfaction in all non-drinking areas of a person's life, so that they can work together to compete with drinking. Significant job dissatisfaction may be due to a variety of factors, but many lend themselves to a problem-solving intervention.

Social/Recreational Counseling

Since CRA's goal is to make an individual's non-drinking activities as reinforcing as his or her drinking activities, considerable attention must be paid to the client's social life. By the time a client enters treatment, it is fairly common for him or her to be totally enmeshed in a "drinking culture" in which friendships and recreational events revolve around drinking. Given that continued contact with these triggers places the client at great risk for relapse, it is necessary to explore the idea of spending time with non-drinking friends, and in developing more non-drinking activities. Unfortunately, many therapists incorrectly assume that individuals will know how to enjoy their free time, and consequently devote little energy to the topic. CRA therapists set aside segments of most sessions to check on the density of reinforcement in the client's social life, and to address it if indicated.

Most clients need some assistance in identifying new non-drinking activities, whether it means generating lists of options, completing new functional analyses for non-drinking behaviors, or using problem-solving to overcome obstacles to participating. CRA therapists rely on a technique called Systematic Encouragement (Sisson & Mallams, 1981) to maximize the chances of the client actually sampling the newly selected activity. The three components of this technique include:

1. Never assume that the client will initiate the first contact on his or her own. Use role-plays to simulate phone calls to the organization, and after sufficient rehearsal and feedback, have the client place the actual call during the session.
2. If feasible, locate a contact person for the activity, and have the client call this individual prior to the event. Arranging to have the contact person watch for the client at the activity improves the likelihood that the client will attend.
3. Review the experience with the client at the next session to determine the activity's reinforcement value. If the client does not plan on attending again, employ problem-solving to address any difficulties that arose, or select a new activity and repeat the procedure.

If the CRA program is being offered to a group of individuals, one might consider organizing a Social Club similar to the one used in several studies (Mallams et al., 1982; Smith et al., in press). The purpose of this club is to demonstrate that alcohol-free social activities can be enjoyable, and to provide an event that competes with drinking during high-risk times (e.g. Friday nights, weekends). Depending on clients' interests, a clinic could host something as simple as free video showings and refreshments.

CRA Relationship Therapy

If a problem drinker is living with a loved one, then in all probability the relationship is strained. Often the loved one either argues with the drinker over the excessive alcohol use, or withdraws and stops communicating with the drinker altogether. Given that substance abusers tend to cope with stress by drinking, the constant arguments or the partner's isolation begin to serve as cues for even more imbibing. CRA therapists believe that focusing exclusively on the client's drinking, while ignoring the interpersonal problems the drinking has stemmed from or created, seriously limits the benefits the drinker may derive from treatment. Consequently, partners typically are invited to participate in segments of the client's program.

CRA relationship therapy focuses on improving the couple's communication and teaching them how to set and obtain realistic goals with each other. The objective is to have each individual work toward making the relationship more reinforcing for both of them (Azrin, Naster, & Jones, 1973; Stuart, 1969). In the event that the client is considering disulfiram use, the partner first will be invited to attend a session in order to learn the disulfiram compliance procedure. Regardless, the Relationship Happiness Scale, which is the relationship equivalent of the Happiness Scale, is administered next. Each individual independently indicates his or her degree of satisfaction with the *partner* in 10 categories: household responsibilities, raising the children, social activities, money management, communication, sex and affection, job/school, emotional support, partner's independence, and general happiness.

Upon examining the Relationship Happiness Scales, the therapist shares the findings with the couple, and a discussion of their discrepant perceptions often ensues. A category with at least a moderate degree of satisfaction for both individuals is then selected for practice in goal setting. The Perfect Relationship form is introduced, and the client is informed that the "rules" for completing it are similar to those learned for the Goals of Counseling form; namely, to be brief, positive, and specific (measurable terms). However, this time the goals will be stated for one's *partner*. Each person takes a turn in formulating and then presenting to the loved one a request for some type of behavior change. The therapist assists with modifying the wording in accordance with the "rules".

Assume that a couple is working on the household responsibilities category, and the wife of the drinker wishes to go first. She may begin by stating, "I want him to stop throwing his dirty towels in a heap on the bathroom floor every morning."

The therapist would reinforce her for being brief and specific, but would ask if she could put her request in positive terms, by saying what she *would* like to see. Eventually the wife would write on the Perfect Relationship form something similar to, "I want him to place his wet towels either in the hamper or back on the towel rack every morning." The husband would then be given his turn to make a request. Assume he states, "I want her to serve dessert with dinner more." With prompting, the husband would take this brief, positive statement and make it more specific: "I want her to serve dessert with dinner 3 nights a week." Sometimes a negotiation period is required before both parties are willing to try complying with the request in the upcoming week. Depending on the couple, an additional request may be practiced, or its formulation may be given as an assignment.

Communication skills training follows naturally from the Perfect Relationship exercise, as it builds on the three basic rules and adds the four that were already introduced to the client in an individual session: label your feelings, make an understanding statement, accept partial responsibility, and offer to help. If the client has worked on these skills previously, then he or she can assist in teaching the partner. The last four rules are presented as "advanced" communication skills, and usually the statements written on the Perfect Relationship form are simply modified and practiced verbally. For example, the wife would take her request about hanging up the wet towels, and eventually her communication would approximate, "I would like you to place your wet towels in the hamper or back on the towel rack each morning. I know that you're always rushed in the morning (understanding statement), and it probably doesn't help to have me tying up the bathroom so long (partial responsibility), but it still bothers me (feelings). Maybe it would help if I moved the hamper out of the corner and put it near the towel rack as a reminder (offer to help)." The therapist spends time discussing the different feelings evoked by the polished communications as opposed to the rough initial attempts. The fact that each individual is more likely to have a request honored when it follows most of these guidelines is highlighted.

Another major component of CRA relationship therapy revolves around the Daily Reminder To Be Nice form. In the beginning stages of couples therapy, most individuals sadly report that they no longer exchange many "pleasing" behaviors that used to show how much they cared about each other. The therapist explains that one goal will be to strive for a relationship that once again maintains a higher ratio of pleasant, caring interactions than unpleasant ones. In an effort to "jump start" this process, the Daily Reminder To Be Nice form is given to each individual. The one-page sheet simply lists a variety of small, positive behaviors down the left column, and leaves room for tracking the frequency of engaging in these behaviors throughout the week. Although the categories certainly may be modified to suit a particular couple, the ones used on the form include:

1. Did you express appreciation to your partner today?
2. Did you compliment your partner today?
3. Did you give your partner any pleasant surprises today?
4. Did you visibly express affection to your partner today?

5. Did you spend some time devoting your complete attention to pleasant conversation with your partner   today?
6. Did you initiate any of the pleasant conversations today?
7. Did you make any offer to help before being asked today?

Couples are told that initially they may feel resentful about having to do something pleasant for the partner, but that this is a first step toward making many aspects of their relationship enjoyable again. And so they are asked to be sure that a day does not slip by without attempting at least one of these behaviors. The therapist will review their sheets in the next session, and will have them discuss what it felt like to have their loved one doing pleasant things for them again. In short, if a relationship starts to feel supportive and reinforcing for both individuals, then chances are greater that it will be able to regularly reinforce a non-drinking life-style.

CRA's Relapse Prevention

Relapse prevention actually begins with the first CRA session, since a functional analysis outlines the antecedents for drinking and identifies high-risk situations. Immediately plans are set into motion to develop behaviors that compete with the drinking. In the event that a lapse occurs, a separate CRA Functional Analysis for Drinking Behavior (RelapseVersion) is available. Modeled after the initial assessment version, the relapse chart simply focuses on the one episode and the specific context in which it occurred. This exploration may be followed with problem-solving or additional skills training.

Another manner in which CRA therapists discuss relapse prevention is in terms of an Early Warning System. Essentially, the behavioral chain of events that lead up to a drinking episode are diagrammed, and the client is asked to point out behavioral warning signals early in the process. For example, assume a client said that she drank a glass of wine at a friend's house when she only intended to have an iced tea. In recreating the scenario, the client would come to understand that there were actually several warning signals along the way:

1. Feeling angry and upset about a work incident, and hopping into the car to distract herself.
2. Deciding to stop at a coworker's house; one who always has alcohol available.
3. Sitting down in the coworker's living room where many drinking episodes have taken place in the past.
4. Hearing her coworker say that she needs a drink to even begin discussing the work incident.
5. Seeing her coworker coming into the living room with 2 glasses of wine, and hearing her say, "One glass won't hurt."
6. Taking the glass from her coworker and drinking it.

The therapist would remind the client that a number of her old drinking triggers could have served as warning signals: feeling angry and upset, seeking the company of a coworker who drinks readily, going into a setting associated with excessive drinking, and being handed a drink with the assurance that one will not be a problem. The next step would entail formulating a non-drinking plan that starts at the top of the behavioral chain and deals with her angry feelings.

General Clinical Comments

As with all behavior analytic programs, CRA is only as good as the therapists who administer it. Consequently, if a therapist does not possess good basic clinical skills, the program will be limited. Furthermore, too often therapists become totally committed to using the various CRA techniques, but in the process lose sight of the overall purpose: to help make the person's non-drinking life-style as reinforcing as his or her drinking life-style. In order to do this one must constantly be aware of the client's reinforcers in all areas of his or her "community", including family, job, and social activities. Having access to these reinforcers on a regular basis is critical in terms of effecting and maintaining change.

Literature Review

Inpatient Trials

The first study to demonstrate the effectiveness of CRA was conducted approximately 25 years ago (Hunt & Azrin, 1973). In this matched-control trial, eight alcohol-dependent clients were selected and matched with eight others on demographic variables, drinking history, family stability, and employment pattern. Random assignment determined which member of each pair was to be placed in the CRA condition, and which was to receive the hospital's traditional Alcoholics Anonymous (A.A.) program. Participants in this early version of CRA received instruction in how to identify and access nondrinking reinforcers. In conjunction with this they were provided with both job and recreational counseling. They also were encouraged to participate in an alcohol-free Social Club. Additionally, relapse prevention was addressed during home visits, and married clients received behavioral marital therapy.

At the time of the 6-month follow-up, CRA group members were on average drinking on 14% of the follow-up days while traditional treatment participants were drinking on 79% of the days. In terms of employment stability, the CRA group was unemployed only 5% of the follow-up time, in contrast to the traditional group's 62% unemployment rate. The superior findings for CRA participants extended into the areas of hospitalization and marital stability as well. This study was an extremely important one for the field, despite its small sample size. To begin with, it was one of the few alcohol treatment projects of the time to include a control group. Furthermore, a novel program based on operant reinforcement theory demonstrated dramatically altered drinking patterns, as well as improvements in many other life areas.

A second study contrasted an expanded CRA protocol with an A.A. condition in a matched-control design with nine pairs of inpatients (Azrin, 1976). The revised CRA program added a prescription for disulfiram (Antabuse) along with a compliance program for monitoring and reinforcing its participants, an early warning monitoring system for identifying high-risk behaviors, and a buddy system as a source of continued social support. Finally, CRA services were provided primarily in a group as opposed to an individual format.

Once again participants randomly assigned to the CRA group significantly outperformed their control group counterparts at the 6-month follow-up. Specifically, the CRA participants spent an average of 2% of the follow-up days drinking, compared with 55% in the traditional treatment. Unemployment time was reported as 20% for the CRA group and 56% for the control. At the time of the 2-year follow-up, 90% of the CRA participants were still abstinent. These excellent results were obtained despite the fact that the median number of counseling hours dropped from 50 in the first study to 30.

Outpatient Trials

The third CRA study was the first one to be conducted with outpatients (Azrin, Sisson, Meyers, & Godley, 1982). Its major purpose was to examine the contribution of the disulfiram compliance program introduced in the last study (Azrin, 1976) by contrasting it with the traditional method for dispensing disulfiram. The compliance component involved training a concerned family member or friend to administer the disulfiram to the drinker, and to provide verbal reinforcement. There were three treatment conditions: Traditional, disulfiram assurance, and CRA plus disulfiram assurance. The traditional group received 12-step counseling and a disulfiram prescription. The disulfiram assurance group received this same program, but additionally the participants were trained in the disulfiram compliance protocol. The final group received CRA treatment and disulfiram compliance training. The new CRA components this time included a motivational procedure called sobriety sampling, disulfiram administration during the first session, and both drink-refusal and relaxation training.

As predicted, the two groups containing the disulfiram compliance component reported the most success during the 6-month follow-up, with the CRA program averaging 97% and the 12-step condition reporting 74% of the last 30 days abstinent. In contrast, the traditional 12-step group which received only the disulfiram prescription had an abstinence rate of only 45% of the days. Interestingly, the couples within the disulfiram assurance group performed much better than the group's single participants, even to the point of matching the CRA group's outcome on several variables. One might hypothesize that the monitoring was more reliable and the verbal reinforcement was more effective when a spouse served as the disulfiram monitor, as opposed to a friend. In terms of employment, the largest differences at 6-months were found between the CRA plus disulfiram assurance and the traditional conditions. Unemployment rates averaged 7% for the former group and 36% for the latter. Noteworthy is the fact that the average number of therapy hours for the CRA condition was five.

A second outpatient study investigated the contribution of one of the CRA components: the alcohol-free Social Club (Mallams, Godley, Hall, & Meyers, 1982). The purpose of the club was to provide enjoyable, nondrinking social activities during high-risk drinking times. Although it was open to both experimental and control group members, the former received repeated reminders and encouragement to attend. Additionally, they were afforded transportation and problem-solving assistance to overcome attendance obstacles. The experimental group not only attended the club significantly more than the control group, but significantly decreased their daily alcohol consumption in comparison as well. The study was limited by the absence of information regarding participants' degree of involvement in their regular rural treatment program and by a small sample and short follow-up period. Nevertheless, the behavioral procedures employed to encourage individuals to attend a potentially valuable activity appeared quite promising.

Homeless Population Trial

Given that CRA's multifaceted behavioral program demonstrated some of its greatest relative treatment gains with its least socially stable clients (Azrin, et al., 1982), the decision was made to test its efficacy with a homeless population. The CRA treatment was offered in group format by behaviorally-trained advanced clinical psychology graduate students. The comparison group was the standard treatment offered by the large day shelter in which the study was conducted. In addition to having access to the shelter's basic services (e.g. free showers, meals, clean clothes, telephone and mail service), an experienced masters-level 12-step counselor offered individual sessions. Furthermore, A.A. meetings were held on site, a job program arranged temporary employment, and case managers were available for the dually diagnosed.

During the three months of the program all participants were housed in grant-financed apartments. A contingency was in place whereby individuals who had obtained a job and saved a specified amount of money were offered a fourth month of free housing. Abstinence was required of all participants during the time they were housed. CRA group members were checked for compliance with random breathalyzer tests at the apartments, and offenders were suspended from housing for 1-2 weeks, depending on whether it was their first offense. Although the standard treatment members were not routinely checked with breathalyzer tests, they were suspended from housing if drinking or disruptive behavior was reported.

The study was set up as a 5-condition design. However, just the primary prediction, which involved collapsing the three CRA groups (n=59) and contrasting them with the two combined standard groups (n=42), will be reported here. The main hypothesis of the study was that members of the CRA group would significantly outperform the standard group members in terms of decreased alcohol consumption and increased employment and housing stability.

A complete description of the study sample and the results may be found in Smith, Meyers, and Delaney (in press). Briefly, 106 alcohol dependent individuals comprised the intent-to-treat sample. They primarily were white (64%), male (86%), high school graduates who were an average of 38 years old. At the time of the intake only 9% were employed even part-time, and only 3% were married. Since the design did not allow for official dropouts from the standard treatment, all dropouts (n=5) were from the CRA condition. Thus, the treated sample was comprised of 101 individuals.

Follow-up rates for the five follow-up periods ranged from 93.4% at the 2-month follow-up to 76.4% at the 12-month. The rates were comparable across the two conditions. The three primary drinking variables examined were: total number of drinks (standard ethanol content: SECs) per week, number of drinking days per week, and estimated peak blood alcohol content. In general, alcohol results significantly favored the CRA group, with the strongest effects found for the first four follow-up periods. In terms of employment and housing progress, there were marked improvements for both treatment conditions throughout the follow-ups (see Smith et al., in press, for complete results).

One limitation of the CRA treatment is the fact that a small subset of CRA participants drank heavily throughout the 1-year follow-up period. Strengths of the study include its low dropout and high follow-up rates. As far as clinical significance, an empirically-supported behavioral treatment that was administered in a cost-effective group format by student therapists obtained promising results with a difficult population.

Working Through Concerned Significant Others

CRA procedures also have been used to work through Concerned Significant Others (CSOs) in an effort to get treatment-resistant individuals to seek substance abuse therapy. In the earliest trial (Sisson & Azrin, 1986) 12 non-drinking family members were randomly assigned to either a traditional 12-step condition or to a CRA program. The latter included training in how and when to suggest treatment to the drinker, when to offer and withdraw reinforcement, how to allow the drinker to experience the natural consequences for excessive alcohol use, how to schedule activities that competed with drinking, how to handle potentially dangerous situations, and the importance of increasing the social activities of the non-drinking family member. Six of the seven drinkers whose CSOs were in the CRA group initiated treatment, whereas none of the control group drinkers sought therapy. Furthermore, drinkers affiliated with CSOs in the CRA group reduced their alcohol use by more than half during the time that only the nondrinker was in treatment. This pattern was not repeated in the comparison group.

Currently called CRAFT (Community Reinforcement and Family Training), this approach is being studied through grants under the direction of William Miller (principal investigator) and Robert Meyers (co-investigator). Both treatment-resistant alcohol and drug-dependent individuals are being examined. Preliminary reports of the ability of CRAFT-trained CSOs to engage their resistant substance-abusing loved ones into treatment are very promising (see Meyers & Smith, 1997 and Meyers, Smith & Miller, in press, for descriptions of CRAFT procedures).

Treating Cocaine and Heroin Problems with CRA

With the exception of the one ongoing CRAFT project, the studies mentioned thus far have used CRA for individuals with a primary substance abuse diagnosis of alcohol dependence. Studies also have utilized CRA to treat cocaine and heroin problems. Noteworthy support for CRA was found in three separate cocaine studies that used it in combination with a contingency management program that rewarded clean urines (Budney, Higgins, Delaney, Kent & Bickel, 1991; Higgins et al., 1991; 1993). Another study demonstrated the efficacy of CRA for an opioid dependent population that was also receiving methadone maintenance (Abbott & Moore, 1997).

References

Abbott, P. J., Weller, S. B., Delaney, H. D., & Moore, B. A. (in press). Community reinforcement approach and relapse prevention in the treatment of opiate addicts. *The American Journal of Drug and Alcohol Abuse.*

Azrin, N. H. (1976). Improvements in the community reinforcement approach to alcoholism. *Behaviour Research and Therapy, 14,* 339-348.

Azrin, N. H. & Besalel, V. A. (1980). *Job club counselor's manual.* Baltimore, MD: University Press.

Azrin, N. H., Naster, B. J., & Jones, R. (1973). Reciprocity counseling: A rapid learning-based procedure for marital counseling. *Behaviour Research and Therapy, 11,* 365-382.

Azrin, N. H., Sisson, R. W., Meyers, R. J. & Godley, M. D. (1982). Alcoholism treatment by disulfiram and community reinforcement therapy. *Journal of Behavior Therapy and Experimental Psychiatry, 3,* 105-112

Budney, A. J., Higgins, S. T., Delaney, D. D., Kent, L., & Bickel, W. K. (1991). Contingent reinforcement of abstinence with individuals abusing cocaine and marijuana. *Journal of Applied Behavior Analysis, 24,* 657-665.

Dougher, M. J. & Hackbert, L. (1994). A behavior-analytic account of depression and a case report using acceptance-based procedures. *The Behavior Analyst, 17,* 321-334.

D'Zurilla, T. J., & Goldfried, M. R. (1971). Problem solving and behavior modification. *Journal of Abnormal Psychology, 78,* 107-126.

Finney, J. W., & Monahan, S. C. (1996). The cost-effectiveness of treatment for alcoholism: A second approximation. *Journal of Studies on Alcohol, 57,* 229-243.

Higgins, S. T., Budney, A. J., Bickel, W. K., Hughes, J. R., & Foerg, F., & Badger, G. (1993). Achieving cocaine abstinence with a behavioral approach. *American Journal of Psychiatry, 150,* 763-769.

Higgins, S., Delaney, D., Budney, A., Bickel, W., Hughes, J., & Foerg, F. (1991). A behavioral approach to achieving initial cocaine abstinence. *American Journal of Psychiatry, 148,* 1218-1224.

Holder, H., Longabaugh, R., Miller, W., & Rubonis, A. (1991). The cost effectiveness of treatment for alcoholism: A first approximation. *Journal of Studies on
Alcohol, 52,* 517-540.

Hunt, G. M. & Azrin, N. H., (1973). A community-reinforcement approach to
alcoholism. *Behavior Research and Therapy, 11,* 91-104.

Mallams, J. H., Godley, M. D., Hall, G. M. & Meyers, R. J. (1982). A social-systems
approach to resocializing alcoholics in the community. *Journal of Studies on
Alcohol, 43,* 1115-1123.

Marlatt, G. A. (1980). Relapse prevention: A self-control program for the treatment
of addictive behaviors. Unpublished manuscript.

Meyers, R. J. & Smith, J. E. (1995) *Clinical guide to alcohol treatment: The Community
reinforcement approach.* New York: Guilford Press.

Meyers, R. J. & Smith, J. E. (1997). Getting off the fence: Procedures to engage
treatment-resistant drinkers. *Journal of Substance Abuse Treatment, 14,* 467-472.

Meyers, R. J., Smith, J. E., & Miller, E. J., (in press). Working through the concerned
significant other: Community reinforcement and family training. In W. R.
Miller & N. Heather (Eds.) *Treating addictive behaviors: Processes of change* (2nd
ed.). New York: Plenum Press.

Miller, W. R., Brown, J. M., Simpson, T. L., Handmaker, N. S., Bein, T. H., Luckie,
L. F., Montgomery, H. A., Hester, R. K. & Tonigan, J. S. (1995). What works?
A methodological analysis of the alcohol treatment outcome literature. In R.
K. Hester & W. R. Miller (Eds.), *Handbook of alcoholism treatment approaches:
Effective alternatives* (2nd ed.). Needham, MA: Allyn & Bacon.

Monti, P. M., Abrams, D. B., Kadden, R. M. & Cooney, N. L. (1989). *Treating alcohol
dependence: A coping skills training guide.* New York: Guilford Press.

Sisson, R. W. & Azrin, N. H. (1986). Family-member involvement to initiate and
promote treatment of problem drinkers. *Journal of Behavior Therapy and Experimental Psychiatry, 17,* 15-21.

Sisson, R. W. & Mallams, J. H. (1981). The use of systematic encouragement and
community access procedures to increase attendance at Alcoholics Anonymous and Al-Anon meetings. *American Journal of Drug and Alcohol Abuse, 8,*
371-376.

Smith, J. E. & Meyers, R. J. (1995). The community reinforcement approach. In R.
Hester & W. Miller (Eds.), *Handbook of alcoholism treatment approaches: Effective
alternatives* (2nd ed.). New York: Pergamon Press.

Smith, J. E., Meyers, R. J., & Delaney, H. (in press) The community reinforcement
approach with homeless alcohol-dependence individuals. *Journal of Consulting
and Clinical Psychology.*

Stuart, R. B. (1969). Operant-interpersonal treatment for marital discord. *Journal of
Consulting and Clinical Psychology, 33,* 675-682.

Chapter 10

An Acceptance-Based Performance Enhancement Intervention for Collegiate Athletes

Laura M. Little
Tracy L. Simpson
University of New Mexico

The discipline of applied sport psychology rests on the assumption that peak athletic performance is partially a consequence of psychological factors. Researchers in the field have sought to describe the psychological states characteristic of peak performance and to develop effective psychological interventions for improving performance. A review of the recent literature on performance enhancement reveals that cognitive psychology is the dominant paradigm in applied sport psychology (Whelan, Mahoney, & Meyers, 1991). Several cognitive-mediational models have been proposed by sport psychologists to account for the influence of an athlete's cognitive processes on performance. These models generally postulate a mediational role played by cognitive appraisal in the relationship between the competitive sport situation and an athlete's performance.

Basic research in sport psychology supports many of the predictive relationships suggested by these models (Whelan et al., 1991). In turn, these conceptual models have informed a great many of the interventions currently being implemented in psychological skills training programs. It should come as no surprise, then, that in this broad conception, the private events of athletes are given a special, causal status in performance enhancement theories. Consequently, the most widely used performance enhancement interventions target thoughts and emotions as factors needing to be changed in order to enhance athletic performance.

Traditional Models of Athletic Performance Enhancement

Peak performance is characterized by exquisite focus and concentration, and many sport psychologists have developed strategies to improve these skills. Attention control interventions often involve techniques that are explicitly intended to reduce the negative impact of cognitive interference from worry and catastrophic thinking (Smith, 1996). Techniques such as refocusing and mental rehearsal provide "cognitive options" for the athlete experiencing attention control difficulties. In each of these strategies, cognitive interference is resisted by substituting different, task relevant, cognitions for the negative ones. For example, Nideffer

(1985) suggests that baseball players respond to negative thoughts by turning to a single positive self-instruction and then to the ball, timing this mental activity so that it is completed as the pitcher begins delivery of the ball.

Peak performance is also associated with athletes' perceptions of confidence (Garfield & Bennett, 1984), and psychological skills training programs often attempt to improve performance by creating or strengthening positive, confident attitudes. Many investigators and practitioners go on to posit causal relationships between self-confidence and success. Bunker, Williams, and Zinsser (1993) maintain that "thoughts directly affect feelings and ultimately actions [of athletes]," and that "their [confident athletes] confidence programs them for successful performance (p.225)." In this vein, Ellis (1982) argues that athletes often suffer from poor performance because they accept and endorse self-defeating, irrational beliefs. Confidence building interventions often teach self-talk strategies in which performance enhancing thoughts are produced and disabling thoughts eliminated. These techniques are believed to increase self-efficacy (Bandura, 1977), change mood (Bunker, Williams, & Zinsser, 1993), and provide appropriate affective cues for performance (e.g., Meichenbaum, 1975).

Researchers in sport psychology have also devoted considerable effort to studying the relationship between self-efficacy and sport performance (Feltz, 1992). Field studies generally have shown that perceived self-efficacy and performance are strongly and positively correlated (e.g., Barling & Abel, 1983; Gayton, Matthews, & Burchstead, 1986; Lee, 1982), and laboratory studies confirm these correlations (e.g., Weinberg, Gould, & Jackson, 1979). Researchers have attributed effects of cognitive-behavioral interventions, such as goal-setting strategies and imagery techniques, to perceived increases in self-efficacy (e.g., Bandura, 1977). Robert Weinberg, a leading sport psychology researcher, has suggested that the mere belief in the effectiveness of a performance enhancement strategy increases self-efficacy among athletes (1985). However, in sport psychology, perspectives other than cognitive mediational theories have not been developed, and approaches other than cognitive-behavioral strategies have not been evaluated. It remains to be demonstrated whether changes in cognitions or emotions are the specific mechanisms responsible for performance gains.

A Behavior Analytic Formulation of Performance Enhancement

An account of the relationship among the variables studied by sport psychologists might also be examined from a behavior analytic perspective in which the effects of goal-setting and other performance enhancement techniques would not necessitate the invocation of internal mediating constructs such as self-efficacy or confidence. From this perspective, the cognition or the emotion associated with the overt behavior of athletic performance would be seen as arising from the same variables that give rise to the performance itself.

A loss of self-confidence accompanying poor performance, for example, would be seen as being associated with a lack of strong positive reinforcement. Skinner (1974), had this to say about an athlete's self-confidence:

A tennis player reports that he practices a particular shot "until he feels confident"; the basic fact is that he practices until a certain proportion of his shots are good. Frequent reinforcement also builds faith. A person feels sure, or certain, that he will be successful. He enjoys a sense of mastery, power, or potency.... In all this the behavior is erroneously attributed to the feelings rather than to the contingencies responsible for what is felt. When reinforcement is no longer forthcoming, behavior undergoes "extinction" and appears rarely, if at all. A person is then said to suffer a loss of confidence, certainty, or sense of power. Instead, his feelings range from a lack of interest through disappointment, discouragement, and a sense of impotence to a possibly deep depression, and these feelings are then said – erroneously – to explain the absence of the behavior. (p. 64)

Viewed this way, targeting the cognitions or feelings (e.g., of frustration, discouragement) themselves in order to effect behavior change (performance enhancement) would not be the most effective course of action. Behaviorists would view the **reactions** to the loss of confidence as the source of difficulty for athletes, not the loss of confidence itself.

Very few athletes routinely produce perfect performances. Free throw shots are missed, batters are walked, and serves are hit into the net. This is the nature of sport at all levels. How an athlete responds to such mistakes and his or her ability to recover effectively is of the utmost importance. Athletes are commonly encouraged to "shake off" thoughts and feelings about mistakes or errors. Indeed, athletes at all levels are taught that experiencing doubts about one's ability is bad and that good performance can only be achieved in the absence of (crippling) self-doubt. The typical formal strategies for handling such self-doubt or loss of confidence include distracting oneself from it, replacing it, or engaging in thought stopping. Evidence from the literature on thought suppression indicates that when people are instructed to suppress emotional thoughts, emotional response to the suppressed thoughts is magnified, and continues to be magnified even when thought suppression is discontinued (Wegner, Shortt, Blake, & Page, 1990).

From a behavior analytic perspective there are three key problems with thought suppression in a sport context that could be hypothesized to lead to interference with effective recovery from mistakes or errors. First, for the athlete who is unwilling to feel anxiety or to have negative thoughts about his or her ability, the occurrence of those feelings or thoughts is likely to cause greater anxiety and worry. Such a reaction is likely to compromise one's ability to respond adaptively to the problem signalled by the negative thoughts or feelings and may further disrupt concentration and focus. Second, for the athlete who is consumed by attempts to replace unwanted thoughts and feelings with acceptable ones, the effort expended making these replacements may cause further cognitive interference. Both of these potential problems may contribute to a third problem; the informational value in the negative self-evaluation is lost in the attempt to be rid of it. Instead of cueing performance correction responses that would facilitate recovery from error, the cycle spirals away from this helpful feedback loop.

Rather than attempting to change the cognitions and emotions associated with a loss of confidence, a preferable strategy would be to change the function of those thoughts and the responses that are cued by them. An acceptance-based intervention would unpack the verbal rules that underlie the athlete's evaluation of the loss of confidence following an error. This unpacking would reveal the twin beliefs that thoughts and feelings cause behavior and that good performance can only occur in the absence of self-doubt. If thoughts and feelings are seen as informational nuggets, and not causes per se, then there is no need to fear them, react to them, struggle against them, nor control or change them (Dougher, 1993). The intervention would then proceed by clarifying the values that are reinforcing to the athlete and helping her make a commitment to take action toward changing the quality of her performance. For example, the infielder who has experienced drastic performance decrements and a loss of self-confidence in her fielding ability might reaffirm her desire to "do the best she possibly can" and then go about accumulating reinforcing behaviors by fielding 50 ground balls in practice day after day until her performance is once more consistently effective. A by-product of this effort would likely be a feeling of increased confidence, signaling to the athlete that she is indeed performing more consistently.

This perspective holds a great deal of promise for sport psychology. For many athletes the notion that it is permissible to have worries or a loss of confidence as a result of poor performance may have an organic appeal. Understanding that these responses are natural reactions to a loss of reinforcement, rather than harbingers of further performance decrement, might free the athlete to correct ineffective skill responses.

An Acceptance-Based Sport Intervention

An acceptance-based intervention was recently developed for use in a sport context. Both the feasibility of implementing such a program and the effectiveness of the intervention were evaluated. In addition, the relationship between changes in athletic performance and the frequency of suppression of unwanted thoughts and feelings was explored.

The Setting for the Intervention

The intervention was developed for an NCAA Division I collegiate women's fastpitch softball team at a large public university. The program had achieved national prominence in years past, but recently suffered several consecutive losing seasons, despite fielding players with substantial talent. A sport psychology program was instituted, and the acceptance-based intervention was implemented during the 1997 spring season.

Screening and Assessment

All members of the team participated in a traditional sport psychology program, but the acceptance-based intervention was specifically designed for players exhibiting high levels of thought suppression and emotional avoidance. During an assessment phase all players completed three pencil-and-paper questionnaires designed to identify those who were reporting frequent thought suppression or emotional avoidance. Those instruments were the White Bear Suppression Inventory (WBSI; Wegner & Zanakos, 1994), the Fear of Sadness Test (FOST; Zanakos & Wegner, 1993), and an experimental questionnaire developed specifically for fastpitch softball. The WBSI requires responses on a 5-point Likert scale from strongly disagree (1) to strongly agree (5) for 15 individual items. These items include statements such as "Sometimes I really wish I could stop thinking" and "I often do things to distract myself from my thoughts." The FOST was constructed to measure the degree to which individuals find negative thoughts disturbing. This measure requires responses on a 5-point Likert scale from strongly disagree (1) to strongly agree (5) for 16 items. These items include statements such as "When I am unhappy, I feel weak" and "Having negative thoughts makes me nervous."

The experimental questionnaire, the Frequency and Suppression of Thoughts During Competition Questionnaire (FSTDC), was designed to assess the degree to which players report both positive and negative thoughts during games and the degree to which they report trying to suppress these thoughts. Items were selected from both player interviews and focus groups. The questionnaire design was based on the Thought Occurrence Questionnaire (Sarason, Sarason, Keefe, Hayes & Shearin, 1986); items were rewritten in order that they be relevant to athletic competition, and particularly to softball. The questionnaire requires responses on a 5-point Likert scale from very often (4) to never (0) for 30 items. Participants were asked first, "How often did you have this thought?" and then "How often did you try to get rid of it?" Items include such statements as "Thought: I can't make another error" and "Thought: My coaches are really unhappy with me."

Players whose responses to these questionnaires indicated either that they frequently suppressed thoughts or emotions or that they found negative thoughts particularly distressing were invited to participate in the experimental phase of the study. Six players participated in and completed the program.

Study Design

The effectiveness of the program was evaluated using a single-subject, staggered baseline design. Baseline measures were taken for the initial three, six, and nine weeks of the conference season, corresponding to four, seven, and nine doubleheaders. The baseline condition consisted of regular team meetings emphasizing supportive, educational intervention by a sport psychology consultant. Topics considered during meetings included team building, communication skills, and responding to criticism. Players began the experimental program after one of the three designated baseline periods. The intervention was implemented immediately following the end of baseline assessment.

The Intervention

During the experimental phase, individual one-half hour training sessions were held during the two to three days prior to each doubleheader. At each session, the fundamental aspects of the intervention were reiterated and discussed, the player's performance in the previous doubleheader was analyzed, and the appropriate strategies for performance enhancement were integrated into this analysis.

Throughout the experimental phase the sport psychology consultant provided information to each player regarding possible acceptance responses to the unwanted thoughts and feelings that might occur either during competition or training. During individual sessions players were encouraged to identify those areas in which they desired improvement, and efforts were made to identify the thoughts and emotions associated with these problem areas. Appropriate intervention-specific strategies were developed for responding to unwanted thoughts and feelings, and each player was encouraged to describe how she would use the strategy in the upcoming games. Each player was also given a printed guide explaining the fundamental tenets of the acceptance-based intervention. This guide is reprinted in the appendix following.

The goals of the intervention were to help the athletes learn to take a different perspective on their thoughts and feelings, to give up efforts to control or extinguish them, and to pursue those behaviors that characterize desired athletic effort and performance. Thus, the elimination of distressing thoughts and feelings was not a goal. Instead, the athletes were taught that a critical distinction must be made between having unwanted thoughts or feelings and responding to them in a manner that interferes with their athletic performance. Athletes were encouraged to be mindful of their private events (whether they be feelings of anxiety, frustration, or disappointment), understand them for what they are, and get on with the pursuit of improving their skills and overall performance.

Player Response to the Intervention

Overall the players were receptive to the acceptance-based intervention. At times they found the striking differences between the acceptance strategies and the traditional sport psychology approach confusing. Players had been told for so long that they must feel confident in order to play better, that occasionally the notion that confidence itself had very little to do with causing good performance was rejected. They also were constantly reminded of the traditional model; although the coaches were familiar with the intervention's approach, they continued to apply conventional models of sport psychology in their talks with individual players and the team as a whole. However, in general, the players expressed relief that their thoughts and feelings did not have to be seen as problematic. One player had this story to tell: she had struck out in her previous two at bats, and found herself standing at the plate scolding herself over thinking about her last at bats. Realizing that this approach was contrary to the program's tenet of accepting her thoughts, she laughed out loud. When the opposing team's catcher asked her what was so funny, she replied, "It's a long story!" Then she hit a double.

Other players in the program described the intervention as "cool" and "a good idea." In general, their perception was that the freedom to stop fighting with their thoughts and feelings helped them to prepare mentally and focus on the game.

Evaluating the Program

The effects of an acceptance-based intervention were examined on both molecular changes in athletic performance (e.g., probabilities of recovering from immediately prior poor performance) as well as on more global measures of athletic performance (e.g., batting average, earned run average). Performance variables were measured for each scheduled doubleheader. The performance variables for hitters included batting average (BA), on-base percentage (OBA), and number of strikeouts.

Four of the five offensive players who participated in the program showed increases in overall batting average and on-base average from baseline to intervention. The average increase in batting average was .104 and for on-base average was .150. However, these increases were not significantly greater than increases in the same performance variables shown by players not participating in the program. The decrease from baseline in a global measure of strikeouts per inning for players in the program also was not significantly different from those not participating.

The ability of a player to recover from a poor offensive showing (operationally defined as a strikeout for any given at bat) by getting a base hit or drawing a walk in her next at bat was considered to be a marker of recovery from error. Each offensive player in the program either showed increases from baseline in the probability of getting a hit or drawing a walk given a strikeout in the previous at bat or did not strike out at all during the intervention portion of the program. By player, those increases were from probabilities of 0.00 to .75, .14 to 1.00, and 0.00 to 0.43. These increases compare favorably to non-program player statistics. Timelines corresponding to the 3, 6, or 9 week baseline for non-program players were constructed, and results showed mean decreases in the probability of recovering from a strikeout in the previous at bat for 6 and 9 week "baselines" and a small increase from .08 to .161 for the 3 week "baseline."

Defense (fielding) performance measures for position players (non-pitchers) were largely invariant because so few fielding errors were made at any point during the season. Global measures of performance improvement were thus not analyzed. However, conditional probabilities were examined for all position players. The conditional probabilities of interest were whether the player could have a good offensive game in spite of performing poorly on the field. Only one position player had sufficient fielding opportunities and errors for analysis. This player showed an encouraging improvement in the probability of having a good offensive game (above average on-base percentage) while having a poor defensive game (fielding or throwing errors). The odds for this player having a good offensive game versus a poor offensive game, given she was having a poor defensive game, increased from one to one to six to one, demonstrating for this player a greater ability to rise above poor performance in a given area of her game. Overall performance variables for pitchers included earned run average (ERA), walks given up, hits given up per inning, homeruns given up per inning, and strikeouts. The two pitchers participating in the program showed performance enhancement in each of these five areas.

Because these two were the only pitchers throwing in the time frames corresponding to baseline and intervention phases, no statistics for non-program pitchers are available for comparison.

Unlike the results for hitters, conditional probabilities indicating recovery from poor performance were unchanged for pitchers. Poor performance was defined as walking a batter or giving up a homerun, and recovery was defined as achieving a strikeout or put-out of the subsequent batter. For the two pitchers in the program, the probabilities of recovering from poor performance increased only sightly, from .631 to .667 and from .688 to .692.

The effectiveness of this intervention was also gauged by the discontinuation of the struggle against unwanted thoughts and feelings during competition. All players participating in the intervention showed decreases in suppression as indicated by the experimental questionnaire, which they completed immediately after each doubleheader. During the baseline phase each player reported at least one occasion in which she often or very often tried to suppress thoughts. Two players showed decreases from "often" trying to get rid of unwanted thoughts to "a few times," each doubleheader, while the remainder of the players suppression decreased generally from "a few times" per doubleheader or "once" per doubleheader to "never." By the end of the season all but two players were reporting "never" trying to get rid of unwanted thoughts. As a gauge of the overall amount of effort players spent trying to suppress negative thoughts or emotions, a composite score was computed for each player as the product of "unwanted thought frequency" score and "effort to get rid of that thought" score. Each player showed a large decrease from baseline in this total suppression effort measure. The acceptance approach did not generalize to unwanted thoughts and feelings outside the sport context, however. All but one player failed to show similar decreases in their overall tendency to chronically suppress thoughts and negative affect as measured by the White Bear Suppression Inventory and the Fear of Sadness Test.

Concluding Remarks

Acceptance-based therapies have been studied in clinical populations, and generally have been shown to be effective in reducing targeted behaviors (see Hayes, Wilson, Gifford, & Follette, 1997 for a review of the outcome literature for acceptance based approaches). While this approach has been shown to be effective in clinical populations, its usefulness has not yet been demonstrated outside a clinical context. This project was an attempt to explore the feasibility of implementing an acceptance-based intervention in a sport context. Particularly critical to this exploration was whether athletes would adopt such a radically different perspective on their thoughts and feelings and how these relate to their athletic performance. Overall, the softball players who participated showed a genuine appreciation of this new way of looking at their mental and physical behavior. Their enthusiasm was not entirely matched by improvement in all aspects of their competitive performance. The program was altogether too brief and the coaching staff not sufficiently involved to fairly test the true effectiveness of the acceptance-based approach. As the softball players might say, "It wasn't pretty, but you got on base." We'll accept this evaluation, extract a few informational nuggets, and work to make the appropriate performance correction responses.

References

Bandura, A. (1977). Self-efficacy: Toward a unifying theory of behavioral change. *Psychological Review, 84,* 199-215.

Barling, J., & Abel, M. (1983). Self-efficacy beliefs and tennis performance. *Cognitive Therapy and Research, 7,* 265-272.

Bunker, L., Williams, J. M., & Zinsser, N. (1993). Cognitive techniques for improving performance and building confidence. In J. M. Williams (Ed.), *Applied sport psychology: Personal growth to peak performance* (pp. 225-242). London: Mayfield.

Dougher, M. J. (1993). On the advantages and implications of a radical behavioral treatment of private events. *The Behavior Therapist, 16,* 204-206.

Ellis, A. (1982). Self-direction in sport and life. In T. Orlick, J. Partington, & J. Salmela (Eds.), *Mental training for coaches and athletes* (pp. 10-17). Ottawa: Coaching Association of Canada.

Feltz, D. L. (1992). Understanding motivation in sport: A self-efficacy perspective. In G. C. Roberts (Ed.), *Motivation in sport and exercise.* Champaign, IL: Human Kinetics.

Garfield, C. A., & Bennett, H. Z. (1984). *Peak performance: Mental training techniques of the world's greatest athletes.* Los Angeles: Tarcher.

Gayton, W. F., Matthews, G. R., & Burchstead, G. N. (1986). An investigation of the validity of the physical self-efficacy scale in predicting marathon performance. *Perceptual and Motor Skills, 63,* 752-754.

Hayes, S. C., Wilson, K. G., Gifford, E. V., Follette, V. M. & Strohsal (1996). Emotional avoidance and behavioral disorders: A functional dimensional approach to diagnosis and treatment. *Journal of Consulting and Clinical Psychology, 64,* 1152-1168.

Lee, C. (1982). Self-efficacy as a predictor of performance in competitive gymnastics. *Journal of Sport Psychology, 7,* 283-295.

Meichenbam, D. (1975). Toward a cognitive theory of self-control. In G. Schwartz & D. Shapiro (Eds.), *Consciousness and self-regulation: Advances in research.* New York: Plenum.

Nideffer, R. M. (1986). *Athlete's guide to mental training.* Champaign, IL: Human Kinetics.

Sarason, I. G., Sarason, B. R., Keefe, D. E., Hayes, B. E., & Shearin, E. N. (1986). Cognitive interference: Situational determinants and trait-like characteristics. *Journal of Personality and Social Psychology, 51,* 215-226.

Skinner, B. F. (1974). *About behaviorism.* New York: Alfred A. Knopf.

Smith, R. E. (1996). Performance anxiety, cognitive interference, and concentration enhancement strategies in sports. In I. G. Sarason, G. R. Pierce, & B. R. Sarason

(Eds.), *Cognitive interference: Theories, methods, and findings* (pp. 261-283). Mahwah, NJ: Lawrence Erlbaum.

Wegner, D. M., Shortt, J. W., Blake, A. W., & Page, M. S. (1990). The suppression of exciting thoughts. *Journal of Personality and Social Psychology, 58,* 409-418.

Wegner, D. M., & Zanakos, S. I. (1994). Chronic thought suppression. *Journal of Personality, 62,* 615-640.

Weinberg, R. S. (1985). Relationship between self-efficacy and cognitive strategies in enhancing endurance performance. *International Journal of Sport Psychology, 17,* 280-293.

Weinberg, R. S., Gould, D., & Jackson, A. (1979). Expectations and performance: An empirical test of Bandura's self-efficacy theory. *Journal of Sport Psychology, 1,* 320-331.

Whelan, J. P., Mahoney, M. J., & Meyers, A. W. (1991). Performance enhancement in sport: A cognitive behavioral domain. *Behavior Therapy, 22,* 307-327.

Zanakos, S. I., & Wegner, D. M. (1993). The Fear of Sadness Test (which used to be called the Depression Sensitivity Scale). An unpublished scale available through the authors at the Department of Social Psychology, University of Virginia, Charlottesville.

Appendix

A Guide to Responding to Unwanted
Thoughts and Feelings During Competition

For most athletes mental abilities such as concentration and focus are seen as keys to optimal performance. Internal processes such as thoughts and feelings that are thought to interfere with concentration and focus are often targeted for change or elimination. For example, most athletes, by the time they reach elite or collegiate levels of competition, have been told, and generally believe, that negative thoughts and feelings are problematic and should be controlled. This old approach looks good on the face of it, but it actually has a tendency to backfire.

The purpose of this guide is to provide a new perspective on how to handle thoughts and feelings that make you uncomfortable while you are engaged in your sport. What you will learn from this manual and from the individual sessions you will have with your sport psychology consultant is that you do not need to block out or otherwise battle with thoughts and feelings that you do not want to have. Instead, by learning to accept those thoughts and feelings, you will find new ways of mentally preparing for and succeeding in competition.

Unwanted Thoughts

You have probably experienced many times the situation where you have "too much time to think." You probably found that when you were in this situation you missed an easy lay-up, a routine fly ball, or a perfectly set up overhead. You probably also found that the next time this happened, your thinking centered on thoughts such as "I can't miss this lay-up" or "I'll be benched for sure if I miss this fly ball." Of course these thoughts are troublesome. You may have already learned that these thoughts themselves lead you to make the bad play. But they don't.

How about the times your coach has told you, "Negative thoughts and worry will destroy you," or "If you think you can't, you won't." You have probably learned that in order to succeed, you must have self-confidence. Well, self-confidence is a wonderful feeling to have, but it cannot be felt on demand. What do you do when you find yourself thinking, "This team is going to have us for lunch," or "This pitcher really has my number"? Do you tell yourself that these thoughts are wrong – that you must think positive thoughts instead?

Unwanted Feelings

Performance anxiety: the jitters, the nervous stomach, the sweaty palms just before a game. You are told that you must play without fear, without worry. The term "choking" is often used to describe the clear lowering of performance that happens when an athlete is unable to cope with high levels of anxiety in competition. How do you cope with anxiety? You may have been taught relaxation techniques to deal with overarousal. You may also have been taught as a result that anxiety is a bad thing to have and that you must not be anxious. As you tell yourself to calm down, relax, don't be nervous, you may find that you also become upset or annoyed with yourself because you are nervous. Being nervous seems to be a signal that you are not mentally prepared, that you will have a bad game unless you can get rid of that nervousness. You get more nervous and worried simply because you are nervous and worried to begin with. Does that make sense?

Responding to Your Thoughts and Feelings

An athlete may report that she is feeling flat or anxious; that she gets caught up in thinking about striking out or worrying about making another error; that she is unable to keep her mind on the game; that she wants to yell back at her coaches. These kinds of troublesome emotions and thoughts almost always come hand in hand with the belief that they need to be changed or eliminated in order to raise the athlete's level of performance. Sport psychologists and consultants commonly offer techniques designed to achieve the goal of changing the thoughts or feelings in order to solve the performance problem. Anxiety management, cognitive restructuring, and thought stopping are all common methods used by psychologists to change thoughts and feelings, and sport psychology has adopted these methods and others. However, a different perspective can be taken. It is based on the notion that avoiding our thoughts and feelings is often the real problem that athletes are dealing with, and that the effort taken to avoid those mental states usually is what truly interferes with your performance.

Here's something to consider: you have played softball many years. You have had thousands of "at bats." You have not always been successful; sometimes you strike out. When you report that you have become overly fearful of striking out, to the point that you are often thinking about not striking out when you step into the batter's box, it is not really the striking out that you fear. It is rather feelings and thoughts you have associated with striking out in the past that you dread. Your major dilemma has become trying not to think about striking out; trying not to fear.

For example, can you imagine stepping into the batter's box and facing a .23 ERA pitcher and successfully hitting off of her while you think to yourself over and over again, "She struck me out last time . . . I can't strike out here. . . . I shouldn't even think about striking out. . . . I need to feel confident. . . . I can't be thinking these negative thoughts. . . ?"

Try this: while you continue to read the next few sentences, try NOT to think of WARM JELLY DOUGHNUTS.

Unfortunately, trying to escape from what you are feeling and thinking creates a problematic cycle. Trying so hard not to worry, not to be nervous, not to think about striking out itself interferes with your attention, concentration, and focus. You make a fielding error, take a called third strike, or miss a target, and the thoughts and feelings intensify. Attempts to avoid these thoughts and feelings reinforce the idea that they are "bad" and something to worry about, and something to avoid, and so on.

Have you been trying to not think of those warm jelly doughnuts? If so, did you notice that while you tried to not think of a warm jelly doughnut you actually were thinking about that warm jelly doughnut? This is what happens when we tell ourselves not to think about something.

The reasons we are stuck with this old approach to feelings and thoughts that you don't want are twofold: first, we have somehow come to believe that our thoughts and feelings are real causes of our behavior, of our performance; second, we have come to believe that these thoughts and feelings are "bad." The new approach that this guide proposes is that you begin now to turn the tables on these reasons – that you decide here and now to "opt out" of this setup that almost inevitably leads you to develop performance difficulties.

How Does the New Approach Differ From the Old One?

You have worked hard to become a top notch softball player. You're playing in a difficult league at a high level. Yet you know you can perform even better. You may ask, "Why am I not hitting as well now as I did in junior college or high school?" or "I'm committing these fielding errors because I need more _____ (fill in the blank with your favorites: willpower, confidence, emotional control)." A common issue that an athlete comes to the sport psychology consultant with is that the mental or psychological aspect of their performance difficulty is related to undesirable content of feelings or thoughts, and that these undesirable internal states in turn arise from some undesirable situation. Athletes often expect sport psychologists to help them improve their performance by changing the situation. Traditionally the sport psychologist has responded by stating that the problem is not that the athletic situation is too stressful, for example, but that the stressful situation is troublesome because the athlete is having the wrong thoughts or feelings. What you are thinking and feeling becomes the target: change your thoughts and feelings, and your problem will go away.

Let us consider another alternative: perhaps the agenda (change your thoughts or your moods and your performance behavior will change) is wrong. Recently psychologists have introduced an innovative approach to understanding the role of unwanted thoughts and feelings in human behavior. Much of what they have learned will apply to the athlete in competition. These psychologists suggest that it is the effort to rid oneself of distressful thoughts and feelings that guides behavior rather than the thoughts and feelings themselves, and that ACCEPTANCE of the thoughts and feelings, rather than efforts to remove or replace them, leads to beneficial behavior change.

Most people have thoughts and feelings that they do not want from time to time. As human beings we have learned that certain thoughts are "bad" or "wrong." As an athlete you have learned that feelings of a loss of confidence are "wrong" and that you should replace them with feelings of "confidence" instead. We know that athletes perform better when they are confident. But we make the mistake of assuming that the feelings of confidence and the thoughts associated with confidence are responsible for the better performance. This explanation may seem to make sense, but when we stop to consider what gives rise to the increased confidence, we realize something else: the feelings of confidence and the enhanced performance are both the results of nailing down the specific behaviors (skills) that it takes to improve performance. For example, when you've fielded 50 ground balls to your left in practice day after day until you can make the play without error over and over again, you begin to feel confident of your ability to field balls to your left AND you perform this play again and again in competition without error.

How does this relate to your feelings? Athletes commonly are unwilling to feel anxiety or to have negative thoughts about his or her ability. A loss of confidence is seen as a sign of "weakness" and of being a "loser." But it is the athlete's reaction to the loss of confidence that becomes the source of difficulty, not the loss of confidence itself. For an athlete who is unwilling to have negative feelings about her ability, the occurrence of those feelings or thoughts is likely to cause greater anxiety and worry. This begins a dangerous spiral that is difficult to put a stop to. But you can.

First of all, you must realize that having worries or a loss of confidence as a result of poor performance is natural. You may have been led to believe that successful athletes never doubt their abilities, but this is highly unlikely. It is their response to self-doubt and worry that has helped them to become successful. Chances are, that athlete did not spend a great deal of effort trying to control those thoughts and feelings. Instead she went about doing those things that she needed to do in order to get better, to perfect her skills.

The Acceptance Approach to your unwanted thoughts and feelings (be they related to your abilities, about your coaches, about your life in general) is based in part on the idea that by understanding your worries or loss of confidence as being a natural result of poor performance or inconsistency, rather than indications that your poor performance is due to psychological factors, will free the athlete to correct inappropriate skills rather than focusing on those thoughts and feelings.

Once you see your thoughts and feelings as common, natural, and understandable reactions to your past performance or some other historical event, your next step is to CLARIFY the values that are important to you. Some may be related to softball, and some may not be. That's fine.

What do you value? Not everyone has the same values, and there are no "correct" or "incorrect" values. Consider each of the following areas: friendships/social relations, athletics, employment, education, family relations, physical well-being, recreation. Try to think about each area in terms of both concrete goals you might have, and also in terms of more general life directions. Now let's focus specifically on softball (athletics). How would you put your values into action. What behaviors specifically would lead to achieving your goal(s)? What direction would you take?

This "taking a direction" is important, not because the outcome is important, but because the PROCESS matters. Choosing how you will act to reach your goals is more than making a decision: choice involves taking the risk of feeling your feelings and having thoughts about your actions once you have acted, once you have made your choice. For example, you may choose to be a more consistent in hitting an outside pitch. You take the actions necessary to improve this aspect of your game; you work hard during batting practice every day before the next game. Are you willing to feel discouraged? Are you willing to feel confused over what you're doing right or wrong? The critical issue here is experiencing what you're feeling or thinking as what it really is. You must be willing to expose yourself to emotional discomfort and disturbing thoughts. If you are not willing to worry about not getting any better, then you are not very likely to try to get better, are you?

A large part of what the Acceptance Approach is about is making a commitment and following through. Once you have come to understand what you value, and you understand the choices you must make to head in that direction, you must commit to behaving in ways that take you in that direction. Can you make a commitment and keep to it? Remember, your commitment is based on the things you value. Keeping a commitment requires that you be willing to accept the thoughts and feelings that you may have along the way.

Commitment to Excellence in Your Athletic Pursuits.

We have come a long way from talking about how changing thoughts and feelings can result in improved performance. Instead of offering negative thoughts and emotions as excuses (or reasons) for athletic performance, we can now understand that it is precisely this process that leads the athlete away from making the changes necessary to improve performance.

Learning to accept the feelings and thoughts you have as you practice and as you compete is an important aspect of improving your athletic performance. Whether you are feeling tired, worried, unhappy, or nervous, your commitment to getting the job done on the field is what really matters. You needn't become involved in the struggle of getting rid of those thoughts and feelings. Instead, HAVE those emotions, HAVE those thoughts. And THEN CONTINUE to perform the behaviors that are associated with improved performance, whether they be focusing on the ball, reminding yourself of where this batter went last time at bat, positioning yourself properly, taking extra batting practice with outside pitches, practicing relaxation training exercises, or talking with your coach about pitch selection. It is the DOING of these behaviors, whatever they specifically are, that ultimately leads to your improved performance. And it is the ACCEPTANCE of the feelings and thoughts, even though you MIGHT NOT WANT to have them, that will allow you to implement those behavior changes to make you a better, more successful player.

Chapter 11

Decreasing the Prevalence of Marital Conflict: A Public Health Perspective for Clinical Research

Barbara Kistenmacher
University of Oregon and Oregon Research Institute
Anthony Biglan
Oregon Research Institute

A Public Health Perspective For Clinical Psychology

Research in clinical psychology and psychiatry has made enormous progress in the past forty years. In the 1950's, empirically validated treatments were not available for any psychological or behavioral problems. Now one can point to multiple randomized controlled trials that have validated "treatments of choice" for most of the common psychological or behavioral problems, including phobias (Barlow, 1988), depression (Hollon & Beck, 1994), panic disorder (Hollon & Beck, 1994), social anxiety (Glaser, Biglan, & Dow, 1983), smoking (The Smoking Cessation Clinical Practical Guideline Panel and Staff, 1996), children's conduct problems (Taylor & Biglan, in press), attention deficit disorder (Pisterman, et al., 1989), harsh or coercive parenting (Taylor & Biglan, in press), and autism (Lovaas, 1987).

One might think that all of this progress would have resulted in a substantial reduction in human suffering. Yet, despite the fact that many treatments of choice have been known for 20 years, there is no evidence that our knowledge of how to treat clinical problems has resulted in widespread benefits. Because ongoing monitoring of the incidence and prevalence of psychological disorders is not yet underway, there is no empirical evidence that we have reduced the incidence or prevalence of any disorder.

Clinical research is reaching the point of diminishing returns. Although we are seeing increasing refinement of our clinical interventions and of the experimental evaluations of those interventions, we seem to be approaching limits on further improvements of these interventions. It is difficult to improve on treatments that already benefit the majority of clients, and many of the factors that interfere with treatment efficacy for clients who don't benefit from treatment are beyond the power of clinicians to affect.

We suggest that it is time to expand the paradigm for clinical research. Rather than focusing only on the efficacy of clinical interventions for treating patients who seek treatment, we should embrace a public health perspective (e.g., Biglan & Metzler, in press.) for clinical research. The essence of the public health perspective is a focus on the incidence or prevalence of a problem in a defined population. For example, rather than simply asking whether we can treat children's conduct problems, one would ask whether we can reduce the prevalence of children of any given age who have conduct problems. The ultimate justification for our society putting resources into clinical research is that it contributes to reducing the proportion of the population that has psychological or behavioral difficulties. Only if we expand the agenda for clinical research beyond tests of the efficacy of clinical interventions will we be able to realize this ultimate benefit of all the excellent work that has been done.

Once one embraces the goal of affecting the prevalence or incidence of a problem in a defined population, many new research questions become apparent. For example, are the efficacious treatments, that have been primarily tested in clinical research settings, effective in service settings? If empirically supported interventions do work in service settings, how can one ensure that a larger proportion of the people who have a problem are able to obtain and benefit from these treatments? This creates a demand for research on how to identify people with the problem and effectively refer them for treatment. For example, in the area of parenting skills training, studies are being conducted on how to recruit parents to programs (Spoth & Redmond, 1994). This is an important line of research. However, even very successful methods of recruiting people to treatment will founder on the fact that treatment is too expensive for some and there are not enough therapists to provide effective treatment. This question implies the need for research on how to make treatments less expensive and more efficient by, for example, providing them in brief, self-administered, or group formats. It points to the likely value of research on whether treatment can be provided by persons other than clinical psychologists, psychiatrists, and social workers. For example, health care providers such as nurses and pediatricians could systematically screen young children for conduct problems and provide brief or self-administered parent training for the parents (e.g., Webster-Stratton, Kolpacoff, & Hollinsworth, 1988; Webster-Stratton, 1992).

Even if we are enormously successful in reaching more people with more efficient, less expensive treatments, it is unlikely that we will ever have enough treatment providers to deal with psychological problems solely through clinical means. Moreover, why must we wait until the problems develop in order to do something about them?

Thus, in addition to expanding the effectiveness, reach, and efficiency of clinical treatment, we need to develop (a) nonclinical means of affecting problems and (b) methods of preventing them. Among the nonclinical means of addressing psychological problems are the use of mass media and the development of policies that affect known influences on the problem. In the area of tobacco control, where the public health model has been in use for some time (Biglan, 1995), there is evidence that mass media has contributed to the reduction in the prevalence of smoking (Flay, 1987 a,b). Public policies that would discourage tobacco use are being researched and promoted. For example, increasing the cost of cigarettes has been shown to reduce the number of young people who take up smoking (U.S.D.H.H.S., 1994), and reductions in illegal sales of cigarettes to minors are being achieved through the promotion of better law enforcement and more stringent laws (U.S.D.H.H.S., 1994).

Although efforts to prevent problems are newer than treatment efforts, a prevention research paradigm has been developed over the last 20 years and it is beginning to bear fruit. In areas such as adolescent tobacco use (Biglan, 1995), marital discord (e.g., Markman, Floyd, Stanley, & Lewis, 1986), and antisocial behavior (e.g., Webster-Stratton et al., 1988), risk factors for the development of problems have been identified (e.g., Hawkins, Catalano, & Miller, 1992) and programs and policies to prevent problems by modifying these risk factors are being developed and evaluated. Yet despite the promising developments in prevention research and nonclinical means of affecting problems, the vast bulk of our research resources continue to be put into clinical research. A public health perspective is lacking.

Behavior Analysis and the Public Health Perspective

Behavior Analysis and a public health perspective are quite compatible. As noted above, a public health perspective means that one is concerned with the incidence or prevalence of a problem in a defined population. When we are concerned with the incidence or prevalence of behaviors, we first need an effective analysis of the behavior of individuals. Biglan (1995) argued that behavior analysis provides a basic building block for developing a science for changing the incidence or prevalence of problematic behaviors. In its most generic form, behavior analysis seeks to identify *any* variable that affects the probability of behavior (Biglan & Hayes, 1996; Biglan & Kass, 1977). As we identify the variables affecting the behavior of individuals, we can use that information to develop interventions to affect the incidence and prevalence of behavior. A framework for research of this sort has been articulated by Biglan (1995). That framework uses behavior analysis to understand the behavior of individuals within social systems. However, it requires concepts that go beyond the analysis of the behavior of individuals. These include the concepts of incidence and prevalence, the actions of organizations, and meta-contingencies affecting the practices of groups or organizations (Biglan, 1995; Glenn, 1988).

Much of the promise of a better society which B. F. Skinner articulated requires that we find ways to translate our understanding of the solutions to the behavior problems of individuals into widespread benefits. We cannot achieve societal changes without our basic understanding of individual behavior. But, if we do not develop a better science of larger social systems, the knowledge we have that can benefit individuals will only diffuse through the culture in a slow and haphazard fashion.

Marital Discord From A Public Health Perspective

The present chapter attempts to spell out the case for a public health perspective as it applies to marital discord. Marital discord is a major problem in this country and in other countries in which it has been studied. For example, 55% of American marriages, 45% of Australian marriages, 42% of English marriages, and 37% of German marriages end in divorce (McDonald, 1995 as cited in Halford, Kelly, & Markman, 1997). Moreover, not all couples who stay together are satisfied with their marriage. Compared to happy marriages, discordant marriages are characterized by ineffective communication and conflict management (Halford, Hahlweg, & Dunne, 1990; Weiss & Heyman, 1990), the reciprocal exchange of negative behaviors (Jacobson, Follette, & McDonald, 1982), and withdraw (Christensen & Shenk, 1991). Further, discordant couples tend to selectively attend to their partner's negative behavior and attribute this behavior to stable and global personality traits (Eidelson & Epstein, 1982; Floyd & Markman, 1983).

Marital discord has many deleterious consequences. Poor marital adjustment is a risk factor for many psychological disorders such as depression in wives (Beach, Arias & O'Leary, 1986; Beach & O'Leary, 1986; Beach, Sandeen, & O'Leary, 1990), and alcohol abuse in husbands (Halford & Osgarby, 1993). Furthermore, phobias in husbands and panic disorder in husbands and wives are associated with low marital quality for both spouses (McLeod, 1994). Marital discord also contributes to inadequate parenting which, in turn, contributes to antisocial behavior and other developmental problems in children (Conger, Patterson, & Ge, 1995). Finally, separated and divorced adults are more likely to have a diagnosable psychiatric disorder than married adults (Standsfield, Gallacher, Sharp, & Yarnell, 1991). Clearly our society would benefit from more effective strategies for reducing the proportion of marriages that end in divorce or continue in misery.

The Efficacy of Behavioral Marital Therapy

Although there are several empirically validated treatments for marital discord (e.g. Insight-Oriented, Emotionally-Focussed, Cognitive, Cognitive-Behavioral), and no treatment has consistently outperformed another in clinical trials, Behavioral Marital Therapy (BMT) is the most widely researched and practiced marital intervention. For that reason, Jacobson and Addis (1993) assert that BMT is the "closest thing that couple treatment has to an established treatment" (p. 4). BMT is heavily rooted in social learning principles. Although there are many variants of BMT, all models of BMT involve increasing the reciprocal exchange of positive behaviors, communication skills training, and problem-solving which includes negotiating and contracting.

Over 30 studies have been published in the past 20 years that focus on the efficacy of BMT. Most of these studies have been covered in one of four major reviews (Baucom & Hoffman, 1986; Gurman, Kniskern, & Pinsof, 1986; Jacobson & Addis, 1993; Lebow & Gurman, 1995) or in one of three meta-analyses (Dunn & Schwebel, 1995; Hahlweg & Markman, 1988; Shadish, et al., 1993). All studies draw the same basic conclusion about the efficacy of BMT, namely that BMT is more efficacious than wait-list control conditions.

Baucom and Hoffman (1986) and Gurman, et al., (1986) reviewed controlled outcome investigations where distressed couples were randomly assigned to treatments. They concluded that BMT is efficacious in reducing the amount of negative communication and decreasing the number of couples' problem areas and requests for behavior change compared to nonspecific treatment and wait-list control. Further, BMT has proven to be more efficacious than wait-list control in terms of showing a greater increase in marital adjustment and happiness. However, BMT has not proven to be more efficacious than nonspecific marital therapy or attention control groups in terms of showing a greater increase in overall marital adjustment and happiness. Finally, BMT did not prove to be successful in helping distressed couples increase positive communication.

Although meta-analytic studies vary in their criteria for inclusion, they are similar in their conclusions that BMT is more efficacious than wait-list control. Hahlweg and Markman (1988) reported the results of their meta-analysis of 17 published BMT studies involving 613 couples. They found strong support for the efficacy of BMT with an average effect size of .95 for BMT versus control or placebo groups. Using less stringent inclusion criteria for their meta-analysis, Shadish, et al. (1993) reported on 27 published and unpublished family and couple therapy outcome studies. Efficacy of marital therapy was based on either global relationship satisfaction or specific presenting problems. The mean effect size across all studies was .60 and rose to .71 when only those studies that evaluated therapy success by global relationship satisfaction were considered.

The most recent, and most conservative meta-analysis was conducted by Dunn and Schwebel (1995) who reviewed 15 marital outcome studies conducted between 1980 and 1993 that met the following inclusion criteria: 1) couples were randomly assigned to treatment groups, 2) a control group was included, 3) there were no major threats to internal validity, 4) sufficient data was reported to allow for a meta-analysis, and 5) treatment procedures were clearly described. The results of their meta-analysis indicated that BMT was more effective than no treatment, with an average effect size of .79 for BMT.

Although the marital outcome literature clearly indicates that BMT is more efficacious than wait-list control, no strong evidence exists for the superiority of BMT compared to other treatment approaches. BMT has been compared to a systems approach, a group-analytic strategy, communication training emphasizing emotional expressiveness and listening skills, cognitive restructuring plus BMT, a group interaction approach, and an experiential intervention (Baucom & Hoffman, 1986). With a few exceptions (Hahlweg, Revenstorf, & Schindler, 1982; Johnson & Greenberg, 1985; O'Farrell, Cutter, & Floyd, 1983), no treatment approach has been found to be superior to another. In the few studies where a certain approach has been shown to be more successful, it is always in the direction of the allegiance and expertise of the investigators. Baucom and Hoffman (1986) suggest that one explanation for the finding that treatment approach does not seem to matter is because the individual needs of the couples were not considered when they were randomly assigned to treatment groups. This would suggest the need for more matching research investigating what treatment works best for what couples. However, it is also possible that differences among active treatments of marital discord have not been found because studies comparing these treatments require, but have not had, sample sizes larger than those needed to compare an active treatment condition with a no-treatment control.

Jacobson and Addis (1993) caution consumers of BMT outcome research to remember the difference between statistical and clinical significance. They point out that we should not necessarily be impressed with the fact that all marital outcome studies have shown that treatment outperforms control groups because marital adjustment in distressed couples is likely to deteriorate over time if not treated. In other words, it does not take a large amount of change in marital satisfaction to achieve statistically significant results compared to no treatment. When indices of clinical significance of change are used to evaluate outcome research, the effectiveness of BMT is modest (Whisman & Snyder, 1997). Furthermore, we can be less confident about the long-term effects of BMT, as longitudinal studies (Jacobson, Schmaling, & Holtzworth-Munroe, 1987; Snyder, Wills, & Grady-Fletcher, 1991) have shown a relapse rate of between thirty and thirty-eight percent.

In sum, the results of meta-analytic and review studies clearly indicate that BMT is more effective than wait list control when statistical significance is used as the criterion. More specifically, BMT is effective in reducing the amount of negative communication, and decreasing the number of couples' problem areas and requests for behavior change compared to wait-list control and nonspecific treatment control, and in increasing couples' global marital adjustment compared to wait-list control. Further, no type of marital therapy has been empirically proven to outperform the other, although more research, with sample sizes large enough to detect differences between treatment conditions, needs to be conducted before any firm conclusions can be drawn. When clinical significance and long-term effects are used as criteria for efficacy, the success of BMT in reducing marital distress is modest.

Thus, it appears that clinical research has identified a set of interventions that can be of significant value in reducing marital discord. There appears to be substantial room for improvement in clinical efficacy, however. Continuing research is needed to (a) identify relationships between components of marital therapy and the types of relationship problems they affect, (b) identify ways to prevent relapse, and (c) increase the overall efficacy of treatment. It is nonetheless, not too early to expand the agenda for research in this area.

The Effectiveness of Marital Therapy

Increasingly, clinical and prevention researchers are distinguishing between efficacy and effectiveness trials (Flay, 1986; Shadish, Ragsdale, Glaser, & Montgomery, 1995; Weiss & Weisz, 1995). An efficacy trial refers to an experimental evaluation of an intervention in which there is tight control over the delivery of the intervention. Typically, the interventionists are highly trained and closely supervised professionals who are directly under the supervision of a researcher. In clinical research, efficacy studies are typically conducted in clinical research settings, rather than in clinical service settings. Often, the participants in the research are selected according to fairly narrow criteria. An effectiveness trial, on the other hand, involves an evaluation of the intervention under conditions that more closely approximate the conditions under which the intervention is likely to be provided if it had come into widespread use. For example, Taylor, Schmidt, Pepler, and Hodgins (in press) compared behavioral parent training with usual care in a public mental health center in which families seeking treatment were randomly assigned to these conditions, and each type of therapy was provided by regular clinical treatment personnel.

The distinction between efficacy and effectiveness trials has been made because most of our clinical research consists of efficacy trials, and there is a concern that we will not be able to achieve the same kind of results in effectiveness trials. If we cannot, then our clinical research cannot be taken as a measure of what can be achieved in clinical service settings. More importantly, it would point to the need for our clinical research to deal with how we can translate successful efficacy trials into effects in the "real world."

In marital therapy research, we are aware that two effectiveness trials exist, although we were only able to locate one. Based on Weisz, Weiss and Donnenberg's (1992) criteria for clinic therapy, Shadish, et al. (1995) tried to locate a true effectiveness study in the field of marital therapy. In a pool of 71 studies, they were able to find one study that met Weisz et al.'s criteria, although they failed to cite which study it was. The other effectiveness study, including 84 counselors from Germany and Austria and 495 clients, showed an average effect size of .28 at posttreatment and .44 at the six month follow-up (Hahlweg & Klann, 1997). However, methodological weaknesses of the study (lack of wait-list control group, extremely high attrition rate, and no information about what type of therapy counselors performed) made it difficult to make any solid interpretations about effectiveness. This landmark study paves the way for future research in that it raises important issues to be grappled with in effectiveness trials.

The majority of outcome studies that are the subject of reviews and meta-analyses are randomized controlled studies conducted in lab clinics. Baucom and Hoffman (1986) acknowledge that "This research design imposes a major limitation regarding the implications of the results for clinicians treating individual couples" (p. 609). However, instead of making a plea for researchers to conduct studies in clinical settings to see if the results obtained in research settings can be replicated in service settings, they make a plea for clinicians to glean useful information from the results of controlled outcome studies. They suggest that clinicians use the case study method to assess whether their clients are benefiting from treatment.

Although Baucom and Hoffman's (1986) suggestion has merit, it would seem more valuable for marital researchers to begin to conduct randomized trials in service settings using regular clinical personnel. However, as Hahlweg and Klann (1997) discovered, this is no small task; there are obstacles to executing randomized controlled studies such as therapist compliance and ethical concerns. Further, research showing that therapist allegiance and expertise are important variables in determining the efficacy of a particular treatment (Hahlweg, et al., 1982; Johnson & Greenberg, 1985; O'Farrell, et al., 1983), implies that it may be difficult to replicate the results of BMT studies in applied settings if the therapists in these settings adhere more strongly to another orientation.

Other researchers suggest the inclusion of more complicated cases (e.g. one or more partners involved in substance abuse) as a way to increase the generalizability of lab study findings to service settings (Markman, Halford, & Cordova, 1997). Conducting treatment studies in community settings would automatically allow for the inclusion of complicated cases, with the addition of including more "externally valid" interventionists.

Experimental evaluations in service clinics would be difficult to carry out, but in the absence of such studies, we will never know whether marital discord can be effectively treated in clinical service settings. In the absence of such evidence, why should service provider organizations adopt the treatment practices that have been developed by marital therapy researchers?

But there is perhaps a more important reason for shifting some of our resources to effectiveness trials. In attempting to do clinical trials in service settings, marital researchers will have to confront many of the problems that have been obstacles to the widespread adoption of BMT. For example, it will be necessary to find effective ways to train and supervise the services of clinic personnel in order to produce good outcomes. The specification of these training and supervisory procedures will constitute a major step toward identifying how ongoing clinical service settings can be assisted in adopting and maintaining effective marital therapy.

Disseminating BMT

One means of reducing the prevalence of discordant marriages would be to ensure that existing treatment facilities are using the most efficacious interventions. The evidence reviewed above suggests, though far from conclusively, that behavioral marital therapy is the best available method of treating discord. This conclusion is tentative both because effectiveness trials have not be conducted to test whether such benefits can be reliably replicated in service settings and because we know little about the particular types of marital problems that are affected by different components of marital therapy. Nonetheless, it seems appropriate to devote some resources to exploring how to influence existing service providers to use the marital therapy that has the most evidence of efficacy.

In a PsycInfo search, we could not find a single study on dissemination of behavioral marital therapy (or any other form of marital therapy). As noted above, even effectiveness trials are a step in the right direction, since they at least give marital therapy researchers some experience in grappling with the problem of how to get service providers to adopt their intervention with integrity.

Ultimately, however, we will need experimental studies to evaluate programs' ability to influence service providers to adopt BMT. In such studies, it will be the behavior of the therapist in providing treatment that will be the dependent variable. The independent variable will be some set of procedures for getting therapists to agree to try BMT as well as procedures for training them to do so effectively. The ultimate test of the success of such studies will be whether they show that therapists so influenced produce significantly better outcomes than do therapists providing usual care.

Delivering Behavioral Marital Therapy Efficiently

If a large proportion of the population of discordant marriages is going to be reached, we will need to search for more cost-effective ways of providing treatment. Despite the pivotal role that marital discord plays in many other psychological problems (e.g. depression, alcohol abuse, etc.), health insurance seldom covers marital therapy. The increasing industrialization of health care (Hayes, 1997) could affect this situation, though the nature of the effect is uncertain. As Hayes (1997) notes, managed care makes it less necessary to assign a diagnosis to the patient. Rather, managed care organizations take responsibility to provide assistance (in a limited number of sessions) for whatever problems the patient presents. Under these circumstances, the organization may be willing to meet a patient's needs for marital therapy. On the other hand, given the nature of the capitation system, there will be heavy pressure on providers to make the intervention as cost-effective as possible.

The field of marital research seems to be moving in the direction of measuring the cost-effectiveness of different types of interventions. For example, O'Farrell, et al. (1996) conducted a cost-benefit and a cost-effectiveness analysis of BMT with and without relapses prevention sessions in a population of male alcoholics and their spouses. A cost-benefit analysis, which includes comparing the monetary cost of delivering an intervention to the monetary benefit of receiving the intervention, addresses the question of whether an intervention is economically justified. Monetary benefits usually included reduced utilization of health care services posttreatment. Cost-benefit research would help managed care institutions determine whether treatment is more justified than no treatment. A cost-effectiveness analysis, which involves calculating the cost per unit of clinical effect, addresses the question of which means of accomplishing a health-related objective is the most efficient and least costly. Cost-effectiveness research would aid managed care settings in determining which type of treatment to deliver. Although there are few marital studies that directly measure cost-benefit or cost-effectiveness, there are a number of studies comparing the effectiveness of various BMT treatment modalities that provide promise for the utilization of efficient ways of delivering marital therapy.

Self-administered treatment. In a randomized, controlled study of 64 white middle class married couples, Ford, Bashford, & DeWitt (1984) compared (a) couples participating in six individually administered weekly one hour sessions of communication skills training, (b) couples watching a videotaped version of the six weekly sessions, (c) couples doing homework exercises by mail with weekly telephone contact and (d) a wait-list control group. There were no differences among the three treatment groups in couple-reported cohesion, expressiveness, and perceived marital satisfaction, and all three treatment groups faired better than the wait-list control group. Comparing these three groups on observer-rated communication skills, they found that the direct contact and video groups did better than the homework and control groups. It must be noted that these couples were not terribly distressed, and that further analyses revealed that different client variables were differentially predictive of outcome success in different interventions. For example, the video group benefited to the extent that they began training with higher levels of marital satisfaction and confidence in family cohesiveness, and the homework clients benefited to the extent that they had a background in therapy. Direct contact seemed to be more necessary for less satisfied, less expressive couples. These results point to the importance of conducting more matching research on client factors and treatment modalities which could eventually guide us in determining how to best use our resources.

In a study of 23 maritally stable couples where the wife had secondary orgasmic dysfunction, husband and wife self-report indicated that participants improved on all specific sexual performance measures and affectional contact and communication measures, regardless of whether they received 15 sessions of standard couple therapy, 15 meetings of group therapy, or 14 weeks of minimal-contact bibliotherapy (Libman, et al., 1984). When there were differences in outcome among the three groups, they were usually in favor of standard couple therapy. More research is needed to understand the relationship between treatment benefits and treatment modality. In other words, what type of treatment gains can be made with a lower cost, minimal contact treatment, and what type of gains require a more expensive standard couple format?

A problem with the Libman, et al. (1984) study is that they did not have a no-treatment or wait-list control condition. Where the self-administered treatment did as well the therapist delivered treatment, it could be because the therapist delivered treatment was not very effective. It would be more convincing to show that self-administered treatment outperformed a no treatment control condition, as Webster-Stratton has done in her evaluations of self-administered parenting skills training (Webster-Stratton, et al., 1988; Webster-Stratton, 1992).

Zeiss (1978) found that a minimal-contact bibliotherapeutic program for premature ejaculation was as effective as a therapist-directed program, but that a totally self-administered program was much less effective than the other formats due to extremely poor subject compliance. These findings suggest promise for at least some type of minimal contact programs. More research needs to be conducted to determine what participant characteristics are associated with compliance and what types of therapy can be delivered with minimal therapist contact.

In their multiple baseline analysis of 5 clinically distressed couples, Bornstein, et al. (1984) tested the efficacy of a self-help behavioral marital bibliotherapy program. They found no significant treatment effects on any measures of marital adjustment, with the exception of a decrease in observer-coded negative behaviors. Perhaps the lack of success was due to the couples' level of distress.

The results of these studies suggest the need for more research on cost-effective ways to deliver marital therapy. Self-administered treatments using books or videos may be of value, but their effectiveness may have to be supplemented by at least minimal contact with a therapist. Moreover, they may not be effective for the most serious cases of marital discord. Further studies will benefit from the inclusion of no-treatment control conditions and examination of the relationship of couple characteristics to treatment outcome as well as to the value of specific components of therapy.

Group treatment. In addition to self-administered and minimal-contact marital therapy, group treatment is a viable modality to explore in future research. If effective, this modality would have obvious benefits in reducing the cost of marital therapy. There are a number of studies that suggest group therapy is indeed a viable method of ameliorating marital discord for many couples.

Revenstorf, Schindler, and Hahlweg (1983) evaluated group therapy, although the assignment of couples to group vs. individual couple conditions was nonrandom because they wanted the groups to be homogeneous with respect to age and number of children. Fifty couples were randomly assigned to either wait-list control or BMT and within BMT, couples were nonrandomly assigned to group or individual couple conditions. Couples in both BMT conditions showed a significant increase in their daily communication, tenderness, and general relationship happiness compared to the control group, and there were no significant differences between the two BMT modalities. However, the authors did state that conjoint treatment is probably the "gold standard" for more difficult couples as it gets the couple to focus more quickly on their core problems. Group therapy can be efficacious if the couples are more or less equally improving, but the effectiveness of the therapy can be challenged by members of the group who are not improving (Revenstorf, et al., 1983).

Wilson, Bornstein, and Wilson (1988) found similar results with respect to the promise of group treatment. They compared group couples therapy with individual couples therapy in a randomized controlled design in which couples were assigned to either of these conditions or to a wait-list control condition. Couples in both treatment conditions showed significant improvements compared to wait-list couples. In an earlier randomized study however, Wilson found that treatment modality success was dependent upon which outcome variables were assessed; couples in individual couple treatment improved more than those in group treatment on sharing feelings, whereas distressed couples in group treatment improved more on communication skills, sexual relations, and childrearing (Wilson, 1987).

In two randomized studies conducted by Bennun (Bennun, 1984; Bennun, 1985), including a total of 93 couples, martial therapy was effective across group and conjoint modalities (Bennun, 1984) and across group, conjoint, and individual modalities (Bennun, 1985), although conjoint treatment worked faster than group or individual modalities.

In sum, it appears that a group format is a viable option for the treatment of marital discord, depending on what outcome variables are being targeted and depending on how fast you want results. Even if it is true, as Revenstorf, et al. (1983) suggest, that the most severe couples will require individual couples therapy, the total number of couples that are helped per therapist could be increased if group treatment were used. At the same time, it should be noted that this will be true only if one succeeds in recruiting and retaining a sufficient number of couples for group treatment. This is because when considering the cost-effectiveness of group therapy compared to conjoint therapy, one must calculate the average number of minutes each therapist spends on each couple. Most groups are run by two therapists and last for 2 to 2.5 hours. The groups is only cost-effective to the extent that you have enough couples to reduce the amount of time per couple (per session) to under 1 hour (Revenstorf, et al., 1983).

Masters level therapists. Another method of reducing the cost of marital therapy would be to train masters level providers. Although many masters level graduate students serve as clinicians in published outcome studies, we are not aware of any studies that have directly evaluated whether the extent of clinical training or credentials makes a difference in marital therapy outcome. If our goal is to reduce the prevalence of discordant marriages, we will need to consider conducting research on the value of having masters level providers deliver marital services.

Nonclinical Means of Ameliorating Marital Conflict

If our goal is reduce the number of discordant marriages in a certain community, then we need to extend out efforts beyond clinical avenues. The public health perspective includes utilizing nonclinical, as well as clinical, means of ameliorating marital conflict. This approach is more proactive than the clinical approach of waiting for someone to come to our door seeking help. A key step for organizing communities to reduce the prevalence of discordant marriages would be to ensure that any agencies that come in contact with distressed couples screen them and take steps that might help them ameliorate their problems. The screening might result in referral for treatment or it might trigger the delivery of brief or automated therapy, such as the self-administered programs discussed above. We will mention a few of the agencies most likely to be able to make a difference.

Health care providers. Although we are unaware of studies, it seems likely that many people who are in troubled marriages present to their primary care physician at some point. For example, during a routine checkup, a woman may present to her physician that she is feeling depressed. Her physician may give her a prescription for Prozac, continue with the routine physical, and send her on her way. If her physician probed a little about why she was feeling depressed, she may reveal that she and her husband are having trouble communicating (as depression and marital difficulties are often comorbid for women). Upon further questioning, she might continue to explain that her husband never wants to talk about things and she feels like she has to nag him just to get him to pay attention to her. This extra information about why she is depressed would provide her physician with an opportunity to give her a pamphlet or video on demand/withdraw communication that she could take home and read/watch with her husband. The self-help video could focus on basic communication skills and offer suggestions about where to get more information/ help. The video could be funded by drug companies that sell medication for depression, and marketing personnel could join forces with clinical psychologists to create the video. They would have an interest in providing the funding for this service because the free video would serve as an incentive for doctors to write prescriptions for their product as opposed to a competitor's product. Ideas such as these open the door for innovative research on decreasing the number of discordant marriages in a community.

Physicians can also play a role in helping battered women find resources they need. Most battered women present to a doctor before they present to a psychologist. How a physician responds to a woman's first effort at getting help can play a pivotal role in what she decides to do to protect herself. Physicians should be taught how to screen for domestic violence and how to talk to a victim of domestic violence. In terms of screening, they should routinely question any woman who presents with injuries such as cuts, bruises, scratches, and broken bones. In terms of talking to a victim, they should learn the appropriate language to use to avoid victim-blaming and to encourage her to seek support so that she can make an informed choice about her marriage. They should also have crisis line cards available in their offices for referrals.

Research could be conducted at many levels of the process. For example, women presenting in the emergency room could be given the choice of filling out a questionnaire about their experiences with emergency room physicians and/or nurses to measure whether domestic violence training programs for health care providers are effective in getting the providers to actually screen and provide referrals for domestic violence situations. Another line of research could focus on whether contact with health care providers was helpful in terms of her finding support.

Police officers. Like physicians, police officers are often one of the first people to make contact with a battered woman, and they can play a pivotal role in the decisions she makes. All police officers should be trained on how to respond to a domestic dispute call. If the officer is unsure who the victim is, he/she should at least know how to talk to the couple in a general way that stresses the seriousness of the "crime" and encourages them to get help. Referrals to shelters and batterers treatment programs should be a routine part of every call, although it should not necessarily replace arrests. Since the 1970's, police forces have made tremendous progress in terms of educating their officers about the dynamics involved in domestic violence. For example, the community of Eugene, Oregon (as well as other communities) has created a domestic violence council that includes battered women's advocates, police officers, lawyers, and therapists who meet monthly to discuss issues and policies related to domestic violence. These meetings often include training workshops for officers and other officials on how to deal with domestic violence situations. Systematic research investigating whether participation in these training workshops translates into behavior change on the part of police officers is sorely needed.

The outcome of domestic dispute calls should be informed by the literature. For example, police officers should know that there are different subtypes of batterers (Holtzworth-Munroe & Stuart, 1994), and that jail-time is most likely the only effective "treatment" for the type of batterer who is a repeat offender, has an arrest record outside of the domestic violence crimes, and has other problems such as substance abuse. If our goal is to decrease the number of discordant marriages, we cannot ignore the fact that many of these marriages involve violence. As a matter of fact, about 50% of the couples presenting to a marital clinic have experienced at least one act of violence in the past year (Holtzworth-Munroe, et al., 1992). Therefore, decreasing the prevalence of marital violence is an integral part of reducing the incidence of marital discord.

Ministers. Because 50% of marriages end in divorce, getting married should be considered a risk factor for divorce. Ministers could play a role in helping couples prevent divorce by requiring them to participate in a premarital therapy program before they will marry them. Many churches already do this; for example the Catholic church has premarriage encounter weekends. However, these programs often provide information to couples as opposed to teaching them skills (Markman, et al., 1997). Research testing the effectiveness of having clergy deliver premarital services is already being conducted by Markman and his colleagues. They are comparing couples participating in PREP (Prevention and Relationship Enhancement Program) delivered by clergy, couples receiving traditional marital counseling, and couples who participate in PREP in a University-based setting on relationship functioning and stability. Once a couple is married and experiencing difficulties, the minister still can play a role, as many couples will talk to a minister about their problems before they will talk to a counselor.

Employers. Two main components of standard behavioral couples therapy are improving communication and increasing relationship "fun." Some couples depend on two incomes, and some couples work opposite shifts (husband may work swing shift and wife may work a typical 9 to 5 shift). Couples that don't have quality time together cannot possibly have quality communication, let alone have time for fun. Employers could play a role in facilitating couples to spend quality time together. For example, they could have special "family days" or "partner days" that are separate from sick days or vacation days. Not only could the day itself facilitate couples spending time together, but the symbolic act of having these days could foster a norm that favors couples devoting time to enjoying their relationship. The government could provide tax benefits to companies that provide these days.

Work organizations also could provide marital therapy as part of their benefits package. Research examining the relationship between marital satisfaction and job productivity could be conducted to inspire companies to value marital mental health benefits. Finally, organizations could sponsor marital workshops where they hire a marriage counselor to provide a half-day of communication skills training for workers and their spouses.

Social service agencies. Data are needed on the proportion of couples contacted by child and family welfare agencies that are having marital difficulties. If, as we suspect, the rate of marital discord among couples contacted by these agencies is high, then steps should be taken to develop ways in which the agencies can screen for marital discord and engage in effective referral and/or brief counseling.

Courts. The principles and procedures by which the court system operates needs to be empirically driven and consistent with the goal of decreasing the prevalence of discordant marriages, especially in domestic violence situations. Batterers are often mandated to treatment as punishment for beating their wives. This is a step in the right direction; however, the court system needs to pay attention to the literature which strongly suggests that certain types of batterers will probably never do well in psychological treatment. Too often, the courts nondifferentially apply the same sentence to first-time offenders.

Media. Although it is difficult to do well-controlled studies of the effects of media, their potential for affecting the prevalence of discordant marriages should not be overlooked. A wealth of evidence indicates that media can affect other aspects of people's behavior. Flay's (1987 a, b) review of the effects of media on smoking concluded that mass media can motivate people to change their behavior and, in conjunction with support, can assist them in quitting smoking. Barber, Bradshaw and Walsh (1989) showed that alcohol consumption can be influenced via mass media, and evidence indicates that media campaigns have affected drunk driving (Niensted, 1990).

With the help of major television stations, Sanders and his colleagues in Australia are producing a series of television shows based on his successful parenting program. We could model a marital program after their work by using the media to educate individuals about healthy ways to deal with relationship conflict and stressors, and to promote realistic beliefs about relationships (Markman, et al., 1997). There has not been any research conducted to date on the efficacy of such programs (Van Widenfelt, Markman, Guerney, Behrens, & Hosman, 1997).

Studies are also needed on the impact that entertainment media have on relationships between couples. A huge proportion of entertainment depicts relationships between men and women. Much of it depicts conflict, little of it models effective problem solving. We know from research on the modeling effects of media that depictions of aggression can influence viewers to be more aggressive (Bandura, 1973). It has been argued that both entertainment and news media have deleterious influences on the relationships between men and women (e.g., Faludi, 1991). From the perspective of its potential to influence couples' relationships in positive or negative directions, the lack of empirical research on the influence of mass media on couples relationships is a huge oversight.

Prevention of Marital Discord

Clinical approaches. The adoption of a prevention paradigm to target marital discord is not new to the field of marital research. Researchers working in the area of prevention have provided several rationale for conducting such research. First of all, because the focus is on health as opposed to sickness, we may reach a segment of the population that may otherwise not present for treatment. There is less stigma attached to participating in an education program than there is attached to getting treatment for relationship dysfunction (Van Widenfelt, et al., 1997). Second, prevention work allows us the advantage of starting with happy couples so we can help them maintain their high levels of adjustment rather than following the standard marital therapy trajectory of making distressed couples less distressed (Markman & Hahlweg, 1993). Third, because martial distress is a risk factor for many other forms of psychopathology, preventing marital distress may prevent other disorders (Bradbury & Fincham, 1990). Fourth, although there is no research to date that directly compares the cost of delivering therapy to distressed couples to the cost of delivering prevention programs to happy couples, prevention programs are more cost-effective in theory because they could be delivered by paraprofessionals and would require fewer sessions (Van Widenfelt, et al., 1997). Finally, Bradbury and Fincham (1990) pose the question that, if we can alleviate marital suffering early, why should we wait until couples have endured years of problems to treat them?

Marital prevention programs vary along several dimensions, including the settings in which they are delivered, the length of the program, the amount of group vs. dyadic interaction that occurs, the phase of marriage to which they are targeted, the extent to which they adopt a psycho-educational versus experiential approach, and the level of training of group leaders (Bradbury & Fincham, 1990). Although the distinction between prevention and promotion is not always clear, promotion involves targeting populations without defined risk, whereas prevention involves searching for and then trying to influence specific risk factors. Most marital prevention/promotion research is aimed at primary prevention which means targeting currently satisfied couples. By nature, prevention efforts are in line with the public health model in that the goal is to reduce the probability of new discordant marriages in the future. The two most popular prevention/promotion programs are PREP and RE.

The development of Markman's PREP program was inspired by research that identifies the factors that distinguish maritally distressed couples from maritally satisfied couples. Based on these risk factors, the goals of the program are centered around improving communication skills such as problem-solving and validation, cognitions such as relationship expectations and attributions about relationship problems, and sexual intimacy (Van Widenfelt, et al., 1997).

Guerney's RE (Relationship Enhancement) promotion program is designed to help couples enhance the positive parts of their relationship. The specific goals of this skills-based program are to increase caring, giving, honesty, understanding, trust, openness, sharing, compassion, and harmony in the relationship (VanWidenfelt, et al., 1997).

Giblin, Sprenkle, and Sheehan (1985) provide the most comprehensive review of the effectiveness of premarital enrichment programs. They included 85 experimental or quasi-experimental studies conducted between 1971 and 1982 that focused on premarital, marital, or family enrichment, They did not limit their review to published studies, studies of happy couples, studies of engaged couples, or methodologically sound studies, although methodologically weak studies were not weighted the same as methodologically sound studies. For the enrichment studies, they obtained an average effect size of .44 which means that the enrichment participants were better off than 67% of the untreated control participants. When only the 12 premarital prevention studies were considered, the effect size was .53. Stronger effect sizes were found with behavioral measures versus self-report measures. The authors suggested that this could be due to response shift bias where couples base their posttreatment self-report ratings of a certain marital variable on a higher standard than their pretreatment self-report ratings. Further, they found stronger effect sizes for skills-based outcome measures versus satisfaction or personality/perceptual measures. This could be due to the fact that behaviors are easier to influence than overall adjustment and/or because there are ceiling effects to begin with for overall adjustment.

Hahlweg and Markman, (1988) calculated an average effect size of .79 for the seven prevention studies that were included in their meta-analysis of 17 BMT studies. Perhaps this effect size is larger than the effect size (.53) reported by Giblin et al. (1985) because the studies in the Hahlweg and Markman (1988) were more methodologically sound than the combination of studies used in the Giblin, et al. (1985) analysis. At this stage in prevention research, it is probably safe to say that prevention interventions show at least modest effects.

The results of previous prevention studies pave the way for several directions in future research. First and foremost, because the purpose of prevention research is to prevent the relationship dissolution that naturally occurs over time, researchers must focus on long-term effectiveness. Of the 85 studies that were reviewed by Giblin, et al. (1985), the longest follow-up assessment was 12 months, and only 40% of the studies included follow-up measures at some point after posttest (Bradbury & Fincham, 1990). Since the Giblin et al. study, four and five year follow-up data has been provided for Markman's prevention program. PREP couples outperformed control couples in conflict management, communication, relationship stability, and relationship satisfaction at the four year follow-up, although only PREP husbands showed a significant advantage over the control group on communication and relationship satisfaction at the five year mark (Markman, Renick, Floyd, Stanley, & Clements, 1993). The results of this study not only indicate the need for longitudinal research to assess the true effectiveness of prevention programs, but also indicate the need for research focused directly on how to maintain treatment effects.

Another important methodological issue in prevention research is the fact that larger effects sizes are achieved with behavioral measures (Giblin, et al., 1985). Giblin, et al. (1985) suggest that future researchers should try to understand this inconsistency between modes of measurement. They offer the possible explanation that self-reported present behavior is influenced by recent past behavior; in other words, it may take longer for a partner to perceive and report change in behavior than it does for an outside observer.

Although longitudinal evaluations of program effectiveness are necessary and an understanding of measurement issues is paramount to future prevention research, Bradbury and Fincham (1990) caution us about moving forward too fast without closely looking at where we came from. Prevention programs are based on findings from basic research, a lot of which is cross-sectional, that differentiate distressed and nondistressed couples. However, they caution against relying too heavily on cross-sectional basic research for designing prevention programs because the direction of the relationship between marital satisfaction and behavior is unclear and because the results of some longitudinal studies (Filsinger & Thoma, 1988; Gottman & Krokoff, 1989) contradict the results of cross-sectional research. We do not know if behaviors drive satisfaction or if satisfaction drives behaviors. Besides, behavior only accounts for a portion of the variance in marital satisfaction. Therefore, the future of prevention research relies heavily on basic research that addresses the directionality problem inherent in cross-sectional designs, and that identifies other predictors of marital satisfaction besides behavior.

Finally, prevention program development needs to borrow from what we know about the relationship between marital distress and physical/sexual abuse, substance abuse, and infidelity. To date, prevention programs do not touch on these risk factors. There is also a need for research on how to recruit "at-risk" couples; for example, are young, lower SES couples (who are at risk) more likely to attend a program at a University, church, or community center? (Van Widenfelt, et al., 1997).

Assuming we do create a marital prevention program that is based on replicated longitudinal studies differentiating distressed and nondistressed couples, that shows strong effects over a long period of time assessed by state of the art measures, and that includes modules to address some of the more complicated issues involved in marital discord such as abuse and infidelity, we then need to investigate ways to measure the effectiveness of the program in clinical settings and ways to ensure the widespread dissemination of the prevention program. As we have learned from the field of traditional marital therapy, this is no small task. Even the widespread dissemination of such a program will not ensure that we reach the majority of the population that needs marital services. That is why we need to explore nonclinical means of preventing marital discord.

High school courses on relationships. The purpose of prevention programs is to catch problems before they occur. Prevention researchers in the marital filed have typically tried to accomplish this goal by focusing on either happy premarital or happily married couples. Marital researchers need to consider a broader definition of prevention by investigating the effectiveness of programs geared toward young individuals about to enter the dating arena. Courses could be offered in middle school or high school that focus on intimate relationships. Course content could challenge traditional socialization that teaches boys to be tough and uncaring and girls to be solicitous and caring. In addition, communication and problem-solving skills could be taught. Such courses could be coupled with already existing sex education programs. Capaldi's research suggests that the level of violence in adolescent relationships is comparable to that of violence in marital relationships (Capaldi & Crosby, 1997). This finding underscores the importance of catching problems early, and hopefully changing patterns before they become a part of an individual's relationship repertoire. Of course the systematic evaluation of these programs, as well as other similar community programs designed to prevent relationship discord, is needed to see whether it is worth investing resources such as teacher classroom time and school funds into such prevention efforts.

Policy changes. There is increasing recognition that the incidence or prevalence of problematic patterns of behavior can be affected by laws or regulations. For example, in the area of tobacco control, research has shown that the prevalence of adolescents who use tobacco use can be reduced by influencing communities to restrict illegal sales of tobacco to young people (Forster, et al., in press). Thus, it is important to examine what laws or regulations would facilitate the reduction in marital discord? We are unaware of research on this topic. In this section, we will simply mention ways in which laws or regulations might be modified to affect the prevalence of discordant marriages. We stress, however, that empirical work will be needed to determine whether any of the changes we suggest will have the influence that we hypothesize they will have.

Domestic disputes/spousal abuse. Many states have adopted laws making it mandatory to arrest the abusing spouse in cases of spousal abuse, regardless of whether the victim is willing to press charges. There are some negative consequences to such laws. For example, police officers may have trouble determining who the perpetrator is and may arrest the wrong person, and families may lose the perpetrator's income while he is in jail. Nonetheless, the results of a randomized clinical trial in Minneapolis indicated that the rate of victim and police-reported subsequent abuse is reduced by such laws (Sherman & Berk, 1984). However, the small sample size in the Minneapolis experiment and the fact that replication studies revealed the findings were dependent on which city the study was conducted in and on the employment status of the perpetrator, raises questions about the effectiveness of mandatory arrest in reducing recidivism (Sherman, 1992). At the very least, the results of the Minneapolis study suggest the possibility that policy changes can play a role in reducing the incidence or marital discord. Another potential advantage of a mandatory arrest policy is that the value that violence is not acceptable in a marriage is communicated through this law, although this communicated value would only be important to the extent that it in some way affects abusing behavior. More research needs to be conducted to determine how well such laws work and whether they contribute to reducing marital discord.

Courts/handling of divorce. When thinking about how court-related policies could influence the prevalence of marital discord, we need to be clear about what our goals are. Are they to reduce the incidence of divorce, abuse, marital discord, or all of the above? Certainly, we do not want to force unhappy couples to stay together, especially in instances of spousal abuse. However, policies centered around offering marital counseling and/or mediation for those couples presenting to the court system for divorce could contribute to the goal of reducing the prevalence of unhappy marriages. Many courts are already offering mediation for divorcing couples, although the rationale for doing so comes more from an overworked court system than from social science research aimed at relieving human suffering. What is needed is the experimental evaluation of sets of procedures that are evaluated in terms of the proportion of participating couples that stay together and find happiness, stay together and remain discordant, and divorce. Most of our public responses to important social problems are based on ideologically driven solutions that have never been empirically examined. It is time that we base court procedures/policies on what we learn from social science research.

Screening of those getting married. Not only can we try to reach couples near the end of their marriage, as in the case of creating policies around how courts handle divorce, but we can also create policies that target couples in the early stages of their marriage. When filing for a marriage license, couples could be required (or given the opportunity) to fill out a battery of questionnaires that screen for marital discord risk factors. Referrals for marital enrichment programs could be provided, or couples could be required to attend a prevention program before getting married. There are definite disadvantages to this approach. First of all, it may be unethical to inform couples that they are destined for poor marital adjustment because it may create a self-fulfilling prophecy. Second, mandating premarital counseling would create bureaucratic difficulties (Markman, et al., 1997). Finally, Markman, et al. (1997) point out there are virtually no data on the effectiveness of mandated programs. It is important to have data on this because, as we know from the batterer's literature, not all mandated clients are motivated to change. Research on the effectiveness of mandated programs needs to be conducted before creating policies on premarital counseling.

Summary

The field of Behavioral Marital Therapy has made tremendous progress over the past thirty years. One can point to countless randomized controlled clinical trials showing that BMT is more efficacious in altering marriage-specific behaviors and increasing overall marital adjustment than wait-list control. Further, the recent emergence of true effectiveness trials is evidence that researchers are starting to pay attention to the importance of generalizing the effects we see in lab research to service settings in the community. However, we have a long journey ahead if we want to decrease the prevalence of discordant marriages in our communities.

A public health perspective challenges us to reacquaint ourselves with the practitioner side of the scientist-practitioner model by allowing clinically-rooted questions drive our research endeavors. We need to step into unfamiliar, albeit often uncomfortable, territory by examining and utilizing all of the elements in our communities that influence the prevalence of marital discord.

References

Bandura, A. (1973). *Aggression: A social learning analysis*. Englewood Cliffs, NJ: Prentice-Hall.

Barber, J. G., Bradshaw, R., & Walsh, C. (1989). Reducing alcohol consumption through television advertising. *Journal of Consulting and Clinical Psychology, 57*, 613-618.

Barlow, D. H. (1988). *Anxiety and its disorders*. New York: Guilford.

Baucom, D. H., & Hoffman, J. A. (1986). The effectiveness of marital therapy: Current status and application to the clinical setting. In N. S. Jacobson & A. S. Gurman (Eds.), *Clinical handbook of marital therapy* (pp. 597-620). New York: Guilford.

Beach, S. R., Arias, I., & O'Leary, K. (1986). The relationship of marital satisfaction and social support to depressive symptomatology. *Journal of Psychopathology and Behavioral Assessment, 8*, 305-316.

Beach, S. R. & O'Leary, K. D. (1986). The treatment of depression occurring in the context of marital discord. *Behavior Therapy, 17*, 43-49.

Beach, S. R. H., Sandeen, E. E., & O'Leary, K. D. (1990). The marital discord model of depression. In D. H. Barlow (Ed.), *Depression in marriage: A model for etiology and treatment* (pp. 53-84). New York: Guilford.

Bennun, I. (1984). Evaluating marital therapy: A hospital and community study. *British Journal of Guidance and Counseling, 12*, 84-91.

Bennun, I. (1985). Behavioral marital therapy: An outcome evaluation of conjoint, group an one-spouse treatment. *Scandinavian Journal of Behaviour Therapy, 14*, 157-168.

Biglan, A. (1995). *Changing cultural practices: A contextualist framework for intervention research*. Reno, NV: Context Press.

Biglan, A. & Hayes, S. C. (1996). Should the behavioral sciences become more pragmatic? The case for functional contextualism in research on human behavior. *Applied and Preventive Psychology 5*, 47- 57.

Biglan, A., & Kass, D. J. (1977). The empirical nature of behavior therapies. *Behaviorism, 5*, 1-15.

Biglan, A. & Metzler, C. W. (in press). A public health perspective for research on family-focused interventions. NIDA monograph. Washington, DC: National Institute on Drug Abuse.

Bornstein, P. H., Wilson, G. L., Balleweg, B. J., Weisser, C. E., Tepper-Bornstein, M., Andre, J. C., Woody, D. J., Smith, M. M., Laughna, S. M., McLellarn, R. W., Kirby, K. L., & Hocker, J. (1984). Behavioral marital bibliotherapy: An initial investigation of therapeutic efficacy. *The American Journal of Family Therapy, 12*, 21-28.

Bradbury, T. N., & Fincham, F. D. (1990). Preventing marital dysfunction: Review and analysis. In F. D. Fincham & T. N. Bradbury (Eds.), *The psychology of marriage* (pp. 375-401). New York: Guilford.

Capaldi, D. M. & Crosby, L. (1997). Observed and reported psychological and physical aggression in young, at-risk couples. *Social Development, 6*, 184-205.

Christensen, A., & Shenk, (1991). Communication, conflict, and psychological distance in non-distressed, clinic, and divorcing couples. *Journal of Consulting and Clinical Psychology, 59*, 458-463.

Conger, R. D., Patterson, G. R., & Ge, X. (1995). It takes two to replicate: A mediational model for the impact of parents' stress on adolescent adjustment. *Child Development, 66*, 80-97.

Dunn, R. L., & Schwebel, A. I. (1995). Meta-analytic review of marital therapy outcome research. *Journal of Family Psychology, 9*, 58-68.

Eidelson, R. J., & Epstein, N. (1982). Cognition and relationship maladjustment: Development of a measure of dysfunctional relationship beliefs. *Journal of Consulting and Clinical Psychology, 50*, 715-720.

Faludi, S. (1991). *Backlash: The undeclared war against American women.* New York: Doubleday.

Filsinger, E. E., & Thoma, S. J. (1988). Behavioral antecedents of relationship stability and adjustment: A five-year longitudinal study. *Journal of Marital and Family Therapy, 50*, 785-795.

Flay, B. R. (1986). Efficacy and effectiveness trials (and other phases of research) in the development of health promotion programs. *Preventive Medicine, 15*, 451-474.

Flay, B. R. (1987a). Mass media and smoking cessation: A critical review. *American Journal of Public Health, 77*, 153-160.

Flay, B.R. (1987b). *Selling the Smokeless Society: 56 Evaluated Mass Media Programs and Campaigns Worldwide.* Washington, DC: American Public Health Association.

Floyd, F. J., & Markman, H. J. (1983). Observational biases in spouse observation: Toward a cognitive/behavioral model of marriage. *Journal of Consulting and Clinical Psychology, 51*, 450-457.

Ford, J. D., Bashford, M. B., & DeWitt, K. N. (1984). Three approaches to marital enrichment: Toward optimal matching of participants and interventions. *Journal of Sex and Marital Therapy, 10*, 41-48.

Forster, J. L., Murray, D. M,. Wolfson, M., Blaine, T. M., Wagenaar, A. C., &. Hennrikus, D. J. (in press). The effects of community policies to reduce youth access to tobacco. *American Journal of Public Health.*

Giblin, P., Sprenkle, D. H., & Sheehan, R. (1985). Enrichment outcome research: A meta-analysis of premarital, marital, and family interventions. *Journal of Marital and Family Therapy, 11*, 257-271.

Glaser, S. R., Biglan, A., & Dow, M. G. (1983). Conversational skills instruction for communication apprehension and avoidance: Evaluation of a treatment program. *Communication Research, 10,* 582-613.

Glenn, S. S. (1988). Contingencies and metacontingencies: Toward a synthesis of behavior analysis and cultural materialism. *The Behavior Analyst, 11,*161-179.

Gottman, J. M., & Krokoff, L. J. (1989). Marital interaction and satisfaction: A longitudinal view. *Journal of Consulting and Clinical Psychology, 57,* 47-52.

Gurman, A. S., Kniskern, D. P., & Pinsof, W. M. (1986). Research on the process and outcome of marital and family therapy. In S. L. Garfield & A. E. Bergin (Eds.), *Handbook of psychotherapy and behavior change* (pp. 565-624). New York: Wiley.

Hahlweg, K. & Klann, N. (1997). The effectiveness of marital counseling in Germany: A contribution to health services research. *Journal of Family Psychology, 11,* 410-421.

Hahlweg, K., & Markman, H. J. (1988). The effectiveness of behavioral marital therapy: Empirical status of behavioral techniques in preventing and alleviating marital distress. *Journal of Consulting and Clinical Psychology, 56,* 440-447.

Hahlweg, K., Revenstorf, D., & Schindler, L. (1982). Treatment of marital distress: Comparing formats and modalities. *Advances in Behaviour Research and Therapy, 4,* 57-74.

Halford, K., Kelly, A., & Markman, H. J. (1997). The concept of a healthy marriage. In K. Halford & H. J. Markman (Eds.), *Clinical handbook of marriage and couples intervention* (pp. 3-41). New York: Wiley.

Halford, W. K., Hahlweg, K., & Dunne, M. (1990). The cross-cultural consistency of marital communication associated with marital distress. *Journal of Marriage and the Family, 52,* 487-500.

Halford, W. K., & Osgarby, S. (1993). Alcohol abuse in clients presenting with marital problems. *Journal of Family Psychology, 6,* 1-11.

Hawkins, J. D., Catalano, R. F., & Miller, J. Y. (1992). Risk and protective factors for alcohol and other drug problems in adolescence and early adulthood: Implications for substance abuse prevention. *Psychological Bulletin, 112,* 64-105.

Hayes, S. C. (1997). Technology, theory, and the alleviation of human suffering: We still have such a long way to go. *Behavior Therapy, 28,* 517-525.

Hollon, S. D. & Beck, A. T. (1994). Cognitive and cognitive-behavioral therapies. In A. E. Bergin & S. L. Garfeild (Eds.), *Handbook of psychotherapy and behavior change* (4th ed.) (pp. 428-466). New York: Wiley.

Holtzworth-Munroe, A., & Stuart, G. (1994). Typologies of male batterers: Three subtypes and the differences among them. *Psychological Bulletin, 116,* 476-497.

Holtzworth-Munroe, A., Waltz, J., Jacobson, N., Monaco, V., Fehrenbach, & Gottman, J. (1992). Recruiting non-violent men as control subjects for research on marital violence: How easily can it be done? *Violence and Victims, 7,* 79-88.

Jacobson, N. S., & Addis, M. E. (1993). Research on couples and couples therapy: What do we know? Where are we going? *Journal of Consulting and Clinical Psychology, 61,* 85-93.

Jacobson, N. S., Follette, W. C., & McDonald, D. W. (1982). Reactivity to positive and negative behavior in distressed and non-distressed married couples. *Journal of Consulting and Clinical Psychology, 50,* 706-714.

Jacobson, N. S., Schmaling, K. B., & Holtzworth-Munroe, A. (1987). Component analysis of behavioral marital therapy: 2-year follow-up and prediction of relapse. *Journal of Marital and Family Therapy, 13,* 187-195.

Johnson, S. M. & Greenberg, L. S. (1985). The differential effects of experimental and problem solving interventions in resolving marital conflict. *Journal of Consulting and Clinical Psychology, 53,* 175-184.

Lebow, J. L., & Gurman, A. S. (1995). Research assessing couple and family therapy. *Annual Review of Psychology, 46,* 27-57.

Libman, E., Fichten, C. S., Brender, W., Burstein, R., Cohen, J., & Binik, Y. M. (1984). A comparison of three therapeutic formats in the treatment of secondary orgasmic dysfunction. *Journal of Sex and Marital Therapy, 10,* 147-159.

Lovaas, O. I. (1987). Behavioral treatment and normal educational and intellectual functioning in young autistic children. *Journal of Consulting and Clinical Psychology, 55,* 3-9.

Markman, H. J., & Hahlweg, K. (1993). The prediction and prevention of marital distress: An international perspective. *Clinical Psychology Review, 13,* 29-43.

Markman, H. J., Halford, K., & Cordova, A. D. (1997). A grand tour of future directions in the study and promotion of healthy relationships. In K. Halford & H. J. Markman (Eds.), *Clinical handbook of marriage and couples intervention* (pp. 695-716). New York: Wiley.

Markman, H. J., Floyd, F. J., Stanley, S. M., & Lewis, H. C. (1986). Prevention. In N. S. Jacobson & A. S. Gurman (Eds.), *Clinical handbook of marital therapy* (pp. 173-195). New York: Guilford.

Markman, H. J., Renick, M. J., Floyd, F. J., Stanley, S. M., & Clements, M. (1993). Preventing marital distress through communication and conflict management training: A 4- and 5-year follow up. *Journal of Consulting and Clinical Psychology, 61,* 70-77.

McLeod, J. D. (1994). Anxiety disorders and marital quality. *Journal of Abnormal Psychology, 103,* 767-776.

Niensted, B. (1990). The policy effects of a DWI law and a publicity campaign. In R. Surette (Ed.) *The media and criminal justice policy: Recent research and social effects* (pp. 193-203). Chicago: Thomas.

O'Farrell, T. J., Choquette, K. A., Cutter, H. S. G., Brown, E., Bayog, R., McCourt, W., Lowe, J., Chan, A., & Deneault, P. (1996). Cost-benefit and cost-effectiveness analyses of behavioral marital therapy with and without relapse prevention sessions for alcoholics and their spouses. *Behavior Therapy, 27,* 7-24.

O'Farrell, T. J., Cutter, H. S., & Floyd, F. J. (1983). The class on alcoholism and marriage (CALM) project: Results on marital adjustment and communication from before and after therapy (Tech. Rep. No. 4-1). Brockton, MA: Brockton/West Roxbury Veterans Administration Medical Center.

Pisterman, S., McGrath, P., Firestone, P., Goodman, J. T. Webster, I., & Mallory, R. (1989). Outcome of parent-mediated treatment of preschoolers with attention deficit disorder with hyperactivity. *Journal of Consulting and Clinical Psychology, 57*, 628-635.

Revenstorf, D., Schindler, L., & Hahlweg, K. (1983). Behavioral marital therapy applied in a conjoint and a conjoint-group modality: Short- and long-term effectiveness. *Behavior Therapy, 14*, 614-625.

Shadish, W. R., Montgomery, L. M., Wilson, P., Wilsom, M. R., Bright, I., & Okwumabua, T. (1993). Effects of family and marital psychotherapies: A meta-analysis. *Journal of Consulting and Clinical Psychology, 61*, 992-1002.

Shadish, W. R., Ragsdale, K., Glaser, R. R., & Montgomery, L. M. (1995). The efficacy and effectiveness of marital and family therapy: A perspective from meta-analysis. *Journal of Marital and Family Therapy, 21*, 345-360.

Sherman, L. W. (1992). The influence of criminology on criminal law: Evaluating arrests for misdemeanor domestic violence. *The Journal of Criminal Law and Criminology, 83*, 1-45.

Sherman, L. W. & Berk, R. A. (1984). The specific deterrent effects of arrest for domestic assault. *American Sociology Review*, 261-279 .

Snyder, D. K., Wills, R. M. & Grady-Fletcher, A. (1991). Long-term effectiveness of behavioral versus insight-oriented marital therapy. *Journal of Consulting and Clinical Psychology, 59*, 138-141

Spoth, R., & Redmond, C. (1994). Effective recruitment of parents into family-focused prevention research: A comparison of two strategies. *Psychology and Health, 9*, 353-370.

Stansfield, S. A., Gallacher, J. E. J., Sharp, D. S. & Yarnell, J. W. J. (1991). Social factors and minor psychiatric disorder in middle-aged men: a validation study and a population survey. *Psychological Medicine, 21*, 157-167

Taylor, T. K. & Biglan, A. (in press). Behavioral family interventions for improving childrearing: A review of the literature for clinicians and policy makers. *Clinical Child and Family Psychology Review.*

Taylor, T. K., Schmidt, F., Pepler, D. & Hodgins, C. (in press). A comparison of eclectic treatment with Webster-Stratton's Parent's and Children Series in a children's mental health center: A controlled trial. *Behavior Therapy.*

The Smoking Cessation Clinical Practical Guideline Panel and Staff. (1996). Consensus statement: The Agency for Health Care Policy and Research Smoking Cessation Clinical Practice Guideline. *Journal of the American Medical Association, 275*, 1270-1280.

U.S. Department of Health and Human Services. (1994). *Preventing tobacco use among young people: A report of the Surgeon General.* Atlanta, GA: U. S. Department of Health & Human Services, Public Health Service, Centers for Disease Control & Prevention, National Center for Chronic Disease Prevention & Health Promotion, Office on Smoking & Health.

VanWidenfelt, B. V., Markman, H. J., Guerney, B., Behrens, B. C., & Hosman, C. (1997). Prevention of relationship problems. In K. Halford &. H. J. Markman (Eds.), *Clinical handbook of marriage and couples intervention* (pp. 651-675). New York: Wiley.

Webster-Stratton, C., Kolpacoff, M., & Hollinsworth, T. (1988). Self-administered videotape therapy for families with conduct-problem children: Comparison with two cost-effective treatments and a control group. *Journal of Consulting and Clinical Psychology, 56*, 558-566.

Webster-Stratton, C. (1992). Individually administered videotape parent training: "Who benefits?" *Cognitive Therapy and Research, 16*, 31-52.

Weiss, R. L., & Heyman, R. E. (1990). Observation of marital interaction. In F. D. Fincham & T. N. Bradbury (Eds.), *The psychology of marriage: Basic issues and applications* (pp. 87-117). New York: Guilford.

Weiss, B., & Weisz, J. R. (1995). Relative effectiveness of behavioral versus nonbehavioral child psychotherapy. *Journal of Consulting and Clinical Psychology, 63*, 317-320.

Weisz, R., Weiss, B. & Donenberg, G. R. (1992). The lab versus the clinic: Effects of child and adolescent psychotherapy. *American Psychologist 47*, 1578-1585.

Whisman, M. A., & Snyder, D. K. (1997). Evaluating and improving the efficacy of conjoint marital therapy. In K. Halford & H. J. Markman (Eds.), *Clinical handbook of marriage and couples intervention* (pp. 679-693). New York: Wiley.

Wilson, G. L. (1987). The comparative efficacy of alternative treatments in the resolution of marital dysfunction. *Dissertation Abstracts International, 47*, 3129-3130.

Wilson, G. L., Bornstein, P. H., & Wilson, L. J. (1988). Treatment of relationship dysfunction: An empirical evaluation of group and conjoint behavioral marital therapy. *Journal of Consulting and Clinical Psychology, 56*, 929-931.

Zeiss, R. A. (1978). Self-directed treatment for premature ejaculation. *Journal of Consulting and Clinical Psychology, 46*, 1234-1241.

Chapter 12

Emotion and The Relationship in Psychotherapy: A Behavior Analytic Perspective

Barbara S. Kohlenberg

*Veterans Affairs Medical Center, Reno, Nevada
and the University of Nevada School of Medicine*

There are few things more pervasive than the interest that most people have in relationships. Relationships that are associated with strong affect are particularly salient, and are of interest in our lay discussions as well as characterize much of what is discussed in a therapy office. Both being *in* these relationships, or talking or thinking *about* them, characterizes a significant portion of the daily verbal activity of many adults. While all relationships that we have are of interest, the relationships that stimulate intense affect are of particular interest—such as the relationships we have with parents, children, spouses, friends, lovers, and therapists, to mention a few. It is surprising, in a sense, that despite the behavior analyst's interest in behavior change, to date minimal attention has been focused on attempting a thoroughgoing analysis of such a powerful, pervasive force in our lives. It is true that there is a substantial empirical body of work oriented around the study of problematic relationships (such as couples therapy research). However, the focus in this work has traditionally been on the study of communication and problem solving skills, behavioral exchange systems, and more recently, acceptance based communication skills (Jacobson & Christiansen, 1996). These approaches have generally focused on understanding and exerting influence over very specific functional relationships occurring in the relationship of interest. What has been less studied is the value and function of intense affect such as love, passion, hate, etc., in marriages and in any kind of relationship for that matter.

Behavior analysts who are interested in the therapeutic relationship are actually interested in a small, defined slice of these general issues: How is it that the relationships that we have influence behavior change? How is it that relationships that we have become meaningful and valued for us? How can we better understand the intense feelings present for us in some relationships, and the absence of such feelings in other relationships? A clinical behavior analyst might ask the following question: "How might it be understood that, after completing a course of therapy characterized by two people talking with one another, a client describes themselves as not only "doing better", but also as feeling better, being more satisfied with their lives, feeling more sure of their relationships, and, to borrow from Freud, generally experiencing more enjoyment in their work, play and relationships?"

It will be the purpose of this chapter to discuss traditional behavioral/behavior therapy accounts of the therapeutic relationship and behavior analytic accounts of the psychotherapy relationship. A behavior analytic analysis is one that is directly influenced by the Skinnerian philosophy of radical behaviorism. This is distinct from methodological behaviorism, or "traditional behaviorism" (for elaboration's on the distinctions between these two forms of behaviorism, see Day, 1969; S. C. Hayes, 1987; Moore, 1981).

This chapter will pay special attention to the affect or emotional reactions occurring in the therapy relationship. Many clients present in their therapist's offices complaining of difficulties with their feelings—they assert that they are too unhappy, too bored, too angry, too filled with hate, not in love, in love with the wrong person. Sometimes the feelings that clients struggle with also occur in the therapy relationship. These feelings—such as love, hate, longing and sorrow will be considered, behavior analytically, in the context of their function in psychotherapy. When relevant, behavioral accounts will be presented in relation to non-behavioral approaches to psychotherapy—particularly some facets of psychodynamic psychotherapy, which have taken the therapeutic relationship and its relation to therapy outcome as a central focus. Furthermore, on close inspection, some areas of psychodynamic therapies have values which converge with a behavior analytic approach, particularly their focus on the individual case, their focus on the use of raw data (therapy transcripts) to evaluate their theory and technique (Dahl, 1978; Weiss & Sampson, 1986), their interest in a coherence, rather than a correspondence notion of truth and accordingly a constructivist epistemology (Hanly, 1992; Sandler & Sandler, 1984, Schafer, 1982), and their sensitivities to interpretation rather than strict experimental method (Hanly, 1992).

What is Radical Behaviorism and What are Some Therapy Implications?

While there are many views on radical behaviorism, this author chooses to highlight the following aspects of the philosophy. First, radical behaviorism considers all of human experience as being legitimate subject matter for scientific inquiry. Second, radical behavioral theory is essentially a contextualistic theory (e.g., Hayes, 1987; Pepper, 1957). And third, radical behaviorism embraces the analytic practice of "functional analysis". What are the therapy implications of these three aspects of radical behaviorism?

Let us consider the idea that all of human experience is legitimate for scientific inquiry. This allows the behaviorist to consider such all private events (such as thoughts and feelings) are just as real and legitimate to study scientifically as overt physical behavior. This move, of legitimizing the study of private events, then allows full and complete consideration of anything and everything that can be seen or felt and even the absence of such things (as in latent content or unconscious material).

How does a contextualistic position influence the study of psychotherapy? A contextualistic position would assert that there is no objective "truth". Nothing can be considered or defined independent of its context. Thus, a complete account of an observed event must include a full and complete account of the events surrounding the observer observing that event. A therapist ascribing certain meaning to a client statement is as amenable to analysis as is the client statement. And, the meanings of client utterances must be understood in the context of the interaction and in the context of the client's life, rather than at face value. This essentially invites attending to the "process" as well as to the "content" of psychotherapy. It further recognizes that the therapist is not a technical instrument who is objective in any way. The thoughts and feelings of the therapist thus become an important source of data as to the meaning of the client's statements, and also invite considerations of what is generally called "countertransference".

What is a functional analysis and what are therapy implications? Skinner defines a functional analysis as one that specifies the "external variables of which behavior is a function" (Skinner, 1953, p. 35). For the purposes of psychotherapy, the critical aspects of performing a functional analysis are as follows. First, any and all behavior that occurs in the session—ranging from overt motor behavior to the content of verbal behavior, to feelings and emotional states that occur in the session must be understood by focusing on the interactions between the client and the therapist. Utilizing the concept of functional analysis absolutely focuses the analysis on the within session behavior between the client and the therapist.

Consider a client who presents in therapy and describes herself as, from time to time, feeling "flat," or "emotionally frozen" in relationships. Consider that these private events are reported by the client as they occur in the session. A functional analysis would entail noting the kinds of behaviors (public and private) that occurred between the therapist and the client that occasioned the client's report and experience of her flat emotions. Say, for example, that the client became "emotionally frozen" shortly after the therapist expressed his feelings of affection, support and caring for her. A clinical behavior analyst might explore why such antecedent conditions might occasion such a feeling. Perhaps it would be learned that the client had in the past, been harmed in relationships when she had been first praised and valued, and numbing or avoiding her feelings served the function of minimizing emotional pain. Or, they might learn that the client has had a history of having to work very hard to retain the interest of an important person to her and thus the therapy interaction evoked feelings that she would soon lose the affection of the therapist, which then occasioned the behavior that she would emotionally withdraw first so as to minimize the emotional pain. One aspect of the above exchange is quite likely, and that is that becoming "emotionally frozen" is probably a way of avoiding and thus not being in contact with the feelings and with the environmental events that occasioned the feelings. This kind of emotional avoidance serves to detract from intimate relationships in the present because when she is "frozen" the client is unsure of what to communicate about. Conducting a functional analysis of the occurrence of the client's feeling "emotionally frozen" implies that the behavior of "freezing up" will be best understood by analyzing the conditions in the session that gave rise to that behavior. This analysis would then lead to further exploration of the meanings or "truths" as they exist for the client, and then to the development of new repertoires of behavior when confronted with other functionally similar circumstances.

Functional Analytic Psychotherapy (FAP, Kohlenberg, R., & Tsai, M., 1991) is a psychotherapeutic framework based upon the above principles. Before FAP is more fully elaborated, consider the following analytic and conceptual activities that provide a context other than Skinnerian radical behaviorism, for the development of a relationship oriented behavior analytic psychotherapy.

The Therapeutic Relationship Puzzle

Several studies have found that the quality of the therapy alliance is a very important predictor of outcome (Gaston, Thompson, Gallagher, Cournoyer & Gagnon, 1998; Horvath & Symonds, 1991; Howard & Orlinsky, 1972, Orlinsky & Howard, 1986; Samstag, Batchelder, Muran, Safran & Winston, 1998; Strupp, 1996). Many researchers who investigate psychotherapy outcome suggest that therapy alliance may be the "quintessential integrative variable" across theoretical conceptions of psychotherapy because it is so consistently shown to be predictive of good outcome, appearing to be more important than treatment technique (Safran, & Muran, 1995). While the term "therapeutic alliance" has had many meanings over the years, contemporary empirical researchers generally use Bordin's definition (Bordin, 1979) which defines alliance as agreement on tasks, on goals, and the bond. Even in studies comparing the effects of medications with psychotherapy, measures of therapist effectiveness (defined in terms of therapy outcome) tend to overshadow differences attributable to the treatments employed—that is, some therapists do consistently better than other therapists regardless of treatment condition (Luborsky, Crits-Christoph, McLellan, Woody, Piper, Liberman, Imber, & Pilonis, 1986), and measures of therapy alliance are found to be significantly related to outcome in the Treatment of Depression Collaborative Study (Krupnick, Sotsky, Simmens, Moyer, Elkin, Watkins, and Pilkonis, 1996). One psychiatrist in the treatment of depression collaborative study, in fact, attained the best outcomes of any other therapist in the study, whether administering the active medication or placebo (Blatt, Stanislow, Zuroff, & Pilkonis, 1996). How might these findings be understood?

Numerous nonbehavioral researchers in recent years have been studying the relationship between affect (both positive and negative) in the therapy relationship, and outcome in psychotherapy. Investigators have studied such behavioral sequences as alliance ruptures, alliance rupture resolutions, and corrective emotional experiences (e.g., Greenberg & Safran, 1987; Safran & Muran, 1995; Watson & Greenberg, 1995). An alliance rupture is a description of an observable interaction, between the therapist and client, characterized by deterioration in the relationship between them. This deterioration is thought to be an opportunity for furthering the therapeutic process (e.g. Newirth, 1995; Safran & Muran, 1995, 1996; Omer, 1995; Watson & Greenberg, 1995). Safran and Muran (1995) assert that their research in the area of alliance has lead them to focus on the interaction between the client and the therapist, with the alliance rupture and subsequent resolution being the central focus of therapy. Similarly, the notion of "negative process," which refers to the ways in which therapists struggle with their own negative reactions to hostile exchanges in the therapy session, is also being examined (Binder & Strupp, 1997). It is generally found that training the therapist to "metacommunicate" about their aversive reactions makes an important contribution to good therapy outcome. Metacommunication, in many ways, seems to refer to the ability of the therapist to do a functional analysis of their own aversive feelings and overt behaviors, which then allows them to increase the probability that they will react in the best interests of the client rather than solely to reduce their own painful affect.

Positive transference and positive countertransference, or the strong positive feelings that a client and a therapist may experience toward each other in the therapy relationship, are also areas that have been extensively discussed, primarily in psychoanalytic circles. Contemporary theorists (Cohen, 1996) argue that some of the reasons why analytically oriented therapists embrace the notion of counter-transference and transference (terms which primarily are metaphorical, referring to enacting past conflicts and repertoires in the present) and distinguish it from "real" feelings is to diffuse the intensity of the emotional content between the analyst and the client. He argues that it is safer for the analyst to respond to intense emotional feelings for a client if it is under the guise of metaphorical activity. Many analytically oriented writers also note the arbitrary nature of the present/past distinction, often refereed to as "real" vs. metaphorical or transferential activity. Many contemporary analytic thinkers assert that the present therapy interaction represents a person's past history as well as the current very real interaction, however it is unclear how much weight to give each in the present moment. It is this author's opinion that this is where a functional analytic approach would offer much guidance, since contingent responding to client within session behavior is the mechanism by which behavioral change occurs (both public and private), no matter what one's theoretical orientation. In short, the therapist runs the risk of becoming less effective when distanced from feelings about the client, and because of this distancing, fails to give the client access as to how their behavior affects them on a private level. Of course, not all private reactions that a therapist has are beneficial to share with a client, however they are all worthy of consideration and one's behavior should ultimately be consequated by client improvement or deterioration.

It is the consensus among those who study therapy alliance and therapy outcome that there is something that transpires in the therapeutic exchange between client and therapist that facilitates behavior change beyond the actual treatment delivered (Binder & Strupp, 1997, Safran & Muran, 1998). How has an analysis of the therapeutic relationship been accounted for in the behavior analytic literature to date?

Traditional Behavioral Accounts of the Therapeutic Relationship

Until recently, behavioral scientists and practitioners have placed little emphasis on investigating the therapeutic relationship. This posture is in contrast to other empirically based scientists who recognize that the therapist-client relationship is an important though complex variable in the conduct of psychotherapy, and that the stronger the therapeutic alliance, the better the outcome (Horvath & Symonds, 1991; Howard & Orlinsky, 1972, Orlinsky & Howard, 1986; Strupp, 1996). Behaviorists have most often viewed the therapy relationship ancillary to technique (O'Donohue, 1995; Rimm & Masters, 1979; Wilson & O'Leary, 1980; Wolpe, 1958). That is, having a "good relationship" is merely a tool to employ to keep the client coming back so as to allow the use of other behavioral techniques—which are the actual active ingredient in promoting client change (DeVoge & Beck, 1978; Turkat & Brantley, 1981; Wilson & Evans, 1977).

The behavioral tradition has considered the therapist to be largely a neutral stimulus, one which imparts potent interventions that are themselves responsible for behavior change. It is this kind of position that has influenced the development of treatment manuals, an endeavor designed to create adherence to and dissemination of specific treatment techniques. However, the use of treatment manuals remains controversial in light of the alliance and outcome data, because it appears that, while a treatment manual can improve therapy technique, there is a cost in that other interpersonal and interactional elements of therapy may, in fact, deteriorate (Henry, Strupp, Butler, Schacht & Binder, 1993). There are questions about whether the therapist's capacity to establish a strong alliance can be trained (Dobson & Shaw, 1993; Luborsky, 1993).

This lack of interest in the therapeutic relationship by behavioral psychologists is curious for several reasons. First, it departs from early functional analytic traditions which emphasize careful, fine-grained analyses of clinical problems and of the immediate contingencies present in the therapy session (e.g. Ferster, 1972a, Ferster, 1972b, Ferster, 1973). Early studies in verbal conditioning also were driven by an interest in studying the effects of contingent responding on the emission of verbal material (e.g. Greenspoon, 1955). Early applications of verbal conditioning procedures have been applied to the reporting of early memories in session (Quay, 1959), and how interpretations in psychoanalytic therapy function as verbal reinforcers (Noblin, Timmons, & Reynard, 1963). It is unclear exactly why such endeavors never made an impact on behavioral accounts of psychotherapy, nor why they failed to capture the interest of the clinicians of the day.

Even the earliest studies in operant and respondent conditioning implicitly focused on the experimenter, the subject, and the observable contingent relationship between them. Whether classically conditioning a response in a subject such as "little Albert" or using operant conditioning procedures with institutionalized patients (e.g. Allyon & Azrin, 1965; Wolf, Risley & Mees, 1964), the primary focus was always on the contingencies operating between experimenter and subject. The subject would emit behavior, and the experimenter would contingently respond to that behavior. Importantly, these early studies demonstrated the vast power of operant and respondent techniques and served as the basis for the emergence of contemporary behavioral therapies. This early work exemplifies the importance of the direct, contingent relationship between the experimenter and subject.

While behavior analysts were busy empirically testing operant techniques with confined populations or in analogue situations, where the experimenter was directly intervening with the subject and then observing results, nonbehavioral psychologists and practitioners were busy trying to understand the active ingredients present in the psychotherapy relationship. Conceptual work on the therapeutic relationship in outpatient, adult psychotherapy was being done by scientists and practitioners trying to distinguish between such aspects of the therapy relationship as transference (positive and negative), countertransference, real relationship, alliance, and working relationship (e.g., Adler, 1980; Greenson, 1965; Klee, Abeles, & Muller, 1990; Zetzel, 1956). Empirical and conceptual work by contemporary theorists and practitioners has focused on the study of alliance and its relationship to positive therapeutic outcome, the ebb and flow of alliance within a therapeutic relationship, the requirements needed (both in session interactional requirements and client characteristics) for alliance to occur, and the role of alliance ruptures in therapy (e.g. Horvath & Luborsky, 1993; Omer, 1995; Safran & Muran, 1995; 1996; Watson, 1996). While these research and conceptual endeavors have emerged from nonbehavioral traditions, they engage the spirit of behavior analytic traditions in that they are focused on trying to understand the variables that are important in psychotherapy, and they are sensitive to the contextual nature of knowledge and the centrality of the both the researcher and the clinician being participant/observers.

Behavioral input regarding the above issues has been quite minimal, consisting of interpretive analyses of traditional psychodynamic therapies (Alexander, 1963; Ferster, 1972b; Greenspoon & Brownstein, 1967; Hobbs, 1962; Mowrer, 1939; Rosenfarb, 1992, Shaffer, 1947; Shaw, 1946; Shoben, 1949; Skinner, 1953), or critical analyses (Salter, 1963; Wolpe, 1958; 1981). This lack of attention to developing our own approach or to collaborating with the efforts of others is curious given that focus on in-session behavioral sequences, or "process" is very much in line with traditional functional analytic analyses.

Contemporary Behavior Analytic Accounts of Therapy Relationship

Functional Analytic Psychotherapy

FAP is a behavior analytic approach to psychotherapy designed for outpatient settings and for clients who are likely to display the problems that they have in their daily lives, in the therapy session. This does not include all clients, certainly. It specifically includes clients whose difficulties are manifest in intimate or potentially intimate interpersonal relationships. FAP considers the interactions between the therapist and the client, or the therapy relationship, to be potentially *the most effective* variable in producing change resulting from psychotherapy (R. J. Kohlenberg & Tsai, 1991). FAP also rests on the notion that there are functional similarities between the therapeutic relationship and the relationships that clients have outside of therapy, thus the behaviors evoked in session are functionally similar to those behaviors occurring outside of the session. FAP embraces the well tested finding that the time and place of reinforcement is an important parameter in creating behavior change, and thus contends that the contingencies present in the actual therapy session present critical opportunities for the therapist to influence behavioral change. While theoretically consistent with our behavioral training, this approach departs significantly from the practice of mainstream behavior therapy with outpatient adults.

In general, mainstream behavior therapy has embraced the empirical strategy of implementing "a therapy procedure" and evaluating its effect on dependent measures of interest. FAP is more of a framework of how to respond effectively to the moment to moment contingencies in the therapy interaction, and thus does not have specific content to be delivered. This presents certain challenges for empirical investigations of FAP. Currently, research and conceptual activity is occurring in an attempt to investigate further the mechanisms by which the therapeutic relationship becomes a sufficient (and perhaps necessary) condition for client behavioral change (e.g., Callaghan, Naugle, & Follette, 1996, Follette, Naugle, & Callaghan, 1996; B. Kohlenberg, Yeater & R. J. Kohlenberg, 1998; R. J. Kohlenberg & Tsai, 1991; R. J. Kohlenberg & Tsai, 1994a; R. J. Kohlenberg & Tsai, 1994b; R. J. Kohlenberg, Tsai, & B. Kohlenberg, 1996).

FAP is an approach to therapy that is characterized by psychotherapy sessions that are intensive, in depth, emotional, involved, and authentic. It is these experiences that provide critical opportunities for producing clinically significant change. In a nutshell, FAP is an emotion based, relationship focused psychotherapy that is guided by behavioral principles. Although FAP can be used as an "add in" to complement and enhance almost any type of treatment (R. J. Kohlenberg, Tsai, & Dougher, 1993; R. J. Kohlenberg & Tsai, 1994a; R. J. Kohlenberg & Tsai, 1994b), this chapter will focus on FAP as a stand alone approach.

The typical behavioral reader (not to mention the nonbehavioral reader) might find this confusing. Are not behavioral therapies generally characterized by the absence or at least the minimization of relationship focus and emotional intensity, with the corresponding deliverance of a potent treatment technique? As previously discussed, behavior therapy has not traditionally focused on the therapeutic relationship, though it is theoretically consistent to do so. Generally, mainstream behavior therapy and cognitive behavior therapy with outpatient adults typically relies on the report of behavior occurring outside of the session, and thus does not attend specifically to relationship factors. Functional analytic psychotherapy, conversely, focuses on any and all behavior (including emotions, bodily sensations, thoughts, talk, and physical behavior) that occurs in session, between the client and the therapist.

FAP: Possible Mechanisms of Action

One very important aspect of FAP is the emphasis placed upon in-vivo demonstrations of problem behaviors and their improvements. The therapist is in the position of being able to directly shape, in the session, via contingent feedback, client behavior. This move of in-vivo demonstrations of behavior coupled with in-vivo shaping of that behavior not only characterizes FAP but also is an essential component of any behavioral strategy directed toward effecting behavior change.

The focus on in-vivo behavior also allows for the process of extinction to occur regarding problematic public and private behaviors. That is, if a person feels fear when confronted with intimacy with another person, and fear occurs in the session, the client and therapist have opportunities to sustain the feeling while noting that current circumstances are different than those of the past. It is well known that treating circumscribed PTSD, anxiety disorders, and phobias works best when exposure to the feared stimulus is present (Foa & Rothbaum, 1998). It is philosophically consistent to also claim that if a person's problems both started and are manifest within close interpersonal relationships, then a close interpersonal relationship, such as is had in psychotherapy, would elicit the problematic behaviors.

The notion of verbal behavior and rule-governance is also critical. As FAP is both a verbal and an experiential therapy, clients are encouraged to both directly experience the relationship and to talk about the relationship. Specifically, clients are encouraged to do their own functional analyses of the controlling variables present in the session as well as historically. The argument is that generating accurate rules about controlling variables increases the chance that the client maximizes reinforcement and minimizes aversive experiences both in therapy and out of therapy.

The Practice of FAP

The basic structure of all adult outpatient psychotherapy is very simple. A client generally comes to therapy because of difficulties in daily life. Usually, the client attends therapy once per week and pays for the session. The interventions made by the therapist occur strictly in the context of the therapy hour. No observations are made of the client outside of therapy, and the therapist never directly intervenes in the client's life outside of the therapy hour. Essentially, all forms of adult, outpatient psychotherapy utilize the above structure. What are the conditions created in therapy which can make a difference in the life of the client?

As previously noted, FAP is a system of therapy that essentially rests upon the idea that therapy will work best when the problem behaviors of interest occur in the session. The FAP therapist must become adept at noticing instances of problematic client behavior, becoming aware of occasioning these behaviors (such as by asking the client what the client is feeling about the therapist or a statement made by the therapist), and being able to reinforce instances of improvement (being more attentive to the client when the client engages rather than avoids a traditionally troublesome topic). The principles of discrimination and consequential responding are the core principles that guide FAP therapy.

FAP divides therapy up into two general categories. The first category consists of the three most relevant client behaviors that occur during the therapy session, and the second category consists of the five rules that comprise the therapeutic technique. A description of these aspects of the therapeutic interaction follows (for elaboration's on these categories, see R. J. Kohlenberg & Tsai, 1991).

Three Clinically Relevant Client Behaviors (CRB1, CRB2, CRB3)

CRB1's consist of actual demonstrations of the problematic behaviors of interest which occur during session. At times, these problems may be avoidance behaviors—that is, behaviors that serve to help the client avoid experiencing difficult material. The client who states that she always feels rejected by others and "like a piece of shit", and who in the therapy session rarely gives eye contact, talks incessantly about work problems, changes the topic immediately when emotional subject matter comes up, gets angry about being misunderstood, and who accuses the therapist of making her feel "like shit—just like everyone else," would be demonstrating CRB1's in session .

CRB2's consist of improvements in CRB1's. The woman described above might be demonstrating a CRB2 when she gives the therapist eye-contact and utters a sincere sounding comment when she sees that the therapist is wearing a cast on her foot. Or, a CRB2 might involve staying with emotional subject matter even a few seconds longer than usual, or who might give the therapist direct, assertive feedback rather than rage when the therapist forgot a piece of her history.

CRB3's involve the client observing and then describing his or her own behavior in terms of environmental events, (this of course includes verbal behavior). The client learns to use statements about contingent, functional relationships that occur between behavior and the events that surround it. During the course of therapy, the client will acquire the skills to describe or interpret their own behavior. This skill requires that the client have also developed the ability to "observe" his or her own behavior. An example of a CRB3 would involve a client stating to the therapist "When you forgot the name of my ex-husband, I immediately felt that you did not care about me, and I immediately started to talk about work. I am aware that in doing this, I avoided my feelings, which results in me hiding from you, which makes me feel like I am a "complete shit"—so here I am, trying to let you know how I feel so that we can talk about it, because in the past I always feel stronger and better when I reveal myself rather than hide." The acquisition of CRB3 repertoires serve to help the client become more aware of the variables that contribute to and maintain their behavior, thus engendering the possibility that the client can develop more satisfying relationships both in and out of therapy.

The Five Rules of FAP Therapeutic Technique

The techniques of FAP are provided in the form of five basic rules, or principles, intended to guide therapeutic technique.

The first rule of FAP is for the therapist to notice clinically relevant behaviors. If the therapist does not notice problematic behaviors, there are no opportunities for the direct shaping of those behaviors, and thus no progress is made in the therapy. Consider a client who has great fears of being rejected and thus is overly compliant and has difficulty expressing anger. Imagine that the therapist announces that he will be moving his office shortly. Consider further that the client responds in a compliant, agreeable way but in fact is very inconvenienced and angry about the therapist's move—perhaps the client is thinking—"doesn't he know that I already have to take two buses to get here and pay for a baby-sitter, now I will have to rework the whole thing and all for what, so Dr. Hedonist can have a bigger office." Therapy will be greatly enhanced if the therapist is able to notice that a CRB1 has occurred (the avoidance of expressing anger), and works with the client on this issue. If the therapist simply accepts the client's compliant behavior and moves to the next issue, a precious therapeutic opportunity would have been lost.

Rule 2 consists of evoking CRB's. The most effective therapy relationship is one that evokes CRB1 and provides those therapeutic, interactional opportunities, which allow for the development of CRB2. This rule basically rests on the formal similarity between therapy and "real life". If a client enters therapy because of problems related to being involved in intimate relationships, and if the therapeutic relationship is evocative of CRB1, then it is likely that the relationship is providing opportunities for intimacy that are both difficult and potentially helpful for the client. For example, the client who avoids expressing anger and who states that her relationships feel constricted and flat and who denies feeling "anything" when her therapist is 15 minutes late for a session is demonstrating CRB1. If a client has difficulty with intimacy, and the therapeutic relationship begins to feel intimate, CRB1 will be evoked.

The therapeutic relationship must be real and genuine if CRB that is functionally the same as what occurs in relationships outside of therapy is to occur in session. If the therapist tries to "role play" or otherwise contrive responding in order to intensify therapeutic interactions, the client might recognize the contrived nature of these responses and consequently fail to emit further CRB. Role playing may also interfere with the generalization of CRB2 outside of therapy because the contrived nature of the interaction which would bring about a behavioral topography that would be functionally dissimilar to the actual CRB. A therapist who fakes a response, however, might produce even worse effects than a failure to generalize. Consider the therapist who gushes over a picture of a client's child, when in fact the therapist does not like children. The client may detect the insincerity and avoid showing further pictures or even discussing the intensity of her feelings toward their child. In short, it could be destructive to the therapeutic relationship and therefore to the therapy outcome if the therapist contrives responses in order to elicit CRB during the course of therapy.

CRB3's consist of reinforcing CRB2's. In terms of reinforcers, the therapist must find all their reinforcers in the context of the therapy. Thus, the actual reactions that the therapist has to the client's behavior are what consequate and thus affect the behavior of the client. The problem is that the more the therapist *tries* to be reinforcing, the more the risk that the reinforcement will be arbitrary in nature, which can be very problematic.

The distinction between natural and arbitrary reinforcement, as first articulated by Ferster (1967) is critical. Arbitrary reinforcement is reinforcement that would not be found in the natural environment for the particular behavior of interest. For example, rewarding eye contact with tokens, or rewarding a child for learning to say "apple" by giving him candy, would be examples of arbitrary reinforcement. Natural reinforcement, conversely, specifies reinforcers that are typically found in the natural environment. Good eye contact would be rewarded with the increased interest of the therapist, a baby learning to say "apple" would be rewarded by being given an apple. The therapist who reinforces a difficult self-disclosure by a client by stating enthusiastically, "that was good sharing," might in fact be perceived as phony and might punish the behavior it was designed to reward. A more natural response to the client's revealing their inner feelings would be increased interest, increased attention, emotional behavior on the part of the therapist, and so on.

For many clients, arbitrary reinforcement could be harmful. It creates behaviors that are insensitive to context. Self-disclosing so that the therapist will praise you is actually a different behavior than self-disclosing that results in increased intimacy and respect. Furthermore, arbitrary reinforcement generally exists for the benefit of the person doing the reinforcing, not for the person whose behavior is being reinforced. The use of arbitrary reinforcement for people with histories of being exploited by others might be destructive in that behavior reinforced would reflect changes that the therapist wanted, but would not necessarily help the client learn to engage in relationships in which their own wants and needs are carefully considered.

Rule 4 consists of encouraging the therapist to observe the potentially reinforcing effects of therapist behavior in relation to CRB's. In FAP, therapist behavior is effective when it "works" to impact client behavior in a favorable manner. In short, behavior that is reinforced or punished by the therapist will alter the rate of responding by the client on future occasions. If the therapist is able to notice and respond to the reinforcing effects of their own behavior upon the client during the session, the therapist will increase the likelihood that they are being effective therapists. This means that therapists should evaluate the progress of their patients frequently, using video or audio tape review, consultation, or supervision.

Rule 5 is to give an interpretation of the variables that affect client behavior. Therapists model the formulation of statements that accurately identify the antecedents and consequences of behavior. Essentially, the therapist conducts functional analyses out loud, with the goal of helping clients learn to be aware of how their own reactions and behavior are related to environmental events. Awareness of this kind can help the client obtain more positive reinforcement in their daily life. A therapist might say "I notice that you haven't once talked about the 6 months of emergency health related leave I had to take–I wonder if you might be avoiding something. I realize that when your mother died when you were a kid after a lengthy illness with many absences, you had no power with her and your feelings really couldn't bring her back so you thought that they were not important."

Interpretations, or statements such as these would model for the client ways to describe their own behavior and the variables that contributed to its occurrence.

To summarize, if the problems that the client struggles with manifest themselves in the session, and the therapist can discriminate instances of these in-vivo demonstrations of the client's behavior, the therapist will then be able to naturally reinforce client improvements. These procedures, based upon the behavioral principles of discrimination and reinforcement, will (by definition) result in behavior change. This change will be strengthened if the client can also learn to generate statements (or verbal rules specifying contingent relationships) regarding the relationship of their feelings, thoughts, and overt behaviors to actual events that occur in the relationship.

ACT and FAP

While FAP (Kohlenberg, R. & Tsai, M., 1991) is the only behavior analytic therapy to specifically focus on the therapeutic relationship, Acceptance and Commitment Therapy (ACT) (Hayes, Strosahl, & Wilson, in press; Hayes & Wilson, 1994) does articulate a perspective on the therapeutic relationship. Hayes & Wilson (1994) argue that an intimate therapeutic relationship is created when the ACT therapist models ACT principles by being fully open and present to the client's pain. They further note that the therapy environment "...may mirror the context in which avoidance repertoires were established in the first place. Many of our clients indicate difficulties in their interpersonal relationships, especially intimate ones. Thus, an intimate therapeutic relationship may bring to bear important contextual variables that have been associated with problematic functioning" (Hayes & Wilson, 1994, p 297). While it is true that ACT pays tribute to the importance of a good therapeutic relationship, it does not explicitly focus on client-therapist interactions as the material to be worked on in treatment. It is possible that ACT would be strengthened if focus was placed on the relationship in part out of recognition of the strong feelings that exist between client and therapist in ACT or in any therapy.

ACT and FAP are both distinguished by being the only therapies with radical behavioral underpinnings that have been developed for outpatient, adult clients. Each can be described as developing well-articulated, comprehensive therapy systems. A FAP therapist might be strengthened by using ACT principles and techniques around emotional acceptance, thus assisting in the full realization of affect in the session. ACT therapy may be enhanced by attending more closely to the notion of emotional acceptance and emotional avoidance that exist between the client and the therapist in the therapy relationship itself.

Love and Hate (and Other Strong Emotions) in the Therapeutic Relationship.

The notion of actually cultivating and anticipating strong affect, such as love, hate, longing and disappointment are, at first glance, antithetical to behavioral therapies. As stated previously, the emphasis in behavioral treatments has been to develop specified technologies, and the emotional connection between the therapist and the client has been viewed as useful only insofar as the emotional connection would then allow the implementation of the specified technology. The notion of actually cultivating love and other intense emotions between the therapist and the client is, on one hand, quite a deviation from traditional behavioral views of therapy. On the other hand, the cultivation of these emotions is actually very much in line with a behavior analytic tradition.

It is perfectly justifiable, in a behavioral sense, to argue that if a person has difficulties with the affect (and corresponding overt behaviors) associated with interpersonal relationships, than the best possible way to treat such a problem would be to see and contingently respond to such behaviors in-vivo. Whether one is shaping a rat to emit a particular behavior, working with a retarded child to eliminate injurious head banging, working with panic, or trying to modify *any* behavior, the most important behavioral principle is that the delivery of the consequence occurs immediately after the behavior of interest. Thus, the more "in vivo" the therapy, the closer in time the consequences are delivered.

There exists a wealth of data that demonstrate that actually experiencing a feared stimulus and the associated affect produces better treatment outcomes than imagining that stimulus and one's reactions (e.g. Barlow, 1988; Foa & Rothbaum, 1998; Goldfried, 1985). We know as well that respondent events spread via verbal relations (Dougher, Auguston, Markham, & Greenway, 1994). This is further justification for the elicitation of strong clinically relevant affect in the therapy session.

We also know that contingency shaped behavior is more flexible and responsive to change than is rule-governed behavior (e.g. Hayes, 1989). This has been demonstrated in areas such as social skills training (Azrin & Hayes, 1984) and clinical supervision (Follette & Callaghan, 1995). The evidence collected in both basic and applied behavioral laboratories is compelling and warrants caution in equating change brought about quickly, largely via instruction, verses change shaped slowly, via contact with natural contingencies. The effectiveness of procedures that involve immediate reinforcement, in vivo exposure, and contingency shaped approaches to learning lead one to strongly consider the benefits of establishing "real" relationships in therapeutic contexts.

People present in therapy with anxiety, depression, substance dependence, and many other diagnostic categories. It is clear that many times these disorders involve some form of emotional avoidance (Hayes, Wilson, Gifford, Follette, 1996). Further, this emotional avoidance often manifests in some way in interpersonal relationships. This would seem to be an inevitable result of an interpersonal relationship where the therapist listens well, tries to be helpful, is stable, reliable, kind, and clearly develops positive, caring feelings for the client? How could disappointment, longing, wishing for more, anger at the boundaries, relief about the boundaries, wanting and not having, not occur? Moreover, what kinds of opportunities are lost when the therapist does not see the behavior of this sort evolving before him or her? Of course, there are times when symptom reduction via empirically supported treatments is the appropriate course of action. However, when these do not work or the client is interested in other kinds of behavior change, the therapy relationship offers much significant material.

Clinical radical behaviorists who are interested in studying psychotherapy very likely will continue to struggle with how to understand what transpires in the therapy session. The laboratory of the psychotherapy session continues to encompass all of the "stuff of life", – love, loss, hope, –as well as the "stuff of behavior analysis" – discrimination, consequences, and exposure, to name a few. It is fascinating to consider what might come from applying the elegance and precision of behavioral analysis to an analysis of the therapeutic relationship.

References

Adler, G. (1980). Transference, real relationship, and alliance. *International Journal of Psychoanalysis, 61,* 547-558.

Alexander, F. (1963). The dynamics of psychotherapy in light of learning theory. *American Journal of Psychiatry, Nov,* 440-449.

Allyon, T & Azrin, N. H. (1965). The measurement and reinforcement of behavior of psychotics. *Journal of the Experimental Analysis of Behavior, 8,* 357-387.

Azrin, R. D., & Hayes, S. C. (1984). The discrimination of interest within a heterosexual interaction: Training, generalization, and effects on social skills. *Behavior Therapy, 15,* 173-184.

Barlow, D. (1988). Anxiety and its disorders. New York: Guilford Press.

Binder, J. L. & Strupp, H. (1997). "Negative Process": A recurrently discovered and underestimated facet of therapeutic process and outcome in the individual psychotherapy of adults. *Clinical Psychology: Science and Practice 4,* 121-138.

Blatt, S., Sanislow, C., Zuroff, D., & Pilkonis, P. (1996). Characteristics of effective therapists: Further Analyses of data from the national institute of mental health treatment of depression collaborative research program. *Journal of Consulting and Clinical Psychology, 64,* 1276-1284.

Bordin, E. S. (1976). The generalizability of the psychoanalytic concept of the working alliance. *Psychotherapy: Theory Research and Practice, 16,* 252-260.

Callaghan, G. M, Naugle, A. E, & Follette, W. C. (in press). Useful constructions of the client-therapist relationship. *Psychotherapy.*

Cohen, S. J. (1996). Love between therapist and patient: A review. *American Journal of Psychotherapy, 50,* 14-27.

Dahl, H. (1978). Countertransference examples of the syntactic expression of warded off contents. *Psychoanalytic Quarterly, 47,* 339-363.

Day, W. (1969). Radical behaviorism in reconciliation with phenomenology. *Journal of the Experimental Analysis of Behavior, 12,* 315-328.

DeVoge, J. T. & Beck, S. (1978). The therapist-client relationship in behavior therapy. *Progress in behavior modification, 6.* New York: Academic Press.

Dobson, K. & Shaw, B. (1993). The training of cognitive therapists: what have we learned from treatment manuals? *Psychotherapy, 30,* 573-577.

Dougher, M. J., Auguston, E., Markham, M. R., & Greenway, E. E. (1994). The transfer of respondent eliciting and extinction functions through stimulus equivalence classes. *Journal of the Experimental Analysis of Behavior, 62,* 331-351.

Ferster, C. B. (1967). Arbitrary and natural reinforcement. *Psychological Record, 22,* 1-16.

Ferster, C. B. (1972a). An experimental analysis of clinical phenomena. *The Psychological Record, 22,* 1-16.

Ferster, C. B. (1972b). Psychotherapy from the standpoint of a behaviorist. In J. D. Keehn (Ed.), *Psychopathology in animals: Research and clinical implications* (pp. 279-304). New York: Academic Press.

Ferster, C. B. (1973). A functional analysis of depression. *American Psychologist, 28,* 857-870.

Foa, E. B., & Rothbaum, B. O. (1998). *Treating the trauma of rape: Cognitive behavioral therapy for PTSD.* New York, Guilford Press.

Follette, W. C., & Callaghan, G. M. (1995). Do as I do, not as I say: A behavior-analytic approach to supervision. *Professional Psychology: Research and Practice, 26,* 413-421.

Follette, W. C., Naugle, A. E., & Callaghan, G. M. (1996). A radical behavioral understanding of the therapeutic relationship. *Behavior Therapy 27,* 623-641.

Gaston, L., Thompson, L., Gallagher, D., Cournoyer, L. & Gagnon, R. (1988). Alliance, technique, and their interactions in predicting outcome of behavioral, cognitive, and brief dynamic therapy. *Psychotherapy Research, 8.* 190-209.

Goldfried, M. G. (1985). *In vivo* intervention or transference? In W. Dryden (Ed.), *Therapist dilemmas* (pp. 71-94). London: Harper & Row.

Greenberg, L. S., & Safran, J. D. (1987). Emotion in psychotherapy. *American Psychologist, 44,* 19-27.

Greenspoon, J. (1955) The reinforcing effect of two spoken sounds on the frequency of two responses. *American Journal of Psychology, 68,* 409-416.

Greenspoon, J. & Brownstein, A. J. (1967). Psychotherapy from the standpoint of a behaviorist. *The Psychological Record, 17,* 401-416.

Greenson, R. (1965). The working alliance and the transference neurosis. *Psychoanalytic Quarterly, 34,* 155-181.

Hanly, C. (1992). *The problem of truth in applied psychoanalysis.* New York: Guilford Press.

Hayes, S. C. (1989), *Rule-governed behavior: Cognition, contingencies and instructional control.* New York: Plenum Press.

Hayes, S. C., Strosahl, K., & Wilson, K. G (1999). *Acceptance and commitment therapy: Treating human suffering.* New York: Guilford Press.

Hayes, S. C. & Wilson, K. G. (1994). Acceptance and commitment therapy: Altering the verbal support for experiential avoidance. *Behavior Analyst, 17,* 289-303.

Hayes, S.C., Wilson, K. G., Gifford, E. V. Follette, V. M, & Strosahl, K. (1996). Experiential avoidance and behavioral disorders: A functional dimensional approach to diagnosis and treatment. *Journal of Consulting and Clinical Psychology, 64,* 1152-1168.

Henry, W., Strupp, H., Butler, S., Schacht, T., & Binder, J. (1993). Effects of training in time-limited dynamic psychotherapy: Changes in therapist behavior. *Journal of Consulting and Clinical Psychology, 61*, 434-440.

Hobbs, N. (1962). Sources of gain in psychotherapy. *American Psychologist, 17*, 741-747.

Horvath, A. O., & Luborsky, L. (1993). The role of the therapeutic alliance in psychotherapy. *Journal of Consulting and Clinical Psychology, 61*, 561-573.

Horvath, A. O., & Symonds, B. D. (1991). Relation between working alliance and outcome in psychotherapy: A meta-analysis. *Journal of Counseling Psychology, 38*, 139-149.

Howard, K. I., & Orlinsky, D. I. (1972). Psychotherapeutic processes. *Annual Review of Psychology, 23*, 615-658.

Jacobson, N. S. & Christensen, A. (1996). *Integrative couples therapy: Promoting acceptance and change.* New York, W. W. Norton & Co.

Klee, M. R., Abeles, N., & Muller, R. T. (1990). Therapeutic alliance: Early indicators, course, and outcome. *Psychotherapy, 27*, 166-172.

Kohlenberg, B., Yeater, E. & Kohlenberg, R. J. (1998). Functional analytic psychotherapy, the therapeutic alliance, and brief psychotherapy. In J. Safran and J. Muran, (Eds.), The therapeutic alliance in brief psychotherapy. Washington DC, American Psychological Association.

Kohlenberg, R. J. & Tsai, M. (1991). *Functional analytic psychotherapy: Creating intense and curative therapeutic relationships.* New York: Plenum.

Kohlenberg, R. J. & Tsai, M. (1994a). Functional analytic psychotherapy: A behavioral approach to treatment and integration. *Journal of Psychotherapy Integration, 4*, 175-201.

Kohlenberg, R. J. & Tsai, M. (1994b). Improving cognitive therapy for depression with functional analytic psychotherapy: Theory and case study. *The Behavior Analyst, 17*, (pp. 305-320).

Kohlenberg, R. J., Tsai, M. & Dougher, M. J. (1993). The dimensions of clinical behavior analysis. *The* Behavior Analyst, 16, 271-282.

Kohlenberg, R. J., Tsai, M., & Kohlenberg, B. (1996). Functional analysis in behavior therapy. In Hersen, M., Eisler, M., and Miller, P. (Eds.), *Progress in behavior modification,* New York: Plenum.

Krupnick, J. L., Sotsky, S. M., Simmens, S., Moyer, J., Elkin, I. Watkins J., & Pilkonis, P. (1996). The role of the therapeutic alliance in psychotherapy and pharmacotherapy outcome: Findings in the National Institute of Mental Health Treatment of Depression Collaborative Research Program. *Journal of Consulting and Clinical Psychology, 64*, (pp. 532-549).

Luborsky, L., (1993). Recommendations for training therapists based on manuals for psychotherapy research. *Psychotherapy, 30*, 578-586.

Luborsky, L., Crits-Christoph, P., McLellan, A. T., Woody, G., Piper, W., Liberman, B., Imber, J., & Pilonis, P. (1986). Do therapists vary much in their success? Findings from four outcome studies. *American Journal of Orthopsychiatry, 56*, (pp. 501-512).

Moore, J. (1981). On mentalism, methodological behaviorism, and radical behaviorism. *Behaviorism, 9*, 55-77.

Mowrer, O. H. (1939). A stimulus-response analysis of anxiety and its role as a reinforcing agent. *Psychological Review, 46*, 553-565.

Newirth, J. (1995). Impasses in the psychoanalytic relationship. *In Session: Psychotherapy in Practice, 1*, 73-80.

Noblin, C. Timmons, E. & Reynard, M. (1963). Psychoanalytic interpretations as verbal reinforcers: Importance of interpretation content. *Journal of Clinical Psychology, 19*, (pp. 479-481).

O'Donohue, W. (1995). The scientist-practitioner: Time allocation in psychotherapy. *The Behavior Therapist, 18*, (pp. 117-119).

Omer, H. (1995). Troubles in the therapeutic relationship: A pluralistic perspective. *In Session: Psychotherapy in Practice, 1*, 47-57.

Orlinsky, D., & Howard, K. (1986). Process and outcome of psychotherapy. In S. Garfield and A. Bergin (Eds.), *Handbook of psychotherapy and behavior change: An empirical analysis.* New York: Wiley.

Pepper, S. C. (1957). *World hypotheses.* Berkeley: University of California Press.

Quay, H. (1959). The effect of verbal reinforcement on the recall of early memories. *Journal of Abnormal and Social Psychology, 59*, (pp. 254-257).

Rimm, D. C., & Masters, J. C. (1979). *Behavior therapy: Techniques and empirical findings* (2nd ed). San Francisco: Academic Press.

Rosenfarb, I. S. (1992). A behavior analytic interpretation of the therapeutic relationship. *The Psychological Record, 42*, 341-354.

Safran, J. D., & Muran, J. C. (1995). Resolving therapeutic alliance ruptures: Diversity and integration. *In Session: Psychotherapy in Practice, 1*, (pp. 1-12).

Safran, J. D., & Muran, J. C. (1996). The resolution of ruptures in the therapeutic alliance. *Journal of Consulting and Clinical Psychology, 64*, 447-458.

Safran, J. D., & Muran, J. C. (1998). The therapeutic alliance in brief psychotherapy. Washington DC: American Psychological Association.

Salter, A. (1963). *The case against psychoanalysis.* New York: The Citadel Press.

Samstag, L. W., Batchelder, S. T., Muran, J C., Safran, J. D & Winston, A. (1998). Early identification of treatment failures in short-term psychotherapy: An assessment of therapeutic alliance and interpersonal behavior. *Journal of Psychotherapy Practice and Research, 7*, (pp. 126-139).

Sandler, J., & Sandler, A. (1984). The past unconscious, the present unconscious, and the interpretation of the transference. *Psychoanalytic Inquiry, 4*, (pp. 367-399).

Schafer, R. (1982). The relevance of the "here and now" transference interpretation to the reconstruction of early development. *International Journal of Psychoanalysis, 63*, (pp. 459-467).

Shaw, F. (1946). A stimulus-response analysis of repression and insight in psychotherapy. *Psychological Review, 53*, (pp. 36-42).

Shaffer, L. F. (1947). The problem of psychotherapy. *American Psychologist, 2*, (pp. 459-467).

Shoben, E. J. (1949). Psychotherapy as a problem in learning theory. *Psychological Bulletin, 46,* (pp. 366-392).

Skinner, B. F. (1953). *Science and human behavior.* New York: Macmillan.

Strupp, H. H. (1996). Some salient lessons from research and practice. *Psychotherapy, 33,* (pp. 135-138).

Turkat, I. D., & Brantley, P. J. (1981). On the therapeutic relationship in behavior therapy. *The Behavior Therapist, 4,* (pp. 16-17).

Watson, J. C. (1996). The relationship between vivid description, emotional arousal, and in session resolution of problematic reactions. *Journal of Consulting and Clinical Psychology, 64,* (pp. 459-464).

Watson, J. C. & Greenberg, L. S. (1995). Alliance ruptures and repairs in experiential therapy. *In Session: Psychotherapy in practice, 1,* (pp. 19-31).

Weiss, J., Sampson, J. & the Mount Zion Psychotherapy Research Group. (1986). *The psychoanalytic process: Theory, clinical observations, and empirical research.* New York: Guilford Press.

Wilson, T. G. & Evans, I. M. (1977). The therapist-client relationship in behavior therapy. In A. Gurman and A. Razin (Eds.). *Effective psychotherapy: A handbook of research.* (pp. 544-565). New York: Pergamon Press.

Wilson, T. G. & O'Leary, K. D. (1980). *Principles of behavior therapy.* New Jersey: Prentice Hall Inc.

Wolf, M. M., Risley, T., & Mees, J. L. (1964). Application of operant conditioning procedures to the behavior problems of an autistic child. *Behavior Research and Therapy, 1,* (pp. 305-312).

Wolpe, J. (1958). *Psychotherapy by reciprocal inhibition.* Stanford: Stanford University Press.

Wolpe, J. (1981). Behavior therapy verses psychoanalysis: Therapeutic and social implications. *American Psychologist, 36,* (pp. 159-164).

Zetzel. E. R. (1956). Current concepts of transference. International Journal of Psychoanalysis, 37, (pp. 369-376).

Chapter 13

Interpretation in Clinical Behavior Analysis

David R. Perkins
Lucianne Hackbert
Michael J. Dougher
University of New Mexico

Consider a hypothetical scenario occurring in a room between a therapist and client engaged in the process of therapy. We assume that the goal of this process is change in the client's behavior, which may take a variety of forms. The client shares his story as the therapist listens intently, observing the client's behavior in the room and formulating hypotheses regarding the client's behavior both inside and outside the therapy context. Given the limitations of the setting, the therapist cannot have access to all of the information necessary to draw conclusive inferences about the client's behavior. In service of the goal of behavior change, the therapist has a number of nonexclusive options based upon the hypotheses formulated to account for the client's behavior. As is characteristic of traditional behavior therapy, the therapist could implement techniques intended to alter the effects of the current variables maintaining the client's reported symptomatology, and give relatively little attention to the client's reported history. Another option would be to implement interventions that are directly focused on the hypothesized historical determinants of the client's behavior, and these may or may not be shared with the client. A third option is interpretation.

In the most general sense, interpretation can be defined synonymously with explanation. In this case, therapeutic interpretations would involve presenting clients with some reason for their behavior. If the therapist decides that providing interpretations to the client would be a useful facilitator of behavior change, the next decision would be to determine the form that the interpretation would take and the principles upon which the interpretation is based. In other words, the consideration of therapeutic interpretation raises two questions: "Are interpretations useful, and, if so, what type of interpretation should be given?" Our position is that interpretations are potentially valuable tools for behavior change, and that the principles of behavior analysis can be applied in clinical contexts to maximize their usefulness.

To Interpret or Not To Interpret

An interpretation provides clients with an explanatory system by which their behavior can become more understandable. Interpretations can take a variety of forms, ranging from spiritual, to psychoanalytic, to behavior analytic. By providing an explanation, interpretations are similar to attributions, a topic that has been the subject of a good deal of social psychological research. The primary focus of this research has been on the behavioral effects of different types of attributions (e.g., Harris, 1994; Nair, 1994). Although this research has not typically investigated the clinical effects of attributions or involved clinical samples, clinical inferences can, nevertheless, be drawn from these studies. In general, attributions can provide short-term alleviation of anxiety and reduce confusion and concern regarding one's behavior (Masling & Cohen, 1987). In addition, attributions can provide guidance for future behavior. For example, even scientifically untenable explanations, such as those based on astrology (e.g., "you have strong emotional reactions because you are an Aries"), can lead an individual to make decisions tailored to the perceived strengths of this astrological sign.

The types of interventions a therapist decides to use and the assessment of their effectiveness depends on the goals of treatment. Depending on the goals adopted, interpretations can be either helpful or harmful. Even scientifically untenable interpretations may alleviate immediate distress, but they may also interfere with more general or long-term goals such as helping a client achieve more autonomy, authenticity, or satisfaction from interpersonal relationships. A good deal of social psychological research concludes that the long-term effects on behavior can vary greatly depending upon the type of attributions an individual makes (e.g. Flett & Hewitt, 1990; Langer, 1992). Thus, while interpretations can be given to promote behavior change, some kinds of interpretations might inhibit behavior change or interfere with therapeutic goals. A better understanding of the potential behavioral functions of interpretations would provide useful information to help shape effective therapeutic interventions.

Interpretation in Behavior Analysis

The process of explaining real "in the world" behavior can be quite challenging given that the variables that determine human behavior are, in many cases, quite complex and temporally remote. Skinner (1957) has argued for the use of interpretation in situations that do not allow for more rigorous experimental analyses of behavior. He states that the function of interpretation is to extend empirical findings to situations where direct experimental manipulation is difficult. More recently, Donahoe and Palmer (1994), define interpretation as "the process whereby principles derived from experimental analysis are used to account for observations that, themselves, cannot be subjected to experimental analysis (p. 362). They go on to argue that interpretation is indispensable in scientific explanations of human behavior. In their words, "even when experimental analysis has identified all of the relevant processes, understanding complex phenomena usually requires interpretation" (p. 127). Further, "Most complex behavior, especially human behavior, is the provenance of the interpretive rather than the experimental-analytic aspects of the biobehavioral science" (p. 362).

There are numerous example of the use of interpretation in the behavior analytic literature. Skinner's book, *Verbal Behavior*, is a self-described exercise in interpretation, and examples of interpretation abound in *Science and Human Behavior* and *About Behaviorism*. Willard Day is the probably the best known behavior analytic writer on the topic of interpretation. His interest in the interpretation of ongoing verbal behavior as it occurred in natural settings led him to develop an interpretive methodology that he labeled behavioral phenomenology (Day, 1992; Leigland, 1989; Dougher, 1989). He also wrote about the use of interpretive methods in the study of intention and private events (Day, 1992).

In their discussion of the role of interpretation in scientific explanations of behavior, Donahoe and Palmer (1994) describe three types of interpretations: verbal, organismic, and formal (pp. 126-129). "Verbal interpretation is when we apply empirically established principles of behavior to make sense out of our daily lives" (p. 126). It applies to situations when all the relevant variables cannot be identified or manipulated, and when exact prediction is not possible. Organismic interpretation refers to situations when the learner (organism) is provided with the experiences that previous experimental analyses indicate are sufficient to produce a behavioral phenomenon.

Organismic interpretation attempts to simulate in the laboratory the naturally occurring conditions thought to produce selected behaviors. "Most research with human subjects falls into the category of organismic interpretation because, with very few exceptions, not all of the variables affecting human behavior are under the investigator's control. Although research with human subjects may very carefully control the variables *within* an experiment, the subjects' differing pre-experimental histories *outside* the study cannot be completely controlled or, often, even described" (p. 128).

Formal interpretation is typified by computer simulation wherein a computer is given a program that represents principles established by experimental analysis. These principles are then repeatedly applied in an attempt to determine whether they can generate the behavioral phenomena of interest. As Donahoe and Palmer emphasize, it is important that the principles upon which the computer programs are based be "restricted to those that are derived from research on the biobehavioral processes" (p. 128). This is what distinguishes biobehavioral interpretations from artificial intelligence or those that use principles inferred from the behavior that they are intended to explain.

Of the three types of interpretations identified by Donahoe and Palmer, verbal interpretations would seem to be the most relevant in clinical situations. These situations are characterized by primarily verbal interactions between a client and therapist and relatively little control by the therapist over relevant contingencies of reinforcement occurring outside of the therapy context. The variables that have shaped and maintain clients' behavior are generally not accessible and often temporally remote. The data available to therapists consist primarily of client reports and in session observations. Formal experimentation is generally not possible. The basis for an interpretation exists when a therapist observes a possible functional relation between reported events and reported behavior or can observe certain functional relations occurring in the therapeutic context.

At the end of *Verbal Behavior* (1957), in a section entitled "No Black Scorpion," Skinner provides an example of verbal interpretation that has particular relevance for clinical behavior analysts. Here, Skinner describes an interaction where he attempts to explain his new science of behaviorism to the renowned mathematician/philosopher, Alfred North Whitehead. At the conclusion of his presentation, Professor Whitehead challenges Skinner to account for his behavior of saying, "No black scorpion is falling at this table." Skinner compared this task to asking a physicist to explain the change in the temperature in a room without having the critical information to derive a solution, and admitted that the best that could be done was to offer a guess. In this case, Skinner guessed that the black scorpion was a metaphor for the new science of behaviorism. This interpretation incorporated known variables including the immediate conditions ("a few relevant facts") as well as a bit of information regarding earlier conditions under which this professor had previously behaved ("Those who knew Professor Whitehead"). Skinner concluded the section with a discussion of the variables that he identified as important for the analysis of Whitehead's behavior including the inaccessibility of critical historical variables, and the social contingencies that were operating at the time.

Although Skinner and other behavior analysts have advocated the use of interpretation in appropriate situations, they all argue that interpretations should be based on environmental events, not hypothetical entities or processes that are inferred from the very behavior that they are intended to explain. This, of course, stems from behavior analysis's primary goals of prediction and influence (Dougher & Hayes, this volume, Hayes & Brownstein, 1986; Morris, 1988), and it is what distinguishes behavior analytic interpretations from psychoanalytic or even cognitive interpretations. This is not to say, however, that other types of interpretations can never be useful. As Donahoe and Palmer state: "Psychoanalytic accounts may be every bit as intricate as biobehavioral accounts, but in psychoanalysis the principles are inferred from the very types of observations that they seek to explain. In biobehavioral research the principles arise from independent experimental analyses. Unless a principle is the result of an experimental analysis, it is difficult to identify the origins of any problems that can arise in interpreting the complex phenomena" (p. 127). We would argue that the same restrictions apply to clinical interpretations.

Interpretation in Psychotherapy

Interpretation has long been considered a cornerstone of all approaches to psychotherapy. Fennichel (1945) defined interpretation as "The procedure of deducing what the patient actually means and telling it to him..." (p. 25). In reviewing the role of interpretation as outlined by Freud, Gill, Kohut, and Rogers, Kahn (1997) concluded that, although the specific content of interpretations may differ, they are consistently used in individual psychotherapies that acknowledge the importance of the interpersonal interaction between the client and therapist. Given the critical role that interpretation has played in a wide variety of psychotherapies, it is not surprising to find clinical behavior analysts articulating their support for its use. Interpretation has been mentioned as a mechanism for change in Acceptance and Commitment Therapy (ACT; Hayes, Follette, & Follette, 1995) and as an integral part of Functional Analytic Psychotherapy (FAP; Kohlenberg & Tsai, 1991). Kohlenberg & Tsai argue that all psychotherapy involves interpretations, and these vary according to the orientation of the therapist. In their words, "... a psychotherapist's observations and interpretations of behavior are a function of history, including his or her clinical and theoretical background" (p. 37). Accordingly, psychoanalytic therapists interpret behavior in terms of intrapsychic conflicts, developmental crises and personality styles. Humanistic therapists tend to interpret behavior in terms of conditions of worth and fragmented selves. Cognitive therapists appeal to cognitive deficits, faulty beliefs, and distorted schema. As stated behavior, behavior analysts interpret behavior in terms of the contingencies of reinforcement that control behavior

Although we have been describing behavior analytic interpretations as postulated explanations of behavior based on established behavioral principles, there is tremendous variability in the form, focus and scope of the interpretations that therapists actually deliver. Interpretations can be extensive, as when long-standing behavior patterns are related to complex learning histories, or they can be relatively simple. They can include all of the elements of reinforcement contingencies and relevant establishing operations (e.g., "What you seemed to have learned from previous relationships is that it's best to avoid intimacy if you want to avoid getting hurt."), or focus on individual elements (e.g., "You don't like people getting close to you," or "That must have really hurt when he said that."). They can pertain to behavior occurring outside of the session (e.g., "Not finishing your dissertation is one way of not having to leave the support and stimulation you have in your current situation."), inside the session (e.g., "You seem annoyed when I ask you about your feelings."), or both ("I think your anger in here serves the same distancing purpose as it does in your relationships"). The can be about what appear to be obvious functional relationships or, as in the "Black Scorpion" scenario, they can attempt to reveal the hidden meaning or purpose of behavior (e.g., " I think your telling a story about your demanding boss has something to do with my asking you about coming late to our sessions."). The specific type of interpretation a therapist chooses will depend upon its intended purpose and the context of the therapy.

In line with the underlying pragmatism of clinical behavior analysis, the value of interpretations should be assessed in terms of their effects on clients' behavior. In that regard, it seems reasonable to argue that interpretations should be cast in the language system of the individual client. Although the function of behavior analytic interpretations is to identify the variables controlling clients' behavior, the use of technical behavior analytic terms may need to be sacrificed in favor of a vocabulary more familiar to clients. Interpretations that capture perfectly those contingencies operating on the behavior of the individual phrased in behavioral terms may not be understood or accepted by the client. Speaking in the language of the client may facilitate the interpretation. Consider for example a client who reports difficulty in interpersonal relationships, including a relationship with parents who were described as being emotionally absent or unavailable to the client. In this situation, statements by the therapist regarding a lack of intimacy in past relationships are likely to be more understandable and effective than statements regarding a history of insufficient reinforcement and/or punishment.

Although behavior analytic interpretations appeal to relevant contingencies of reinforcement, we would argue that interpretations that appeal only to immediately controlling contingencies of reinforcement may be inadequate, depending upon the goals of treatment. Interpretations of this type provide only partial explanations of behavior. At the very least, they leave unexplained how those contingencies have come to exert control. This is often a very important question for clients, and the answer may have important therapeutic benefits.

An adequate answer to the question of why certain contingencies exert control over a client's behavior requires an appeal to historical variables. This is, of course, perfectly in line with the view that, unlike other approaches to psychology, behavior analysis takes an historical approach to the study of behavior (e.g., Donahoe & Palmer, 1994). Hineline (1992) describes behavior analysis as an approach that emphasizes the contextual analysis of the "dynamic interplay between environment and behavior," and one grounded in a philosophical orientation that would find explanations based merely on immediate contingencies to be inadequate. As Chiesa (1992) persuasively puts it: "Personal history is neglected in the episodic account by a commitment to contiguous causation, whereas the causal mode of variation and selection draws attention to the effects of past experience on present behavior. Personal history (experience) is a necessary part of explanations of present behavior in the variation and selection causal mode" (p. 129). Although we would argue that an adequate account of behavior must consider historical variables, we are not suggesting that simply providing an historical interpretation of a client's behavior is sufficient to produce therapeutic change. However, as we will try to clarify below, it is our contention that such interpretations in themselves can have salutary effects and can assist in the formulation of effective interventions.

Thus far, we have advocated the use of interpretation in therapy, described the kinds of interpretations that follow from a behavior analytic perspective, and mentioned some factors that might enhance the effectiveness of interpretations. We turn our attention now to a discussion of the possible functions of therapeutic interpretations.

Possible Functions of Clinical Interpretations

Within the clinical behavior analytic literature, interpretation has been most thoroughly discussed by Kohlenberg and Tsai (1991). As radical behaviorists, Kohlenberg and Tsai advocate functional analytic interpretations, which they describe as having two main functions: They help generate more effective rules, and they increase contact with controlling contingencies of reinforcement.

The first function is based on the assumption that some rules are more effective than others. Specifically, rules that accurately describe controlling relations are better than those that do not because they suggest specific interventions. For example, a statement that a client engages in self-destructive behavior "because he is a Virgo" doesn't imply a specific intervention for change, although it may alleviate distress in the short run by offering an "explanation" for the client's behavior. In comparison, if the client were to be told that his self destructive behavior occurs when he thinks that nothing less than perfection is acceptable, a number of interventions are conceivable.

In addition to suggesting possible interventions, identifying the external and historical determinants of clients' behavior may also remove the onus of blame or personal weakness associated with having a clinical disorder. Owing in part to our culture's view of psychological distress, clients who seek therapy frequently see themselves as deficient, weak, or diseased. They often view their problems as resulting from some mental, cognitive, or emotional disorder, and the very presence of feelings like anxiety, sadness, loneliness, and insecurity validates their beliefs that something is wrong with *them*. Obviously having such a belief can, in itself, be very distressing, and it can be a source of relief for clients simply to discover that their behavior, including their thoughts and feelings, are the result of their personal histories, and not some infliction. This can free clients to restructure their environments and explore alternative ways of behaving rather than focusing on ways to eliminate or remedy their personal deficiencies.

With respect to the second function of interpretations described by Kohlenberg and Tsai, many individuals who seek psychotherapy engage in patterns of behavior that prevent contact with environmental contingencies that could affect positive change. They persist in behaving in ways that lead to aversive consequences and they fail to behave in ways that could produce reinforcement. These behavior patterns often are the result of attempts to avoid the possible unpleasant consequences that are inherent in the pursuit of desired consequences. Keeping an emotional distance in interpersonal relationships may successfully avoid the pain associated with rejection, but it also precludes the development of intimate relationships. Interpretations that describe these kinds of controlling relations can increase clients' awareness of the effects of their behavior and of alternative ways of acting that may foster reinforcement

In addition to the functions suggested by Kohlenberg & Tsai, we are suggesting that interpretations may also alter the behavioral functions or effects of relevant events. That is, they may also function as establishing operations. Michael (1982; 1993) provides the most detailed discussion of establishing operations. Setting factors and setting events are terms that have also been used by behavior analysts in reference to function-altering variables (e.g., Kantor, 1959; Bijou & Baer, 1961), but, partly due to Michael's detailed discussion, establishing operations seems now to be the most commonly used term. According to Michael, establishing operations are events, stimuli, or conditions that operate on all the elements of the three-term contingency. As such, they a) alter the reinforcing effectiveness of relevant behavioral consequences, b) alter the probability of behaviors that have produced those consequences in the past, and c) alters the control of relevant discriminative stimuli. While establishing operations increase the reinforcing effectiveness of relevant consequences, evoke relevant behaviors, and enhance the control exerted by relevant discriminative stimuli, abolishing operations decrease the reinforcing effectiveness of relevant stimuli, decrease the probability of relevant behaviors, and decrease the control exerted by relevant discriminative stimuli. Food deprivation is an example of an establishing operation. It potentiates food as an effective reinforcer, evokes behaviors that have been reinforced by food, and enhances the control exerted by stimuli correlated with the availability of food reinforcement. Food satiation is an example of an abolishing operation. For purposes of convenience, we will use the term establishing operation as a generic description of function altering procedures unless discussing specific abolishing operations.

Although few have actually been investigated, a number of potential establishing operations or setting factors have been identified. These include deprivation, conditions of the organism, ambient temperature, variables related to sexual arousal, painful stimulation, previous learning histories, instructions, and events that elicit emotional reactions. Physical abuse, for example, could function as an establishing operation with potentially long lasting effects (Dougher & Hackbert, in press). Among other behavioral effects, it could render reinforcing the infliction of pain on others, while rendering intimacy and care taking aversive. In general, any event that alters the functions of other events can be considered to be an establishing operation.

There are at least two ways that interpretations can function as establishing operations. First, interpretations can serve simply as rules, instructions, or verbal statements that alter the functions of relevant stimuli. To take a non-clinical example, the statement that eating tofu is good for you can effectively alter the behavioral functions of tofu. Where it once might have had punishing and negatively reinforcing effects, it now may function as a positive reinforcer. By providing clients with alternative explanations of their behavior, interpretations can alter the behavioral effects of certain stimuli and experiences. Consider, for example, a client who experiences considerable anxiety in interpersonal situations. This anxiety leads the client to avoid interpersonal contexts and to make self-deprecating comments about his clumsy social skills and lack of self-confidence. The therapist offers a different explanation for the client's anxiety and interprets it as the natural result of the client's particular history and experiences. He adds that most people also feel at least some anxiety in social situations, especially with people they don't know well. This verbal statement could alter for this client the behavioral effects of anxiety and interpersonal contexts. By seeing his reaction as a natural result of his history rather than some personal flaw, the client has less reason to avoid anxiety or the conditions that evoke it. Thus, the therapist's interpretations would have abolished the negative reinforcing effects of anxiety and situations that elicit anxiety.

The second way that interpretations can function as establishing operations is by evoking previous experiences and clinically relevant behaviors in the therapy setting. Although we have restricted our definition of interpretations to postulated explanations of behavior, the fact that they are verbal means that they can functionally bring the events to which they refer into the psychological present (see Hayes & Wilson, 1993; Wilson and Blackledge, this volume). Statements by therapists that refer to a client's previous combat experiences, sexual abuse, parental abandonment, etc. can evoke in the therapy session some very intense emotional reactions. However, the consequences of these reactions are different in the therapeutic setting; they occur without punishment and may even be reinforced. Moreover, they can be explored and interpreted in new and more effective ways.

Kohlenberg and Tsai advocate evoking clinically relevant behaviors in the therapy session primarily so that the functions of these behaviors can be explicated and the behaviors themselves can be consequated. Inappropriate behaviors can be extinguished or punished, and appropriate behaviors can be reinforced. We agree, but suggest that there is also a function-altering effect that can occur when emotional reactions and previous experiences are evoked in therapy sessions. Extinction, punishment, and reinforcement not only alter the impact of relevant stimuli and the frequency of relevant behaviors, they are, themselves, establishing operations. As an example, consider extinction-based therapies, like systematic desensitization, that repeatedly expose clients to feared stimuli in the absence of any aversive consequences. Not only do these stimuli loose their respondent elicitation functions, the extinction procedures also alter the operant functions of the relevant stimuli.

The potential function altering effects of the emotional reactions evoked by an interpretation is illustrated by the following clinical example. The client reported a history of repeatedly trying but failing to please his excessively demanding father. As he reported it, regardless of his accomplishments, his father would focus on the imperfections and encourage better performance the next time. His father was also intolerant and critical of any displays of emotion. As an illustration of his interactions with his father, the client reported an incident that happened in the fifth grade. He had been struggling with math and found fractions to be particularly challenging. His father routinely criticized his inability to grasp the concepts and suggested openly that the client might have limited intellectual abilities. Despite this lack of encouragement, the client persisted and eventually learned to do the calculations. He received an A- on his next test, which he proudly brought home for his father to see. According to the client, his declared, "Jesus, you just can't go all the way, can you?" He then berated his son for making careless mistakes and made him do the problems that he missed. The client related the incident with a conspicuous absence of affect, and when the therapist asked him how he felt about his father's response, he reported that he didn't know. The therapist then interpreted the client's reaction as the resulting from his father's intolerance of emotional displays and suggested that his father's comments must have been very painful. This comment evoked a very strong expression of sadness by the client, the first demonstration of any emotional reaction thus far in the therapy.

The evocation of a strong emotional reaction by the therapist's comment can be seen as an extinction trial. By evoking the response in the safe and supportive context of the therapy setting, the client's emotional reactions were not punished and efforts to suppress emotional responding were not negatively reinforced. But this extinction trial can also be seen as a potential establishing operation or, more accurately, an abolishing operation. The very having of a strong emotional reaction in the therapy in the absence of any punitive consequences may have altered its aversive properties and diminished its effectiveness as a negative reinforcer or punisher. Once the emotional expression occurred, there was no longer any reason to avoid it; the experience itself may have changed or at least diminished its behavioral function. Of course, this is a conceptual not an empirical analysis, and the single occurrence of an emotional reaction in therapy likely would not be sufficient in itself to overcome the client's history with respect to emotional reactions. However, repeated occurrences of emotional reactions in therapy evoked either by interpretations or other clinical interventions could eventually abolish their negatively reinforcing and punishing effects.

We do not wish to be understood as advocating emotional expression as the ultimate goal of all therapeutic encounters. It is certainly possible to construct contingencies where the elicitation of emotional expression is not recommended, and in fact may be damaging. However, we believe that it is important to acknowledge that interpretations can lead to emotional expression, and this expression appears in many cases to be related to progress in treatment. The concept of "catharsis" has little use for us, and we believe it is worthwhile to consider a more effective conceptualization of what occurs at these moments that could potentially be useful for the client.

In addition, it is important to acknowledge that no interpretation or subset of interpretations will constitute a "magic bullet" that will lead to immediate reformulation of rules or contact with new contingencies. Long-standing behavior patterns are often chained up with other related behavior patterns and verbal formulations. Thus, the process of interpretation in therapy often becomes an iterative one, where interpretation is responded to with novel behavior and a re-contextualization of experience, which then leads to further description and interpretation on the part of the therapist.

Conclusions

All therapeutic interventions derive from certain implied or explicit goals and values. While it is, of course, possible to affect important behavior change with therapeutic approaches that focus on directly modifying clinical symptoms, we have come to value interpretation. Form our perspective, understanding the events and processes that have resulted in the tendencies, preferences, and patterns that characterize who we are is a worthwhile therapeutic goal. We would agree with Socrates's' assertion that "the unexamined life is not worth living." More than that, however, knowledge of the historical and contemporaneous determinants of one's behavior provides individuals with the ability to serve as their own mediators of change. According to Skinner (1957), "...men will never become originating centers of control, because their behavior will itself be controlled, but their role as mediators may be extended without limit. In addition, Follette, Bach, and Follette (1993) argue that "People who become psychologically 'stuck' operate as if their history is also their future, whereas the healthy individual recognizes and behaves as if his or her history is simply what it is." It is our contention that behavior analytic interpretations can allow for the explication of historical sources of control over an individual's

References

Bijou, S. W. & Baer, D. M. (1961). *Child development I: A systematic and empirical theory.* Englewood Cliffs, NJ.: Prentice-Hall.

Day, W. F. (1992). Methodological problems in the analysis of behavior controlled by private events: Some unusual recommendations. In S. Leigland (Ed.), *Radical behaviorism: Willard Day on psychology and philosophy.* Reno: Context Press.

Day, W. F. (1992). Analyzing verbal behavior under the control of private events. In S. Leigland (Ed.), *Radical behaviorism: Willard Day on psychology and philosophy.* Reno: Context Press.

Donahoe, J. W., & Palmer, D. C. (1994). *Learning and Complex Behavior.* Needham Heights, MA: Allyn & Bacon.

Dougher, M. J. (1989). A functional analysis of a researcher's functional analysis. *The Analysis of Verbal Behavior, 7,* 19-23.

Dougher, M. J., & Hackbert, L. (in press). Establishing operations, cognition and emotion. *The Behavior Analyst.*

Flett, G. L. & Hewitt, P. L. (1990). Clinical depression and attributional anxiety. *British Journal of Psychology, 29,* 339-340.

Follette, W. C., Bach, P. A., & Follette, V. M. (1993). A behavior analytic view of psychological health. *The Behavior Analyst, 16,* 303-316.

Harris, M. J. (1994). Self-fulfilling prophecies in the clinical context: Review and implications for clinical practice. *Applied and Preventive Psychology, 3,* 145-158.

Hayes, S. C., & Brownstein, A. J. (1986). Mentalism, behavior-behavior relations, and a behavior analytic view of the purpose of science. *The Behavior Analyst, 9,* 175-190.

Hayes, S. C., Follette, W. C., & Follette, V. M. (1995). Behavior therapy: A contextual approach. In A. S. Gurman & S. B. Messer (Eds.) *Essential Psychotherapies: Theories and Practice.* New York: Guilford.

Hayes, S. C. & Wilson, K. G. (1993). Some applied implications of a contemporary behavior analytic account of verbal behavior. *The Behavior Analysts, 16,* 283-301.

Kantor, J. R. (1959). *Interbehavioral psychology.* Granville, OH: Principia Press.

Kohlenberg, R. J., & Tsai, M. (1994). *Functional analytic psychotherapy: Creating intense and curative therapeutic relationships*. New York: Plenum.

Langer, E. J. (1992) Matters of mind: Mindfulness/mindlessness in perspective. *Consciousness and Cognition, 1,* 289-305.

Leigland, S. (1989). A functional analysis of mentalistic terms in human observers. *The Analysis of Verbal Behavior, 7,* 5-18.

Masling, J. & Cohen, I. S. (1987). Psychotherapy, clinical evidence, and the self-fulfilling prophecy. *Psychoanalytic Psychotherapy, 4,* 65-79.

Michael, J. (1982). Distinguishing between discriminative and motivative functions of stimuli. *Journal of the Experimental Analysis of Behavior, 37,* 149-155.

Michael, J. (1993). Establishing operations. *The Behavior Analyst, 16,* 191-206.

Morris, E. K. (1988). Contextualism: The worldview of behavior analysis. *Journal of Experimental Child Psychology, 46,* 289-323.

Nair, E. (1994). How do prisoners and probationers explain their predicament? An attributional analysis. *Psychologia, 37,*66-71.

Skinner, B. F. (1953). *Science and human behavior*. New York: The Free Press/Macmillan.

Skinner, B. F. (1957). *Verbal behavior*. New York: Appleton-Century-Crofts.

Skinner, B. F. (1974). *About behaviorism*. New York: Alfred A. Knopf, Inc.

Titles of Related Books by CONTEXT PRESS

Clinical

Treating Depression in Primary Care
Living Life Well: New Strategies for Hard Times
Scientific Standards of Psychological Practice
Acceptance and Change: Content and Context in Psychotherapy
Prescription Privileges for Psychologists: A Critical Appraisal

Applied and Basic Behavior Analysis

Autism: Behavior Analytic Perspectives
Ethical Issues in Developmental Disabilities
Handbook of Applied Behavior Analysis
Behavioral Psychopharmacology

Community and Social Psychology

Analyzing Social Behavior: Behavior Analysis and the Social Sciences
Changing Cultural Practices: A Contextualist Framework for
    Intervention Research

Developmental

Developmental Psychology: Dynamical Systems and Behavior Analysis
Behavior Analysis of Child Development
New Directions in Behavioral Development

Language and Cognition

Understanding Verbal Relations
Context and Communication Behavior
Behavior Analysis of Language and Cognition
Dialogues on Verbal Behavior

Contextual Philosophy

Varieties of Scientific Contextualism
Radical Behaviorism: Willard Day on Psychology and Philosophy
Investigations in Behavioral Epistemology

You can examine all of these volumes and more at
www.contextpress.com